D1556010

Guide to
Advanced Software Testing

Second Edition

For a listing of recent, related titles,
turn to the back of this book.

Guide to
Advanced Software Testing

Second Edition

Anne Mette Hass

ARTECH
HOUSE

BOSTON | LONDON
artechhouse.com

Library of Congress Cataloging-in-Publication Data

A catalog record for this book is available from the U.S. Library of Congress.

British Library Cataloguing in Publication Data

A catalogue record for this book is available from the British Library.

ISBN-13: 978-1-60807-804-2

Cover design by John Gomes

© 2014 ARTECH HOUSE, INC.
685 Canton Street
Norwood, MA 02062

10 9 8 7 6 5 4 3 2 1

*This book is dedicated to my family: my husband, Finn,
my daughter, Lærke, and my dog, Pippin.*

*It is also to my ISO "family,"
especially, Tafline Ramos and Stuart Reid.*

Contents

9   Test Tools and Automation   **379**

Acknowledgments

Many people have contributed to this book.

First and foremost I'm very grateful to DELTA, who supported my writing the first edition of the book, and now has given me permission to write this second edition. My 16 years at DELTA taught me so much and made it possible for me to develop as a tester and a person. They also gave me a friend for life in my former boss Jørn Johansen.

I have since moved on from DELTA, and I'd also like to thank Devoteam, where I worked for a couple of years. They made it possible to continue the work on the ISO 29119 standard; and the belief in me and the continuous encouragement that my boss there, Tanja Rye, gave me, have made a difference in my life.

As mentioned above, the work in the ISO working group has been fantastic; not always easy, but definitely the most professionally and personally enriching experience I have ever had. I would like to thank everybody I have worked with in the group for longer or shorter periods of time. Thanks for all the fruitful and sometimes difficult professional discussions, for all the work, and for all the fun and good food we have shared. A very special thanks to Tafline Ramos (neé Murnane), without whose compassion for people and unbreakable patience, the standard would not have been; and to Stuart Reid, without whose incredible stamina and courage, the standard would not have been either.

There is no way I can mention all the people who have taught, inspired, and helped me during my testing career—be it managers, colleagues, developers, customers, tutors at courses, authors of books, or speakers at conferences. Thanks to you all; I hope you know how much you mean to me!

I also need to thank my longtime friend Pernille Lemvig-Fog for listening to all my talk about the book and the writing process, and for her never-ending support.

Finally yet importantly, I had the full support of my husband, Finn, and my daughter, Lærke, throughout the long days, evenings, and weekends of writing. I am very grateful to you all.

Preface

"Write a test book? Never!" This was my position for many years, when the thought occurred to me or when colleagues or course delegates suggested it. I had and still have great respect for all the very good testing books already out there.

I did, however, write the first edition of this book and had it published in 2008. It was a great experience for me, and it has since given me pride and joy to hear that people have read the book and found it useful.

Many interesting things have happened in the testing world since then. The two most significant, I believe, are that:

▶ ISTQB released a new Foundation syllabus in 2011 and a full set of Advanced syllabi in 2012.

▶ The ISO 29119 Standard for Software has seen the light of day, and Parts 1, 2, and 3 of the five planned parts were published in September 2013. Part 4 was to follow in 2014.

I have been fortunate enough to follow the ISTQB syllabi close and to be part of the ISO 29119 working group since 2008, most of the time as editor for Part 3.

The proposal to write a new version of this book seemed almost heaven-sent. It gave me the opportunity to update the original book to comply with the new ISTQB syllabi, and at the same time the opportunity to introduce the ISO 29119 standard in a book and compare the two. This was a dream come true, and I hope I have managed both.

The ISO 29119 standard is based on the ISTQB syllabi, and, as far as I understand, the intention is for the ISO 29119 testing process and testing documentation definitions to be adopted by ISTQB over time.

Since the first version of this book came out, many more testing books have been published, but still no book, no course, no person can provide THE truth about testing. The book is intended as another voice in the constant dialog going on among people with an interest in testing where thoughts and ideas are being exchanged. I hope the book will work as such, and as an inspiration and an aid to testers wanting to listen to yet another voice in the choir.

I also hope that it will further help the promotion of the ISTQB certification, as I find this a great opportunity for testers to develop a common language and work together to strengthen the understanding of testing in the entire software development industry.

Remember:

- ▶ Testing is difficult.
- ▶ Testing requires overview.
- ▶ Testing requires creativity.
- ▶ Testing requires systematic work.
- ▶ Testing requires imagination.
- ▶ Testing requires courage.
- ▶ Testing is fun.

A Guide to Professional Testing

Contents

This book is a paradox. It is written for testers who want to become real advanced testing practitioners, but there is no way you can become a practitioner just by reading. A guide, however, can be good for preparing for the journey and for obtaining help on the way.

This book is based on the ISTQB Certified Tester, Advanced Level Syllabi, Version 2012, namely, Test Manager, Test Analyst, and Technical Test Analyst. ISTQB is the International Software Testing Qualification Board, an independent organization made up of member boards from more than 40 countries around the world. See more at www.istqb.org.

The book also takes ISO 29119:2013, *Standard for Software Testing*, into consideration. The standard is to some extent inspired by ISTQB, and it is the intention that future ISTQB syllabi will be based on ISO 29119.

The main purpose of this book is to inspire you to be an even better tester than you already are; it is a guide for already experienced testers on their way to becoming truly professional testers. According to the *Collins Pocket English Dictionary* a professional is engaged in and worthy of the standards of an occupation requiring advanced education!

The book can also be used as an extension to the ISTQB syllabi to support you if your goal is to take one or more of the ISTQB Advanced Level certificates.

A professional tester is a person who puts test knowledge into action in a professional way. He or she must have knowledge and understanding of the basics of testing, and some experience in deploying the knowledge in testing practice. An advanced education goes further than knowledge and understanding and aims at providing the tester with abilities to analyze complete and complex test assignments.

Do not forget that testing is not a natural science.

There is no absolute solution to how software testing must be done; in fact there are many different schools and convictions for the approach to testing. This book represents one, mine in combination with that expressed by ISO 29119 and ISTQB. You will find that you agree and disagree as you read; the important thing is for you to find what you believe to be the "right" way.

I.1 Reading Guidelines

This book contains this basic introduction and 10 chapters, each covering a topic in the syllabus. The 10 chapters are:

1. Testing in Context;
2. Testing Processes Overview;
3. Test Management;
4. Static Testing (Review);
5. Dynamic Testing;
6. Test Case Design Techniques;
7. Testing of Quality Characteristics;
8. Incident and Defect Management;
9. Test Tools and Automation; and
10. People Skills.

The chapters are structured in the same way:

- A very short appetizer to the contents of the chapter, including an overview of the sections in the chapter;
- The text; and
- A list of questions, which may be used for repetition or as basis for discussions in a study group.

Some chapters have appendices with additional information.

A number of vignettes are used in the margin to attract attention to specific information. These are explained in Appendix I.A at the end of this chapter.

Examples are marked in light gray.

I.1.1 Certified Tester, Advanced Level

The ISTQB advanced certification is briefly explained below; this section can be skipped if you do not intend to be certified.

The advanced level certification is aimed at people who have achieved an advanced point in their careers in software testing. To receive advanced level certification, candidates must hold the Foundation certificate.

The advanced level syllabus is split into three distinct syllabi:

▶ Advanced Level Syllabus, Test Manager;
▶ Advanced Level Syllabus, Test Analyst; and
▶ Advanced Level Syllabus, Technical Test Analyst.

To pass the exam, candidates must also demonstrate that they have achieved the learning objectives provided in the syllabus.

The syllabi cover all aspects for each of the three different certification paths and explain in great detail what you need to know and be able to do for each of them.

The syllabi also explain how the examination is conducted.

This book does not replace the syllabus in terms of what must be learned and understood for the certification. Where there are discrepancies between the syllabus and this book, the syllabus prevails if you want to pass the exam!

The structure of the book follows the structure of the syllabi to a very large extent. A few sections are placed differently and a few sections are left out, because the descriptions in the syllabi are comprehensive.

This book, unlike the syllabi, is monolithic; that is, each topic is covered comprehensively in one place, even though the individual topics have different weights for the different paths in the certification scheme. The syllabi explain in detail what the learning objectives are for each topic for each of the certification paths. It is up to the reader to figure out which sections to study extensively and which to skim or even skip.

The ISTQB Software Testing Advanced Level Certification is a demanding professional education in testing, based on the ISTQB/BCS Software Testing Foundation Certification.

If we compare the testing education with getting a driver's license and driving a car, then the Foundation certification is like getting the theoretical part and basing the license on that and a little bit of supervised practice. You have to learn all the traffic rules by heart, not necessarily understand them, and only be able to apply them in a limited environment. The advanced driver has driven a car many times, and in many different situations: in nice weather, in the rain, and maybe even on an icy surface. The advanced driver has driven different cars, and perhaps even driven in places where they drive on the "wrong" side of the road. Maybe the advanced driver would not be able to pass the theoretical driver license test again, but he or she drives around every day using a deep understanding of that foundation.

An advanced level certification does not come easy. You have to

▶ Listen to the experiences and opinions of other testing professionals.

▶ Read as many of the books from the syllabus reference list as you can manage.

▶ Think about what you have heard and seen and compare it to your own experiences: what have I seen, what was similar and what was different, and how and why and with what effect.

▶ Use what you learn in your daily work as much as possible.

▶ Discuss what you hear, read, think, experience and write with your colleagues and your boss—maybe try to get a mentor.

▶ Write things down. When we put pen to paper, things take another form in our brain, so when you have read and talked about a topic write down what it means to you and how you may apply it. Use drawings, tables, and lists to get an overview. Just make it simple; you don't have to write a book.

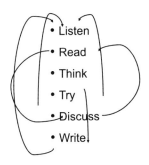

In doing all this in any mixture, the theory you get from books and courses will be transformed into active knowledge and practice: You will become a truly advanced and, it is hoped, also professional tester.

There are a number of lists of things that you will have to learn by heart. Isn't that a wonderful concept: learn by heart! You don't have to memorize things just to see if it is possible for you to remember them; you should do it because the things you have to memorize are the very cornerstones of your profession: those things that should be closest to you professional heart.

I.2   Necessity of Testing

There should be no need to tell the readers of this book this, but we'll do it anyway: It is necessary to test!

"*Errare humanum est*" ("It is human to err") is imputed to a number of people. One source quotes a certain Hieronymus (ca. 345–419). Cicero is quoted to have said: "*Errare humanum est, ignoscere divinum*" or "To err is human, to forgive divine" (Philippicae orationes).

Another quote without a source is "*Cuiusvis hominis est errare, nullius nisi insipientis in errore perseverare*" or "Anybody can err, but only the fool persists in his defect."

It seems to be a recognized condition of life that we are not perfect and, hence, mistakes happen.

Mistakes are not made on purpose!

Human beings are not machines that perform their tasks mechanically step by step. There are a number of life conditions that cause us to err.

Most people are able to handle 7 +/– 2 issues at the time. When this limit is passed, we forget things or mix information. We also tend to neglect or postpone issues that seem to be too difficult for us to handle. Sometimes we believe or hope that if we close our eyes to a problem it will somehow go away.

In our daily work we get distracted and disturbed numerous times. Streams of thoughts get cut, and important information is unintentionally left out.

People also seem to have a tendency to get used to things that in the beginning seem wrong. Little by little we internalize it and make the mistake ourselves—it is called the "adaptive testing syndrome"—but it also exists outside testing. For example, this is one of the reasons why our languages change over time.

Sometimes we don't express ourselves clearly, and that can lead to very dangerous guesswork if we don't go back to the source and ask for clarification. Just consider this requirement:

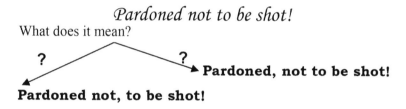

Wrong assumptions, whether they are conscious or not, may also cause mistakes—and here the worst ones are the unconscious assumptions, so be very aware of those.

An accounting system was once implemented by a small software house. After a while it appeared that some invoices had identical numbers. It turned out that the developer didn't know that invoice numbers were not to be reused, even if an invoice had been "deleted" or archived. The accountant who had written the specification had not mentioned this issue, because "I thought it was common knowledge."

I.3   Software Testing Basics

In any profession you must have a firm understanding of the basic concepts of the profession. I'll therefore briefly go over the most important issues in testing to make sure that the fundamentals are present in the back of our heads at all times.

I.3.1   Definition of Testing

So what is testing all about? Most of us have an idea of what testing is—
something about finding defects. But further than that the confusion is fairly big.

Let's try to seek help in the standards.

> ▶ IEEE 610 (Software Engineering Terminology): "The process of
>   operating a system or component under specified conditions, ob-
>   serving or recording the results, and making an evaluation of some
>   aspect of the system or component."
>
> ▶ IEEE 829 (Test Documentation): "The process of analyzing a soft-
>   ware item to detect the difference between existing and required
>   conditions (that is, bugs) and to evaluate the features of the soft-
>   ware items."
>
> ▶ BS 7925-1 (Software Testing—Vocabulary): "Process of exercising
>   software to verify that it satisfies requirements and to detect errors."
>
> ▶ ISTQB Glossary of Terms Used in Software Testing, V 1.0: "The
>   process consisting of all life cycle activities, both static and dynamic,
>   concerned with planning, preparation and evaluation of software
>   products and related work products to determine that they satisfy
>   specified requirements, to demonstrate that they are fit for purpose
>   and to detect defects."
>
> ▶ ISO 29119 (Standard for Software Testing—Part 1) "Set of activities
>   conducted to facilitate discovery and/or evaluation of properties of
>   one or more test items."

There is one term they all agree on, although ISO 29119 expresses it a little
differently: process. Testing is a process.

So what does that process entail? IEEE 610 and BS 7925-1, respectively,
talk about "operating" and "exercising"; that is the idea that testing requires
the software to run on a computer. This is also called "dynamic testing."
IEEE 829 broadens the idea to "analyzing," thus including "static testing."
ISTQB takes the full step and includes both "dynamic and static." ISO 29119,
for political reasons, only includes "dynamic testing" and no "static testing"
at the moment, but it is hoped that sometime in the future static testing will
be included.

In this book *testing can be both dynamic and static.*

What is it we test? The object of the testing in the definitions ranges
from "system or component," "software item," and "software" to "software
products and related work products." ISO 29119 does not attempt to limit or
outline what we can test, but only states "one or more test items."

In line with testing being both dynamic and static, we have to conclude
that *testing can be done on any work product or product.*

The difference between a "product" and a "work product" is that work products are not delivered to the customer, but, like a product, are produced during the course of the development project or the ongoing maintenance.

And last but not least: why? The reasons given include "observing," "evaluate," "detect the ... bugs/errors," "to verify/determine ... satisfaction," "to demonstrate ... fit for purpose." We shall see later, that all this boils down to *testing gathers information about the quality of the object under test.*

The quality is the amount of fulfillment of expectations. On the one hand, we have some expectations and, on the other, we have the product that should fulfill these expectations. The question is "Does it?" We test to be able to answer that question.

Talking about quality—how does testing relate to quality assurance? IEEE 610 defines: "*Quality assurance:* A planned and systematic pattern of all actions necessary to provide adequate confidence that an item or product conforms to established technical requirements."

Is there any difference between testing and quality assurance here? Not really. At least within the framework of this book, testing and quality assurance of the work products and the product will be considered one and the same thing.

As Lee Copeland puts it:
Testing is comparing what is to what should be
and we could add:
and share the information obtained.

I.3.2 Testing Terms

There is no universal set of definitions of test concepts. That is a fact we have to live with, and part of being an advanced tester is the ability to map one set of definitions to others.

This book is based on the ISTQB Glossary of Terms, version 2.2, 2012.

ISO 29119 also provides a comprehensive list of terms and definitions with almost 100 test-related terms.

I.3.3 Handling Failures, Defects, and Mistakes

In a professional software development context, it is not precise enough to talk about errors as indiscriminately as we do in everyday language.

Mistake:
Human action
that produces an
incorrect result.

Defect:
Manifestation
of a mistake in
software.

Failure:
Deviation of the
software from its
expected deliv-
ery or service.

We therefore operate with three different terms: mistake (or error), defect (or fault or, indeed, a bug), and failure, as illustrated below.

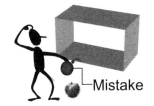
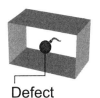

What happens is that a mistake, made by a human being, causes a defect to be placed in a product—for example in a software component. The defect causes no harm as long as it is not encountered by anybody. But if it is "hit" during the use of the product, it will give rise to a failure; that is, the product will react in a way other than expected.

Remember that the product—the test item—can be anything from the first requirements specification to the final product to be delivered to the customer.

It is important to distinguish between the concepts of "mistake," "defect," and "failure."

This is because they appear for different reasons, as can be seen above, and because they are to be treated very differently in the organization.

The job of the tester in static testing is to find as many defects as possible, and the job of the tester in dynamic testing is to provoke as many failures as possible before the product reaches the customer.

When the tester sees a failure, he or she must report it; in dynamic testing this means filling in an incident report, describing what happened, and giving this report to whomever is responsible for deciding what is then going to happen.

Incident reporting enables the person or the group of people responsible for the analysis of the defects to find the defects and to correct those that must be corrected. *The actual defect correction is not part of the testing process*, but a task for development or maintenance.

Process improvement uses analysis of incident reports and root causes to find areas where future mistakes may be prevented by new ways of working (new processes) or caught earlier by using better quality assurance processes, or using the existing one in appropriate ways, as the case might be.

These three steps are illustrated below.

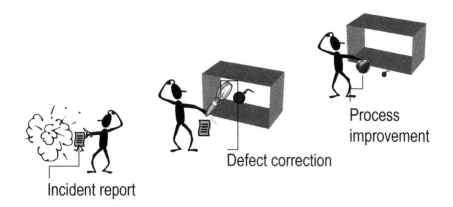

Process
improvement

Defect correction

Incident report

A tester is testing the discount calculation in a sales support system. She enters the item she wants to "buy" and the number of units she wants. The system shows the price for one unit and calculates the total price. In the case where the tester "buys" 9 units the price that the system shows is too high compared to what the tester has calculated beforehand and hence expects. The tester notes that she has seen a failure. It turns out that the system calculates a discount when the number of units is equal to or greater than 9. But the requirement states that a discount shall be calculated if the number of units is 10 or more. There is a defect in the statement that determines if a discount shall be calculated or not. It further turns out that the designer happened to get it wrong when he wrote the detailed design for the requirement, and this was not discovered during the review of the design.

I.3.4   Testing Is Multidimensional

The universe of *testing is multidimensional*. It changes its composition and look all the time depending on the context. It is like looking into a kaleidoscope on a richly faceted picture.

Unfortunately the different facets that make up this universe can only be presented one at the time in a sequential way in a book. Even in a three-dimensional drawing, it would not be possible to capture the complexity of the testing universe.

It is your task and challenge as an advanced tester to grasp all the facets—one by one—and be able to make different pictures of the testing universe depending on the context you find yourself in at any given time. An unlimited number of different pictures of the testing universe may be made, and not two pictures will ever be exactly identical.

The testing universe facets include, but are not necessarily limited to, those listed here (in alphabetical order). Some of them might not mean anything to you at the moment, but at some point in time they all will.

Coding languages
Development models
Development paradigms
Incident handling
Incidents
Maturity models
Money
People skills
People types
Product architectures
Product paradigms
Product risks
Quality assurance activities
Quality factors
Quality goals
Resources
Risk willingness
Standards
Test approaches
Test basis
Test effort
Test levels
Test objectives
Test policy
Test process improvement
Test processes
Test project risks
Test scopes
Test techniques
Test tools
Test types
Testing obstacles
Testing progress
Time

All these facets are discussed in this book—some in great detail, some just superficially; none to exhaustion.

Don't despair. Read and reread the chapters and sections in any order. Read other books. Try things out. Discuss with colleagues, both testing colleagues and others. Figure out what each facet means to you, and how the facets can relate to each other in your world. Train and train again in making the picture that suits the context you are in.

I.4 Business Value of Testing

On the face of it testing adds no value. The product under test is, in principle, not changed after the test has been executed.

But we are paid to test, so we must add some value to the business. And we do!

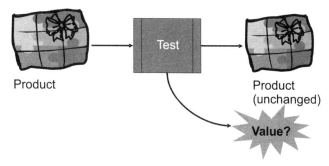

The business value of testing lies in the savings that the organization can achieve from improvements based on the information the testing provides.

Improvements can be obtained in three places:

▶ The product under development;
▶ The decisions to be made about the product; and
▶ The processes used in both testing and development.

It may, however, sometimes be difficult to understand and express what the value is, both to us and to others in the organization.

It is essential that test managers know and understand the value of testing and know how to express it to others to help them understand as well. *Test managers must communicate the value both to the testers, to other project participants, and to higher management.*

Testers are often engrossed in the testing tasks at hand and don't see the big picture they are a part of; higher management is often fairly remote from the project as such and don't see the detailed activities.

I.4.1 Purpose of Testing

What testing does and therefore the *immediate purpose of testing is getting information about the product under test.* We could say (with Paul Gerrard, founder of Gerrard Consulting): "Testing is the intelligence office of the company."

The places we gather our raw data from are the test logs and the incident reports, if these are used sensibly and updated as the testing and the incident are progressing. From the raw data we can count and calculate a lot of useful quantitative information.

A few examples of such information are:

- Number of passed test cases;
- Coverage of the performed test;
- Number and types of failures;
- Defects corrected over time; and
- Root causes of the failures.

Most of this information is "invisible" or indigestible unless we testers make it available in appropriate formats. There is more about this in Section 3.6. This section also discusses how the information can be used to monitor the progress of the development in general and the testing in particular.

I.4.2   The Testing Business Case

It is not straightforward to establish a business case for testing, since we don't know in advance what savings we are going to enable. We don't know how many defects in the product we are going to unveil

A well-established way to express the value of testing for the product is based in the cost of quality. This can be expressed as the value of product improvement:

Value of product improvement =
(cost of failure not found – cost failure found) – cost of detection

To this we can add

Value of decision improvement =
(cost of wrong decision – cost of right decision) – cost of getting decision basis

Value of process improvement =
(cost using old process – cost using better process) – cost of process improvement

These three aspects add up to form the entire business case for testing. The aim is to get as high a value as possible.

A value may be expressed either quantitatively or qualitatively. Quantitative values can be expressed in actual numbers—euros, pounds, or dollars, or numbers of something else. Qualitative values cannot be calculated like that, but may be expressed in other terms or "felt."

I.4.2.1   The Value of Product Improvement

The value of product improvement is the easiest to assess.

One goal of all development is reliability in the products we deliver to the customers. Reliability is the probability that software will not cause a failure of the system for a specified time under specified conditions.

A product's reliability is measured by the probability that faults materialize in the product when it is in use.

No faults
= 100% reliability

Many faults
= x% reliability

The fewer failures that remain in the product we release, the higher is the reliability of the product and the lower the risk of the product failing and thereby jeopardizing its environment. Project risks range from ignorable to endangering the lives of people or companies. Risk-based testing in discussed in more detail in Section 3.3.

The earlier we get a defect removed, the cheaper it is. Static testing finds defects and dynamic testing finds failures, enabling the correction of the underlying defects.

The cost of correcting a defect depends on when the defect is found. Defects found and corrected early are much cheaper to correct than defects found at a later point in time. Research shows that if we set the cost of correcting a defect found in the requirements specification to 1 unit, then it will cost 10 units to make the necessary correction if the defect is first found in the design.

If the defect remains in the product and is not found until encountered as a failure in dynamic test, it costs 100 units to correct it. The failures found during development and testing are called internal failures, and they are relatively cheap.

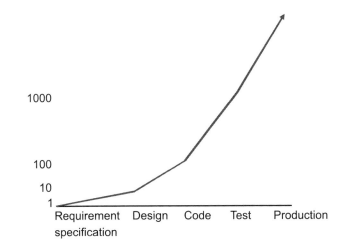

This graph is provided by Grove Consultants, UK; other sources for similar research results are IBM and Brüel & Kjær, Denmark.

If a customer experiences a failure in production—an external failure—it may cost more than 10,000 units to make the necessary corrections, including the cost that the customer may incur. The analysts and programmers who can/must correct the defects may even have been moved to new assignments, which are then in turn delayed because of (emergency) changes to the previously delivered product.

The basic reason for this rise in cost is that defects in software don't go away if left unattended; they multiply. There are many steps in software development—from a requirements specification to manufacturing—and for each step a defect can be transformed into many defects, as illustrated below.

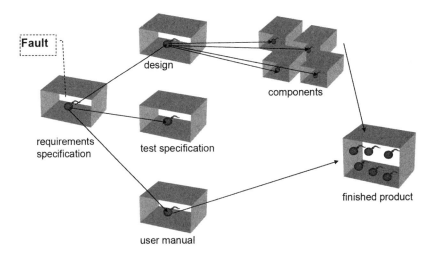

There is some element of estimation in preparing the business case for product improvement. Many organizations don't know how many defects to expect, how much it costs to find defects and how much it costs to fix them, or how much it would have cost to fix them later. The more historical data about testing and defect correction an organization has, the easier it is to establish a realistic business case.

Let's look at a few calculation examples.

If we assume that it cost 4 units to correct a defect in the requirements phase, and 6 units to detect and correct a defect or a failure, we can make calculations like:

Value of finding a defect in system testing rather than in production at the customer's site = (4,000 – 400) – 6 = 3,594 units

Value of finding a defect in requirements specification rather than in system test = (400 – 4) – 6 = 390 units

Other research shows that about 50% of the defects found in the entire life of a product can be traced back to defects introduced during the requirements specification work. This is illustrated in the following figure where the origins of defects are shown.

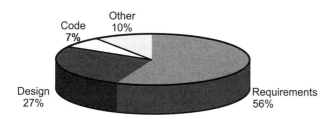

If we combine these two pieces of research results, we have a really strong case for testing, and for starting testing early on in the project!

To get the full value of testing, it should start as early as possible in the course of a development project, preferably on day 1!

I.4.2.2   The Value of Decision Improvement

From the point of view of decision making such as decisions concerning release (or not) of a product, the confidence in the product and quality of the decisions are proportional to the quality and the amount of the information provided by testing. As testing progresses, more and more information is gathered and this enhances the basis for the decisions.

The more knowledge the decision makers have about what parts of the product have been tested to which depth—coverage—and which detected defects have been removed and which are still remaining, the more informed are the decisions made. The value of more informed decisions rather than less informed decisions is qualitative; it is very rarely possible to calculate this quantitatively.

It follows from the concept of test as an information collection activity that it is not possible to test good quality into a product. But the quality of the test is reflected in the quality of the information it provides.

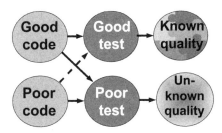

Good testing provides trustworthy information and poor testing leaves us in ignorance.

If the starting point is a good product, a good test will provide information to give us confidence that the quality is good.

If the starting point is a poor product, a good test will reveal that the quality is low.

But if the test is poor, we will not know if we have got a good or a poor product.

The line from "poor code" to "good test" is dashed because poor coding and a good test are not often seen together. Our goal as professional test practitioners is to reduce the occurrence of poor testing.

More important decisions may also be based on the information from testing. A test report with documentation of the test and the test results can be used to prove that we have fulfilled contractual obligations, if needed. It may even in some (hopefully rare) cases provide a juridical shield for the company in that it provides evidence against suits for negligence or the like. This is of qualitative value to the business

I.4.2.3   The Value of Process Improvement

From the process improvement point of view, the information gained from testing is invaluable in the analysis of how well processes fit and serve the organization. The results of such analyses can be used to identify processes that could be subject to process improvement. The processes to improve may be both testing processes and other processes in the development or maintenance life cycles.

As time goes by the information can tell us how a process improvement initiative has worked in the organization.

When the testing process improves, the number of failures that end up happening to customers decreases, and the organization's reputation for delivering quality products increases (all else being equal). The value of this is qualitative.

Process improvement is discussed in more detail in Section 1.4.

Questions

1. What is the number of the new ISO standard for testing?
2. What appears at the end of each chapter of this book?
3. What is the difference between a Foundation and an Advanced Level certification?
4. Which study techniques should you use?
5. Why is testing necessary?
6. What is testing?
7. Name the two overall types of testing.
8. Which list of terms is used in this book?
9. What is the difference between "mistake," "defect," and "failure."
10. Explain the business value of testing.
11. Name some facets that influence testing.
12. What is the purpose of testing?
13. What is reliability?
14. Explain the cost of correcting a defect through the development life cycle.
15. What is the result of a poor test?
16. How can testing support process improvement?

Appendix I.A   Vignettes

The vignettes used in the margins of this book are shown here to make it easier to refer to them when you are reading the book.

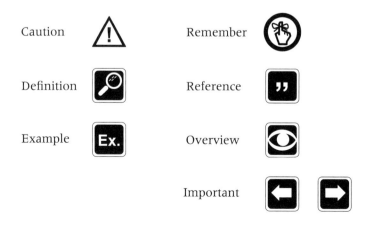

Caution

Definition

Example

Remember

Reference

Overview

Important

Testing in Context

Testing is never performed in isolation; it is a process that is always performed in a context, and that context must be known and respected for the test effort to be successful. The context may be complex, but nonetheless it needs to be understood to ensure that the testing is efficient and effective.

The context has many aspects, and the more important of these will be discussed in this chapter. You do not have to read the sections in this chapter in depth from the beginning. Familiarize yourself with the different aspects, and return to study them closer when the need arises.

Testing in the context of this book is supposed to be performed in a commercial or nonprofit professional organization using and/or manufacturing software products. The reader should understand that no matter how important testing might seem, it has its place in an organization among many other processes and activities.

An important context aspect is the development model or maintenance model chosen, since testing will have to fit into this. Testing is a support process—meaningless without a development project or ongoing maintenance, and not producing anything in its own right: nothing produced means nothing to test.

Testing will also have to fit into the other support processes. These will affect the testing to be done; just like the testing will affect them. We'll only look at the support processes of project management, quality assurance, and configuration management here, because these are the most important ones for testing.

Testing is a process and may be the subject of process improvement in an organization. This has an impact on the way we shall/should/may test, and constantly improving the test process should be high on the priority list for people working with testing and with development in general.

The last aspect of the context in which testing may be performed is standards. There are not many standards dedicated to software testing; in fact, the only comprehensive standard is ISO 29119, *Standard for Software Testing*. However other standards may influence the test work and some of these are discussed at the end of this chapter.

1.1   Testing in a Business Context

Software testing is not the center of the world. It may (almost) be to me, because it takes up all my working life, and some of my spare time; but as important as it is, it is only a small piece in the big jigsaw that an organization is.

1.1.1   Organizational Context

The purpose of an organization is to stay in business by fulfilling the business's goals. These may be to produce software to sell; but more often the core business is something else, and the software is just a means to the end—a necessary good.

Organizations are structured, usually in overlapping organizational layers, such that each layer has a specific responsibility and purpose; and the layers interact and support each other. This is illustrated in the figure below.

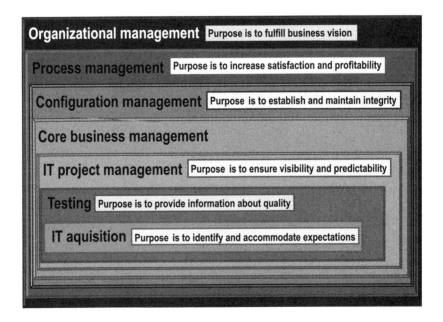

Organizational management, or top management, is ultimately responsible for fulfilling the business goals. Top management supports the entire organization and all activities therein.

Process management is responsible for defining and improving work process descriptions, making them available, and improving adherence to the processes. This level of management may support the entire organization or a part of it.

Configuration management covers identification, storage, and change control of selected work products and products. Configuration management may be supporting all other layers, in the sense that artifacts produced by any layer may need to be kept under configuration management.

Core business is what the business goals are about. Core business may be any conceivable type and size of business, because software is used (almost) everywhere. The core business is supported by the organizational management, and process and configuration management. The core business may be software development, but the vast majority of businesses have other business goals.

IT project management is responsible for continuously being able to provide the software necessary to support the work being performed throughout the organization.

The *acquisition* of the necessary software may occur through development in-house, by buying software, by using open-source software, or through a mixture of these methods. The software will also need to be maintained on an ongoing basic, including corrections of defects and adding, changing, or removing features.

The necessary software must be tested—or subjected to quality assurance processes—no matter how it gets into the organization. For software developed in-house or maintained in-house the entire testing is the responsibility of the organization. For software brought in from outside, the responsibility for the testing is split, with only some carried by the organization itself.

If the core business of the organization is to produce software, then this software must, of course, also be tested.

1.1.2 Product Paradigms

The use of computers to assist people in performing tasks has developed dramatically since the first huge (in physical size) computers were invented around the middle of the previous century. The first computers were about the size of a family home and you could only interact with them via punch cards or tape and printed output. Those were the days.

Today we as testers may have to cope with a number of different product types or product paradigms, and with different development paradigms and coding languages. Not all of us encounter all of them, but it is worth knowing a little bit about the challenges they each pose on us.

We always need to be aware of the product and development paradigm used for the (testing) projects with which we are involved. We must tailor our test approach and detailed test processes to the circumstances and be prepared to tackle any specific obstacles caused by these as early as possible.

Product paradigms include, but are not limited to:

- Client-server;
- Embedded;
- Mainframe;
- Mobile-based;
- PC-based;
- Real-time;
- Safety critical;
- Web-based systems.

A few, but significant product paradigms are discussed here.

1.1.2.1   System of Systems

A system of systems is the concept of integrating existing systems into a single information system with only limited new development. The concept was first formulated by an American admiral, Admiral William A. Owens, in his book *Lifting the Fog of War*. The concept was primarily used for military systems, but is spreading more and more to civilian systems as well.

The idea is to use modern network technologies to exploit the information spread out in a number of systems by combining and analyzing it and using the results in the same or other systems to make these even more powerful.

A tiny example of a system of systems is a sprinkling system at a golf course. The gardener can set the sprinkling rate for a week at a time. Using a network connection this system is linked to a system at a meteorological institute where hours of sunshine, average temperatures, and rainfall are collected. This information is sent to a small new system, which calculates the needed sprinkling rate on a daily basis and feeds this into the sprinkling system automatically. The gardener's time, water, the occasional flooding, and the occasional drying out of the green is saved.

Systems of systems are complicated in nature. The final system is usually large and complex and so may each of the individual systems be. Each of the individual systems may in itself consist of a number of different subsystems, for example software, hardware, network, documentation, data, data repository systems, license agreements, services (e.g., courses, and upgrades), and descriptions of manual processes. Few modern systems are pure software products, though they do exist.

Even if the individual systems are not developed from scratch, these systems pose high demands on the supporting processes; especially project management, but also configuration management and product quality assurance. In the cases where some or all of the individual systems are being developed as part of the construction of a system of systems this poses even higher demands in terms of communication and coordination.

From a testing point of view, there are at least three important aspects to take into account when working with a system of systems:

- ❯ System testing of the individual systems;
- ❯ Integration testing of systems;
- ❯ Regression testing of systems and integration.

A system of systems is only as strong as the weakest link, and the completion criteria for the system testing of each individual system must reflect the quality expectations toward the complete system of systems. The system testing of each individual system is either performed as part of the project or assurance of its performance must be produced, for example, in the form of test reports from the producer.

Systems of systems vary significantly in complexity and may be designed in hierarchies of different depths, ranging from a two-layer system where the final system of systems is composed of a number of systems of the same "rank," to many-layered {system of [system of (system of systems)]}. Integration of the systems must be planned and executed according to the overall architecture, observing the integration testing aspects described in Section 1.2.2.3.2.

It is inevitable that defects will be found during system and integration testing of a system of systems and significant iterations of defect correction, confirmation testing, and regression testing must be anticipated and planned for. *Strict defect handling is necessary to keep this from getting out of control*, resulting, for example, in endless correction and recorrection cycles. Systems of systems may well contain systems of different paradigms; see the list above.

1.1.2.2 Safety Critical Systems
Any system presents some risk to its owners, users, and environment. Some present more risk than others and those that present the most are what we call safety critical systems.

The risk is a threat to something valuable. All systems have something of value, which can be jeopardized, inside them, and their usage may jeopardize some value outside of them. A system should be built to protect the values both from the results of ordinary use of the system and from the result of malicious attacks of various kinds.

A typical categorization of values is:

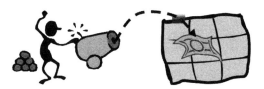

- Safety;
- Economy;
- Security;
- Environment.

Many regulatory standards address how to determine the safety criticality of systems and provide guidelines for the corresponding testing. Some of these are listed in Section 1.5.4.

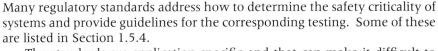

The standards are application specific and that can make it difficult to determine what to do if we have to deal with multidisciplinary products. Nonetheless standards do provide useful guidance.

The most generic of the standards is IEC 61508; this may always be used if a system does not fit into any of the other types.

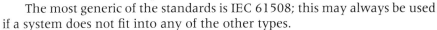

All the standards operate with so-called "software integrity levels" (SILs), a measure of how bad it can get.

The concept of SILs allows a standard to define a hierarchy of levels of testing (and development). A SIL is normally applied to a subsystem; that is, we can operate with various degrees of SILs within a single system or within a system of systems. The determination of the SIL for a system under test is based on a risk analysis.

This table shows an example of a classification.

SIL Value	A	B	C	D
Safety	Many people killed	Human lives in danger	Damage to physical objects; risk of personal injury	Insignificant damage to things; no risk to people
Economy	Financial catastrophe (the company must close)	Great financial loss (the company is threatened)	Significant financial loss (the company is affected)	Insignificant financial loss
Security	Destruction/ disclosure of strategic data and services	Destruction/ disclosure of critical data and services	Defects in data	No risk for data
Environment	Comprehensive and irreparable damage to the environment	Reparable, but comprehensive damage to the environment	Local damage to the environment	No environmental risk

The standards concerning safety critical systems deal with both development processes and supporting processes; that is, project management, configuration management, and product quality assurance.

As an example the CEI/IEC 61508–E/E/P Safety-Related Systems recommends the use of test case design techniques depending on the SIL of a system. This standard defines four integrity levels: SIL4, SIL3, SIL 2, and SIL1, where SIL4 is the most critical.

For a SIL4 classified system, the standard says that the use of equivalence partitioning is highly recommended as part of the functional testing. Furthermore, the use of boundary value analysis is highly recommended, whereas the use of cause-and-effect graphs and error guessing are only recommended. For white-box testing the level of coverage is highly recommended—although the standard does not say which level of which coverage.

The recommendations are less and less strict as we come down the SILs in the standard.

For highly safety critical systems, the testers may be required to deliver a compliance statement or matrix, explaining how the pertinent regulations have to be followed and fulfilled.

1.1.3   The Where and Who of Testing

Not all the work in an organization needs to be performed in the same place by people employed by the same organization. In today's world of easy communication and globalization, there are many ways of organizing the work inside and/or outside the responsible organization.

1.1.3.1   Ways of Organizing Test Work

Here we concentrate only on test work, but the principles described below are equally relevant to other processes in an organization, such as design and coding.

The ways of organizing the test work, which will be discussed here, are:

▶ Distributed testing;
▶ Outsourced testing;
▶ Insourced testing.

Distributed testing is the term for people employed by the same organization, but working at one or more other locations than where the rest of the work is done, performing the test.

This may happen for various reasons; one reason is that an organization may have offices in various places in the same country, and that one of these offices has been selected to be the place where the testers are located.

Another reason may be that the organization has concentrated testing in offices placed in other parts of the world to benefit from the different time zones around the globe.

Outsourced testing is related to the above way of organizing work, but the testing is done by independent organizations, that is, by people employed by another organization than the one performing the rest of the work.

Outsourced testing may be divided into *offshore testing*, where the test work is performed on another continent, and *near-shore testing* where the test work is performed in another country, but within the same continent.

This way of organizing the testing is done for economic reasons. For example, time can be saved if the company is able to benefit from the different time zones, and money can be saved if work is outsourced to people being paid less compared to the people in the outsourcing organization.

Insourced testing is the opposite of outsourced testing; the term means that the testing is performed at the same place as the other work, but by people employed by an independent organization. This may also be known as testing done by external consultants posted inside the organization.

The reason for this form of test work organization is usually to get highly experienced and skilled people to perform the testing quickly, and perhaps also to be able to use these people only for a limited amount of time.

1.1.3.2 Issues for Consideration

A number of issues must be considered in connection with distributed, outsourced, and insourced testing.

First we must consider trust. When people are to work together they need to trust each other, both as people and as colleagues. Trust is generally difficult to establish and easy to destroy.

If people working together don't trust each other, they may behave in strange and counterproductive ways, like insisting on too much control or doing things twice. It may also cause people to feel bad about themselves and/or about others and it may cause stress and depression.

The better people know each other, the easier it is to establish and keep trust. Experience shows that it is a good investment for people working together across even short distances to meet physically or at least see each other.

A Danish company was outsourcing some of its testing to a test company in India. Things were not going quite as smoothly as expected, and a trip was arranged for the testers in Denmark to visit the testers in India. They spent a week together in workshops and working together in small groups of two or three people. Time was also set aside for fun and sport, where the Danes excelled in running and lost terribly in cricket—to the enjoyment of everybody. After the trip work efficiency and employee satisfaction rose significantly in both countries.

If visits are not possible, modern communication techniques, such as video conferences, enable other ways of "almost being there in person" and should be used as much as possible.

Another issue is communication. Good communication is the foundation of all working (and personal) relationships. In all the different ways of organizing the test work, great care should be taken to ensure the best possible communication between the people filling the test roles and all of the stakeholders.

An obvious obstacle in working together is the language. Consider a situation in which some people working together are using their mother tongue, while others need to use a second or third language that they have not mastered quite as well as their mother tongue. Those using their mother tongue must be considerate, for example, by speaking slowly and using common simple words, and those speaking a foreign language must be considerate by speaking as clearly as possible; most often problems arise from pronunciation rather than lack of a rich vocabulary.

Methods of communication are an issue in this context. The further physically apart people working together are, the more formal the ways of communicating become, for better and for worse. Written communication is less likely to be misunderstood and/or forgotten; on the other hand, written information may exclude information that might otherwise have been exchanged.

Clear expectations facilitate a good working environment in all circumstances, and even more when work is organized as distributed, outsourced, and/or insourced testing. Therefore, well-defined processes are especially important.

Process descriptions define lines of authority, roles and responsibilities, activities to be formed, techniques to use, and expected deliverables and their expected structure. If processes are not well defined, inefficiencies may result and ultimately mistrust.

Well-prepared, documented, communicated, and maintained plans are a means of communicating clear expectations to testers, and their value should not be underestimated.

The last issue to be discussed here is *cultural differences*. Culture may differ between people in the same city, the same country, the same continent, the same world. Culture has to do with our values and our behavior in the broadest sense. Some cultural differences are easy to identify, such as ways of dressing and ways of preparing and eating food, while others are more subtle, such as how words are understood and messages interpreted.

The answer to this situation is to learn as much as we can about the culture of those we are working with and to respect it. Many courses and books about various cultures are available, providing plenty of examples of where people may misunderstand each other with small or huge effects.

An open mind is always advisable and it may also be a good idea to observe the old saying "When in Rome, do as the Romans do."

1.2 Testing in the Software Life Cycle

The intention of product development is to get from the vision of a product to the deployment of the final product. When the product is deployed, its real life begins. The product's life lasts until the product is disposed of.

The period of time from the initial idea for a product until it is disposed of is called the product life cycle; or *software life cycle*, if we focus on software products.

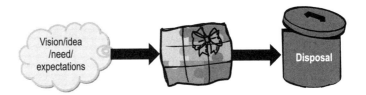

A product may be acquired in many different ways, including in-house development, use of open-source code, bespoke development by a supplier, standard system bought off-the-shelf, or a mixture of some of these. But no matter what, somebody will have to develop it.

The period of time from the initial idea for a product until it is ready for deployment is the *development life cycle*.

While the product is in use, its behavior will have to be monitored. The product will also have to be maintained in terms of defect correction and possibly evolution of the product.

The period of time from deployment until the product is disposed of is the *production and maintenance life cycle*.

Testing, both dynamic and static, is an important part of the development project and of the production and maintenance life cycle. The next section describes how dynamic testing may be fitted into various development models.

1.2.1 Development Models

Everything we do in life seems to follow a few common steps, namely, conceive, design, and implement.

The same activities are recognized in software development, although here they are normally called:

▶ Requirements engineering;
▶ Design;
▶ Coding.

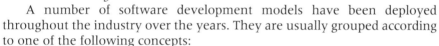

R D C

Building blocks

In software development we call the building blocks "stages," "steps," "phases," "levels" or "processes." Here we will use the term "processes."

You'll see that a test process is not shown as a building block here. That is because testing is a support process; a software product may be developed and delivered without any testing—it is not wise, but it can be done.

The way the development processes are structured is the development life cycle or the development model. A life cycle model is a specification of the order of the processes and the transition criteria for progressing from one process to the next; that is, completion criteria for the current process and entry criteria for the next.

Many software projects have experienced problems because they pursued their development without proper regard for the processes and the transition criteria.

The reason for using a software development model is to produce better quality software faster. That goal is equal for all models. *Using any model is better than not using a model at all.*

A number of software development models have been deployed throughout the industry over the years. They are usually grouped according to one of the following concepts:

▶ Sequential;
▶ Iterative/incremental; or
▶ Agile.

The building blocks—the processes—are the same; it is only a matter of their lengths and the frequency with which they are repeated.

There is no "best" development model. Each organization will have to define its own so that it fits with the nature of the products and the organization; this is the responsibility of the process management or project management. The test will have to be fitted into any model that is used.

1.2.1.1   Sequential Development Models

Historically the first type of sequential model was the *waterfall model*. A pure waterfall model consists of the building blocks ordered in one descending sequence, illustrating that work flows downward from one process to the next—and not back again.

In the waterfall model there is one single test process to be performed after the coding (and any necessary integration).

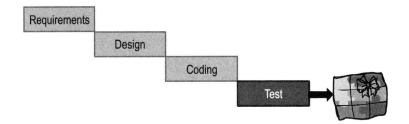

The *assumptions* when using a sequential model are:

- The customer knows what he wants.
- The requirements are frozen once the requirements specification process has been completed (changes are exceptions).
- Phase reviews are used as control and feedback points.

The *characteristics* of a successful sequential development project are:

- Stable requirements;
- Stable environments;
- Focus is on the big picture;
- One, monolithic delivery.

The goals of the sequential models are achieved by enforcing fully elaborated documents as phase completion criteria, and formal approval of these as entry criteria for the next.

The V-model is an expansion of the pure waterfall model that introduces test levels corresponding to the requirements and design processes.

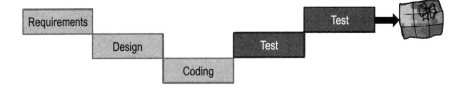

The V-model describes a course where the left side of the V reflects the processes to be performed in order to produce the components that make up the product, for example, the software code. The processes on the right side of the V are test levels to ensure that we get what we have specified as the product is integrated.

The pure V-model may lead you to believe that you develop first (the left side) and then test (the right side), but that is not how it is supposed to work.

In a V-model the idea is that the test work, that is, the production of testing work products, starts as soon as the basis for the testing has been produced. The V-model may therefore also be drawn as shown below.

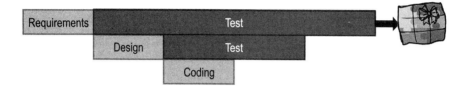

When working like this we describe what the product must do and how (in the requirements and the design), and at the same time we describe how we are going to test it (the test plan and the specification). This means that we are starting our testing at the earliest possible time.

The planning and specification of the test against the requirements should, for example, start as soon as the requirements have reached a reasonable stage.

A V-model–like development model provides a number of advantages:

- ▶ More time to plan and specify the test;
- ▶ Extra test-related review of documents and code;
- ▶ More time to set up the test environment(s);
- ▶ A better chance of being ready for test execution as soon as something is ready to test.

For some classes of software (e.g., safety critical systems, or fixed price contracts), a V-model may be the most appropriate.

1.2.1.2 Iterative and Incremental Development Models

In iterative and incremental models, the project strategy is that some changes should and will happen during development. To cater to this, the basic processes are repeated in shorter cycles, iterations. These models can be seen as a number of mini V-models; testing must be incorporated in every iteration within the development life cycle.

An iterative or incremental development model could be illustrated like this:

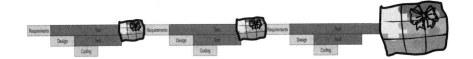

Note that the difference between the two models discussed here is:

▶ In iterative development the product is not released to the customer until all the planned iterations have been completed.
▶ In incremental development a (sub)product may released to the customer after each iteration if it is deemed useful.

The project goals are achieved through various prototypes or subproducts in these models. The subproducts are developed and validated in the iterations. At the end of each iteration an operational (sub)product is produced, and hence the product is expanding in each iteration. The direction of the evolution of the product is determined by the experiences with each (sub)product.

The *assumptions* for an iterative and incremental model are:

▶ The customer cannot express exactly what he wants.
▶ The requirements will change.
▶ Reviews are done continuously for control and feedback.

The *characteristics* of a successful project following such a model are:

▶ Fast and continuous customer feedback;
▶ Floating targets for the product;
▶ A focus on the most important features;
▶ Frequent releases.

The iterative/incremental model matches situations in which the customer says: "I can't tell you what I want, but I'll know it when I see it"—the last part of the sentence often expressed as "IKIWISI."

These models are suited for a class of applications where there is close and direct contact with the end user, and where requirements can only be established through actual operational experience.

Testing is perhaps even more important in iterative and incremental development than in sequential development. The product is constantly evolving and extensive regression testing of what has previously been agreed on and accepted is imperative in every iteration.

A number of more specific iterative models are defined. Among these the most commonly used are the RAD model and the spiral model.

The *RAD model* (Rapid Application Development) is so named because it is driven by the need for rapid reactions to changes in the market. James Martin was the first to define this model. Since then the term RAD has more or less become a generic term for many different types of iterative models.

The original RAD model is based on development in time-boxes in few—usually three—iterations on the basis of a fundamental understanding of the goal achieved before the iterations start. Each iteration basically follows a waterfall model.

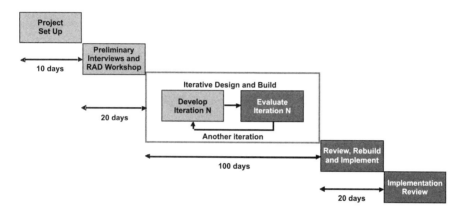

When the last iteration is finished, the product is finalized and implemented as a proper working product to be delivered to the customer.

Barry Boehm has defined a so-called *spiral model*. This model aims at accommodating both the waterfall and the iterative model. The model consists of a set of full cycles of development, which successively refines the knowledge about the future product. Each cycle is risk driven and uses prototypes and simulations to evaluate alternatives and resolve risks while producing work products. Each cycle concludes with reviews and approvals of fully elaborated documents before the next cycle is initiated.

The last cycle, when all risks have been uncovered and the requirements, product design, and detailed design approved, consists of a conventional waterfall development of the product.

1.2.1.3 Agile Development Model

The latest addition to development models is the *agile development model*. In this type of model the emphasis is placed on values and principles, as described in the "Manifesto of Software Development."

The development is carried out by a loosely structured small team, where people with different skills such as designing, programming, and testing are working closely with the customer in short development cycles.

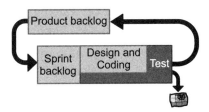

A development cycle usually only lasts 4 to 8 weeks, and in principle there can be any number of cycles; the highest number I have heard of is 58 cycles and still counting.

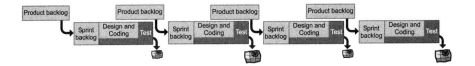

The *assumptions* when using an agile model are:

> ⏵ The team can produce workable features in each cycle.
> ⏵ The requirements (user stories) are constantly being added and changed in a product backlog, and implemented in the development cycles.
> ⏵ People are excelling when allowed to manage themselves and not having to follow defined processes.

The *characteristics* of a successful agile development project are:

> ⏵ Evolving requirements;
> ⏵ Very close cooperation in the development team, which includes a user representative;
> ⏵ Continuous testing of what is being produced;
> ⏵ Delivery in small and very frequent increments.

The small teams evolve features and whole products incrementally while introducing new concepts and product ideas along the way. However, because developers are free to innovate as they go along, they must synchronize frequently so product components all work together.

Testing is a truly integrated process in the development cycles, and each cycle is concluded with a demonstration of the product to inform the customer of what the product can do.

1.2.2 Test Types and Test Levels

To be able to divide testing into clear and coherent groups, testing has traditionally been structured into test types and test levels.

The primary division has been to split testing into static testing and dynamic testing.

Static testing is further split into a number of types, as described next.

Dynamic testing has traditionally been divided into dynamic test types and dynamic test levels; these are also described below.

1.2.2.1 Static Test Types

Static testing is performed without code being executed; it is typically performed on documents or drawings, but may be performed on anything you can look at.

Static testing is divided into a number of types, also sometimes called static testing techniques.

These types include:

▶ Informal reviews;
▶ Walk-through;
▶ Technical review;
▶ Management review;
▶ Inspection;
▶ Audit.

The types are further described in Section 4.3.

1.2.2.2 Dynamic Test Types

A dynamic test type is a test that focuses on a specific quality characteristic.

Quality characteristics for software products are described in ISO 25010, which is used here. More quality characteristics have been defined in other contexts.

The quality characteristics and hence the test types for a new system or a new or enhanced feature according to ISO 25010 are:

▶ Functional suitability;
▶ Performance;
▶ Compatibility;

> ◗ Usability;
> ◗ Reliability;
> ◗ Security;
> ◗ Maintainability;
> ◗ Portability.

Note that the last seven quality characteristics are often collectively referred to as nonfunctional.

The test types related to the quality characteristics are described in Chapter 7.

The functional and nonfunctional quality characteristics are guiding the design of new tests to verify the quality attributes of a system not yet subjected to testing.

However, testing may also be used for verifying changes made to a software product that has already been tested. The change-related test types are:

> ◗ Retesting (confirmation of a correction); and
> ◗ Regression testing of specified areas.

Retesting is the execution of tests that failed during the preceding execution, but are expected to pass after defect correction. It is done to determine whether defects have been correctly removed or not.

Regression testing is the execution of tests that have previously passed execution and are still expected to pass. This type of testing is used to determine whether the untouched parts of the system still work as specified after the change has been introduced.

1.2.2.3 Dynamic Test Levels

In the classic V-model, each development process, except the coding, has been assigned a corresponding dynamic test level as shown below.

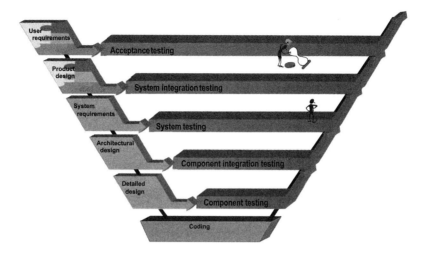

The V-model shown here includes the following dynamic test levels:

▶ Acceptance testing—based on and testing the fulfillment of the user requirements;
▶ System integration testing—based on and testing the implementation of the product design;
▶ System testing—based on and testing the fulfillment of the (software) system requirements;
▶ Component integration testing—based on and testing the implementation of the architectural design;
▶ Component testing—based on and testing the implementation of the detailed design.

Coding does not have a corresponding test level—it is not a specification phase, where expectations are expressed, but actual manufacturing. The code becomes the test object in the dynamic test levels.

No matter how many test levels we have, each test level is different from the others, especially in terms of goals and scope.

The dynamic test levels in the V-model used here are described in detail below.

1.2.2.3.1 Component Testing

Component testing is the test level for which the test planning work is the last to start, the first where test execution can start, and also the first to be finished.

The *goal* is to find defects in the implementation of each component according to the detailed design of the component.

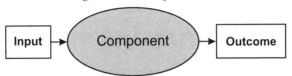

The test object is hence an individual component in isolation, and the basis documentation is the detailed design, and sometimes also other documentation like the requirements specification.

The code must never be used as the basis documentation from which to derive the expected results.

It is not always easy to agree on what a component is. A component could be what is contained in a compilable file, a subroutine, a class, or … the possibilities are legion. The important thing in an organization is to define "a component"—it is less important what a component is defined as.

The scope for one component test is an individual component. The full scope of component testing could be all components specified in the design, although sometimes only the most critical components may be selected for component testing.

The primary focus in component testing is on the functionality that the component is implementing, but nonfunctional requirements or characteristics, such as memory usage, defect handling, and maintainability, may also be tested at the component testing level.

To isolate a component, it may be necessary to have a driver that is able to execute the component. It is also usually necessary to have a stub or a simulator to mimic other components that interface with the component under test. Test stubs are sometimes referred to as test harnesses.

The need for test drivers and stubs must be specified as part of the specification of the test environment. Any needed drivers and stubs must of course be ready before the test execution of each individual component can start.

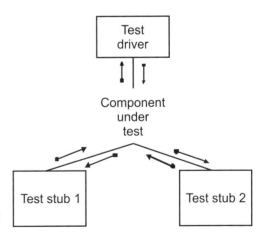

Many tools support component testing. Some are language specific and can act as drivers and stubs to facilitate the isolation of the component under test. Tools are discussed in Chapter 9.

Component *test execution* can start when the component has been deemed ready by the developer. The least we require before test execution can start is that the component be able to compile. It could be a very good idea to require a static test and/or static analysis to be performed and approved on the code before the component test execution.

Measures of time spent on the testing activities, on defects found and corrected, and on obtained coverage should be collected. This is sometimes difficult because component testing is often performed as an integrated development/testing/debugging activity with no registration of defects and very little if any reporting. This is a shame because it deprives the organization of valuable information about which kinds of defects are found and hence the possibility for introducing relevant process improvements.

The component testing for each individual component can stop when the completion criteria for the test have been met.

Any *test procedures should be kept,* because they can be very useful for later testing, including regression testing. Drivers and stubs should be kept for the same reason, and because they can be useful during integration testing.

1.2.2.3.2 Integration Testing

The *goals* of integration testing are to find defects in the interfaces and invariants between interacting entities in a system or a product. Invariants are substates that should be unchanged by the interaction between two entities. This is also called testing coexistence.

The objective is not to find defects inside the entities being integrated—the assumption being that these have already been found during previous testing.

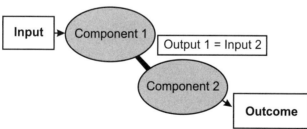

The entities to integrate may be components as defined in the architectural design or different systems as defined in the product design. The principles for integration testing are the same no matter what we are integrating.

There are a number of different strategies for the testing order in integration testing:

- Top down;
- Bottom up;
- Pairwise integration;
- Neighborhood integration;
- McCabe's design predicate approach;
- Big-bang.

These are briefly described below.

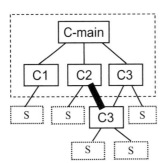

In top-down integration the interfaces in the top layer in the design hierarchy are tested first, followed by each layer going downward. The main program serves as the driver.

This way we quickly get a "shell" created. The drawback is that we (often) need a large number of stubs.

In bottom-up integration the interfaces in the lowest level are tested first. Here higher components are replaced with drivers, so we may need many drivers. This integration strategy enables early integration with hardware, where this is relevant.

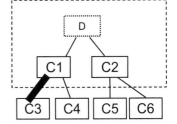

In pairwise integration testing, neighborhood integration, and McCabe's design predicate approach, the actual call relations between the components are studied to design an integration test approach that reduces the need for builds and for stubs and drivers. This way we can reduce the work needed for integration testing, and we may be able to make complete functional areas available more quickly; on the other hand, bugs may be more difficult to locate and the threat of moving into big-bang integration testing is moving closer.

In big-bang integration we integrate most or everything in one go. At first glance it seems like this strategy reduces the testing effort; but it does not—it does the opposite. It is impossible to get proper coverage when testing the interfaces in a big-bang integration, and it is very difficult to find defects; it is like looking for a needle in a haystack. Unfortunately, other integration test approaches often end up as big-bang, even if this was not the initial intention.

Often one of the producers of the entities to integrate has the responsibility for that integration testing, though both should be available.

Both the formality and the level of independence are usually higher for system integration testing than for component integration, but these issues should not be ignored for component integration testing.

The necessary drivers or stubs must be specified as part of the environment and developed before the integration testing can start. Often stubs from a previous test level, for example component testing, can be reused.

The *execution* of the integration testing follows the completion of the testing of the entities to integrate. As soon as two interacting entities have been tested individually, their integration test can be executed. There is no need to wait for all entities to be tested individually before the integration test execution can begin.

Measures of time spent on the testing, on defects found and corrected, and on coverage should be collected.

The integration testing for each individual interface can stop when the completion criteria have been met.

We must keep on integrating and testing the interfaces and the invariants until all entities have been integrated and the overall completion criteria defined in the integration test plan have been met.

1.2.2.3.3 System Testing

The *goal* of the system testing is to find defects in features of the system compared to the way it has been defined in the software system requirements or otherwise expressed expectations. The test object is the fully integrated system.

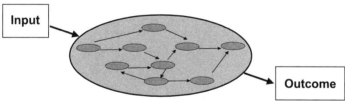

The better the component testing and component integration testing have been performed prior to the system testing, the more effective is the system testing. All too often system testing is impeded by poor or missing component and component integration testing. The *execution* of system testing follows the completion of the entire component integration testing.

Measures of time spent on the testing, on faults found and corrected, and on coverage should be collected. The system testing can stop when the completion criteria have been met.

1.2.2.3.4 Acceptance Testing

The acceptance testing is the queen's inspection of the guard. The *goal* of this test level is not, unlike all other levels, to find defects by getting the product to fail; at the acceptance test level the product is expected to be working and it is presented for acceptance.

The customer and/or end users must be involved in the acceptance testing. In some cases they have the full responsibility for the acceptance testing; in other cases they just witness the performance.

In acceptance testing the test object is the entire product. That could include:

> ❱ The system itself;
> ❱ Business processes in connection with the new system;
> ❱ Manual operations;
> ❱ Forms, reports, documentation.

The system itself should have been tested, and the other test objects should have been subjected to static testing before the acceptance testing.

The acceptance test may be executed by future users applying their domain knowledge and (it is hoped) testing skills to the validation of the product. Extracts of the system test are sometimes used as part of the acceptance test too.

An extra benefit of having representatives of the users involved in the acceptance testing is that it gives these users a detailed understanding of the new system—it can help create ambassadors for the product when it is brought into production.

There may be a number of acceptance test types, namely:

> ❱ Contract acceptance test;
> ❱ Alpha test;
> ❱ Beta test.

The contract acceptance test may also be called a factory acceptance test. This test must be completed before the product is handed over to the customer. It requires clear acceptance criteria to have been defined in the contract. A thorough registration of the results is necessary as evidence of what the customer acceptance is based on.

An Alpha test is usage of the product by representative users at the development site, but reflecting what the real usage will be like. Developers must not be present, but extended support must be provided. Alpha testing is not used particularly often since it can be very expensive to establish a "real" environment. The benefits rarely justify the costs.

A Beta test is usage of the product by selected (or voluntary) customers at the customer site. The product is used as it will be in production. The actual conditions determine the contents of the test. Also here extended support of the users is necessary. Beta tests preferably run over a longer period of time. Beta testing is used for off-the-shelf products—the customers get the product early (and possibly cheaper) in return for accepting a certain amount of immaturity and the responsibility of reporting all incidents.

1.2.3   ISO 29119 Test Sub-Process Concept

There are some difficulties with the concept of test types and test levels. When talking more specifically about the testing being planned or performed, it seems cumbersome to talk about either test types or test levels, as if they are district. The concept of test levels is sometimes difficult to understand because the levels are almost always presented across from a list of (example) development phases, giving the idea that the test levels are fixed phases and not "just" generic.

In ISO 29119 the concepts of test types and test levels have been condensed into the *concept of a test sub-process*. The definition of a test sub-process is a collection of test activities for which the test objective, test basis, and risks are identical.

The test objective, test basis, and risks specific to a test sub-process guide the choice of test activities to be performed, and also how they are being performed.

A test sub-process can be given any name that distinguishes it from other test sub-processes in the same test project.

A test sub-process may cover a number of test items, and include both dynamic testing and static testing performed using relevant techniques. It may also include "first time" testing and/or change-related testing, such as retest and/or regression test, as needed.

The figure below illustrates the principles of test sub-processes.

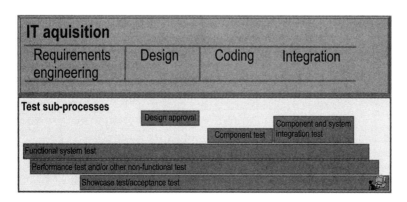

The number of test sub-processes in a test project depends on the test strategy and the life cycle phases defined for the overall project. It does not, however, depend on the development life cycle. The ones in the figure are just a few examples of the many possible test sub-processes that may exist in a development project.

In the figure a number of test sub-processes are defined and named. The figure is not to scale, but it should give the impression that test sub-processes may start early and last long, or be relatively short depending on their objective.

Below a few examples of test sub-processes are described. The examples are chosen to illustrate that a test sub-process may consist of various types and levels of testing and that a number of test items may be involved depending on the objective and the risk associated with any given test sub-process.

System Requirements Verification Sub-process

Test objective(s):   Assessment of quality of system requirements.

Test item(s):   System requirements specification.

Test item specification(s):   Allocated product requirements and internal guideline for requirements.

Test types(s):   Static, for consistency, completeness, and conformance to guidelines.

Test techniques(s):   Technical review (for readiness), inspection (for quality), and informal review (for retest and regression test).

The corresponding test subprocess may look like this:

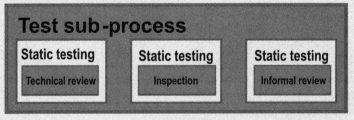

This example represents relatively formal requirements verification. The test sub-process should be scheduled to be complete before a requirements approval milestone.

Acceptance Test

              Test objective(s): Assessment of quality of final system.

                   Test item(s): Final system.

  Test item specification(s): System requirements.

                Test types(s): Dynamic, functional

           Test techniques(s): Use case testing, retest, and regression test.

Generally the objective of the acceptance testing is not to find defects by getting the system to fail, but rather to obtain final validation and acceptance by the customer. The assumption is that the system works after having passed other test sub-processes.

The corresponding test sub-process may look like this:

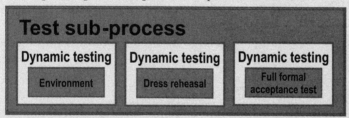

As should be the case for all dynamic test sub-processes, the first test execution cycle should be one to determine if the test environment is ready and valid. Following this a dress rehearsal (or two) may be performed to ensure that the final execution in the presence of the customer will be successful.

Security Test

              Test objective(s): Mitigate the risk of security failure of the system including verification of correct removal of uncovered defects.

                   Test item(s): Detailed design, architectural design, and the final system.

  Test item specification(s): Security requirements and security risks.

                Test types(s): Static and dynamic testing, nonfunctional for security.

           Test techniques(s): Inspection, technical review, attacks.

The corresponding test sub-process may look like this:

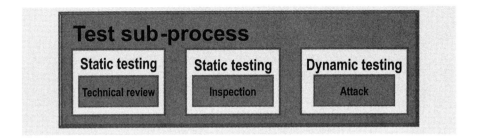

1.2.4 Production and Maintenance

A project set up for continuous maintenance is usually different from a development project, in the sense that an amount of money is budgeted for maintenance in a specific period at an agreed-on level. This may be stated in a service level agreement (SLA) between the customer and the maintenance organization.

The maintenance goal is to maintain a specified level of availability of the system, and will consist of a number of minor changes implemented for the system on a continuous basis. This entails numerous minor test sub-processes for the testing of the changes and regression testing of the rest of the system (or selected parts of it).

1.3 Test and Support Processes

No matter how the development model is structured, there will always be a number of supporting activities, or supporting processes for the development.

The primary supporting processes are:

- ▶ Project management;
- ▶ Quality assurance;
- ▶ Configuration management.

These processes are performed during the entire course of development and support the development from idea to product.

The supporting processes all interact with the test process.

Testing is a product quality assurance activity and hence part of the supporting processes. This is in line with the fact that testing is meaningless without the development processes and not producing anything in its own right.

The test material is itself subject to quality assurance or testing, so testing is recursive. Testing also interacts with project management and configuration management as described in detail in the following.

When the product—or an increment—is deployed, it transfers to the production and maintenance phase. In this phase corrections and possibly new features will be delivered at defined intervals, and testing plays an important role in this.

1.3.1 Project Management

It is obviously important for the development process and the supporting processes to be managed and controlled during the entire project. Project management is the supporting process that takes care of this, from the first idea to the release.

The most important activities in project management are:

▶ Risk analysis;
▶ Estimation;
▶ Scheduling;
▶ Monitoring and control;
▶ Communication.

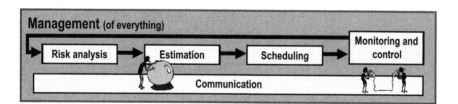

Test management is subordinated to project management.

The estimation, risk analysis, and planning, including scheduling of the test activities, will either have to be done by the test manager in cooperation with the project management or alone by the test manager and consolidated with the overall project planning. The results of the monitoring and control of the test activities will also have to be coordinated with the project management activities.

The communication between project management and the test project is illustrated in the figure below. The details of the test process are described in Chapter 2.

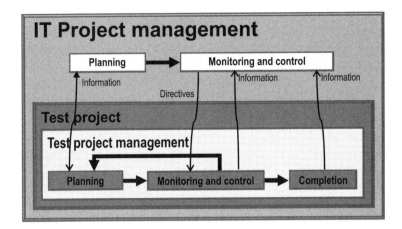

Project management activities are not discussed further here.

1.3.2 Product Quality Assurance

It is not possible to test quality into a product by performing dynamic testing when the development is close to being finished. The quality assurance activities must start early and become an integrated part of the entire development project and the mind-set of all stakeholders.

Traditionally, quality assurance has been treated as a different process area from testing, and there is still no agreement on the relative "hierarchy." Personally I find that testing in the broad sense of both dynamic and static testing is very close to quality assurance.

In this section traditional quality assurance is described, and then it is up to you to judge if you think this is "just" another way of looking at testing, or if there is more to it.

Quality assurance comprises four activities:

 ▶ Definition of quality criteria;
 ▶ Validation;
 ▶ Verification;
 ▶ Quality reporting.

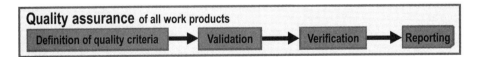

Note that the validation is not necessarily performed before the verification; in many organizations it is the other way around, or in parallel.

First of all the *quality criteria* must be defined. These criteria are the expression of the quality level that must be reached—or an expression of "what is sufficiently good." These criteria can be very different from product to product. They depend on the business needs and the product type. Different quality criteria will be set for a product that will just be thrown away when it is not working than for a product that is expected to work for many years with a great risk of serious consequences if it does not work.

Two quality assurance activities are used for checking if the quality criteria have been met by the object under test, namely:

▶ Validation;
▶ Verification.

They have different goals and different techniques. Unfortunately, they also have different definitions in different standards.

According to ISTQB vocabulary, based on ISO 9000, we have:

> *Validation*: Confirmation by examination and through provision of objective evidence that the requirements for a specific intended use or application have been fulfilled.
>
> *Verification*: Confirmation by examination and through the provision of objective evidence that specified requirements have been fulfilled.

A popular way of expressing the concepts is:
Validation answers the question: *"Are we building the correct product?"*
Verification answers the question: *"Are we building the product correctly?"*

The test processes and techniques presented in this book can be used as part of both the validation and verification activities.

Quality assurance reports on the findings and results that should be produced.

The test object should be placed under configuration management once it has passed the validation and verification stages if that has not been done already.

1.3.3 Configuration Management

Configuration management is another supporting process with which testing interacts. The purpose of configuration management is to establish and maintain the integrity of work products and the product.

Configuration management can be defined as:

▶ Unique identification;
▶ Controlled storage;

> Change management
  (recognition, investigation, action, and disposition);
> Audit;
> Status reporting;

for selected

> Work products;
> Product components;
> Products;

performed during the entire product life cycle.

Audit is a quality assurance activity aimed at the way configuration management is performed in an organization. This is not described further here.

Note that an object under configuration management is called a configuration item (CI).

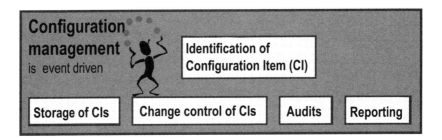

The purpose of *identification* is to uniquely identify each configuration item and to specify its relations to the outside world and to other configuration items. Identification is one of the cornerstones of configuration management, because it is impossible to control something you don't know the identity of.

Each organization must define the conventions for unique identification of the configuration items.

Test Cases
   10.3.1.6 (80)–1.A Test for correct bank identity number

   The identification encompasses:
   Current section number in document: 10.3.1.6
   Running unique number: 80
   Version of test case: 1.A

The purpose of *storage* is to ensure that configuration items don't disappear or become damaged. It must be possible to find the items at any time and have them delivered in the condition in which we expect to find them.

Storage is something physical. Items that are stored are physically present at a specific place. This place is often called the library, or the controlled library.

Configuration items are released from storage to be used as the basis for further work. *Use is all imaginable deployment of configuration items without these being changed,* not just use of the final product by the final users.

For instance, use may be a review if a document is placed under configuration management in the form of a draft and subsequently has to be reviewed. It may be a test of larger or minor parts of the system, integration of a subcomponent into a larger component, or the proper operation or sale of a finished product.

Configuration items of a specific version released from storage must not be changed, ever! But new versions of the configuration item may be issued as the result of change control.

The purpose of *change management* or *change control* is to be fully in control of all change requests for a product and of all implemented changes. Any change should be traced to the configuration item where the change has been implemented.

The initiation of change control is the occurrence of an incident. Incident management is discussed in Chapter 8.

The purpose of *status reporting* is to make available the information necessary for effective management of the development, testing, and maintenance of a product, in a useful and readable way.

Configuration management can be a mine of information.

A few words about the concept of a *configuration item* are needed here. In principle, everything may be placed under configuration management. The list below shows what objects may become configuration items, with the emphasis on the test ware.

- ▶ Test material: test specifications, test data(base), drivers, and stubs;
- ▶ Environments: operating systems, tools, compilers, and linkers;
- ▶ Technical documentation: requirements, design, and technical notes;
- ▶ Code: source code, header files; includes files and system libraries;
- ▶ Project documentation: user manuals, build scripts, data, event registrations, installation procedures, and plans;
- ▶ Administrative documents: letters, contracts, process description, sales material, templates, and standards;
- ▶ Hardware: cables, mainframe, PC, workstation, network, storage, and peripherals.

The communication between configuration management and the test project is illustrated in the figure below. The details of the test process are described in Chapter 2.

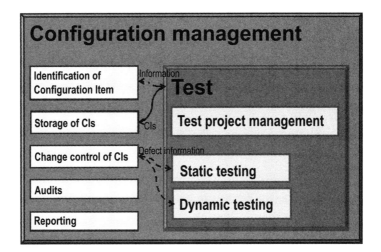

1.4   Test Process Improvement

Maturity is as important for software development as it is for people. When we are immature, we can easily find ourselves in a situation where we lose control and are unable to solve problems—problems we might even have created ourselves.

The demands on the software industry are growing as pervasive software thunders ahead. More and more products include software, and both embedded software and other software products are becoming more and more complex. The potential number of defects in the software is increasing and so is the cost of finding and removing them—not least keeping in mind that the cost of defect correction increases by a factor 10 for each development phase the defects "survive" in the work products.

The solution to the growing demands is more professional software development with a focus on the entire product and hence the entire development process. Software development needs to be able to stay in control, foresee problems, and prevent them or mitigate them in a mature way. Software development needs to grow up, improve, and thereby become a mature industry—and so does testing.

Process improvement is based on the understanding that software development is a process, and that processes can be managed, measured, and continuously improved.

An important assumption is *that the quality of the software produced using a specific process is closely related to the quality of the process.*

This does not mean that it is impossible to produce excellent software using no or a lousy process—or indeed the other way around—but the probability of producing good software rises significantly with the quality of the process.

The urge for improvement can come from many places both outside and inside the organization, and both from the "floor" and from the "top."

▶ Customers or suppliers may push or even demand proof of maturity and ongoing process improvement. More indirectly they may express requirements in terms of quality criteria and time-to-market, whose fulfillment requires a certain maturity in the organization.

▶ Within the organization managers are pressed to obey constraints and to provide growth in the organization.

▶ Employees may be fed up with constant fire-fighting and impossible deadlines requiring them to work overtime and cut corners.

Military organizations usually require their suppliers to be at a minimum of CMMI level 3.

1.4.1   Process Improvement Principles

Process improvement is hard work. More than anything the software quality is dependent on the abilities of the people working in the organization—both the individuals and the teams. People write the processes and the methods and techniques to be used. People follow the processes and use the methods and techniques.

Everything needs to fit together to be efficient and effective.

A popular and long lasting approach to process improvement is the **IDEAL model** (from the Software Engineering Institute at Carnegie University, USA—the home of the CMM and CMMI models):

▶ Initialization;

▶ Diagnosis;

▶ Establishing;

▶ Acting;

▶ Learning.

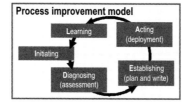

This approach is cyclic as continuous process improvement must be. Organizations performing process improvement must:

▶ Produce process descriptions including methods and techniques.

▶ Introduce the processes to the people working in the organization, and provide adequate training.

▶ Request and support deployment of the processes as appropriate.

▶ Determine the maturity of the processes and their deployment.

▶ Use this information to adjust the processes and/or introduce them again to the people.

▶ Repeat ad libitum.

Tools may be used to support the activities, but tools cannot provide process improvement by themselves.

A process improvement project must be run like any other project. Activities must be prioritized—both in the short term and in the long run. Activities must be planned with defined goals, activities, resources, time, and budget. The responsible person must follow up on the progress. And last but not least: it is important to report on the successes.

Process improvement is not easy. Many organizations fail in their first attempt and that impedes any following attempts.

Research has been done into what make organizations succeed or fail. This research shows that the *organizations most likely to succeed are those where software process improvement is incorporated in the organization's vision and strategy* at the highest level.

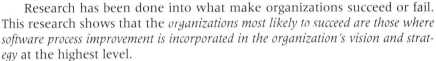

It is important that top management understand that process improvement is an organizational change and that it involves change management. Process improvement is first and foremost about people.

It is hard work that requires continuous focus, but it is also very rewarding work. No organization I have met has ever wished itself back to the "bad old days" of low maturity.

1.4.1.1 A Few Process Improvement Results

More and more assessments are being performed all over the world and companies of all sizes are embarking on structured process improvement. What most of these companies are asking for before starting a process improvement project is the possible return on investment (ROI).

Return on investment can be expressed in a number of ways; the most common, of course, is to express it in economic terms, such as cost and savings. But measures such as defects per 1,000 lines of code and employee satisfaction can also be used. The greatest impediment regarding measuring of ROI is lack of initial measures. Amazingly many organizations have no clue as to how much their work costs them.

SEI has collected data from more than 500 organizations using CMM as the basis for their process improvement. A few of these results are presented here as appetizers.

The graph below shows a typical change in the average and distribution of the performance of a process for organizations moving from maturity level 1 to 5 (the levels are described below).

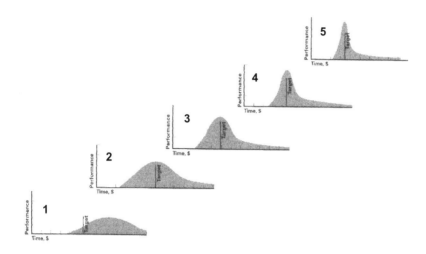

At level 1 the average project is far over the target for the estimated time of completion, and the dispersion is high.

The dispersion decreases as the maturity increases, and the average project actually hit the target. As the maturity increases further, the target is moved to the left. *Mature organizations perform in a more predictable way and they perform better than more immature organizations.*

The table below shows the employees' perception of six aspects of the performance of their organization as the organizations moved from CMM level 1 to CMM level 3.

138 individuals	CMM 1	CMM 2	CMM3
Meet schedule	40	55	80
Meet budget	40	55	65
Product quality	75	90	100
Staff productivity	55	70	85
Customer satisfaction	75	70	100
Staff morale	25	50	60

The table is the result of 138 people being asked to state their opinion of the aspects on a five-step scale ranging from "nonexistent" to "excellent."

The table shows how many percentages answered one of the two highest possibilities.

The percentages of employees answering "good" or "excellent" are increasing with the maturity level for all aspects.

One small exception is "Customer satisfaction" where the high-answering percentage is dropping at level 2. This could well be because the organizations have started to answer "no" to impossible tasks upfront, and maybe also because they are starting to ask the customers for more precise requirements, etc.

1.4.2 Process Maturity Models in General

One of the more reliable ways to determine the maturity of a software-producing organization is by using a certified software process assessment tool set. An assessment tool set consists of two basic parts: a reference model and a method. The model is a description of the domain to be assessed, and the method describes how to perform the assessment in a verifiable and valid way. The model usually also works as a map guiding organizations toward higher maturity levels.

Many assessment tool sets have been produced during the past two decades, but the most important are CMM, BOOTSTRAP, CMMI, and ISO 15504. These have got much inspiration from one another as the "family tree" below shows. BOOTSTRAP was a European tool set now overtaken by ISO 15504.

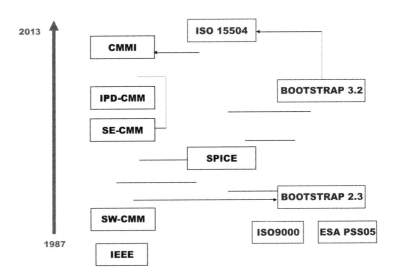

Maybe—it is hoped—the CMMI and ISO 15504 will come together in one standard sometime in the future.

1.4.2.1 CMM

The Capability Maturity Model (CMM) was the first assessment tool set, officially released in 1991. It has now been overtaken by CMMI, but the original definitions of maturity levels still exist.

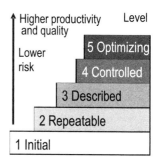

The CMM is staged. This means that each maturity level has a number of associated Key Process Areas (KPAs). CMM KPAs are distributed on maturity levels as shown here.

From a testing point of view, the CMM is not adequate. The concept of testing maturity is not addressed and the model does not include testing practices as a process improvement area. Testing issues are addressed in some of the KPAs, but not in a satisfactory manner.

CMM is still widely used, but CMMI is moving in fast.

1.4.2.2 CMMI

The Capability Maturity Model Integration (CMMI), Version 1.02, was published in 2000, and Version 1.2 was published in 2006. Like CMM, CMMI is developed and supported by the Software Engineering Institute.

CMMI has two representations: staged and continuous. Guidelines are offered on how to choose between the models and how to tailor the chosen model to specific needs.

The *staged* CMMI representation is similar to CMM V. 1.1. Maturity levels in the staged representation apply to an organization's overall process capability and organizational maturity. The result of a staged assessment is one number = the maturity level.

The capability levels in the *continuous* representation can be reached for each process area individually. There are six capability levels, numbered 0 through 5. The result of a continuous assessment is a profile showing the capability level for each process area. This is very much like the result of a ISO 15504 assessment.

CMMI operates with process areas. These are divided into four main groups: Process Management, Project Management, Engineering, and Support.

CMMI is rapidly establishing itself worldwide. The CMMI continuous representation is gaining ground over the staged representation.

From a testing point of view CMMI has more focus on verification and validation than CMM, but testing maturity is still not addressed explicitly.

1.4.2.3 ISO 15504

The ISO 15504 standard for maturity assessments has long been known under the working name of SPICE, and it was finally released in 2003. ISO 15504 is mostly used in Europe and the Far East.

ISO 15504 is a continuous model; that is, the capability is assessed for each of the defined process areas individually in an identical way. The result of an assessment is a capability profile.

The reference model defined in SPICE is two dimensional. One dimension is the capability dimension with six capability levels. The other dimension is the process dimension structured in three process categories.

Each of the process categories is refined into a number of subcategories (called processes). The full structure is shown below.

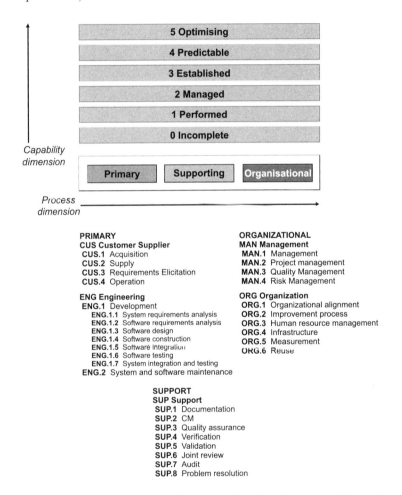

PRIMARY
CUS Customer Supplier
  CUS.1 Acquisition
  CUS.2 Supply
  CUS.3 Requirements Elicitation
  CUS.4 Operation

ENG Engineering
  ENG.1 Development
    ENG.1.1 System requirements analysis
    ENG.1.2 Software requirements analysis
    ENG.1.3 Software design
    ENG.1.4 Software construction
    ENG.1.5 Software Integration
    ENG.1.6 Software testing
    ENG.1.7 System integration and testing
  ENG.2 System and software maintenance

ORGANIZATIONAL
MAN Management
  MAN.1 Management
  MAN.2 Project management
  MAN.3 Quality Management
  MAN.4 Risk Management

ORG Organization
  ORG.1 Organizational alignment
  ORG.2 Improvement process
  ORG.3 Human resource management
  ORG.4 Infrastructure
  ORG.5 Measurement
  ORG.6 Reuse

SUPPORT
SUP Support
  SUP.1 Documentation
  SUP.2 CM
  SUP.3 Quality assurance
  SUP.4 Verification
  SUP.5 Validation
  SUP.6 Joint review
  SUP.7 Audit
  SUP.8 Problem resolution

ISO 15504 has much more focus on the development life cycle, and hence on testing, than CMM and CMMI. This can be seen in the process category Engineering where the subcategory Development is further broken down into detailed development activities, including the processes of Software Testing and Software Integration and Testing.

1.4.3 Testing Improvement Models

This section begins with a word of warning. An old saying goes: "One should stick to one's own class." This is to some extent the case for organizations with regard to maturity. Research has shown that the maturity of organizations influences their ability to work together. The results are shown in the matrix here.

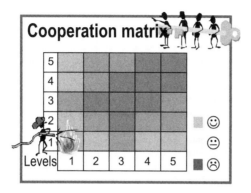

Provided by Jøm Johensen, DELTA

In general, organizations at maturity level 1 are difficult to work with for organizations at level 1 and 2, and at level 4 and 5—even though the reasons are different. A level 3 organization can work with a level 1 organization, but it is not the best constellation.

The higher the maturity on both sides, the better the cooperation—and more importantly, the more equal the maturity, the better the cooperation.

This is worth keeping in mind for test organizations that want to improve. The next section is about testing specific improvement models. Testing organizations can mature using these models, but *the best result for the company as a whole is if the different departments synchronize their process improvements.*

1.4.3.1 TMMI—Testing Maturity Model

Dr. Ilene Burnstein, Institute of Technology, has said: "Testing is a critical component of the software development process. Organizations have not fully realized their potential for supporting the development of high quality software products. To address this issue we are building a Testing Maturity Model (TMM) to serve as a guide to organizations focusing on test process assessment and improvement."

TMMI has been developed based on TMM as a complement to the CMMI. Organizations interested in assessing and improving their testing capabilities are likely to be involved in general software process improvement. To have directly corresponding levels in both maturity models would logically simplify these two parallel process improvement drives.

The Software Engineering Institute's CMMI does not adequately address testing issues. The TMMI is built to overcome this.

The model is structured like the CMMI, but specifically addressing issues important to test managers, test specialists, and software quality assurance staff. Like CMMI, the TMMI contains a set of maturity levels, a set of recommended practices at each level of maturity, and an assessment model that will allow organizations to evaluate and improve their testing process.

The TMMI can be used by a number of stakeholders:

▶ Internal assessment team to identify the current testing capability state;

▶ Upper management to initiate a testing improvement program;

▶ Development teams to improve testing capability;

▶ Users and clients to define their role in the testing process.

The founders of TMMI point out that not only is the TMMI structurally similar to the CMMI, it must be viewed and utilized as a complement to the CMMI, since mature testing processes depend on general process maturity.

In the development of TMMI a historical model provided in a key paper by Gelperin and Hetzel has been used. Their model describes phases and test goals for the periods of the 1950s through the 1990s.

Beizer's evolutionary model of the individual testers' thinking process in many ways parallels the Gelperin-Hetzel model. Its influence on TMMI development is based on the premise that a mature testing organization is built on the skills, abilities, and attitudes of the individuals who work within it.

Beizer's phases in a tester's mental life are shown here.

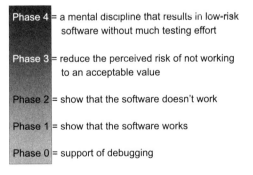

Phase 4 = a mental discipline that results in low-risk software without much testing effort

Phase 3 = reduce the perceived risk of not working to an acceptable value

Phase 2 = show that the software doesn't work

Phase 1 = show that the software works

Phase 0 = support of debugging

The initial period in the Gelperin and Hetzel model is described as "Debugging-Oriented." During that period most software development organizations had not clearly differentiated between testing and debugging. Testing was viewed as an activity to help remove bugs.

In the "Demonstration-Oriented" period, a primary testing goal was to demonstrate that the software satisfied its specification. Testing and debugging were still linked in efforts to detect, locate, and correct faults.

The "Destruction-Oriented" period focused on testing as an activity to detect implementation faults. Debugging was a set of separate activities needed to locate and correct faults.

In the "Evaluation-Oriented" period, testing became an activity that was integrated into the software life cycle. The value of review activities was recognized. The view of testing was broadened and its goals were to detect requirements, design, and implementation faults.

The Gelperin-Hetzel historical model culminates with what they call a "Prevention-Oriented" period, which reflects the optimizing level 5 of both the CMMI and the TMMI. The scope of testing is broadly defined and includes review activities. A primary testing goal is to prevent requirements, design, and implementation defects. Review activities now support test planning, test design, and product evaluation.

1.4.3.2   TPI Next®—Test Process Improvement Model

TPI Next, the Test Process Improvement model, is a dedicated test maturity model. It was developed in Holland in 1997 by Tim Koomen and Martin Pol as TPI, but has since developed into TPI Next.

The model was first developed because the authors needed a model to support their test-focused process improvement activities, and they were unable to find an existing model that satisfied their needs.

TPI Next is built on extensive testing experience, and suggests the following improvement: After initial awareness of the general improvement ideas, the actual improvement work starts with an assessment. The result of this is used to define improvement actions. After planning and implementation of these actions, a new assessment can be performed to define the next actions. Test process improvement is an ongoing, never-ending process.

The authors of TPI Next point out that test process improvement is only one of a much larger group of aspects that influence the total result of system development. Test process improvement should be aligned with other initiatives, such as general software process improvement.

1.4.3.2.1   TPI Next Structure

Like the other models, TPI Next has a well-defined structure, as shown in the figure below.

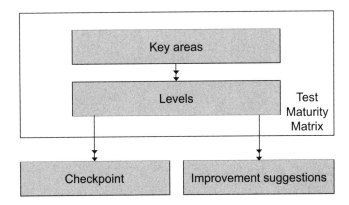

The model defines a number of key areas and for each of these it defines a number of levels. For each level for each specific key area a number of checkpoints are defined. These checkpoints are used to determine if a specific level is achieved for the specific key area. To assist the test process improvement, a number of improvement suggestions is also defined for each specific level for each key area.

TPI Next has 16 key areas that cover the total test process. The areas are grouped into cornerstones or areas:

Stakeholder Relations:

- Stakeholder commitment;
- Degree of involvement;
- Test strategy;
- Test organization;
- Communication;
- Reporting.

Test Management:

- Test process management;
- Estimating and planning;
- Metrics;
- Defect management;
- Testware management.

Test Profession:

- Methodology practice;
- Tester professionalism;

- Test case design;
- Test tools;
- Test environment.

1.4.3.2.2   TPI Assessment

As mentioned above, each level for each key area has a number of check-points to be met. The number of checkpoints varies from key specific level to key specific level.

There is no graduation applied in the model. This means that all check-points have to be fully met before a key area reaches a specific level.

The result of a TPI assessment is a test maturity matrix that indicates how each of the 16 key areas has scored. This is the maturity profile of the test organization. The maturity profile shows the strong areas and the weak areas, and provides the first indication of where to set in with improvement actions.

1.4.3.3   CTP—Critical Testing Processes

In the beginning of this book we established that testing is a process, and that the testing process can be broken down into more and more detailed processes.

The quality of the description of a given process and the way the process is performed influences the quality of the work done. Following well-described and well-fitting processes in a conscientious way provides better results than other combinations, such as following processes in a sloppy way (or not at all) or following ill-fitting processes.

The American Rex Black has introduced the concept of critical testing processing as a guideline for test process improvement.

The basic assumption is that some of the testing processes we can specify and follow are more critical than others. The criteria for a process to be defined as critical are that the process is:

- Repeated frequently;
- Highly cooperative;
- Visible to peers and superiors;
- Linked to process success.

The CTP model is a highly flexible model and the aspects in it should be tailored to the specific context in which it is being used. This includes that the organizations using the model may identify their own specific challenges and their own way of describing a process, and may define the importance of the processes and hence the order of their improvement actions.

The critical processes must fit into the development model in which the testing is a support activity. Each development process must be linked to one or more testing processes and vice versa.

1.4.3.3.1   The 12 Critical Processes

Rex Black has defined the 12 processes he considers to be most critical. These are:

1.   Testing;
2.   Establishing context;
3.   Quality risk analysis;
4.   Test estimation;
5.   Test planning;
6.   Test team development;
7.   Test system development;
8.   Test release management;
9.   Test execution;
10. Bug reporting;
11. Result reporting;
12. Change management.

For each of these processes, the model explains what the heading covers and why the specific process is important.

One example is the first of the critical processes: *the testing process*.

This process encompasses the activities:

▶ Planning: determining what testing to do in the context;
▶ Preparing: designing and build the tests and forming the test team(s);
▶ Performing: getting the test object, making it executable and testable, and testing it;
▶ Perfecting: reporting findings and guiding the process.

This process is important because the result of performing it well will be reducing costs by finding important bugs, providing useful information about less important bugs, reducing risks by identifying what works and what doesn't, and giving management essential information.

Another example is the *test estimation process*. This process encompasses the activities:

▶ Identifying the testing tasks, resources, and dependencies through a work-breakdown structure;

▶ Drawing on test and project team wisdom;

▶ Putting together a budget;

▶ Selling the estimate to management.

This process is important because the result of performing it well will be balancing cost and time required for testing against project needs and risks, forecasting the tasks and duration of testing in an accurate and actionable manner, and demonstration of the return of the testing investment.

1.4.3.3.2 Assessment of the Testing Process

The CTP model includes a guide for assessing the existing test process and its sub-processes in an organization. The assessment process itself may be tailored to the specific context.

The following top five points should however be assessed for the processes:

▶ Effectiveness;

▶ Efficiency;

▶ Pervasion;

▶ Information provision;

▶ Improvement.

The findings for these points can be substantiated by both quantitative and qualitative measurements.

1.4.3.3.3 Improving Critical Processes

The result of a CTP assessment is a profile showing which processes are strong and which are weak. Taking the organizational needs into consideration this provides a prioritized recommendation of which process to improve at this particular point in time. There is no inherited recommendation for the order in which testing processes should be improved in the CTP model.

1.4.3.4 STEP: Systematic Test and Evaluation Process

The last model we are going to look at is in fact the first. The testing methodology called STEP (Systematic Test and Evaluation Process) was developed by Drs. David Gelperin and William Hetzel in 1986. STEP was developed based on ANSI, American National Standards Institute 829: Test Documentation Standard, and 1008: Unit Test Standard. IEEE has since taken over these standards, which is why we now refer to IEEE 829, but it is the same standard.

At the time the STEP presented an entirely new concept, namely, a test process to run in parallel with the development and support validation of the completeness of each phase of development. The STEP model defines four test levels: acceptance test, system test, integration test, and unit test; a concept that holds to this day.

Before STEP, testing was seen as something performed after the system was fully assembled. STEP expanded that original definition of testing to encompass three main steps:

1. Plan the test strategy (develop a master test plan and associated detailed test plans).
2. Acquire testware (define test objectives, design and create test plans).
3. Measure (execute the tests, ensure that tests are adequate and monitor the process itself).

The test planning activities are based on the ANSI Standard 829 requiring a master test plan and a detailed test plan for each of the test levels outlined in the master test plan. The detailed test plans are to be produced during the corresponding development phase.

In the acquisition activity STEP describes how test cases are to be produced to validate each requirement in a requirements-based testing approach for the higher test levels. At the lower test levels test cases are produced to validate the design. The test cases are to be produced in parallel with the development activities and serve as extra quality assurance of, what STEP refers to as inventory items (work products). Traceability matrices between test cases and inventroy items must be produced.

The acquisition activity includes a risk analysis for prioritization of the test cases, and the creation of test procedures, test data, and tools, if any.

During test execution and measurement, a test log is required and incident reports must be made when incidents are discovered. At the conclusion of the test a test report must be made; the findings and experiences made during the test must be analyzed and reported. STEP outlines that the results of these activities, the documents, test data, and tools used are to be preserved for future use.

STEP also covers maintenance testing including regression testing.

In short, we can say that STEP supports the modern understanding of a good testing process in that it promotes and supports:

▶ A requirements-based testing strategy;
▶ Testing starts at the beginning of the life cycle;
▶ Tests are used as requirements and usage models;
▶ Testware design leads software design;
▶ Defects are detected earlier or prevented altogether;

◗ Defects are systematically analyzed;

◗ Testers and developers work together.

STEP is not a process improvement model in the sense discussed above. It presents a test process, whose introduction in an organization is the improvement. The way the STEP process is used may be improved by auditing (assessing) the process and analyzing the measures collected.

1.5 Standards

1.5.1 Standards in General

The word "standard" means a usage or practice that is generally accepted, according to Collins Pocket English Dictionary. Standards document experience gained by many people over a long time.

It is a long and hard job to create a standard. The right people have to be found, they have to be able to meet, and—more importantly—to agree enough on the various subjects to determine what "the standard" is. There is usually also a long period of time set aside for hearings and reviews of the material before a standard may indeed be approved as a standard. In some cases this process can take years.

This is part of the reason why standards don't change very often. They do change when there is a real need because practices, opinions, and experience change, and it is important when working with standards to take care that the right version is used and referenced as applicable—versions are often indicated by the year of the issue of the standard.

A standard is not an expression of a scientific truth, but something made by humans. This is why we have a number of standards on the same subjects; and why standards sometimes are both internally inconsistent and inconsistent with each other. Standards also to some extent disagree; and it can be difficult to determine which, if any, is most "correct." Despite this, standards can be a great help.

Standards come from many sources, for example:

◗ International standards;

◗ National standards;

◗ Domain-specific standards.

Standards may also be specific to an organization, so called in-house standards. Such standards are very useful as guidelines for work to be done.

Test-related standards fall into three categories, depending on the type of information they provide.

- ▶ Quality assurance standards—telling you that *you shall test*. An example of these standards is ISO 9001:2001 quality management system design.
- ▶ Industry specific—telling you that *you shall test this much*.
  Such standards exist for example for aviation, railways, fire alarms, electronic products, vehicles, nuclear plants, and medical devices.
- ▶ Testing standards—telling you *how to actually test*.

Sometimes we are obliged to follow one or more specific standards because of the nature of the product we are developing or because of demands from customers or management.

Even if that is not the case, we as testers should be aware of which standards are relevant for us and from where we can get guidelines and inspiration.

Remember though, that whatever you do, don't do it because a standard says so. Do it because it serves your business.

1.5.2 International Standards

The two most prominent sources of internationally recognized standards are:

- ▶ ISO—International Organization for Standardization;
- ▶ IEEE—Institute of Electrical and Electronics Engineers.

ISO and IEEE recognize each other and some standards are common to the two organizations. These standards have identical numbers in the ISO and in the IEEE series.

1.5.2.1 ISO Standards

ISO is a network of the national standards institutes of 157 countries, on the basis of one member per country, with a Central Secretariat in Geneva, Switzerland (www.iso.org).

The name ISO is derived from the Greek *isos*, meaning "equal," in order for the name to always be ISO whatever the national language is.

ISO is a nongovernmental organization, but occupies a special position between the public and private sectors.

International standardization began in the electrotechnical field: the International Electrotechnical Commission (IEC) was established in 1906. In 1946, delegates from 25 countries met in London and decided to create a new international organization, of which the object would be "to facilitate the international coordination and unification of industrial standards." The new organization, ISO, officially began operations on February 23, 1947.

ISO has developed hundreds, if not thousands of standards. Those of most interest to testers may be:

- ▶ ISO 29119:2013—Software testing processes;
- ▶ ISO 9000:2005—Quality management systems;
- ▶ ISO 9126—Product quality;
- ▶ ISO 12207—Information technology, software life cycle processes.

1.5.2.2   IEEE Standards

The IEEE is a nonprofit organization based in the United States. The association has more than 370,000 members in over 160 countries (www.ieee.org).

The full name of the IEEE is the Institute of Electrical and Electronics Engineers, Inc., although it is referred to by the letters I-E-E-E and pronounced Eye-triple-E.

The IEEE formed in 1963 with the merger of the AIEE (American Institute of Electrical Engineers, formed in 1884), and the IRE (Institute of Radio Engineers, formed in 1912).

IEEE has issued more than 900 active IEEE standards and more than 400 are in development on areas ranging from aerospace systems, computers and telecommunications to biomedical engineering, electric power and consumer electronics among others. Those of most interest for testers may be:

- ▶ IEEE 610:1991—Standard computer dictionary;
- ▶ IEEE 829:1998—Standard for software test documentation;
- ▶ IEEE 1028:1997—Standard for software review and audit;
- ▶ IEEE 1044:1995—Guideline to classification of anomalies;
- ▶ IEEE/ISO 12207:1995—Standard for software life cycle processes.

Note that IEEE 829 has now officially been superseded by ISO 29119, Part 3.

1.5.3   National Standards

Many countries have their own standardization organization, like the British Standard Institution (BSI) in the United Kingdom and Dansk Standard (DS) in Denmark. These organizations issue their own local standards and they may also recognize some of the international standards.

An example of a British national standard of interest for testers is:

BS 7925-2:1998—Software testing. Software component testing.

Note, that this has now officially been superseded by ISO 29119, Part 4.

1.5.4 Domain-Specific Standards

Many regulatory standards mandating the application of particular testing techniques exist. Some of them (but probably not all) are listed below:

▶ IEC/CEI 61508
Functional safety of electrical/electronic/programmable safety-related systems;

▶ DO-178-B
Software considerations in airborne systems and equipment certification;

▶ pr EN 50128
Software for railway control and protection systems;

▶ Def Stan 00-55
Requirements for safety-related software in defense equipment;

▶ IEC 880
Software for computers in the safety systems of nuclear power stations;

▶ MISRA
Development guidelines for vehicle-based software;

▶ FDA
American Food and Drug Administration (pharmaceutical standards);

▶ ECSS
European Cooperation on Space Standardization.

One of the difficulties with the above standards is that they are not directly aimed at software. Each of them has its origin in a specific field, into which software has only relatively recently penetrated. It would be nice if we had one software-specific standard dealing with the aspects of how much to test and how to test software depending on risk analysis. But since that is not the case, we will have to make do with the existing standards.

Questions

1. What are the processes that may be expected to be present in an organization?
2. Name some of the product paradigms in which testing should be included.
3. What characterizes systems of systems?
4. What are the values that may be jeopardized in safety critical systems?

5. How may testing be organized?
6. Name some of the considerations for outsourcing testing.
7. Name the life cycles for a software product.
8. What are the building blocks in software development models?
9. What are the basic development model types?
10. Explain the idea of the V-model.
11. What is the main difference between iterative development and incremental development?
12. What are the characteristics of projects following an agile model?
13. Name some static test types.
14. Name some dynamic test types.
15. Name some test levels.
16. What is the test object in component testing?
17. What are stubs and drivers used for?
18. What are the test objects in integration testing?
19. Which integration strategies exist?
20. What is the goal of system testing?
21. How is acceptance testing different from the other test levels?
22. Explain the concept of a test sub-process.
23. What are the supporting processes discussed in this book?
24. What are the five activities in project management?
25. What are the four quality assurance activities?
26. What is validation?
27. What is verification?
28. What are the five configuration management activities?
29. What can be placed under configuration management from a testing point of view?
30. How does configuration management interact with testing?
31. How does software quality relate to the processes?
32. Explain the IDEAL model.
33. How can process maturity influence delivery estimations?
34. Name some important process improvement models.
35. What are the maturity levels in CMM?
36. Explain the structure of ISO 15504.
37. What should we be aware of when improving test processes?
38. Explain the principles of TMMI.
39. What are the five phases in a tester's mental life according to Beizer?
40. Explain the structure of TPI Next.
41. Explain the idea of CTP.
42. Name some of the critical processes defined by Rex Black.

43. Explain the principles of STEP.
44. What levels of standards exist?
45. Name some ISO standards related to testing.
46. Name some IEEE standards related to testing.

Testing Processes Overview

Everything we do, from cooking a meal to producing the most complicated software products, follows a process or a set of processes. A process is a series of activities performed to fulfill a purpose and produce a tangible output based on a given input.

The process view on software development is gaining more and more interest. Process models are defined to assist organizations with process improvement by making their work more structured and efficient.

Testing is a process.

Testing is, however, not defined as ONE universal process. It is not a scientifically definable process, but something invented and defined by people.

The ISTQB generic test process, introduced in the foundation syllabus, was originally derived from the BS 7925 Software Component Testing. For a number of years, the ISTQB test process has been regarded as a de facto standard, and it is the process on which the ISTQB certifications are based. This test process is introduced here.

Based on the ISTQB test process and a number of other standards in the testing realm, the ISO 29119 test process was published in August 2013. This is in fact a set of test processes arranged in three layers. These processes are also introduced here.

The differences between the ISTQB test process and the ISO 29119 test processes are outlined in the descriptions.

The greatest difference between the two processes is that the ISO 29119 processes include an organizational test process, in which organization-wide test documents, such as a test policy and test strategies, are produced and maintained. This process is described in detail.

The test processes discussed here are only examples of possible test processes. Others are defined, and each organization should define its own, either based on an existing one or from

Contents

scratch. Therefore, this chapter begins with a short introduction to the concepts of a process and a process model.

2.1 Processes in General

2.1.1 The Concept of a Process

A process is a series of activities performed to fulfill a specific purpose. Based on an input to the process and following the activities—also called the procedure—a tangible output is produced.

It is important to remember that the tangible output (for example a specification) is not the goal itself. The goal is to perform the activities, to think, to discuss, to try things out, to make decisions, to document, and whatever else is needed. The tangible output is the way of communicating how the purpose of the process has been fulfilled.

Processes can be described and hence monitored and improved. A process description must always include:

> ▶ A definition of the input;
> ▶ A list of activities—the procedure;
> ▶ A description of the output.

In the basic description of a process, the purpose is implicitly described in the list of activities.

For a more comprehensive and more useful process description, the following information could also be included:

> ▶ Entry criteria—What must be in place before we can start?
> ▶ Purpose—What must be achieved?
> ▶ Roles—Who is going to perform the activities?
> ▶ Methods, techniques, tools—How exactly are we going to perform the activities?
> ▶ Measurements—What metrics are we going to collect for the process?
> ▶ Templates—What should the output look like?
> ▶ Verification points—When do we assert if we are on the right track?
> ▶ Exit criteria—What do we need to fulfill before we can say that we have finished?

A process description must be operational. It is not supposed to fill pages and pages. It should fit on a single page, maybe even a webpage, with references to more detailed descriptions of methods, techniques, and templates.

2.1.2 Monitoring Processes

It is the responsibility of management in charge of a specific area to know how the pertinent processes are performed. For testing processes, of course, it is important for the test manager to know how the testing activities are performed and progressing compared with the plan.

In some organizations internal quality assurance will perform more or less formal audits to assess how processes are being performed. In the safety critical realm, external auditors may perform formal quality assurance audits of how the formal processes are performed in the organization.

People in charge of process improvement may use quality assurance results or otherwise collected information to pinpoint which processes should be the target processes for improvement activities, and to be able to predict and later determine the effect of process improvement activities.

This is why the description for each process should include the metrics we are interested in for the process, and hence the measurements we are going to collect as the process is being performed.

Metrics and measurements are described in Section 3.5, and Section 3.6 discusses how test progress monitoring and control can be performed. In this present chapter, a few metrics associated with the activities in each of the test processes are listed for inspiration.

2.1.3 Processes Depend on Each Other

The input to a process must be the output from one or more proceeding process(es)—except perhaps for the very first, where the infamous napkin with the original idea is the input. The output from a process must be the input to one or more other processes—except perhaps the final process where the product is disposed of.

Processes depend on each other:
Output n = Input m

The dependencies between processes can be depicted in a process model, which shows how outputs from processes serve as inputs to other processes.

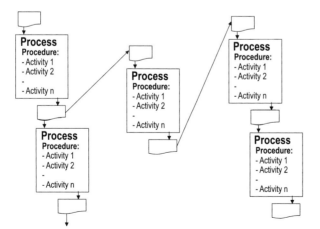

A process model could be in a textual form or it could be graphical, as shown in the figure above. Here, for example, the output from the top-left process serves as input to the top-middle process and to the lower-left process.

The figure only shows a tiny extract of a process model, so some of the processes deliver input to processes that are not included in the figure.

2.2   The ISTQB Generic Test Process

The generic test process defined in the ISTQB advanced syllabi includes the following activities:

- ▶ Test planning, monitoring, and control;
- ▶ Test analysis;
- ▶ Test design;
- ▶ Test implementation;
- ▶ Test execution;
- ▶ Evaluating exit criteria and reporting;
- ▶ Test closure activities.

The activities are described in the chapters targeted at the different roles of testing; that is, test planning, monitoring, and control; evaluating exit criteria and reporting; and test closure activities are described in Chapter 3, whereas test analysis, design, and implementation are described in Chapter 5. The test activities applied to static testing are described in Chapter 4.

The documents produced during the performance of the entire process include the following:

- ▶ Test policy;
- ▶ Test strategy;
- ▶ Master test plan;
- ▶ Level test plan;
- ▶ Test documentation in the form of test conditions, test design, test cases, and test procedures and/or test scripts;
- ▶ Test logs;
- ▶ Reports.

The generic test process is applicable to each of the dynamic test levels to be included in the course of the development and maintenance of a product. So, for example, the process should be used for:

- Component testing;
- Integration testing;
- System testing;
- Acceptance testing.

The test levels are described in Chapter 1.

The test activities need not be performed in strict sequential order. Test planning and control are constant activities in the sense that they are not just done once in the beginning of the test assignment. Monitoring of the process should be done on an ongoing basis, and controlling and replanning activities are performed when the need arises. Sometimes test analysis and design are performed in parallel with test implementation and execution.

The generic test process is iterative—not a simple straightforward process. It must be foreseen that we'll have to perform the activities more than once in an iterative way before the exit criteria have been fulfilled. The iterations to be foreseen in the test process are shown in the figure here.

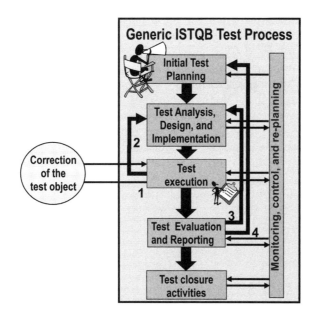

Experience shows that in most cases three iterations must be reckoned with as a minimum before the test process can be completed.

The first activity from which an iteration may occur is the test execution. This is where we detect the failures, when the actual result is different from the expected.

The resulting iterations may be:

1   *The defect is in the test object.*

A calculation does not give the expected result, and it appears that the algorithm for the calculation has been coded wrongly.

When the defect has been corrected we must retest the software using the test procedure that encountered the failure in the first place. We will probably also perform some regression testing.

2   *The defect is in the test procedure.*

A calculation does not give the expected result, but here it appears that the test case was wrong.

The defect must be corrected and the new test case(s) must be executed. This iteration usually goes back to the analysis, design, and implementation activities.

The second activity from which an iteration may occur is the evaluation of the exit criteria. This is where we find out if the exit criteria are met.

The resulting iteration in this situation may be:

3   *More test cases must be specified to increase coverage, and these must then be executed.*

During the checking process it turns out that the decision coverage for a component is only 87%. One more test case is designed and when this is executed the coverage reaches 96%.

4   *The exit criteria are relaxed or strengthened in the test plan.*

The coverage is found to be too small because of an error-handling routine that is very hard to reach. The required coverage for the component is relaxed to 85%.

The generic ISTQB test process is primarily aimed at a scripted test where the test is specified before the execution starts.

But this does not mean that the test process is not useful when other techniques or approaches are used. Even in exploratory testing where you test a little bit and direct the further testing based on the experience gained, you need to plan and control what is going on, to analyze and design (at least in your head), to execute, and to report (very important!), and to close the testing.

2.3 The ISO 29119 Test Processes

Standards are useful. Standards are not meant to be straightjackets, but to assist people in their work, so that they don't have to invent everything themselves and so that they can use a "language" that is common across a professional field.

Many people with a lot of experience have contributed to standards. Even though no standard is perfect and no standard fits any organization completely, they can facilitate the work by providing ideas and guidelines.

2.3.1   ISO Standards in General

The International Organization for Standardization (ISO) is a network of national standards bodies that represent ISO in their respective countries. ISO headquarters is in Switzerland, and the ISO maintain nearly 100 standards.

A new standard has to be approved by ISO before the work can start. After approval a working group is established with volunteers from national bodies and a convener. Stuart Reid from the United Kingdome has been the ISO 29119 convener for its entire tenure.

It takes up to 5 years to produce a standard. Based on the first draft, the working group meets every 6 months to go through the comments that have been sent in from ISO member countries all over the world. Between meetings new—and better—drafts are finalized and released for review and comments.

A standard is not "the truth"; it is to some extent a compromise between many people with extensive experience from all over the world.

The ISO 29119 *Standard for Software Testing* is planned as a six-part standard of which the first three were published in 2013:

     Part 1: Concepts and Definitions;
     Part 2: Test Processes;
     Part 3: Test Documentation;
     Part 4: Test Techniques;
     Part 5: Keyword Driven Testing;
     Part 6: Static Test Techniques.

The ISO 29119 working group with representatives from Korea, Malaysia, China, the United Kingdom, Japan, Denmark, Spain, Chile, New Zealand, Australia, India, the United States, and South Africa.

2.3.2   Overview of the ISO 29119 Test Processes

The test processes according to ISO 29119 are presented in a three-layer model consisting of these processes:

- ▶ Organizational test process;
- ▶ Test management process;
- ▶ Dynamic test process.

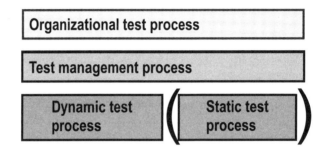

It would seem natural to many testers to have static testing included in ISO 29119, but this has not yet been possible. If it were, static testing would be part of the third level aligned with dynamic testing as shown.

The organizational test management process is described in detail in Section 2.4. The other processes are described in the following chapters, that is, the test management process is described in Chapter 3, the static testing process and techniques are described in Chapter 4, and the dynamic testing process is described in Chapter 5.

2.3.2.1   The ISO 29119 Organizational Test Process

The organizational test management process is used to produce and maintain the highest level of test specifications, usually known as test policy and organizational test strategy. It includes the following activities:

- ▶ Develop an organizational test specification.
- ▶ Monitor and control use of the organizational test specification.
- ▶ Update the organizational test specification.

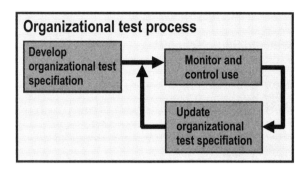

The organizational test process is continuous, ensuring that the organizational test specifications are up to date and aligned with the business and the business's goals.

The organizational test process is described in detail in Section 2.4.

2.3.2.2   The ISO 29119 Test Management Process

The test management process is a generic process that may be used to manage an overall test project, as well as any test sub-processes that may be defined for a specific scope in a specific context.

The concept of a test sub-process was described in Section 1.2.3.

The test management process includes the following activities:

- ◗ Planning;
- ◗ Monitoring and control;
- ◗ Completion.

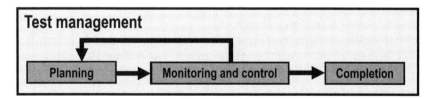

There will be iterations in the test management process when monitoring gives rise to changes in the plan.

The test management process is described in detail in Chapter 3.

2.3.2.3   The ISO 29119 Dynamic Test Process

The dynamic test process is applied for tests executed on a running piece of software, that is, the test item is the running software. This can be anything from an isolated component to a system-of-systems.

The dynamic test process includes the following activities:

▶ Test design and implementation;
▶ Test environment setup;
▶ Test execution;
▶ Incident reporting.

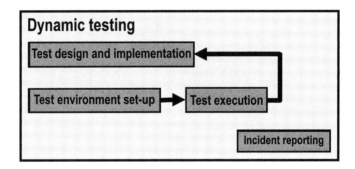

There will be iterations in the dynamic test process if test execution does not achieve the exit criteria and more test cases will have to be designed, implemented, and executed.

The ISO 29119 dynamic test process includes an incident reporting activity to illustrate that raising incident reports is an important part of the dynamic test work, although incident reporting strictly speaking is a configuration management activity that may be applied as a supporting process to many more processes than dynamic testing.

The dynamic test process is described in detail in Chapter 5.

2.3.2.4 Static Testing Process

The static testing process is testing performed on anything but running software. The test item is typically a document, but can be anything written, drawn, or otherwise documented.

ISO 29119 does not include a static testing process. This is one of the compromises that has to be accepted in order to get a worldwide standard approved. One of reasons for this is that static testing is not necessarily performed by testers but may be performed by, for example, developers or managers.

Static testing is, however, covered in this book in line with dynamic testing, as it is in the ISTQB syllabi.

Had the static testing process been included in ISO 29119 it might have included the following activities:

- Preparation of rules and/or checklists;
- Performance of the static test;
- Debriefing and/or reporting.

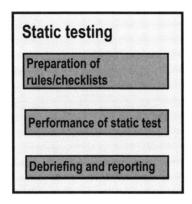

The static testing process does not directly include iterations; if a static test does not perform as expected or if the test item is not accepted, a new static test is planned.

The static testing process is described in detail in Chapter 4.

2.3.3   Overview of ISO 29119 Test Documentation

The following documentation may be produced as a result of performing the ISO 29119 test process:

- Test policy;
- Organizational test strategy/strategies;
- Project test plan;
- Sub-process test plan(s);
- Test specification(s);
- Test environment and test data requirements;
- Test environment and test data readiness report(s);
- Test execution documentation;
- Test status reports;
- Incident reports;
- Sub-process test completion report(s);
- Project test completion report.

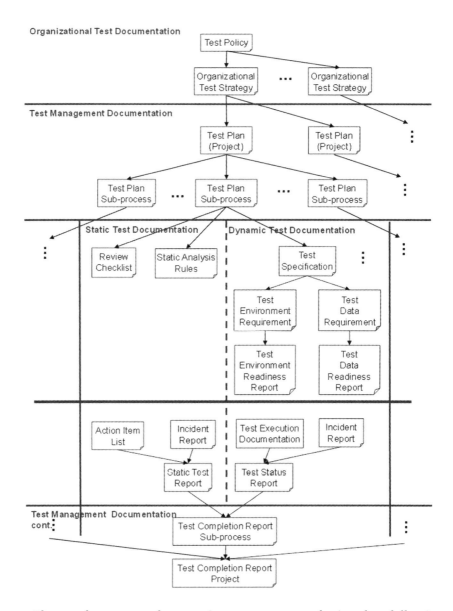

The performance of a static test may result in the following documentation:

◗ Review checklist;
◗ Static analysis rules;
◗ Action item list;

▶ Static test report.

An overview of the full documentation mentioned here is shown above. The lists of documentation do not mean that all the documentation will have to be produced in any test situation. A determination must be made of which documentation is necessary and in which form for each test project and each test assignment.

2.4 ISO 29199 Organizational Test Process

The organizational test management process is used to produce and maintain the highest level of test specifications, usually known as a test policy and organizational test strategy.

It includes the following activities:

▶ Develop organizational test specification.
▶ Monitor and control use of organizational test specification.
▶ Update organizational test specification.

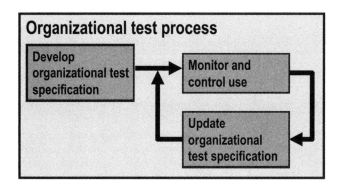

This process may be applied to any kind of overall (test) organizational specifications that the organization chooses to produce. The most common types of organizational test specifications are:

▶ Test policy;
▶ Organizational test strategy.

These specification types are described here.

The organizational test process is ongoing as illustrated in the figure above. Although both the test policy and the organizational test strategy are supposed to be stable documents with long lifetime expectancies, they will have to change over time if significant changes are implemented in the organization. Hence, the use and appropriateness of these documents must be monitored and the documents updated to keep them in line with what is actually going on in the organization.

2.4.1   Organizational Management Responsibility

Top management's responsibility is to fulfill the business goals and govern the organization. Governance relates to decisions that define expectations toward the organization, grant appropriate power to the appropriate employees, and verify performance.

The reason for this process being explicitly described in ISO 29119 is that it is important to get higher management's buy-in on testing. If testing is "just" performed within individual projects, it might not be appreciated and not get the required resources.

Top management's awareness of software testing should reflect the business value of testing; but that is not always the case. In many places the value of software testing could be increased by increased management awareness.

Test-wise it is top management's responsibility to issue a test policy and the relevant test strategies. It may not be the top managers themselves who actually write these documents, but they must at least endorse them, and promote them in the organization.

The presentation of this documentation depends on the organization's needs, general standards, size, and maturity. The presentation can vary from oral (not recommended!) over loose notes to formal documents based on organizational templates. It can also vary from all the information being presented together in one document, or even as part of a bigger document, to it being split into a number of individual documents.

The more mature an organization is, the more the presentation about the test policy and test management documentation is tailored to the organization's needs. The way the information is presented is not important; the information is.

2.4.2   Interaction with Other Processes

The initial development of the organizational documentation in the organizational test process is based on input from the business, from other processes in the organization (e.g., development, maintenance, and configuration management), and not least from the testers.

This is shown in the figure below.

The organizational test process indirectly affects all other test processes through the test policy and the test strategy. It affects the strategy and the planning of the test to be performed in any particular test project, from the identification of relevant test sub-processes to how all the testing should be done and by whom.

The more specific impact is described in the sections where the affected test processes are described.

The organizational test process continues to be affected by the other test processes; that is, by all the tests being performed in the organization and by feedback to the organizational test process about their use of the test policy and the appropriate test strategies. This feedback is used to continually improve the organizational documents to fit the testing being performed.

This is also illustrated in the figure below.

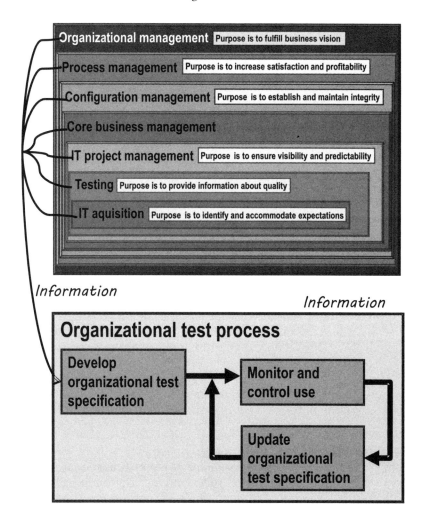

2.4.3 Detailed Activities

The organizational test process is in fact a process improvement process instantiated for testing. The introduction of behavior regulating documents—here the organizational test policy and relevant organizational test strategies—is an organization change process and care should be taken to regard it as such. Testers should work closely with the general process management if such an organizational unit is present in the organization. Section 1.4 provides a bit more discussion about the general process improvement process in relation to testing.

The development of organizational test specifications must be based on the current testing practices within the organization as identified through information soliciting activities such as interviews and workshops with stakeholders and/or document studies.

Other material, such as the business goals, applicable policies and/or strategies, and applicable standards, may also be relevant and should be identified and studied.

The contents of the organizational specifications must be approved by the relevant stakeholders to make sure they are appropriate and to instill ownership in the organization.

It is of course also important to make employees aware of the existence of the organizational specifications and the expectations regarding their use.

The monitoring and control of the use of the organizational test specifications is a classic process quality assurance activity in which employees are encouraged (or forced) to use the contents of the organizational test documentation as described, with actual adherence monitored through interviews, analysis of evidence, and measurements as appropriate.

It may sound very formalistic and bureaucratic, but the monitoring and control will always have to be done in a way that is appropriate to the risk of the products being produced in the organization; that is, low risk means a low level of bureaucracy; high risk level means a high level of control and bureaucracy.

The updating of the organizational test specifications is a learning and improving activity, where the information from the monitoring and control activity and possibly other feedback regarding the use of the organizational test specification should be treated, understood, and implemented if relevant.

As for the first version of the organization test specification, new versions must be approved by the relevant stakeholders, and the employees made aware of the new—and better—organizational test specifications.

2.4.4   Produced Documentation

The tangible outcome of the performance of the organizational test process is one or more organizational test specifications. These are usually in the form of a test policy and/or one or more organizational test strategies.

The contents of the two types of specifications as suggested in ISO 29119 are described below.

2.4.4.1 Test Policy

The test policy defines the organization's philosophy toward software testing. It is the basis for all the test work in the organization and the test policy must be behavior regulating in the good way—*it is like a lighthouse for all the testing activities.* Like every lighthouse has its own signal, every organization must have its own policy, tailored to its specific business needs.

The test policy should be short and to the point. In my opinion it should be able to fit onto a maximum of a couple of pages, so that people can read it quickly and get an overall idea of the testing.

It is the responsibility of the top management to formulate the policy. It may, however, be difficult for top management if they are not familiar with professional testing, so it is often seen that the IT department (or equivalent) steps in and develops the test policy on behalf of the management, who of course will have to endorse it and enforce it. Approval of a test policy must be obtained from the relevant stakeholders, e.g. portfolio manager and quality assurance responsible.

The purpose of a test policy is to define the objectives and principles of software testing to be applied within the organization. An additional purpose is to increase the awareness of software testing and its importance for the organization at the highest relevant management level.

The scope of a test policy is the entire organizational unit in which testing is being performed. It may be an entire company or it may be a significant subdivision.

Test policy statements may be incorporated in the organizational test strategy (described below) where a separate test policy is not appropriate or for other reasons not provided.

2.4.4.1.1 *Test Policy Contents*

Any piece of documentation should provide some document specific information. This should adhere to the organizations convention for document identification, if there is one. The information should include the following as appropriate:

▶ Overview;
▶ Unique identifier, incl. for example title, issue date, and version;
▶ Issuing organization;
▶ Approval authority;
▶ Change history.

Furthermore any document should provide an introduction, which should include:

▶ Scope of the document;

▶ References;
▶ Glossary.

ISO 29119 provides the following table of contents for a test policy. This may of course be tailored to the individual situation.

1.   Objectives of testing
1.1   This section should provide a description of what the organization expects to achieve by testing (purpose and goals), and what testing means in the particular organization (scope).
2   Test process
2.1   This section should provide a description of, or a reference to, an overview of the test process, i.e. of the activities to be performed for testing in the organization.
3   Test organization structure
3.1   This section should provide an overview of the structure of the test organization, including a description of the roles and their responsibilities.
4   Tester training
4.1   This section should state which training and/or certifications are required for the people filling the different roles in the test organization.
5.   Tester ethics
5.1   This section should provide a set of rules for the expected conduct of the people working with test.
6.   Standards
6.1   This section should provide references to standards (both internal and external to the organization) that are applicable
7.   Other relevant policies
7.1   This section should provide references to other organizational policies that impact the work in the test organization.
8.   Measuring the value of testing
8.1   This section should provide a description of reason and methods for determination of the return on investment of testing.
9.   Test asset archiving and reuse
9.1   This section should provide a description of, or a reference to a description of, how test assets should be archived and reused.
10.   Test process improvement
10.1 This section should provide a description of, or a reference to a description of how continuous improvement of the test process is ensured.

2.4.4.1.2 Test Policy Contents Example

The table below provides some examples of contents for each of the entries in a test policy. The examples are rather short, but I hope they may serve as inspiration.

Test Policy for nn organization	
Objectives of testing	"Reducing the number of failures experienced by the users." "Activity to provide information about the quality of the products." "The test must aim at minimizing the product risks."
Test process	"See 'Development and Test Handbook' on the intranet." "The activities in the test process are: test management, dynamic testing, and static testing"
Test organization structure	"The test is anchored in the test knowledge centre managed by Carl Morse" "Each project must have an appointed test coordinator and a number of test analysts depending on the size of the project."
Tester training	"All people actively involved in any test activity must have at least ISTQB Foundation certification." "Test analysts must have at least 5 years' experience in software testing and a relevant higher education."
Tester ethics	"See 'Employee Handbook' on the intranet." "We expect all employees to act in a professional manner, and respect the company's confidentiality agreement."
Standards	"All test work is based on ISO 29119." "The organization must comply with ISO 29119, Parts 1-3."
Other relevant policies	"The Quality Management Policy and the Configuration Management Policy apply for testing."
Measuring the value of testing	"The focus is on test effectiveness, and this shall be measured as Defect Detection Percentage after 3 and 12 months of operation of any new system. The overall average must increase on a yearly basis." "The customers must not be reporting more than 3 severity 1 failures during the first year of use." "The system must not have a breakdown lasting longer than 15 minutes during the first 6 months in production."
Test assets archiving and reuse	"All approved documentation of testing must be stored in the CM system, according to the CM processes." "The complete test environment must be handed over to production, including test data and test tools."
Test process improvement	"A post project workshop where all the observations during the test process are collected shall be held within the first month after turnover to production." "Failure reports shall be analyzed to determine any trends in the defects found in system test." "The root cause shall be found for every severity 1 and 2 defect found during testing, and improvement actions shall be identified."

2.4.4.1.3 Policy Contents Mapping ISQTB / ISO 29119

The ISTQB syllabi mention a test policy as part of the test documentation, but are not explicit in defining its contents. The table below does however present a mapping between the ISTQB description of the contents of a test policy and the table of contents provided in ISO 29119. A blank entry means that there is no equivalence.

ISTQB	ISO 29119:2013
The objectives of testing	Objectives of testing
The typical test process	Test process
	Test organization structure
	Tester training
	Tester ethics
in the strategy	Standards
	Other relevant policies
The value of testing Evaluation of the effectiveness and the efficiency	Measuring the value of testing
	Test asset archiving and reuse
Test process improvement approach	Test process improvement

The order of the entries is not important. Some of the entries not found in the test policy may be found in the organizational test strategy. It is not of great importance where an entry is placed, as long as it is included.

2.4.4.2 Organizational Test Strategy

The Latin word "stratagem" means a plan for deceiving an enemy in war. Note that the enemy here is not the developers—it is the defects!

The strategy outlines how the risks of defects in the product will be fought. It could be said to express the generic requirements for the test. If we keep in the naval realm the strategy is the navigation rules for the testing.

The *organizational test strategy* is based on the policy, and it should of course be compliant with it. It can have the scope of an entire organization or a smaller unit or a program (one or more similar projects).

The test strategy is high level, and it should be short. It should also be readily available to all with a stake in the testing within the scope of the strategy. The strategy could be issued in a document, but it would be a good idea to present it in table form on a poster or on the intranet in the organization.

The organizational test provides guidelines on what testing should be carried out within the organization to achieve the goals in the policy. The organizational test strategy is generic for the projects within the organizational scope it is defined for; it is not project-specific.

Test policy statements may be incorporated in the organizational test strategy where a separate Test Policy is not available or not complete.

More than one organizational test strategy may be needed if the organization performs development and/or maintenance in a number of significantly different ways. Different development ways may be for safety-critical products, for noncritical products, for agile, iterative, or sequential development models, or for small projects and large programs.

Relevant test sub-processes should be identified as part of the organizational test strategy, and separate parts of the strategy should be defined for each of these.

Approval of an organizational test strategy should be obtained from the relevant stakeholders, e.g. product managers and quality assurance responsible.

The life expectancy for an organizational test strategy is long, though it will have to be revised if significant impacting changes are implemented in the organization.

2.4.4.2.1 *Organizational Test Strategy Contents Overview*

Any piece of documentation should provide some document specific information. This should adhere to the organizations convention for document identification, if there is one. The information should include the following as appropriate:

- ▶ Overview;
- ▶ Unique identifier, incl. for example title, issue date, and version;
- ▶ Issuing organization;
- ▶ Approval authority;
- ▶ Change history.

Furthermore any document should provide an introduction, which should include:

- ▶ Scope of the document;
- ▶ References;
- ▶ Glossary.

ISO 29119 provides the following structure and contents for a test strategy where it is divided into a common part and a part for each of the relevant test sub-processes in the scope. This may of course be tailored to the individual organization.

General strategy	
1) Generic risk management 2) Test selection and prioritization 3) Test documentation and reporting 4) Test automation and tools 5) Configuration management 6) Incident management 7) Test sub-processes	
Detailed strategy for 'test sub-process 1' 1) Entry and exit criteria 2) Test completion criteria 3) Test documentation and reporting 4) Degree of independence 5) Test design techniques 6) Test environment 7) Metrics to be collected 8) Retesting and regression testing	**Detailed strategy for 'test sub-process n'** 1) Entry and exit criteria 2) Test completion criteria 3) Test documentation and reporting 4) Degree of independence 5) Test design techniques 6) Test environment 7) Metrics to be collected 8) Retesting and regression testing

2.4.4.2.2 Scope-wide Organizational Test Strategy Contents

The contents for the general or scope-wide part of the organizational test strategy according to ISO 29119 are:

    1.   Generic risk management

    1.1 This section should provide a description of the generic approach to risk management expected to be used in the organization to direct the testing activities. This includes definition of risk scales and risk management processes. Generic lists of test project and/ or product risks may be included or referenced.

    2.   Test selection and prioritization

    2.1 This section should provide a description of how to prioritize the execution of the test procedures, based on ongoing prioritization during test analysis and design.

3. Test documentation and reporting
3.1 This section should provide one or more lists of documents that should be produced during the performance of an entire test project according to the test process specified in the test policy.

4. Test automation and tools
4.1 This section should provide a description of the approach to use of test tools, not least test execution automation. Specific tools to use may be identified. This is an area where the strategy needs to be rather precise in order for tool investments not to go out of hand. Technical people—including testers—love tools. Tools are very useful and can ease at lot of tedious work; but tools can also be expensive. The strategy should include a list of already existing testing tools to be used, and/or guidelines for considering the implementation of new tools. Test tools are described in Chapter 9.

5. Configuration management
5.1 This section should provide a description or a reference to a description of how CM should be performed for the test work products; that is how these should be identified, traced, stored, and made available. Configuration management is a general support process and if a configuration management system is in place, this is of course the one the testers should use, and the one the strategy should refer to.

6. Incident management
6.1 This section should provide a description or a reference to a description of how incidents should be managed during testing; that is how they should be recorded, triaged, corrected as appropriate, and approved. In mature organizations this could be part of the configuration management system, and close cooperation with this is strongly recommended.

7. Test sub-processes
7.1 This section should provide one or more lists of the test sub-processes that should be planned and performed as part of the testing within the scope of the strategy.

2.4.4.2.3 Scope-Wide Organizational Strategy Contents Example

The table below provides some examples of contents for each of the entries in the scope-wide part of an organizational strategy.

Organizational Test Strategy, scope-wide part for an organization	
Generic risk management	The risk management in all test projects must be based on the Risk Management Process described in the QA handbook. The risk management must be performed in close cooperation with the project manager, and have a product risk focus. The standard risk register is found on the QA homepage; this must be used as a starting point for risk identification in a test project, and it must be updated if new general risk areas are identified.
Test selection and prioritization	In all test sub-processes, feature set(s) are defined to cover the entire test item. Test sets must be defined for all feature sets to achieve required coverage. Test cases must be prioritized according to the priority of the requirements the cases are covering. For test procedures the highest priority of the included test cases applies. Test procedures must be executed according to the prioritization. At least one procedure for each feature set shall be executed.
Test documentation and reporting	A test project must provide a project test plan and a project test completion report as outlined in the QA handbook. For each test sub-process a test sub-process plan must be developed, as well as a test specification, test logs, test status reports and a test completion report shall be produced; except for any test sub-processes, where the corresponding development is performed in an agile manner and a test completion report therefore suffices. Tracing between artefacts where-ever possible and appropriate is mandatory.
Test automation and tools	The test management tool described in the QA handbook must be used on all test projects and for all sub-processes. This should also be used to manage traceability to requirements and defect reporting. In the cases where more than 4 regression tests are planned, the project might consider using a capture/playback testing tool.
Configuration management of test work products and incident management	The Configuration Management Process described in the QA handbook must be followed for all test work products to guide identification, storage, and incident and change management.
Test sub-processes	The following test sub-processes shall be included in any test project depending on the risk exposure for the applicable test item: –Component testing (only risk exposure "R") –Component integration testing (only risk exposure "R") –System testing (not risk exposure "G") –Customer acceptance testing (all risk exposures) If corresponding requirements exist, the following test subprocess shall be included in each test project: –Performance test (not risk exposure "G") –Operability test (all risk exposures)

2.4.4.2.4 Test Sub-Process Wide Organizational Test Strategy Contents

Each sub-process should have a section in the organizational test strategy where the sub-process specific strategy statements are provided.

The contents of the organizational test strategy for a specific test-sub-process according to ISO 29119 are (assuming it is the nth defined test sub-process):

1.   Entry and exit criteria
1.1   This section should provide a specification of what needs to be in place before test work in a given test sub-process can start or stop respectively. The entry and exit criteria can be defined for the entire sub-process or for each of the individual test activities, e.g. planning, design, and execution.
2.   Test completion criteria
2.1   This section should provide a description of what should be in place before the test execution can be completed. Test can never be 'finished', i.e. it is not possible to test 'everything', but there is a point for any test sub-process where further testing is not worth the expense.
3.   Test documentation and reporting
3.1   This section should provide a list of the test documentation to be produced for the test sub-process including information about when each document is produced, and the approval process(es) to be applied.
4.   Degree of independence
4.1   This section should describe the level of independence between the producer(s) of the test item and those performing the test analysis and design for the test sub-process.
4.2   Levels of independence may be:

  1.   the producer tests his or her own product;
  2.   tests are designed by another non-tester team member;
  3.   tests are designed by a tester who is a member of the development team;
  4.   tests are designed by independent testers in the same organization;
  5.   tests are designed by organizationally independent testers (consultants or out-sourced);
  6.   tests are designed by external testers (third party testing).

5.   Test design techniques
5.1   This section should provide a list of specific test design techniques to be used during test design and implementation within the test sub-process. The choice of test case design techniques is

very much dependent on the risk—high risk: few, comprehensive techniques to choose from; low risk: looser selection criteria. Test design techniques are described in Chapter 6.

6.   Test environment

6.1   This section should provide a generic description of the test environment, possibly including test data, for the test sub-process; and identify the responsible for the test environment. The specific environment must be described in test environment requirements document. Care should be taken to define the test environment so that the test is valid.

7.   Metrics to be collected

7.1   This section should provide a list of the metrics for which values (measures) are to be collected during the test activities in the test sub-process. In the test policy it has been defined how the test shall be evaluated. It has also been defined what the approach to process improvement is. This governs the measures we have to collect.

7.2   Measures are also necessary to be able to monitor and control the progress of the testing. We need to know how the correspondence is between the reality and the plan. We also need to know if and when our completion criteria have been met.

7.3   Metrics and measurements are discussed in general in section 1.3.

8.   Retesting and regression testing

8.1   This section should provide a description of the approach and activities for retesting and regression testing to be performed in the test sub-process.

2.4.4.2.5   Test Sub-Process Wide Organizational Test Strategy Contents Example

The table below provides some examples of contents for each of the entries in the test sub-process wide part of an organizational strategy.

Organizational System Testing Strategy	
Entry and Exit criteria	The integration test completion report and the system test specification must be approved before the system test execution can begin. All the system test deliverables must be approved before the system test can be considered complete.
Test completion criteria	The system test shall have 100% requirements coverage, and all test procedures must be executed without incidents.
Test documentation	A system test plan and a system test completion report as outlined in ISO 29119 Part 3 must be produced, as must all documents defined for dynamic testing.
Degree of independence	The system test shall be specified by the staff in the test department and executed by students.
Test design techniques	Appropriate black-box test case design techniques are to be used. Error guessing could also be used, if defect information exists for previous versions.
Test environment	The system testing environment shall be identical to the production environment in terms of hardware and software. In the case of embedded systems the system test could be executed on a simulator. Data could be made anonymous, but must otherwise be 100% representative.
Metrics to be collected	The following shall be reported in the system test completion report: –Total number of specified test procedures –Total number of executed test procedures –Total number of testing hours spent on specification –Total number of hours spent on execution and registration of incidents –Total number of hours elapsed for testing –Total number of failures found
Retesting and regression testing	All test procedures resulting in incident reports shall be rerun after defect correction. Regression testing during the system test sub-process is at the test manager's discretion. In the final system test run, all test procedures shall be executed.

2.4.4.2.6   Strategy Contents Mapping ISQTB/ISO 29119

The ISTQB syllabi mention a strategy as part of the test documentation, and suggest its contents. The table below presents a mapping between the ISTQB description of the contents of a test strategy and the table of contents provided in ISO 29119. A blank entry means that there is no equivalence.

ISTQB	ISO 29119:2013
Standards to comply with	*in the policy*
Risks to be addressed	(Generic risk management)
	Test selection and prioritization
an entry for each level	Test documentation and reporting
an entry for each level	Test automation and tools
Defect management	Incident management
Configuration management of testware	Configuration management
Integration procedures	
Test control and reporting	
Levels of testing and their relationships	Test sub-processes
For each level	**For each test sub-process**
Entry criteria	Entry and exit criteria
Exit criteria	
Degree of independence	Degree of independence
Techniques to use	Test design techniques
Extent of reuse	
Environments	Test environment
Test automation Test tools	*one entry in the general part*
Measurements	Metrics to be collected
Confirmation and regression testing	

The order of the entries is not important. Some of the entries not found in the organizational test strategy may be found in the test policy. It is not of great importance where an entry is placed, as long as it is included.

2.5 Test Approaches

Test approach or test strategy or test practice; there are many names for an overall conceptual framework for test.

Even though ISO 29119, and hence this book, applies the overall strategy of risk-based testing, some of the test approaches that have been used over the last couple of decades, and are still widely in use, are listed below along with a short description of each.

The list is not exhaustive, the entries are not necessarily at the same conceptual level, and the descriptions might not even seem correct to you. "Approach" is a word that may have different meanings to different people.

The purpose of this section is to get you to discuss test approaches and agree on what makes sense in your context.

The list is provided in alphabetical order.

- Consultative approach—where test is driven primarily by the advice and guidance of technology and/or business domain experts outside the test team.

- Experience-based approach—where test is guided by the test analyst's or test executioner's previous experience with similar system and/or domain knowledge.
- Heuristic approach—where test is more reactive to events than pre-planned, and where execution and evaluation are concurrent tasks; for example exploratory testing.
- Methodical approach—where testing is guided by a chosen method, for example check-lists, fault taxonomies, and quality characteristics.
- Model-based approach—where test is based on a model of the future system, for example statistical models for usage, or requirements expressed using formal (provable) models.
- Process- or standard-compliant approach—where test is based on industry-specific standards, for example ISO 29119.
- Regression-averse approach—where focus of the test is on reuse of existing test material, extensive automation of regression tests, and standard test procedures.
- Requirements-based testing—where test aims at ensuring that the requirements of the test item have been addressed (i.e. "covered").
- Scripted / Unscripted testing—where test cases and/or test procedures are written down prior to test execution; respectively not written down.

Approaches may be mixed as they address different aspects of testing and more approaches can support each other.

We could for example decide:
    The component test shall be performed in compliance with the tool used for component testing.
    The component integration testing shall be bottom up integration based on a design model and in compliance with standard xxx.
    The system test shall be risk based and scripted and the initial risk analysis shall be supplemented with exploratory testing.

The decisions about approaches have a great influence on some of the decisions that have to be made for specific topics in the strategy. It is up to the individual test project manager, test analyst, and technical test analyst to decide what the appropriate decision is in any particular case.

2.6 Testing Roles

One entry on the test policy is "Test organization structure" and that has to do with the defined roles in testing, and how testing is interfacing with other organizational units and hence testing stakeholders.

The organizational management should define roles and role descriptions for people working in test (as well as for people working in other areas). Experience shows that clearly defined roles align expectations and facilitates cooperation in an organization.

As it is apparent from the description of the testing processes above, testing involves a number of different activities, which will be performed by a number of people with a number of job titles or roles.

ISTQB operates with three overall roles, namely:

- ▶ Test manager;
- ▶ Test analyst;
- ▶ Technical Test Analyst.

Individual advanced certifications and corresponding syllabi are available for each of these.

ISO 29119 defines three overall roles, which are:

- ▶ Test strategist;
- ▶ Test manager;
- ▶ Tester.

These roles defined by ISTQB and in ISO 29119 are rather high-level and more detailed roles can be defined. Below are lists of examples of more detailed roles; these lists are not exhaustive, and organizations may choose to define their own, but the lists may be used as inspiration.

The *test manager role* may be split into more specific roles, for example:

- ▶ Test manager;
  - ▶ Test project manager;
  - ▶ Test manager (dynamic test);
  - ▶ Test manager (static test).

The *tester role* may be split into more specific roles, for example:

- ▶ Tester in dynamic testing:
  - ▶ Test analyst;
  - ▶ Technical test analyst;

- ❯ Test environment responsible;
- ❯ (Test)tool responsible;
- ❯ Test executer;
- ❯ Test automator.
- ❯ Tester in static testing:
  - ❯ Author;
  - ❯ Moderator (inspection);
  - ❯ Reviewer/Inspector;
  - ❯ Reader/Presenter;
  - ❯ Scribe/Recorder.

Other roles may be involved in testing activities, for example:

- ❯ User representative;
- ❯ Domain expert.

Each role may be filled by one or more persons; it is for example common to have more than one reviewer and/or more than one test analyst in a test project. One person, on the other hand, may fill several roles; for example a test manager managing more test projects at the same time (although allocation to a post should be at least 25 % for it to be effective).

The table below provides an overview of the roles listed above in   alphabetical order:

Note: "document" in the followings means a document or another form of documentation that is the test item of static test.

Role	Short description
Author	Person with chief responsibility for the production of the document.
Domain expert	Person with deep business subject matter knowledge.
Inspector	Person who reads and comments on a document as part of an inspection.
Moderator	Person who leads the feed-back meeting as part of a static test, for example an inspection.
Reader	Person who guides a group of reviewers through the document, either by reading it aloud or pointing out the current section.
Reviewer	Person with a specific technical and/or business background who identifies and describes findings (e.g., defects) in the product under review using appropriate static test techniques.

Scribe	Person who documents all the issues, problems and open points that are identified during an inspection meeting. Sometimes called recorder.
Technical test analyst	Person who analyses requirements and other specifications—primarily nonfunctional, and designs test cases and builds test procedures using appropriate test case design techniques. May also be test automator, test executor, and/or test tool responsible.
Test analyst	Person who analyses requirements and other specifications—primarily functional, and designs test cases and builds test procedures using appropriate test case design techniques. May also be test executor.
Test automator	Person who automates test procedures. May also perform test tool installation and maintenance. May also be test executer.
Test environment responsible	Person who is responsible for the state of platform(s), middleware, and or test data on which dynamic test is being executed, both before, during and after execution.
Test executer	Person who executes test procedures, record and check test results and created incident reports as necessary.
Test manager	Person who plans, monitors and controls the dynamic and/ or static testing in one or more test sub-processes.
Test project manager	Person who plans, monitors and controls the testing for an entire test project.
Test strategist	Person who establishes and ensures conformance to a test policy and/or test strategy for an organization.
Test tool responsible	Person who installs and /or maintains specific tool(s) used in performance of the test processes.
User representative	Person who participates in test activities on behalf of specific future users of the system under test.

Everyone in a test team must have a clear understanding of their role(s) and responsibilities to avoid misunderstandings and unrealistic expectations.

Questions

1. Which 3 elements must always be defined for a process?
2. How do processes depend on each other?
3. What are the seven activities in the generic ISTQB test process?
4. Which documents may be produced as a result of following the ISTQB test process?
5. Which iterations are embedded in the generic test process?
6. Which ISO standard defines a set of test processes?

7. Which parts does this standard include?
8. Which are the 3 main processes in the ISO standard.
9. Name the 3 activities in the highest level of the ISO test processes.
10. Name the 3 activities in the middle level ISO test process.
11. Name the 4 activities in the lowest level of the ISO test processes.
12. Name the 3 activities in the static testing process.
13. Which documents may be produced as a result of following the ISO test processes?
14. Which documents may be produced as a result of following the static testing process?
15. Name the 2 most common organizational test documents.
16. What is the primary responsibility of the top management?
17. Explain how top management can get inspiration to produce the organizational test documents.
18. How large should a test policy be?
19. What should always be included in a document?
20. Name the suggested 10 entries in a test policy.
21. Explain how the ISTQB and the ISO test policy match.
22. How many organizational test strategies can an organization have?
23. Explain the structure of an organizational test strategy.
24. What is the first suggested entry in an organizational test strategy
25. Explain the concept of "completion criteria".
26. Explain the concept of "degree of independence".
27. Name some metrics that may be collected during testing.
28. Explain how the ISTQB and the ISO organizational test strategy match.
29. Name some common test approaches.
30. What are the roles defined in ISTQB?
31. Name some of the specific tester roles.
32. What is the main difference between a technical test analyst and a test analyst?

3

Test Management

Test management is the art of planning and directing a test project or a test subprocess to success. It is in many ways like project management, and yet not quite the same.

The fundamental ISTQB test process is described in Section 2.2. This process includes the test management activities of test planning, monitoring, control, and test closure. These activities form the basis for the corresponding ISO 29119 test management activities described here, and they are very similar in nature.

This chapter first describes how a test project management interacts "upward" with the development or maintenance project management it belongs to. This is followed by a description of how the test project management interacts "downward" with the management of its individual test subprocesses. Finally the interaction between the test subprocess management and its dynamic and/or static test processes is described.

Following this introduction, the individual activities in the test management process and their outcomes in the form of documents are described. Mappings are provided between documents defined in ISTQB (IEEE 829–1998) and the corresponding documents defined in ISO 29119.

The central detailed activities to be performed in the course of test management—test stakeholder analysis, test estimation, and test progress monitoring and control—are each described in separate sections in order not to confuse the overview of the process provided in Section 3.1.

Likewise, the two central themes of risk-based testing and test metrics and measurement are described in separate sections.

The order of these special sections follows the order in which the activities and themes appear in the course of the test management process. The order is shown in the section overview on the right.

Contents

3.1 Test Management Process

The test management process defined in ISO 29119 can be used for all test projects and test subprocesses, and it includes the following activities:

> Test planning;
> Test monitoring and control;
> Test completion.

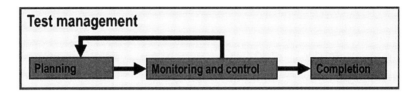

The test management process has iterations when monitoring and control give rise to changes in the plan.

The test management process may be applied to a test project as well as to a test subprocess; this is further explained below.

3.1.1 Test Management Responsibility

The responsibility of any test manager or test leader at any level is to plan the work, follow the progress to completion, and change the plan according to reality as the work progresses.

If you fail to plan—you plan to fail!

It is important to plan activities rather than just jump head first into action. The planning work provides a deeper understanding of the task at hand, and it is much easier to change something you have written down or sketched out on a piece of paper than something that has already taken place in the real world.

Planning takes time and because it is so important, it should be planned so that it can start as early as possible. Take your planning seriously, so that you don't end up like this poster painter once did:

The benefits of starting test planning early are many:

> There is time to do a proper job of planning.

▶ There is more time to talk and/or negotiate with stakeholders.

▶ Potential problems might be spotted in time to warn all the relevant stakeholders.

▶ It is possible to be able to influence the overall project plan.

When you plan, you have to keep in mind that a plan needs to be **SMART**:

Specific—Make it clear what the scope is.
Measurable—Make it possible to determine if the plan still holds at any time.
Accepted—Make every stakeholder agree to his or her involvement.
Relevant—Make references to additional information; don't copy it.
Time specific—Provide dates.

All stakeholders for a test plan must agree to the contents according to their interest and involvement—otherwise the plan is not valid!

Remember that *a plan is just a plan*; it is not unchangeable once written. A plan must be a living document that should constantly be updated to reflect what happens in the real world. Contrary to what many people think, it is not a virtue to keep to a plan at any cost—the virtue lies in getting the plan to align with the real world. No matter how hard you try, you are not able to see what is going to happen in the future when you make the plan.

The planned work must therefore be monitored and any deviation from the plan analyzed and acted on, so that the test project or test subproject is still under control. If, for example, an activity takes longer than expected, decisions must be made about what to do: Should we push the deadline? Should we assign more people? Should we reduce the scope? Should we apply a mixture of these measures? Should we do nothing? This is a very important part of the test management responsibility.

3.1.2 Interaction with Other Processes

A test management process interacts with other test management processes at higher and/lower levels and with other processes depending on the context in which it is applied.

Processes cannot communicate with each other as such. The communications will be in written or in oral form between the people filling the various roles in the performance of the processes.

Test management must be done in close cooperation with project management; sometimes by the same person, sometimes by different people, though the two roles should not be filled by the same person if at all possible.

The test manager is the link between the test team and the development team and between the test team and higher management. It is therefore essential for the test manager to be the ambassador of testing and truly understand how testing contributes to the business goals.

However, this does not mean that testers and developers should not talk to each other directly. On the contrary, the more interaction there is between these two groups and between testers and other stakeholders the better. Such interaction facilitates understanding and respect for each other's work and contributes to the common goal of producing an operational and reliable software product.

3.1.2.1   IT Project Management and Test Project Management

Usually a test project is a subproject under a development project or a maintenance project or contract.

The interactions between any form of an IT project management process and a test project management process are shown in the figure below.

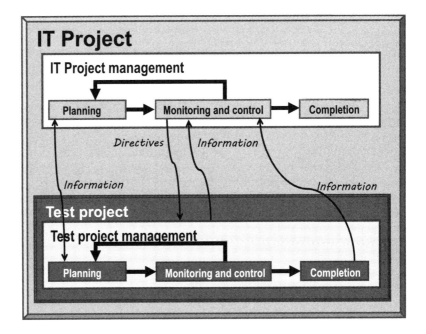

The project test plan must be closely connected to the overall project plan, especially in terms of the schedule and budget. The project test plan could either be referenced from or included in the project plan. During initial planning as well as in subsequent updates of the plans, both in the IT project and in the test project, information is shared between the two planning activities to ensure that the two plans are aligned.

Directives will be issued to the test project management during the course of the test project. This could be, for example, in the form of an announcement from the IT project manager that a specific test subprocess will have to be postponed for whatever reason, or a formal instruction to deliver a test report within a specific time frame.

Information will go the other way from the test project to the IT project to keep the IT project manager aware of progress and/or problems with the test project. This information may be used to update the IT project plan, if needed.

When all test subprocesses for a test project are completed, this must be communicated to the IT project.

3.1.2.2 Test Project Management and Test Sub-Process Management

A test project will comprise at least one and usually a number of test sub-processes, depending on the development or maintenance project with which it is associated.

The interactions between a test project management process and any test sub-process management process are shown in the figure below.

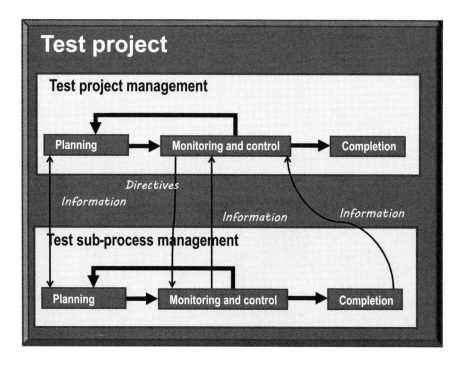

During initial planning as well as in subsequent updates of the plans, both in the test project and in any test sub-process, information is shared between the two activities to ensure that the two plans are aligned.

Directives will be issued from the test project management to the test subprocess manager(s) during the course of the test project. This could be in the form, for example, of the test project manager giving the go-ahead for a planned test execution to begin.

Information will go the other way from any test subprocess to the test project to keep the test project manager aware of progress and/or problems with the test subprocess. This information may be used to update the test project plan, if needed. The information may be relayed to the IT project manager as described above.

When a test subprocess is completed, this must be communicated to the test project.

Note that there should not be any interactions between individual test subprocess management processes; these should communicate through their test management process, so that the test project manager is informed of what is going on and can make the appropriate decisions.

3.1.2.3   Test Subprocess Management and Static or Dynamic Testing

Static and/or dynamic test(s) will be performed in a test subprocess, depending on the development or maintenance project with which it is associated.

The interactions between a test subprocess management process and a dynamic test process or a static test process are shown in the figure below.

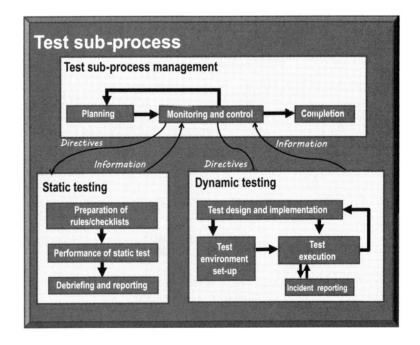

Directives will be issued from the test subprocess management to the dynamic or static test process to initiate or stop action during the course of the test subprocess. This could take the form of, for example, relaying a directive for beginning a planned test execution.

Information will go the other way from any dynamic or static testing process to the test subprocess management to keep the test project manager aware of progress and/or problems with the actual testing. This information may be further relayed and used to update appropriate plans.

When a static or dynamic test is completed, this must be communicated to the test subprocess.

Note that there should not be any interactions between individual static and/or dynamic tests; these should communicate through their test subprocess, so that the appropriate test project manager is informed of what is going on and can make the appropriate decisions.

3.1.3   Detailed Activities

The test management process is in many ways like a classic project management process, only with a specific testing objective. The involved activities are described below.

3.1.3.1   Test Planning

The first activity in the test management process is the test planning. A number of considerations and choices must be made to ensure the most effective and efficient test performance. The results of these choices must be documented as the test plan to guide the test project or test subprocess.

The point is not to create the plan, but to perform the planning activities; that is, to make the necessary decisions about what, how, where, and by whom testing shall be performed.

Test planning requires a firm understanding of the context in which the testing is going to be performed. Relevant material, such as the test policy and/or applicable test strategies, regulatory standards, relevant plans, project documentation, and not least the risk register(s) and the requirements specification(s), must be studied and analyzed.

Creating the testing plan takes time and it should not be "invisible" work (i.e., work that is not scheduled nor reported anywhere). It is part of the planning to include the planning activities in the plan.

The detailed planning activities can be derived from the list of contents of a test plan as suggested, for example, by ISO 29119. This list of contents is described in Section 3.1.4.1.1 below.

Even though the list of contents for a test plan is sequential, the planning activities may be performed in a different sequence and often is an iterative way to make everything fall into place. Consensus of all decisions must be gained from relevant stakeholders.

The test plan, that is, the decisions made as an outcome of performing the detailed planning activities, must be recorded. One purpose of this to be able to remember what the decisions are. Another purpose is to make the decisions available to the relevant stakeholders.

3.1.3.2   Test Monitoring and Control

Monitoring and control is an ongoing activity with the purpose of staying in control of the test project or test subprocess at hand. *If you don't control a project, it will control you.*

Monitoring is performed by collecting measurements and comparing these to the plan; a bit like testing actually. If there is any discrepancy, control actions must be planned and implemented and the relevant stakeholders must be informed.

Planning what metrics to collect and how to collect them as well as how to present and use the actual measurements is described in Sections 3.5 and 3.6 below.

Another important part of monitoring is to *revisit the risks*, and identify possible new risks and/or changes in the already identified risks in the risk register(s).

There are a few rules that you must adhere to when following up on the actual activities. Follow up must be guided by:

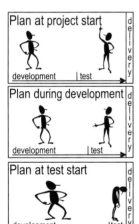

▶   Honesty;

▶   Visibility;

▶   Action.

First of all you need to be honest, not only when you estimate, but also when you collect information about reality. In the long run you lose integrity and trust if you "tailor" the numbers, or come up with "political" results of the monitoring.

You also need to make the information visible to all stakeholders. Again you lose trust if you hide the truth, whether it is a positive truth (we are ahead of schedule) or a negative truth (we are behind schedule). Information about progress and findings must be made readily available to the stakeholders in appropriate forms, including regular test status reports.

The last thing you need to do to stay in control is to take action whenever needed. *It is your duty as test manager to intervene as soon as deviations occur!*

3.1.3.3 Test Completion

The completion activity is about safeguarding the assets that have been produced during the course of the testing covered by the plan and cleaning up the test environment.

The assets can be both tangible, in the form of, for example, test plans, manual and/or automated test procedures, and/or test environment infrastructure, and intangible, in the form of lessons learned.

Tangible assets should be placed under configuration management such that they are clearly identified, safely stored, and available to those who might benefit from them, for example, for the purpose of regression testing during maintenance.

Lessons learned may be collected at a retrospective meeting. This could be both concerning what went well and what did not go so well during the course of the testing. Recommendations for improvement of both testing and other processes may be derived from the lessons learned and reported to those responsible for process improvement. *In this way the testing not only contributes to better quality in the item under test, but also to better quality in future products and better results for the business.*

3.1.4 Produced Documentation

The tangible outcomes of the performance of a test management process are a test plan and a test completion report. These two types of test management documentation belong to a particular test project typically consisting of a number of test subprocesses. Hence, a complete set of test management documentation might consist of:

- One project test plan;
- One or more subprocess test plan(s);
- A number of test status reports;
- One or more subprocess test completion report(s);
- One project test completion report.

The contents of a test plan, a test status report, and a test completion report as suggested in ISO 29119 are described below.

3.1.4.1 Test Plan

The project test plan documents the implementation of the relevant organizational test strategy for a particular project. This is where strategy meets reality for the first time. The project test plan must comply as much as possible with the strategy; any noncompliance must be explained, and the reason reported to the person responsible for the organizational test strategy as input for possible changes.

The plan outlines the journey

A subprocess test plan documents the details for a specific test subprocess, for example, component testing, security testing, or acceptance testing. The size of a subprocess test plan depends on the test subprocess it describes—a component test subprocess plan for single components may be just 5 to 10 lines; a system test subprocess plan may be several pages.

The structure of the test plans, both the project test plan and any subprocess test plans, should be tailored to the organization's needs.

The way the information in a test plan is presented is not important; the information is. A project may have a project test plan and several subprocess test plans, or all the planning for the entire test project may be held in one document. A test plan does not even need to be a document; the various sections could be kept in appropriate tools, such as spreadsheets or dedicated test management tools.

ISO 29119 suggests the following contents for a test plan. This can, of course, be tailored to the individual situation.

Note that Section 3.1.4.1.2 provides an example of a test plan; you might want to look at this as you read the description of the test plan contents.

3.1.4.1.1   Test Plan Contents

Any document should include some document-specific information. This should adhere to the organization's convention for document identification, if there is one. The information should include the following as appropriate:

- ▶ Overview;
- ▶ Unique identifier (e.g., title, issue date, and version);
- ▶ Issuing organization;
- ▶ Approval authority;
- ▶ Change history.

Furthermore any document should provide an introduction, which should include:

- ▶ Scope of the document;
- ▶ References;
- ▶ Glossary.

It is important to get the references precise and correct. Testing is influenced by many aspects, including the organization's test policy, the test strategy, the development or maintenance plan, risks, constraints (time, money, resources), and the test basis and its availability and testability. References must be made to all this information, as applicable—and the information must be respected.

If this chapter gets too voluminous you can place some of the contents in appendices.

1.   Context of the testing

This section should provide an overview of the test covered in the plan. It may be divided into the following subsections.

1.1   Project(s)/test subprocess(es)

This section should provide a very brief description of the test project or the test subprocess(es) that the plan is covering.

In a test project plan the development or maintenance project to which it belongs should be briefly described. In a subprocess test plan, the overall test project should be mentioned.

1.2   Test item(s)

This section should provide precise and explicit identification of the test item(s). It may also contain additional information such as appropriate basis specification, for example, detailed design or requirements specifications, and helpful information such as design guides, coding rules, checklists, a user manual, and relevant test reports.

It may also describe the business purpose of the test item(s), or reference where this information can be found, as well as any procedures for the transfer of the test item(s) from other environments to the test environment.

The test item can be a software unit, interfaces between units, a subsystem, or a complete system depending on the scope of the test plan.

1.3   Test scope

This section should provide a more specific overview of *the features to be tested*.

A feature to be tested could be a specific attribute or set of attributes of the software, a function, an interface, or a business process. Features include both functional and nonfunctional quality attributes.

The decision about which features are to be tested and which not is based on the applicable test strategy, the identified risks, and the mitigation activities for them. The identification of the features to be tested is also closely linked to the specified coverage items.

To set the expectations of the stakeholders right, it is just as important to state what features are not tested as it is to state which are, and hence a list of the features not to be tested should also be provided. A reason must be given as to why each feature is left out.

1.4 Assumptions and constraints

This section should provide descriptions of any assumptions and constraints for the test covered by this plan. This could be based on the test policy and the applicable organizational test strategy, contract issues, project time and cost constraints, and availability of appropriately skilled staff.

1.5 Stakeholders

Relevant stakeholders should be identified and registered along with useful information about them, so that they can be appropriately involved. Stakeholder analysis is described in Section 3.2 below.

This section should provide the result of a stakeholder analysis for the test project or test subprocess.

2. Testing communication

This section should provide a communication plan for how and when to communicate with different stakeholders during the course of the testing.

The section could include a communication or organizational diagram.

The section may also include overview information about the communication lines in defect handling.

3. Risk register

In risk-based testing some of the most important activities are the risk management activities, including identification of ways of treating the risks. The detailed activities in risk-based testing are described in Section 3.3 below.

This section should provide or reference lists of risks to be considered during the test covered by the plan.

It is a good idea to separate product risks and project risks into two separate risk registers as indicated here.

3.1 Product risks

These are risks related to defects that could cause harm during use if they remain in the test item when it is released. A test item may be released for use in production, for example, the complete system, or released for inclusion in other test items, for example, a component to be integrated with other components.

3.2 Project risks

These are risks related to completion of the test project or test subprocess within the constraints (typically time, quality, and cost).

4. Test strategy

This section should provide an outline of the approach to testing for the specified test project or test subprocess, as outlined in the following subclauses.

This test strategy should be based on the organizational test strategy, which outlines the overall test strategy from a business point of view, and the result of the risk management process as described above (because these are the specific risks and mitigation actions for the scope of the test plan).

This section may be divided into the following subsections.

4.1   Test subprocesses

For a project test plan this section should provide an overview of the test subprocesses that will be performed within the test project.

For a test subprocess plan this section may be omitted.

4.2   Test deliverables

This section should provide an overview of everything that is to be produced and delivered to stakeholders during the course of the planned test. This may typically be in the form of documents or contents in databases, general tools, and/or dedicated test tools.

The overview of test documentation presented in Chapter 2 may provide inspiration for which deliverables a test project or test subproject is expected to produce.

Test input data and test output data may also be identified as deliverables, as well as test tools created as part of the testing activity. If documents have been combined or eliminated, then this list will be modified accordingly.

This subsection may include information about when the document(s) should be delivered, and to/from whom, that is, to which defined role in or outside the project of which the testing is a part.

4.3   Test design techniques

This section should provide a list of the specific test design techniques that are to be applied. References may be made to where the techniques are further described, for example, in a test handbook.

The most common test design techniques are described in Chapter 6 along with general guidelines for selecting which technique(s) to use depending on the risk profile for the test item.

4.4   Test completion criteria

This section should provide a description of what must be in place before the test execution activities for the planned test may be considered to be complete.

This will typically include one or more of the following:

- ▶ Specified coverage has been achieved.
- ▶ Specified number of failures found per test effort (test hours) has been achieved.

> ◗ Number of known outstanding defects is below a specified level (possibly per defect category).
> ◗ The benefits of the system are greater than the problems.
> ◗ (The time has run out.)

The last one is usually not a very sensible completion criterion; it is nonetheless often encountered in real life, though rarely documented.

4.5   Metrics to be collected

This section should provide a list of the metrics for which measurements are to be collected during the test activities (typically for use in the monitoring activity).

Test metrics are described in Section 3.5 below.

4.6   Test data requirements

This section should provide a list of the test data necessary for execution of the defined test procedures.

This section in the test plan often only provides overall guidelines for the test data related to the test covered by the plan. Detailed test data requirements are identified during the test design activity and may be documented in a separate test data requirements document that may be referred to from here. This document is described in Chapter 6.

4.7   Test environment requirements

This section should provide a list of the necessary and "nice-to-have" properties of the test environment for execution of the defined test procedures. This could include platform(s), middleware, other systems, testing tools, peripherals, and venue.

As for the corresponding section concerning test data requirements, this section in the test plan often only provides overall guidelines for the test environment related to the test covered by the plan. Detailed test environment requirements are identified during the product design and the test design activities and may be documented in a separate test environment requirements document that may be referred to from here. This document is described in Chapter 6.

4.8   Retesting and regression testing

This section should provide a description of the conditions under which retesting and regression testing will be performed.

This could include a description of the estimated number of test cycles, and should refer to the risk profile for the test item.

4.9 Suspension and resumption criteria

This section should provide a description of any criteria used to suspend and resume all or some of the testing activities. It should also identify who has the authority to suspend and who can resume testing activities.

If test activities have to be repeated when testing is resumed, this should also be specified.

This section may be included in Section 3.2, project risks of the test plan.

4.10 Deviations from the organizational test strategy

This section should provide a list of any deviations from the organizational test strategy introduced in this test plan, along with the approving authority/authorities.

5. Testing activities and estimates

This section should provide an overview of *ALL* activities to be performed for the test covered by the plan. This may be presented in the form of a work breakdown structure, possibly using a general planning or a dedicated test planning tool.

Time and possibly cost estimates should be provided for the activities. Estimation is further described in Section 3.4 below.

Sometimes budget and cost issues are only dealt with in the project plan or in the test project plan.

The detailed overview of activities and estimates for these will evolve as the test progresses. It is not possible, and should not be attempted, to provide the same level of detail for activities just about to be performed and activities to be performed in months or even years into the future.

6. Staffing

This section should provide an overview of the roles that are needed in the test project or test subprocess, and the organizational unit and/or people who are filling these roles.

The preparation of this section is often iterative, going through the detailed descriptions of the role, identifying staff, possibly hiring and training new people, and assigning people to roles several times before the puzzle is completed.

6.1 Roles, activities, and responsibilities

This section should provide a list of the roles needed for the test at hand. This will, of course, include testing roles, but it may also include other roles, for example, operations staff, user representatives, technical support staff, data administration staff, and quality support staff.

A role description including required and possibly also "nice-to-have" skills should be provided or referenced for each role.

The number of people needed for each role should also be identified, for example two test analysts and one half-time technical test analyst.

The list of roles is used to staff the test project; that is, to assign organizational unit and/or named people to roles and define their specific responsibilities. It should also be used to identify staff recruitment and/or training needs.

The result of the identification of activities and staffing can be described in a RACI matrix (responsibility assignment matrix). RACI is short for the responsibilities that can be assigned to roles, namely:

Responsible—the role(s) performing the activity;

Accountable—the role carrying the economic liability;

Consulted—the role(s) that may contribute or influence;

Informed—the roles that must know about the activity and its results.

In a RACI matrix, the activities are often listed vertically, the roles horizontally, and the RACI marked in the intersecting cells.

6.2 Hiring needs

This section should provide a list of the people who may have to be hired, transferred, contracted, or otherwise acquired to fill roles that may not be otherwise filled. It must describe when people are needed and for how long, if not permanent full time. Necessary and wanted skills should also be expressed as precisely as possible.

6.3 Training needs

This section should provide an overview of any training required for the people filling the roles in the test project. The training should be part of the activities to be handled in the schedule.

7. Schedule

This section should provide the detailed schedule created from the tasks and their dependencies, the staffing, and the estimates. This should provide the expected start time and duration for each testing activity and associated test milestones.

This is where it is shown when and for what amount of time each person is allocated to perform which activities.

This is the most versatile part of the plan, since the schedule will change over time, when tasks are being performed and estimates are refined.

3.1.4.1.2   Project Test Plan Contents Example

The table below provides some examples of contents for each of the entries in a specific instantiation of a test plan. The examples are rather short, but I hope they may serve as inspiration.

Note that text in brackets refers to examples in this book.

System Test Plan	
Context of the testing	
Project	This system test is part of the KLOD project.
Test item(s)	The completed KLOD product delivered for system test. This includes the software and the documentation.
Test scope	All functional and nonfunctional requirements specified in the KLOD requirement specification must be covered in this test, except the performance requirements because the dynamic performance test will be carried out by third-party company PTESTIT.
Assumptions and constraints	This plan is based on the constraint that the deadline for decision on go/no go based on the system test is a kill or cure deadline and will be maintained, no matter how far the system test has proceeded by then.
Stakeholders	The identified stakeholders are: (See result of stakeholder analysis in Section 3.2.2.)
Testing communication	
(See result of stakeholder communication analysis in Section 3.2.3.)	
Risk register	
Product risks	(See examples of product risks in Section 3.3.1.2.3.)
Project risks	(See example of project risks in Section 3.3.1.2.4.)
Test strategy	
Test deliverables	–This test plan; –Test specification; –Test data requirements document; –Test environment requirements document; –Specified test environment, including test data; –Logs and test status reports; –System test completion report.
Test design techniques	The following test design techniques must be used, depending on the nature of the each requirement: –Classification tree; –Decision table; –State transition.

Test completion criteria	–100% requirements coverage; –80% test element coverage, as per applied test case design technique for the requirements; –0 known failures of category A; –Max. 2 known defects of category B; –Max. 15 known defects of category C.
Metrics to be collected	(See Section 3.5.)
Test data requirements	The required test data will be documented in a specific test data requirements document that will be produced during the test analysis and design process.
Test environment requirements	The required test environment will be documented in a specific test environment requirements document that will be produced during the test analysis and design process.
Retesting and regression testing	All test cases that have exposed failures must be rerun when the underlying defect(s) has/have been reported, corrected, and component tested. An analysis must be performed and documented for each defect correction to determine the appropriate regression testing to be executed.
Suspension and resumption criteria	Test execution may be suspended if more than 20% of the execution time is spent reporting banal failures, caused by defects that should have been found during component testing. Development must report back when they have performed sufficient component testing. At resumption, 30% of executed test procedures and the same number of as-yet unexecuted test procedures must be executed to ensure that the quality of the test item has improved.
Testing activities and estimates (A work breakdown structure is too voluminous to include here, but it can be derived from the process descriptions.)	
Staffing	
Roles, activities, and responsibilities	This is illustrated in the RACI matrix shown here:

	1	2	3	4	5	6	7
Test manager	A	A	A	I	A	A	A
Development manager	C	C		A	I		I
Test analysts	C	R	I	I	R	R	R
Technical test analysts	C	R	R	I	R	R	R
Quality assurance	I						I
Sales/marketing	I						I
The customer	I						I
Method department	I	C/I	C/I				I

1. Test management
2. Test design
3. Test tools
4. Test environment
5. Test data
6. Test execution
7. Reporting

Responsible **A**ccountable **C**onsulted **I**nformed

Hiring needs	We have to hire a technical analyst to start by September 1 at the latest to fill the technical analyst role.
Training needs	All the staff assigned to this system test must have participated in the half-day introduction to KLOD system test.

Schedule

The schedule is maintained in the ProfProject tool under KLOD, System Test. This is just an example of a Gantt diagram.

Id		Opgavenavn	Varighed	bruar	01. marts	01. april	01. maj	01. juni	01. juli	01. august	01. september	01. oktober	01. novem
				-3	-1	2	4	6	8	10	12	14	16	18	20	22	24	26	28	30	32	34	36
1		Opgave 1	15 dage
2		Opgave 2	10 dage
3		Opgave 3	75 dage
4		Opgave 4	15 dage
5		Opgave 5.1	20 dage
6		Opgave 5.2	20 dage
7		Opgave 5.3	100 dage

3.1.4.1.3 *Test Plan Contents Mapping ISTQB/ISO 29119*

The ISTQB syllabi mention a master test plan and refer to IEEE 289–1998 for contents. The table below therefore presents a mapping between the widely used IEEE description of the contents of a test plan and the table of contents provided in ISO 29119. A blank entry means that there is no equivalence.

Note that IEEE 829 is superseded by ISO 29119.

ISTQB (IEEE 829–1998)	ISO 29119:2013
Test plan identifier	Unique identification of document
Introduction (scope, risks, and objectives)	Introduction (Scope, References, Glossary)
	Context of the testing –Project/test subprocess –Test item(s) –Test scope –Assumptions and constraints –Stakeholders
Test item(s) or test object(s)	(In context, test items)
Features to be tested	
Features not to be tested	
Approach (must at least cover): –The test methods and test techniques to use –The structure of the test specification to be produced and used –The tools to be used –The interface with configuration management –Measurements to collect –Important constraints	Test strategy: –Test subprocesses –Test deliverables –Test design techniques (Test environment requirements) (Metrics to be collected) –Test completion criteria –Metrics to be collected –Test data requirements –Test environment requirements –Retesting and regression testing –Suspension and resumption criteria –Deviations from the organizational test strategy
Item pass/fail criteria (exit criteria including coverage criteria)	(Test strategy: Completion criteria)
Suspension criteria and resumption requirements	(Test strategy: Suspension and resumption criteria)
Test deliverables (work products)	(Test strategy: Test deliverables)
Testing tasks	Testing activities and estimates
Environmental needs	(Test strategy: Test data requirements, and Test environment requirements)
Responsibilities	(Staffing: Roles, activities, and responsibilities)
Staffing and training needs	Staffing –Roles, activities, and responsibilities –Hiring needs –Training needs
Schedule	Schedule
Risks and contingencies	Risk register –Product risks –Project risks
Test plan approvals	Approval authority

3.1.4.2   Test Status Report

The purpose of the test status report is to provide information to relevant stakeholders about the status of the testing that is performed in a specific reporting period.

Status reports should be issued according to the communication plan outlined in the testing communication section in the relevant test plan.

In a test project or test subprocess, a number of different test status reports may be issued depending on the target audience. The people working directly on the test activities may need daily or very frequent, very detailed status reports, whereas management may need less frequent and less detailed status reports.

ISO 29119 suggests the following table of contents for a test status report. This may, of course, be tailored to the individual situation.

Note that Section 3.1.4.2.2 provides an example of a test plan; you might want to look at this as you read the description of the test status report contents.

3.1.4.2.1   Test Status Report Contents

Any document should include some document specific information. This is described in Section 3.1.4.1.1.

1. Test status

1.1 Reporting period

This section should provide information about the period over which the measures presented in the report have been collected, that is, the time period covered by the report.

1.2 Progress against test plan

This section should provide an overview of how the testing has progressed in the covered period compared to the schedule.

If notable deviations are found, these should be listed with the following information:

- ▶ Explanations of the reasons for deviation;
- ▶ Description of any actions;
- ▶ Description of the effects;
- ▶ Implications with regard to planned project objectives.

1.3 Factors blocking progress

This section should provide an overview of the factors that have impeded progress during the reporting period, if any, with descriptions of how the obstacles have been overcome. Any unsolved issues should also be listed with suggested solutions.

1.4 Test measures

This section should provide suitable presentations of the test measures collected during the reporting period and relevant at the end of the reporting period.

This information may be presented graphically. For more details see Section 3.6 below.

1.5 New and changed risks

This section should provide the result of a renewed risk identification and analysis; that is, new risks and updated remaining risks.

1.6 Planned testing

This section should provide a description of the test activities planned for the next reporting period. This information is usually presented as an updated schedule.

3.1.4.2.2   Test Status Report Contents Example

The table below provides some examples of contents for each of the entries in a test status report. The examples are rather short, but I hope they may serve as inspiration.

System Test Status Report	
Test status	
Reporting period	Week 4, 2013 (21.1–25.1)
Progress against plan	All the test procedures were executed according to the plan; except TP 31.C and TP 31.D. These have been postponed to next week, when there should be enough time to execute them.
Factors blocking progress	The test environment concerning the interface to HUNF was delayed 5 hours on Wednesday. We have found an unexpected high number of trivial defects in the report creation functionality. This has caused some delay.
Test measures	(See examples below in Section 3.6.)
New and changed risks	No new risks have been identified. Risk R45 has been removed based on the results of executing PR16.
Planned testing	See updated test schedule on the project wall.

3.1.4.2.3   Test Status Report Contents Mapping ISTQB/ISO 29119

The ISTQB syllabi mention a test report and refer to IEEE 289–1998 for contents. IEEE 829–1998 does not include a test status report and hence there is no mapping possible for the ISO 29119 test status report contents.

3.1.4.3   Test Completion Report

The purpose of test reporting is to summarize the results of a test project or test subprocess and provide evaluations based on these results.

A test report should be issued at the completion of each test level and the end of the entire testing assignment task. The test reports should include analysis of result information to allow management decisions, based on risk, about whether to proceed to the next level of testing or to project implementation, or whether more testing is required.

Top management or other stakeholders may also need test completion reports at other points in time, for example, for regularly scheduled project status meetings or at the end of the project in order to adjust policy and strategy.

ISO 29119 suggests the following table of contents for a test completion report. This may, of course, be tailored to the individual situation.

Note that Section 3.1.4.3.2 provides an example of a test plan; you might want to look at this as you read the description of the test status report contents.

3.1.4.3.1   Test Completion Report Contents

Any document should include some document specific information. This is described in Section 3.1.4.1.1.

1. Testing performed

1.1 Summary of testing performed

This section should provide an overview of the testing performed for the test project or test subprocess covered by the report. The section could refer directly to the test plan. It should be possible to read the summary in isolation and get the main information about the test.

1.2 Deviations from planned testing

This section should provide an overview of the deviations from the planned testing, if any, including what was done and not done compared to the original plan.

1.3 Test completion evaluation

This section should provide an account of whether or not the original (or modified) plan was followed to completion. It should describe which of the planned tests were not performed, if any, and why not.

This is also where a description goes of how the original completion criteria were met. If the completion criteria were modified during the course of the testing, an explanation should be provided here.

Any statistically valid conclusions that can be drawn from these analyses could be used to predict the quality level achieved in the tested product.

1.4 Factors that blocked progress
This section should provide an overview of the factors that have impeded progress during the reporting period, if any, with descriptions of how the obstacles have been overcome.

1.5 Test measures
This section should provide suitable presentations of the test measures collected during the course of the testing.
This information may be presented graphically. For more details see Section 3.6 below.

1.6 Residual risks
This section should provide a list of the risks that have not been resolved at the end of the testing; this may be risks that have not been fully treated by the test and/or any new risks identified as a result of the final monitoring and closure of the test.

1.7 Test deliverables
This section should provide a list of all the test deliverables produced as a result of the test effort and where they are stored. The list should be compared to the corresponding list in the related test plan, and any discrepancies explained.

1.8 Reusable test assets
This section should provide a list of the test deliverables and other artifacts produced during the course of the testing that can be reused. The artifacts should be placed under configuration management or handed to the appropriate stakeholders for storage.

1.9 Lessons learned
This section should provide the result of any lessons learned meetings in a form that is suitable for the organizational unit in charge of process improvement and/or any other relevant stakeholder(s).

3.1.4.3.2   Test Completion Report Contents Example
The table below provides some examples of contents for each of the entries in a test completion report. The examples are rather short, but I hope they may serve as inspiration.

System Test Completion Report	
Test performed	
Summary of testing performed	Activities planned in the system test plan have been performed. We have executed 231 of the 254 specified test procedures. 108 incidents have been reported, hereof −2 category A defects, −11 category B defects, −38 category C defects. The rest are category D defects and misunderstandings. 2 defects were identified in the test procedures; these have been corrected and the test procedures reexecuted.
Deviations from planned test	Due to the delay in setting up the test environment for the interface to the HUNF, the execution of the related test procedures was postponed. This was remedied by executing other test procedures earlier than planned.
Test completion evaluation	We have reached the coverage completion criteria, and the numbers of remaining defects are below the maximum allowed number per category.
Factors blocking progress	None that were not overcome during the test.
Test measures	(See examples in Section 3.6 below.)
Residual risks	Three risks remain; see the Product Test Register in the project room.
Test deliverables	All documentation specified in the system test plan has been delivered. See more details in the project room.
Reusable test assets	The database containing the test data used in this system test has been stored under configuration management for reuse in acceptance testing and possible testing during production and maintenance of the system.
Lessons learned	A report has been delivered. The main lesson learned is that more testing should be performed in the component test step, because about 25% of the defects found in this system test could have been found more efficiently in a more thorough component test.

3.1.4.3.3 *Test Plan Contents Mapping ISTQB/ISO 29119*

The ISTQB syllabi mention a test summary report and refer to IEEE 829–1998 for contents. The table below therefore presents a mapping between the IEEE description of the contents of a test summary report and the table of contents for a test completion report provided in ISO 29119. A blank entry means that there is no equivalence.

Note that IEEE 829 is superseded by ISO 29119.

ISTQB (IEEE 829 - 1998)	ISO 29119:2013
Test plan identifier	Unique identification of document
Summary of testing performed	Summary of testing performed
Variances	Deviations from planned testing
Comprehensiveness, assessment	Test completion evaluation
Summary of results	
Evaluation	
Summary of activities	
	Factors that blocked progress
	Test measures
	Residual risks
	Test deliverables
	Reusable test assets
	Lessons learned

3.2   Test Stakeholder Analysis

One of the rules in warfare is "Know your enemy." Product development and testing is not warfare, and no enemies are involved, but the rule can be modified to "Know your stakeholders," which is just as crucial for success.

A test stakeholder is anybody who will in any way be affected by or will affect the testing of the new product under development. A stakeholder can be a person, an organizational unit, a group of people with similar stakes, or another product.

Stakeholders may have a positive influence; that is, they may be beneficial to the testing process, for example, by providing money and/or expertise. Stakeholders may also have a negative influence; that is, they could represent a risk to testing, for example, by withholding resources.

It is therefore important to know who the stakeholders for a test project or test subprocess are, and how they can be communicated with and drawn into the work as appropriate.

3.2.1   Identifying Test Stakeholders

Basically the way to identify test stakeholders is to ask in relation to the test and the product to be produced and used:

- ▶ WHO knows;
- ▶ WHO feels;
- ▶ WHO benefits;
- ▶ WHO suffers.

Test stakeholders can come from any part of the business and the future user realm.

Techniques for identifying the stakeholders for a project may include:

◗ Checklists from previous projects;
◗ Interviews;
◗ Brainstorm meetings;
◗ Document studies.

Think far and wide when identifying test stakeholders. It is a good idea to "go overboard" and identify too many potential stakeholders, and then discard the irrelevant ones, rather than run the risk of missing somebody.

The following table may be used for inspiration:

Area	Possible Stakeholders
The business	Top management Product line manager Product sponsor Business analysts Finance executives Lawyers Marketing Sales Customers
Users	Users of existing product(s) to be replaced Future users More or less official user groups Future users' management Indirect users (users of the results from the product)
Development	Project management Requirements engineers Architects Designers Programmers
Support processes	Process managers Configuration managers Quality assurance User trainers
Production and maintenance	Operations management Operation personnel Support personnel

List all possible stakeholders by name of people or organizational unit or by role, and expand the list with relevant information as described below.

3.2.2 Test Stakeholder Register

The identified stakeholders should be listed in a stakeholder register, and relevant information provided for each. The relevant information, apart from the name of the stakeholder, could include:

▶ Contact information;

▶ Role;

▶ Responsibilities beyond those implied by the role;

▶ Authority (level of power);

▶ Rights;

▶ Availability;

▶ Relevance;

▶ Knowledge areas and depth of knowledge;

▶ Personal goals and interests;

▶ Possible positive influences;

▶ Possible negative influences;

▶ Possible contributions;

▶ Communication needs.

The list provided here is fairly extensive; the relevant pieces of information for the test stakeholders should be determined for any given test situation.

The list should be reviewed regularly and kept up to date. Information about test stakeholders may change quickly, and an outdated stakeholder register is a potential risk to the test project.

3.2.3 Communication Plan

Stakeholders should be involved as much as possible, both to benefit from their interest and knowledge and to mitigate any opposition toward the product and/or the testing.

It is a very good idea to develop a plan for communication with stakeholders to ensure that each of them gets the information they need in the right format at the right time. Communication with stakeholders can be the "all or nothing" for the success of a project.

The table below shows some examples of communication planned for various test stakeholders.

Stakeholder	Communication
Project manager	Weekly progress meetings Monthly test status report Test completion reports
User representative	Tailored test completion reports
Programmers	Daily overview of new and corrected defects during test execution periods
Testers	Daily overview of new and corrected defects during test execution periods
Quality assurance	Test completion reports

3.3   Risk-Based Testing

The golden rule of testing is:

> **Always test so that whenever you have to stop you have done the best possible test.**

Everybody with some understanding of requirements and testing will know that a requirement like this cannot be verified. What does it mean: the best possible test? It is not immediately measurable.

What is the best possible test then? The answer to that is: It depends!

The best possible test depends on the risk associated with having defects left in the product when it is released to the customer!

The best possible test is determined by the risks we are facing and the risks we are willing to run. Obtaining consensus from stakeholders on the most important risks to cover is essential.

3.3.1   Introduction to Risk-Based Testing

We have to live with the fact that it is impossible to test everything. Testing is sample control. There is a risk involved in all sample control: the risk of overlooking defects in the areas we are not testing.

3.3.1.1   Risk Definition

A risk is defined as "The possibility of realizing an unwanted negative consequence of an incident."

Alternatively a risk may be defined as *"A problem that has not materialized yet and possibly never will."*

There are two important points in these definitions:

▶ A risk entails something negative.
▶ A risk may or may not happen—we don't know.

A risk therefore has two aspects:

▶ Effect (impact—consequence);
▶ Probability (likelihood—frequency).

The two aspects of risk can be combined into:

Risk level = probability × effect

From this it is quite clear that if we have no probability or no effect we have no risk. The risks that do have a risk level greater than zero are the risks we have to deal with.

It is not a risk (to us), if there is no effect of an event that might happen. We can therefore ignore it even if the probability is high.

There is a probability that there are defects in the new version of our database management system, but that will have no effect on the quality of our product if that does happen, because it is not used in our system.

It is not a risk if there is no (or an extremely small) probability that an event will happen, even if the effect would be extremely big, if it did. We can therefore ignore that as well.

There is no (detectable) risk of our department closing down, because we have lots of orders, are making good money, and both management and employees like their jobs. If we did close down, the effect on the project would be pretty bad, if not disastrous.

It is not a risk either if the probability of an event with a negative effect is 100%. In this case we know we have a real problem on our hands, and we will have to deal with that in our planning.

It is a problem—not a risk—that we will have to do without one of our test experts because she has found another job and is leaving in 3 months.

3.3.1.2 Risk Types

It is quite common to treat all the risks we can think of in connection with a development project in one big bundle. This can be quite overwhelming.

It is therefore a very good idea to take a closer look at the risks and divide them into classes, corresponding to where they may hit—or what they are threatening.

Risks hit in different places, namely:

- The business;
- The processes;
- The project;
- The product.

3.3.1.2.1   Business Risks

The business risks threaten the entire company or organization from a "staying-in-business" point of view. This discussion is beyond the scope of this book and is not discussed further.

3.3.1.2.2   Process Risks

Process risks are related to the processes and/or the way work is performed. This is also beyond the scope of this book, but will be briefly discussed because knowledge about processes is indispensable in a modern development organization, and because testing is also performed according to processes.

Process risk threatens the effectiveness and efficiency with which we work on an assignment. Process risks may originate from:

- Missing process(es);
- The organization's lack of knowledge about the processes;
- Inadequate processes;
- Inconsistencies among processes;
- Unsuitable processes;
- Lack of support in the form of templates and techniques.

Process risks jeopardize the way the work in the project is being performed; including the way testing is being performed. These risks should be the concern of the project manager and/or the test manager, and those responsible for the processes in the organization.

Process risks may influence business risks, as well as project and product risks.

3.3.1.2.3   Project Risks

Project risks are related to the project and the successful completion of the project.

A project consists of a number of activities and phases, from requirements development to the final acceptance test. These activities are supported by activities like quality assurance, configuration management, and project management.

Activities in a project are estimated, get resources allocated, and are scheduled. As the project progresses the activities are monitored according to the plan.

Risks concerning the project may originate from:

- People assigned to the project (e.g., their availability, adequate skills and knowledge, and personalities);
- Time (deadlines);
- Money;
- Development and test environment, including tools;
- External interfaces;
- Customer/supplier relationships.

Project risks jeopardize the project's progress and successful completion according to the plan.

Examples of project risks include the following:

- The necessary analysts may not be available when the requirements development is expected to start.
- Two of the senior designers are not on speaking terms and useful information exchange between them is not happening—this may cause the design phase to take longer than expected.
- The complexity of the user interface may have been underestimated.
- The testers may not be adequately trained in testing techniques, so testing may require more resources than expected.
- The integration may be more time consuming than expected.
- The access to external data may not be possible with the technique chosen in the design.

The project risks are the main concern of the project manager and higher management.

The test manager is concerned with the project risks related to the test project as it is specified in the test plan.

3.3.1.2.4 Product Risks

Product risks are related to the final product. They are the risks of defects remaining in the product when it is delivered.

The risks threatening the product are the testers' main concern. This is where we can make a difference.

We want to deliver the required quality and reliability. This cannot be tested into the product at the end of the development, but must be worked into the product through the work products produced during development and in the implementation of the components. Product risks may be originated in functional and nonfunctional requirements in the form of, for example:

▶ Missing requirements;

▶ Ambiguous requirements;

▶ Misunderstood requirements;

▶ Requirements on which stakeholders do not agree.

Research (for example, from IBM) has shown that more than 50% of all defects in products can be traced back to defects in the requirements.

Product risks jeopardize customer satisfaction, and maybe even the customer's life and livelihood.

Product risks may be related to different requirement types, such as functionality, safety, security, and political and technical factors.

Examples of product risks are:

▶ A small, but important functionality may have been overlooked in the requirements and is therefore not implemented.

▶ A calculation of discounts may be wrongly implemented and the customer may lose a lot of money.

▶ The instrument may reset to default values if it is dropped on the floor.

▶ It may be possible to print a report of confidential customer information through a loophole in the reporting facility.

▶ The installation procedure may be difficult to follow, and this may lead to incorrect and/or incomplete installation.

Project risks and product risks can influence and be the cause of each other. A project risk may cause a product risk, and a product risk may cause a project risk. Risk mitigation actions for a risk may also introduce new risks and/or increase (or indeed decrease) the risk levels of other risks.

If a project risk results in time being cut from component testing, this may cause the product risk of an increased number of defects remaining in the components that are not tested or not tested sufficiently. This may further cause the project risk that there may not be sufficient time to perform a proper system test because too many trivial failures are encountered in the system test.

3.3.1.3 Testing and Risk Management

Test and management of risks should be tightly interwoven as they support each other. In risk-based testing, the test strategy and plan are based on the results of risk analysis, and test results give valuable feedback to support continuous risk analysis.

The result of a product risk analysis can be used in the test planning to make the test as effective as possible. It can be used to target the testing effort, since different types of tests are most effective for different risks.

Component testing is most effective for testing in the case where the product risk level related to complex calculations is highest.

The risk analysis results can also be used to prioritize and distribute the test effort. The areas with the highest risk level should be planned to be tested first and given the most time and resources.

Finally the product risk analysis can be used to qualify the testing already done. If the test effort is related to the identified risks, it should be possible to report on resolved and remaining risks at any time.

Testing can, as mentioned above, resolve or mitigate product risks. The probability of sending a product with defects out to the customers is reduced by the testing finding failures and the subsequent correction of the defects.

Testing can also mitigate project risks if an appropriate test strategy is applied, especially if testing is started early.

Even process risks may be reduced by analyzing failure reports and taking appropriate process improvement initiatives.

3.3.2 Risk Management

Risk management consists of the following activities:

▶ Risk identification;
▶ Risk analysis;
▶ Risk mitigation;
▶ Risk follow-up.

In risk identification we are finding out what may be threatening the process, the project, or—in this particular context—customer satisfaction with the product.

The identified risks are evaluated in the risk analysis and ordered relative to each other according to their level. The analysis means that we assign probability and effect to the risks, and based on this we can determine the risk level and hence which risk is the worst and how the others relate to that.

One of the points in risk management is to use the results of analyses to mitigate the risks. Actions can be planned to lower the probability and/

or the effect of the risks. In the context of product risks and testing, test activities can be planned to mitigate the risks by lowering the probability of having remaining defects in the product when it is released. The more defects we can remove from the product as a result of the testing, the more the probability falls. *Testing cannot change the effect of a risk.*

Contingency planning is a part of classic risk management, but this is not relevant for product risks in relation to testing. Testing is concerned with lowering the probability of defects remaining in the product. For the defects that still remain when the product is in production, support and maintenance must be prepared to provide work-arounds and/or corrections and updates.

Risk identification, analysis, and mitigation should not be a one-time activity. It is necessary to follow up on the risks as testing progresses. The results of the testing activities provide input to continuous risk management.

Information about the failure frequency over time can be used to assess if the probability of a risk is falling or rising.

3.3.2.1   Risk Identification

Risk identification is finding out where and how things might go wrong, and writing it down to form the basis for risk analysis.

Risks are found in areas where the fulfillment of expectations may be threatened, that is, where the customer satisfaction is jeopardized. *Satisfying expectations is the way to success!*

All stakeholders have expectations about the product, but we are most concerned with the expectations of the customer. The customer orders the product, pays for it, and takes advantage of it—the latter possibly through end users.

In an ideal world the customer's expectations are expressed requirements. These requirements are transformed into a design, and the requirements are fulfilled in the code and or in other types of subsystems being integrated into the final products.

Customer satisfaction

In lesser ideal worlds expectations may be derived from other sources.

Risks are not always evident. Even when we work with experienced and knowledgeable stakeholders, it can be efficient to use a risk identification technique.

Useful techniques include:

▶ Lessons learned;
▶ Checklists;
▶ Risk workshops;
▶ Brainstorming;

▶ Expert interviews;

▶ Independent risk assessments.

Techniques may be mixed to be even more efficient.

3.3.2.1.1 Lessons Learned and Checklists

Lessons learned and checklists are closely related. A checklist is a list of generic risks, formed and maintained by experience (i.e., lessons learned from previous projects).

Risk checklists are valuable assets in an organization, and should always be treated as such.

One or more product risk checklists should be kept in the organization, depending on the diversity of the nature of the projects performed by the organization.

The checklists used by pilots before take-off are long and must be run through very carefully before every take-off. A pilot was once hurried along by a busy business man who asked him to drop the checklists and get going. The pilot carried on with his work as he answered, "These checklists are written in blood!"

3.3.2.1.2 Risk Workshops

Workshops are an effective way to identify risks. There are no strict rules as to how a workshop should be conducted, but a few guidelines can be given.

As many stakeholders as possible should be involved, though the number of participants should not exceed 10 to 12 in order to give everybody a chance to talk within reasonable intervals.

Risk workshops can get emotional and a neutral facilitator—somebody who is not by any account a stakeholder in the project—should be present to guide the discussions. *Encourage discussions and new ideas, but avoid conflicts.*

Make sure that all participants agree that the objective of the workshop has been reached and that it is clear how work can proceed after the workshop.

3.3.2.1.3 Brainstorming

A brainstorming session (in this context of risk identification) is an informal session designed to identify possible risks connected with the product when it is released.

The only rule that should apply during brainstorming is *that no possible idea must be criticized* in any way by the participants. Ideas should be allowed to flow freely, the rationale being that even the most seemingly stupid, silly, or strange thought may be the inspiration for valuable potential risks.

A brainstorming sessions must have a facilitator who can act as a catalyst if ideas do not flow freely. At the end of the session, the facilitator must make sure that whatever surfaced as possible risks is documented.

Any type of stakeholder may be involved in brainstorming.

3.3.2.1.4 Expert Interviews

Interviews may be conducted as individual interviews or as group interviews. *An interview is not as easy to conduct as many people think.* It requires specific skills and thorough preparation to get as much information as possible from an interview.

First of all, an interview is not like an ordinary conversation. People in an interview have different roles (e.g., the interviewer and the interviewees), and they may have a number of expectations and prejudices related to these roles. Interviews must be prepared. The interviewer must make sure, for example, that the right people are being interviewed and the right information is being gathered. A list of questions or a framework for the course of the interview must be prepared.

Ample notes must be taken and/or the interview can be recorded (with the permission of the interviewees). *The interviewer should extract a list of possible risks from the interview* and get agreement from all the participants.

3.3.2.1.5 Independent Risk Assessments

In cases where conflicts are threatened, external consultants may be called in to identify risks. External consultants could also be used if time is short or if specific expertise is not present within the immediate stakeholders.

The external consultants identify risks and usually also perform or facilitate the risk analysis.

The consultants may be external to the project organization or third-party consultants entirely external to the developing organization.

3.3.2.2 Risk Analysis

Risk analysis is the evaluation of the identified risks. One thing is to identify and list the risks; another is to put them into perspective relative to each other. This is what the analysis of the risks helps us do.

The analysis must be performed by all appropriate stakeholders, because they all have different perspectives, and risk analysis is aimed at providing a common and agreed-on view of the risks. Experts may be called in to contribute if adequate expertise cannot be found among the immediate stakeholders.

Risk analysis can be performed more or less rigorously, but it should always be taken seriously.

3.3.2.2.1   Risk Register

A risk register is a very useful tool in risk management. It can be used to support risk analysis and risk mitigation.

Risk registers can be created using office tools, for example, spreadsheets that support calculations.

A risk register should include:

▶ Risk identification (e.g., number or title);
▶ Risk description;
▶ Probability;
▶ Effect;
▶ Level;
▶ Test priority;
▶ Mitigation action;
▶ Dependencies and assumptions.

3.3.2.2.2   Perception of Risks

The performance of risk analysis is more or less subjective. In fact, most *risk analysis is based on perceptions;* it is usually not possible to determine risk probability and effect totally objectively. There is an element of prediction in risk analysis since we have to deal with something that has not happened and maybe never will.

Perceptions are personal and different people have different "pain thresholds."

Just look around you: Some people use their holidays to explore new places, others always spend their holidays at the same place. In connection with process improvements, we sometimes say that if it blows hard some people build shelters others build windmills.

People in different professions may also have different viewpoints on risks—partly because people choose jobs according to their personalities, partly because job-related experiences influence their perception of different risks.

The following descriptions of job-related risk perceptions are of course gross generalizations, but they can be used as guidelines in understanding different viewpoints on "the same risks." The descriptions encompass the following roles:

▶ Project managers;
▶ Developers;

- ❯ Testers;
- ❯ End users.

Project managers are often under time pressures, and they are used to compromises. They know that even though things may look dark, the world usually keeps standing.

Developers (i.e., analysts, designers, and programmers) are proud of their work, and they know how it was done. They have really done their best, and they are usually reluctant to accept that defects may still remain.

Testers often have a pessimistic view about work products, product components, and products. We remember previous experiences where we received objects for test and got far more failures than we expected.

The *end users* are, despite what we might think, usually highly failure tolerant. They also tend to remember previous experiences, but what they remember is that, even though the system failed, they found a way around it or another way of doing their work. End users use our product as a tool in their job, and nothing more. If it does not help them, they'll find another way of using the tool, another tool, or just live with it.

In risk analysis we must encourage communication and understanding among stakeholders. *Stakeholders need to be able to, if not agree with then at least be aware of and accept others' points of view.* If need be, stakeholders will have to compromise or use composite analysis, as explained below.

3.3.2.2.3 Scales for Risk Analysis

The analysis of risks uses metrics for probability and effect. For all work with metrics, it is mandatory to use agreed-on and understood scales.

We can work with two different kinds of scales: qualitative and quantitative. In a qualitative scale we work with feelings or assessments.

For effect we could use:

bad—worse—worst

For probability we could use:

not likely—likely—very likely

In a quantitative scale, on the other hand, we work with exact measures or numbers.

For effect we could use actual cost in for example $ or €.
Probability could be expressed as:

<= 10%, >10% & <= 50%, >50% & <=80%, > 80%

Whichever way we do it, the test manager must define scales for both probability and effect before we start the risk analysis (that is, before we assign values to the probability of the identified risks actually materializing, and values for the effect if they do).

3.3.2.2.4 Effect

The effect is the impact or consequences of a risk if it occurs. As mentioned above, the first thing we must have is a scale for the effect.

The obvious *quantitative scale* for the effect is the actual cost imparted by a risk occurring. The actual cost can be measured in any agreed-on currency (e.g., $ or €). This is an open scale; in theory, there is no limit to actual cost.

It can be very difficult to assess what the actual cost in real money might be. On the other hand, it can be quite an eye-opener to consider all the sources of extra costs associated with a risk.

Costs may be considered for:

▶ Time for the end user to realize that something is wrong;

▶ Time to report the incident to first-level support;

▶ Time for first-level support to understand the report and try to help;

▶ Time for any double or extra work to be performed by the end users;

▶ Loss of production because the system is down or malfunctioning;

▶ Time for escalation to second-level support;

▶ Time for second-level support to try to help;

▶ Time to investigate the failure and decide what to do about it;

▶ Time for finding the defect(s);

▶ Time for corrections to be implemented and tested in all affected objects;

▶ Time for retest and regression test;

▶ Time to reinstall the new version;

▶ Time to update what has been done by other means while the system was unavailable or malfunctioning.

These are all examples of time to be spent in connection with a failure. Costs may also be associated with, for example, renting or replacing parts of the system or the entire system.

Furthermore, there may be an effect in the form of indirect losses from people getting hurt, the environment being destroyed, or the company getting an adverse reputation or losing trustworthiness.

Failures have been known to cost lives or to put companies out of the market completely. Fortunately, it is usually not that bad, but still the effects of failures can be significant.

Another way to measure effect is by using a *qualitative scale*. Such a scale could be expressed as shown in the table below.

Effect	Description	Score
Critical	Goals cannot be achieved	6
High	Goals will be jeopardized	5
Above middle	Goals will be significantly affected	4
Below middle	Goals will be affected	3
Low	Goals will be slightly affected	2
Negligible	Goals will be barely noticeably affected	1

Inspired
by Paul Gerrard

In the table there is a column for a mnemonic for the effect, a column describing the effect more precisely, and a column for a score.

Use of a numeric score makes it possible to calculate the risk level even when a qualitative scale is used for the effect.

It can be useful to define a scale with an even number of scores. This can mitigate the effect of some people having a tendency to choose the middle value if they are not sure what to score or can't be bothered to think deeper about their opinion. A scale with an even number of scores does not have a middle value, and the stakeholders will have to decide if they want to score over the middle or under.

The important point before the analysis of the effects can start is that *the stakeholders agree to and understand the scale.*

When you perform the analysis of the effect of the risks you have identified, you must keep your focus on the effect. You must *NEVER let the probability influence the effect!* It can sometimes be tempting to give the effect an extra little turn upward if we know (or think) that the probability of the risk materializing is high, but this will give a twisted picture of the risk level and should be avoided.

A simple effect analysis for the risks pertaining to the four top-level architectural areas defined for a product may look like this, using a scale from 1 to 6 where 6 is the worst

The product in the example is from the case story.

Risk Area	Effect
Setup	2
Conveyor	2
Concentration calculation	6
Compound determination	5

Often it is not enough to have one single score for the effect. Stakeholders see the effect from different perspectives. An end user sees the effect in the light of how a failure will influence his or her daily work. A customer may look at the effect of failures on the overall business goals. A supplier organization may assess the effect in terms of correction efforts for failures or loss of credibility in the market.

These different perspectives can be honored if we use a more complex or composite effect analysis. The scale should be the same for all the perspectives, but the descriptions should be tailored to make sense for each of the viewpoints.

A composite effect analysis taking more perspectives into account may look like this:

Risk Area	Effect for Perspective			Final Effect
	User	Customer	Supplier	
Setup	5	3	2	3.3
Conveyor	3	3	5	3.7
Concentration calculation	2	5	2	3
Compound determination	1	5	3	3

Here all perspectives have the same weight, and the final effect is a simple average of the effect contributions.

If the scale is not sufficiently differentiated, the individual perspectives may be assigned independent weights, and the final effect can then be calculated as the weighted average:

Final effect = $\sum(\text{effect*weight})/\sum(\text{weight})$

The effect analysis taking more perspectives into account and assigning different weights to the perspectives may look like that shown below.

Risk Area	Effect for Perspective			Final Effect
	User W=2	Customer W=7	Supplier W=1	
Setup	5	3	2	3.3
Conveyor	3	3	5	3.2
Concentration calculation	2	5	2	4.1
Compound determination	1	5	3	3.9

3.3.2.2.5 Probability

The probability is the likelihood of the materialization of a risk.

Also here we first of all need to agree on a scale. On a *quantitative scale* probability can be measured on a scale from 0 to 1 or a scale from 0% to 100%. For most risks it is, however, almost impossible to determine the probability with such precision.

A *qualitative scale* for probability is usually much more useful, and it could be expressed as shown in the table below where there is a column for probability intervals, a column describing the probability, and a column for the score. Again using numeric scores makes it possible to calculate the risk level even when a qualitative scale is used for the probability.

Probability (%)	Description	Score
99–90	Highly likely	6
89–70	Likely	5
69–50	Above 50–50	4
49–30	Below 50–50	3
29–10	Unlikely	2
9–1	Highly unlikely	1

Focus must be kept on the probability when you perform the analysis of the probability of the risks you have identified. You must *NEVER let the effect influence the probability!* It can sometimes be tempting to give the probability an extra little turn upward if we know (or think) that the effect of the risk if it materializes is high. This will give an untrue picture of the risk level and should be avoided.

The probability of a risk materializing may be a function of many factors, for example:

▶ Complexity of the product or the code;

▶ Size of the product or the code;

▶ The producer of the work product(s) or component(s);

▶ Whether it is a new product or code or maintenance;

▶ The previous defect record for the product or area;

▶ The developers' familiarity with tools and processes.

Just like for the effect, the final probability can be calculated as the weighted average of the probabilities pertaining to the different factors.

Final probability = $\sum$(probability*weight)/$\sum$(weight)

A composite probability analysis may look like this:

Risk Area	Probability for Factor			Final Probability
	Size W=1	History W=5	Complexity W=2	
Setup	4	2	1	2
Conveyor	5	3	5	3.8
Concentration calculation	3	1	2	1.5
Compound determination	3	1	5	2.2

The same quantitative scale must be used for all factors.

3.3.2.2.6   Risk Level

The risk level is calculated for each of the identified risks as

Risk level = final effect × final probability

Using the above examples for final effect and final probability, the final risk level may look like that shown in the table below.

Risk Area	Final Effect	Final Probability	Final Risk Level
Setup	3.3	2	6.6
Conveyor	3.2	3.8	12.2
Concentration calculation	4.1	1.5	6.2
Compound determination	3.9	2.2	8.6

Sometimes some stakeholders will be unhappy with the final level. If a stakeholder has high rates for a particular risk and the risk comes out with a relatively low final risk level, this can "seem unfair." In such cases the perspectives and the scales will have to be discussed once more.

The point of the perspectives and the scales is that they should satisfy every stakeholder's viewpoint. If that is not the case, they should be adjusted. Most of the time, however, stakeholders recognize that the perspectives and scales are OK, and that their viewpoint is fairly overruled by others' different viewpoints.

The distribution of the final risk level over individual risks is used to plan the test activities. It can be used to prioritize the test activities and to distribute the available time and other resources according to the relative risk level. A test plan based on a risk analysis is more trusted than a plan based on "gut feeling."

It is usually not a very difficult task to perform a risk analysis as explained above. A full analysis, including identifying about 30 risks and assessing and calculating the effect, probability, and final level, can be done in a couple of hours. It is well worth the effort because it gives everybody involved a much clearer picture of why testing is necessary and how it should be planned.

It is difficult to predict events, and therefore all risk analysis has some built-in uncertainty. *A risk analysis must be repeated at regular intervals as the testing progresses.*

The test results can be used as input to the continuous risk analysis. If we find more defects than expected in a particular area, it means that the probability is higher than we expected, and the area hence has a higher risk level. On the other hand, if we find fewer defects than expected, the risk level is lower.

3.3.3   Risk Mitigation

We use the results of the risk analysis as the basis for risk mitigation, the last activity in risk management. "To mitigate" means "to make or become milder, less severe or less painful." That is what we'll try to do.

Faced with the list of risks and their individual risk level we have to go through each of the risks and decide

- ❱ What are we going to do?
- ❱ How are we going to do it?
- ❱ When are we going to do it?

3.3.3.1   What to Do to Mitigate Risks

In terms of what to do, we have the following choices:

- ❱ Do nothing;
- ❱ Share the pain;
- ❱ Plan contingency action(s);
- ❱ Take preventive action.

We can choose to do nothing if the benefit of waiting to see how things develop is greater than the cost of doing something.

You would not buy a safe for 1,000 € to protect your jewels if they were only worth 500 € (including the sentimental value). If the jewels were stolen, you could buy new ones and still have money left.

Sharing the pain is outside the scope of testing, but it is a possibility for project management or higher management to negotiate sharing the pain of the effect of a materializing risk with other parties. This other party could be an insurance company or it could be a supplier or even the customer.

Planning contingency action(s) is a natural part of most risk mitigation. The contingency action is what we are going to do to mitigate the effect of a risk once it actually has materialized. For risk types others than product risks and processes other than test, the response to the risk analysis may be the production of contingency plans. But it is not something that is applicable in the test planning for mitigating product risks.

Extra training is planned if it turns out that the system is more difficult to learn than expected.

Testing is one of a number of possible preventive actions. The aim is to mitigate the risks. Testing can be used to mitigate the risk level by lowering or eliminating the probability of the risk.

Product risks are associated with the presence of defects. The effect is associated with the failure of the product in use. The probability is associated with the probability of undetected defects still being present in the product when it is released, which then cause the product to fail in use.

Testing aims at identifying defects by making the product fail—before it reaches the customer. Defects found in testing can be corrected—before the system reaches the customer. Hence testing and defect correction (!) reduce the risk level by reducing the probability.

3.3.3.2   How to Mitigate Risks by Testing

When we have decided to do something to mitigate a risk, we must determine what to do. The nature of the risk can be used to determine what testing to perform to mitigate the risk, and the level of formality applied. The decisions must be documented in the applicable test strategy or test plan.

Certain test subprocesses are especially applicable for certain types of risks. We need to look at the risk source and determine the activities that are most likely to unveil defects.

Some examples are:

Risk Source	Recommended Test Phases
High risk of defects in algorithms	–Review of detailed design –Review of code –Component testing –Functional system test
Risk of problems in the user interface	–Usability evaluation of prototype (requirements review) –Usability test (nonfunctional system test)
Risk of performance problems	–Review of detailed design –Review of code –Performance test (nonfunctional system test)
Risk concerning external interface	–Review of design –Review of code –System integration test

The formality of the test can also be determined from the risk level. The rule is simple:

The higher the risk level => The higher the formality

The formality can change from test subprocess to test subprocess and it can change over the product. Some areas can have more formal testing than others, even within the same test subprocess.

In a test subprocess, for example, a system test, we can have different levels of formality as shown in the following table.

System Test	
Risk Level	**Recommended Test Phases**
High	–Specific test case design techniques to be used –Strict test completion criteria –Strict regression test procedures
Low	–Free choice of test case design techniques –And/or less strict test completion criteria –And/or less strict regression test procedures

3.3.3.3 When to Mitigate Risks by Testing

We can use the results of the risk analysis to prioritize the test activities that we have identified for the risks, and to distribute the test time (and possibly other resources).

In the prioritization we are going to determine the order in which to attack the risks. Even if we are not going to perform all of the testing activities identified for the risks in strictly sequential order, it helps in the planning stage to have them prioritized.

The priority can follow the final risk level. This means that the final level can be used as the sorting criteria. This takes every perspective of the risks into consideration in one go.

With the example from above, the priority of the risks areas can then be as shown below, where 1 is the highest.

Risk Area	Final Risk Level	Priority
Setup	6.6	3
Conveyor	12.2	1
Concentration calculation	6.2	4
Compound determination	8.6	2

The stakeholders could also choose to let the prioritization be guided by either the final effect or the final probability. Or they may even agree to use one particular perspective, for example, the probability related to the complexity, from which to prioritize.

To calculate the distribution of the time to spend on the testing, we need to calculate the sum of the final level.

Risk Area	Final Level
Setup	6.6
Conveyor	12.2
Concentration calculation	6.2
Compound determination	8.6
Total	33.6

The next step is to calculate the distribution of the final levels over the risk areas. This could look as shown here, where the percentages have been rounded to the nearest whole number.

Risk Area	Final Level	% Distribution
Setup	6.6	20
Conveyor	12.2	36
Concentration calculation	6.2	18
Compound determination	8.6	26
Total	**33.6**	**100%**

With a table like this we have a strong planning tool. No matter which resources we have at our disposal, we can distribute them on the risk areas and hence ensure that each area is indeed tested, but neither more nor less than it deserves.

If the project manager allocates, for example, 400 hours for the complete testing of our sample system, we can distribute this time over the areas as shown here:

Risk Area	% Distribution	Hours for Testing
Setup	20	80
Conveyor	36	144
Concentration calculation	18	72
Compound determination	26	104
Total	**100%**	**400**

The list of prioritized risks with their allocated resources and identified testing activities allows us to produce a substantiated plan and schedule for the test.

The list also allows us to immediately assess the results of a proposed change in resource allocation. If the resources we have distributed are cut, we will have to find out how to make do with what is left.

Usually we are operating with time; usually a certain number of hours are allocated for the testing and consequently a number of hours may need to be cut. If time is cut we must ask management what to do with our distribution of time over the risks. We can't leave our plan and schedule untouched—the cut must have an effect. What we can do is in principle:

◗ Reduce testing time proportionally to the cut.
◗ Take risk areas out of the testing completely.

The best thing to do is to reduce the time proportionally. This ensures that all areas are still tested, that is, that we will get some information relating to all risks. We can combine the two approaches, but we should be very careful if we take areas that are still in the scope of the project out completely.

If some testing has already been performed, a renewed risk analysis is necessary before we can act on any cuts. In this case we must distribute the remaining resources over the remaining risks according the new final level, and prioritize as we did before.

3.4   Test Estimation

3.4.1   General Estimation Principles

This section will concentrate on time estimation, but some of the techniques may be applied for estimating elements other than time, for example, number of test cases, number of defects to be found, and number of iterations in the test process needed to fulfill the completion criteria. We may also estimate other costs, such as acquisitions of hardware, tools, etc.

Time estimation is a prediction of how much time it takes to perform an activity. It is an approximation or judgment, not a precise calculation.

There are many ways in which to express estimations, but the best way is in hours. By using hours, we don't have problems with holidays, effective working hours, etc. You must never express estimates using dates—dates and estimates are incompatible. Estimation is input to the scheduling. Only in that activity will we transform the estimated hours into dates.

We should always take our estimations seriously. Be honest when you estimate—even though it is often easier to ask for forgiveness rather than permission. Keep your original estimates for future reference.

In line with this remember that estimation is **not**:

▶ The most optimistic prediction you can think of;
▶ Equal to the last estimate that was made;
▶ Equal to the last estimate + the delay the customer or the boss is willing to accept;
▶ Equal to a given "correct" answer.

Estimates are predictions about the future and predictions are by definition uncertain. The closer we come to the actual result, the less the uncertainty, as illustrated below.

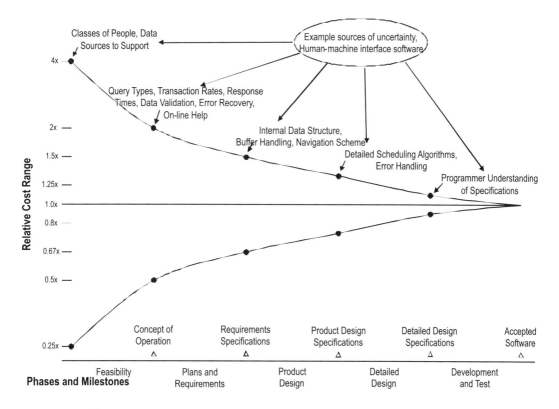

You should always estimate the uncertainty for an estimate and document this uncertainty with the estimate.

Furthermore, estimates should always be accompanied by the rationale or justification for the estimation values along with any assumptions.

3.4.2 Test Estimation Principles

Estimating test activities is in many ways like all other estimation in a project. We need to take all tasks, even the smallest and seemingly insignificant, into account.

The time to complete must be estimated for each task defined in the task section of the test plan, including all the test process activities from test planning to checking for completion.

Even though estimation of testing tasks is in many ways identical to the estimation for any other process, there are also important differences.

The test estimation is different from other project estimation, because the number of failures we will encounter is not known in advance—although it can be estimated as well.

The number of necessary iterations before the completion criteria are met is usually not known either. As a rule of thumb, at least three iterations must be reckoned with—one is unlikely to be enough, unless the completion criterion is a simple execution of all test cases, and independent on the number of outstanding defects and coverage.

Nevertheless, we have to do our best, and the estimation must also include:

▶ Time to report failures (incident registration);

▶ Possible time to wait for defect analysis;

▶ Possible time to wait for defect correction;

▶ Time for retesting and regression testing (minimum of three iterations!).

The reason why we have to cater to the need for several iterations is that, well, "*Errare humanum est!*" When we report incidents and the underlying defects are corrected by development or support staff, experience shows that not all defects are actually corrected; not because the developers couldn't be bothered, but because, for example, they can't find the defect or can only solve part of the problem. Furthermore, defect correction introduces new defects, and defect correction unveils existing defects that we could not see before.

Experience in the testing business shows that *50% of the original number of defects remain after correction*. These are distributed as follows:

Remaining defects after correction: 20%;
Unveiled defects after correction: 10%;
New defects after correction: 20%.

So if we report 100 defects, we have 20 + 20 + 10 = 50 defects to report in the next iteration, 10 + 10 + 5 = 25 defects in the third, and 5 + 5 + 2 = 12 in the fourth. This means that we will have reported and fixed 152 in all if have fixed everything after the fourth iteration.

These are general experience numbers. It is important that you collect your own measurements!

3.4.3 The Estimation Process

Estimation is a process like anything else we do. You should, of course, use your organization's standard process for estimation, if there is one. Otherwise, you can adapt an estimation procedure like the generic one described here.

1. *Define the purpose of the estimation.* Is this estimation the first approach, for a proposal, or for detailed planning?
2. *Plan the estimating task.* Estimation is not a 2-minute task. Set sufficient time aside for it, and include the activities in the plan.
3. *Write down the basis for the estimation.* Here the scope and the size of the work are determined, and all factors that may influence the estimates are registered. This includes factors related to the nature of the processes we are working by, the nature of the project we are working in, the people we are working with, and any risks we are facing.
4. *Break down the work.* This is the work breakdown structure (i.e., the listing of all the tasks to estimate). Do this to a level of detail related to the purpose of the estimation.
5. *Estimate.* Use more than one technique as appropriate.
6. *Compare with reality and reestimate.* This is the ongoing monitoring and control of how the work that we have estimated is actually going.

3.4.4   Estimation Techniques

The following estimation techniques are the most used and an expression of the best practice within estimation, and they are further described below.

- FIA (Finger in the Air) or Best Guess;
- Experience-Based Estimation:
  - Analogies and experts;
  - Delphi technique;
  - Three-point estimation (Successive calculation);

- Model-Based Estimation;
  - Function points;
  - Test points;
  - Percentage distribution.

3.4.4.1   Best Guess (FIA) Estimation

This technique is more or less pure guesswork, but it will always be based on some sort of experience and a number of (unconscious) assumptions. The technique is very widespread, but the estimate is usually highly uncertain it is often not repeatable, and it is not always trusted.

The uncertainty is probably around 200% to 400% for estimates based on best guess. Fortunately, we can do better than that.

3.4.4.2 Analogies and Experts Estimation

In the analogy techniques you base your estimate on something you have experienced before.

For example: "This looks very much like the system I tested in my previous job. That took us 3 months, and we were four people. This is slightly smaller and we are five people—so I guess this will take 2 months to complete."

If you have participated in a testing project that is comparable to the one you are estimating, you might use that as a baseline for your estimation.

Analogies may also be based on metrics collected from previous tests. We may estimate the number of iterations of the test based on recent records of comparable test efforts. We can calculate the average effort required per test on a previous test effort and multiply this by the number of tests estimated for this test effort.

Experts, in the estimation context, know what they are talking about and have relevant knowledge. It is almost always possible to find experts somewhere in the organization.

If experts on this kind of testing are available, then by all means make use of them. They have been there before, so they know what they are talking about.

3.4.4.3 Delphi Technique Estimation

This is a simple technique that has proved remarkably resilient even in highly complex situations.

You must appoint an estimation group as appropriate; members can be stakeholders and/or experts in the tasks to estimate.

The steps in this estimation process for a specific task are:

▶ Each member of the group makes an estimate.
▶ The group is informed about the average and distribution of the provided estimates.
▶ The people giving estimates in the lower quartile and in the upper quartile are asked to tell the rest of the group why their estimates were as they were.
▶ The group estimates again, this time taking the previous result and the provided arguments for the "extreme" estimates into account.
▶ This may continue two, three, four or more times until the variation in the estimates is sufficiently small.

Usually the average of the estimations does not change much, but the variation is rapidly decreased. This gives confidence in the final estimation result.

The Delphi technique can be used in many ways. The people taking part can be in the same room, but they may also be continents apart and the technique used via, for example, e-mail.

The technique can be combined with other techniques. Most often the participants give their initial estimates based on experience and/or they are experts in a specific area. The initial estimates may also be obtained using some of the other estimation techniques to make them even more trustworthy.

3.4.4.4 Three-Point Estimation

Three-point estimation is a statistical calculation of the probability of finishing within a given time. The technique is useful for quantifying uncertainty to the estimate. The technique is also called successive calculation because tasks are broken down and the estimates successively calculated until the variance is within acceptable limits.

Three-point estimation is based on three estimates:

▶ The most optimistic time (ideal conditions);
▶ The most likely time (if we do business as usual);
▶ The most pessimistic time (Murphy is with us all the way).

The three estimates to be used can be provided in a number of ways, usually using another estimation technique high and low values may either be estimated separately (i.e., "What are the best and the worst cases?") or they may be the highest and the lowest of the individual estimates.

From the three estimates, "best, worst, and most likely," it is possible to define the distribution function for the time to finish.

It could look like shown here, where V_o = most optimistic; V_s = most likely; V_p = most pessimistic; and V_m = mean.

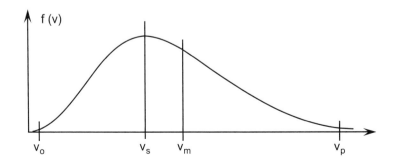

We can use the approximated formula to derive:

$$V_m = (V_o + 3*V_s + V_p)/5 \text{ (weighted mean)}$$

$$S = (V_p - V_o)/5 \text{ (the standard deviation)}$$

Based on this distribution we can calculate the time needed for any probability of finishing the task we want by using the appropriate formula.
For the 5% interval the formulas are:

$$5\%: V_m - 2S \qquad 95\%: V_m + 2S$$

Let us say that for a testing task we have reckoned:

$$V_o = 70 \text{ hours} \quad V_s = 80 \text{ hours} \quad V_p = 110 \text{ hours}$$

We calculate:

$$V_m = (V_o + 3*V_s + V_p)/5 = (70 + 3*80 + 110)/5 = 84$$
$$S = (V_p - V_o)/5 = (110 - 70)/5 = 8$$

The upper value in the 95% interval = 84 + 2*8 = 100.
Therefore if we want to be 95% sure that we'll finish in time, our estimate for the given task should be 100 hours.
All tasks or a selection of the most critical tasks can be estimated using this technique.

Tools are available to support the calculations.

3.4.4.5   Function Point Estimation

This technique is a factor estimation technique initially published by Albrecht in 1979. It has been revised several times, and it now maintained by the International Function Points User Group (IFPUG). The group has been permanent since 1992, and it is still going strong issuing new versions of the technique.

The estimation is based on a model of the product, for example a requirements specification and/or a prototype. Five aspects of the product are counted from the model:

  ▶ External inputs;
  ▶ External outputs;
  ▶ External enquiries;

- Internal logical files;
- External interface files.

The counts are then multiplied with a weight, and the total of the weighted counts is the unadjusted sum. The actual effort in person-hours is then calculated with an adjustment factor obtained from previous project data.

It requires some training to be able to count function points correctly. Continuous comparisons of actual time spent with the estimates are essential to get the best possible local adjustment factor.

The disadvantage of using function points is that they require detailed requirements or other fairly detailed descriptions of the expectations.

3.4.4.6 Test Point Estimation

In 1999 Martin Pol et al. published a dedicated test estimation technique called test points as part of the TMAP method.

The technique is based on the function point technique, and it provides a unit of measurement for the size of the high-level test (system and acceptance tests) to be executed.

The technique converts function points into test points based on the impact of specific factors that affect tests, like:

- Quality requirements;
- The system's size and complexity;
- The quality of the test basis (the document(s) the test is specified toward);
- The extent to which test tools are used.

3.4.4.7 Percentage Distribution Estimation

Unlike all the other techniques discussed here, this technique is a so-called top-down estimation technique. The fundamental idea is that test efforts can be derived from the development effort.

The estimation using this technique is starting from an estimate of the total effort for a project. This estimate may be the result of the usage of appropriate estimation techniques at the project management level, or it may be a period of time that is fixed for some reason.

The next step is to use formulas (usually just percentages) to distribute this total effort over defined tasks, including the testing tasks. The formulas are based on empirical data, and they vary widely from organization to organization.

It is essential that you get your own empirical data and constantly update them according to experiences gained.

If you do not have any data, you could assume that the total testing effort is 25% to 30% of the total project effort. The testing effort should then be spread out on the test subprocess with an appropriate amount for each test subprocess.

This example is from Capers Jones *Applied Software Measurements*. It is for in-house development of administrative systems. The left-hand table shows the distribution of the total effort on overall task, including all testing as one task only. The right-hand table shows the distribution of the effort on detailed testing tasks (the terminology is Capers Jones'.)

Activity	%
Requirement	9.5
Design	15.5
Coding	20
Testing (all test phases)	27
Project management	13
Quality assurance	0
Configuration management	3
Documentation	9
Installation and training	3

All phases	%
Component testing	16
Independent testing	84
	100
Independent testing	**%**
Integration testing	24
System testing	52
Acceptance testing	24
	100
System testing	**%**
Functional system testing	65
Non-functional system testing	35
	100

3.4.5   From Estimations to Plan and Back Again

The estimation is done to provide input to the scheduling activity in the project planning.

In the scheduling we bring the estimates for the defined testing tasks together with the people who are going to be performing the tasks. Based on the start date for the first task and the dependencies between the tasks, we can then puzzle the tasks together and calculate the expected finishing date.

As mentioned above, time estimations should be given in hours. The scheduling provides the dates: dates for when the performance of each of the tasks should begin, and dates for when they are expected to be finished.

When defining the expected finish date for a task, we need to take several aspects into account:

▶ The start and/or finish dates of others tasks that this task depends on to start, if any;

▶ The earliest possible start date for the task;

- The general calendar regarding public holidays;
- The pure estimate for the time to finish the task;
- The efficiency of the employee(s) to perform the task—typically 70% to 80% for a full-time assignment;
- The employee availability on the task (which should NOT be less than 25%).

We should not expect that our estimations will be accepted straightaway. Making plans for a development project is a very delicate balance between resources (including costs), time, and quality of the work to be done. Testing is often on the critical path for a project, and testing estimates are likely to be the subject of negotiations between stakeholders—typically the customer or higher management, the project manager, and the test manager.

The estimating does not stop with the preparation of the first schedule. Once the actual testing has started—from the first planning activities onward—we need to frequently monitor how realities correspond to the estimates. Based on the new information gathered through the monitoring, we must reestimate when the deviations between estimates and reality get too large to stay in control. Only when all of the testing activities have been completed can we stop the monitoring and reestimation.

3.4.6 Get Your Own Measurements

All estimates are based on experience, whether they are very informal (like FIA) or very formal (like function points). The better the basis for the estimation is, the better the estimation gets. Better estimation means more reliable estimations, and that is what we both, management and customers, want.

To get better estimates, we need to collect actual data related to the estimates. The more empirical data we have, the better future estimates will become. In general, we can say that (almost) any empirical data is better than no data.

We do however always need to objectively evaluate the empirical data we have—are they collected from tasks that can be compared with the ones we are dealing with now?

When we use the available empirical data, we also have an obligation to contribute to and refine these empirical data on an ongoing basis. Empirical data for estimation is part of the measurements we are collecting. So we need to chip in to establish a set of simple measurements of time, costs, and size for all projects in which we participate.

This is described in the following section.

3.5 Test Metrics and Measurements

Tom De Marco, one of the testing gurus, once said:

If you don't measure you're left with only one reason to believe you're in control—hysterical optimism.

One of the principles of good planning, both of testing and anything else, is to define specific and measurable goals for the activities. But it is not enough for goals to be measurable; we must also collect facts—measurements—that can tell us if we have indeed achieved the goals.

3.5.1 Measuring in General

For facts or data collection we operate with the following concepts:

▶ Metric—a definition of what to measure. The definition must include data type, scale, and unit.

▶ Measuring method—the description of how we are going to get the data.

▶ Measurements—the actual values collected for the metrics.

An example could be that the metric for the size of a book is "number of pages"; the measuring method is to "look at the last page number"; and the measurement for Alice in Wonderland, ISBN 7409746, is "54."

It is a good idea to establish a measurement plan as part of the project plan or master test plan. This should specify the metrics we want to measure and the measuring methods; who is going to measure; and, perhaps most importantly, how the measurements will be analyzed and used.

Our measurements are derived from raw data such as time sheets, incident reports, test logs, and work sheets. *Direct measurements* are measurements we get directly from the raw data, for example, by counting the number of log sheets for passed test procedures and counting the number of incident reports. *Indirect measurements* are measurements we can calculate from direct measurements.

Most direct measurements have no meaning unless they are placed in relation to something. Number of incidents as such—for example, 50—says nothing about the product or the processes. But if we calculate the defects found compared to the estimated amount of defects it gives a much better indication—either of our estimation or of the quality of the product!

It is a common mistake to think that only objective data should be used. Objective data are what you can measure independently of human opinions. But even though subjective data have an element of uncertainty about them, they can be very valuable. Often subjective data are even cheaper to collect than objective data.

A subjective metric could be: The opinion of the participants in walk-throughs concerning the usefulness of the walk-through activity on a scale from 1 to 5, where 1 is lowest and 5 is highest. This is easy to collect and handle, and it gives a good indication of the perception of the usefulness of walk-throughs.

The metrics should be specified based on the goals we have set and other questions we would like to get answers to, such as how far we have got in performing a specific task in relation to the plan.

3.5.2   Test-Related Metrics

Many, many measurements can be collected during the execution of test procedures (and any other process for that matter). They can be divided into groups according to the possibilities they provide for control. The groups and a few examples of direct measurements are listed here for inspirational purposes; the lists are by no means exhaustive.

Measures About Progress:

▶ Of test planning and monitoring:
  ▶ tasks commenced;
  ▶ task completed.
▶ Of test development:
  ▶ number of specified test procedures;
  ▶ number of approved test procedures;
  ▶ relevant degrees of coverage achieved in the specification, for example for code structures, requirements, risks and/or business processes;
  ▶ other tasks completed.
▶ Of test execution and reporting:
  ▶ number of executed test procedures (or initiated test procedures);
  ▶ number of passed test procedures;
  ▶ number of passed retests;
  ▶ number of test procedures executed for regression testing;
  ▶ other tasks completed.
▶ Of test closure:
  ▶ tasks completed.

For each of these groups we can collect measurements for:

▶ Time spent on specific tasks both in actual working hours and elapsed time;
▶ Cost both from time spent and from direct cost such as license fees.

Measures About Coverage:

▶ Number of coverage elements covered by the executed test procedures (e.g., code structures, requirements, decision combinations, classification tree leaves).

Measures About Incidents:

▶ Number of reported incidents;
▶ Number of incidents of different classes (e.g., defects, misunderstandings, or enhancement requests);
▶ Number of defects reported to have been corrected;
▶ Number of closed incident reports.

Measures About Confidence:

▶ Subjective statements about confidence from different stakeholders.

 All of these measurements should be collected at specific points in time, and the time of the measuring should be noted to enable follow-up on the development over time, for example, the development in number of open incident reports on a weekly basis.

It is also important to prepare to be able to measure and report status and progress of tasks in relations to milestones defined in the development model we are following.

To be able to see the development of measured topics in relation to expectations, corresponding factual and/or estimated total numbers are also needed. A few examples are:

▶ Total number of defined test procedures;
▶ Total number of coverage elements;
▶ Total number of failures and defects;
▶ Actual test object attributes (e.g., size and complexity);
▶ Planned duration and effort for tasks;
▶ Planned cost of performing tasks.

3.5.3   Analysis and Presentation of Measurements

It is not enough to just collect measurements; they must be analyzed and presented in an understandable way to relevant stakeholders to be of real value.

The analysis and presentation of measurements are discussed in Section 3.6 below.

3.5.4   Planning Measuring

It is important that stakeholders agree to the definition of the metrics and measuring methods before any measurements are collected. Unpopular or adverse measurements may cause friction, especially if definitions are not clear and approved. You can obtain very weird behaviors by introducing measures!

Here is some advice you should keep in mind when you plan the measures you are going to collect. You need to aim for:

- ▶ *Agreed metrics*—definitions (e.g., what is a line of code), scale (e.g., is 1 highest or lowest?), and units (e.g., seconds or hours) must be agreed and understood.

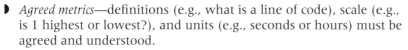

- ▶ *Needed measures*—what is it you want to know, to monitor, and to control?

- ▶ *Precise measures*—appropriate scale must be used.

- ▶ *Comparable measures*—for example, over time or between sources.

- ▶ *Economical measures*—practical to collect and analyze compared to the value of the analysis results.

- ▶ *Creating confidentiality*—never use measurements to punish or reward individuals.

- ▶ *Using already existing measurements*—maybe the measurements just need to be analyzed in a new way.

- ▶ *Having a measurement plan*—the plan should outline what, by whom, when, how, and why the measures are going to be collected.

- ▶ *Using the measurements*—only measure what can be used immediately and give quick and precise feedback.

3.6   Test Progress Monitoring and Control

Continuous monitoring on how the testing is progressing compared to the plan is absolutely necessary to stay in control. If we don't control the test project, it will control us—and that is not a nice experience.

3.6.1   Collecting Data

The data to collect during testing should be specified in the "Metrics to be collected" section in the test plan, based on the metrics requirements outlined in the test policy and the relevant test strategy.

Regardless of which measurements we have planned to collect, it is not enough to just collect them. They must be presented and analyzed to be of real value.

3.6.2   Presenting the Measurements

Test reports are used to communicate test progress. These reports must be tailored to the different stakeholders (see Section 3.2 above). The stakeholders for test monitoring information include the customer, the project and/or product (or higher) management, the test management, and the testers.

The customer and the management above test management need test completion reports. The test management needs information on a continuous basis to keep in control. The testers need to be kept informed about progress on a very regular basis—preferably daily when the execution activities are at their peak.

A picture speaks a thousand words. The best way to present progress information for testing is by using graphics. This holds true for all stakeholders. Graphics used in the right way give an immediate overview of the state of the testing.

The flip side of the coin is that graphics can "lie." You can do it deliberately—which is outside the scope of this book—or you can make it happen accidentally if you are too eager to make your presentation "interesting" and "lively." The truth may look boring, but adding decoration does not help.

One of the common mistakes is to use too many dimensions. Most of our information is two dimensional: the number of something at different points in time. Many graphs are, however, presenting two-dimensional information in a three-dimensional way.

Consider the following information:

Day 1:   2 defects found
Day 2:   5 defects found
Day 3   11 defects found.

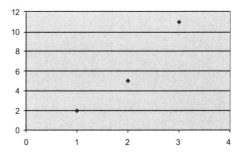

The simplest way to present this is as shown to the right of the raw data. See the trend? Yes, that is perfectly clear! Need anything else? Not really.

But all too often we may see exactly the same information presented like this: or even worse like this:

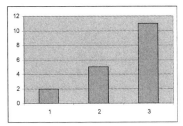
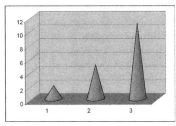

Does that add to the understanding? No. Does it blur the message? Maybe.

There is a "metric" called the ink-factor. That is defined as the amount of ink used in the presentation graph in relation to the ink needed to convey the message in a graph. You should keep the ink-factor as low as possible.

Also *avoid highlighting (read: hiding) the message in decoration, patterns, shading, or color.* A graph that presents the number of failures found each day as the size of the corollas of a line of flowers is perhaps cute, but not very professional.

More obvious ways to misinform is by changing the scale across the axis, or by omitting or distorting the context of the information or the way it has been collected.

Whichever way you choose to present the information you have collected, it is your responsibility to ensure that the recipients understand and interpret the data correctly. In the following some of the most common and useful ways of presenting test progress information are described.

3.6.2.1   S-Curves
Perhaps the most used, most loved, and most useful way of presenting progress information and controlling what's happening is S-curves. They are named so because of the shape of the "perfect" curve.

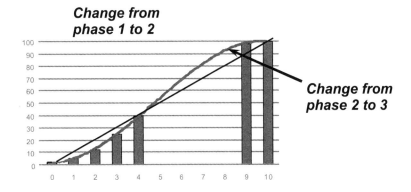

Source:
Marnie Hutcheson
Unicom Seminar
Oct. 95.

The figure shows a graph where the S-curve is the thick black line swinging in an S-shape from the starting point (0,0) to the estimated end point (10,100).

S-curves can be used for many different metrics. You need two sets of metrics that are related to each other; one is typically time, and the other could be :

▶ Test cases (run, attempted, passed, completed);

▶ Incidents (encountered, fixed, retested).

S-curves can give us early warnings of something being wrong. They can also give us reassurance that (so far) things are progressing as planned.

The principle in S-curves is that our work falls in three phases:

▶ Phase 1: slow start—not more than 15% to 25% of the time.

An initial period of reduced efficiency to allow for testing teams to become familiar with the testing task, for example with the test object, the test environment, and execution and logging practices.

▶ Phase 2: productive phase—55% to 65% of the time.

After the initial period, the second phase is the period of maximum efficiency.

▶ Phase 3: the difficult part—10% to 25% of the time.

The final phase reflects the need to be able to ease off the work as the testing window nears completion.

The figure below shows how real data are reported as several S-curves in the same graph.

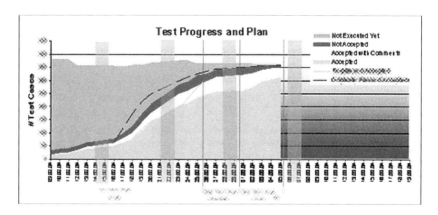

To use an S-curve you need to know the expected start point (usually 0,0) and the expected end point. The end point is your estimation of what needs to be achieved after a specific period of time; for example, 300 test cases passed after 21 days of testing.

You mark the start point and the end point, and you draw (or get a tool to draw) a third-order polynomial that fits.

As the time goes by and you do you work, you plot in your achievements; for example, sum of test cases passed day by day. Follow the progress to see if it fits the predicted curve. If it does, we are happy! This is illustrated in the first graph in this section.

If the upward turn, marking the start of the second phase, set in too late, we are in trouble. But the good news is that we know it and can take action well before the end date! If the curve is rising too fast, we may also be in trouble, and we must investigate what could be wrong. Maybe our test cases are not giving enough failures? Maybe we have run the smallest test procedures first and are pushing work in front of us? Or maybe things are going fine and it is our estimate that is wrong.

3.6.2.2 Pie Chart

Pie charts are used to give an overview of the proportions of different aspects relative to each other.

The graph shown here gives a nice impression of the testing going well.

But think about the ink-factor— maybe the third dimension is not needed to present the information.

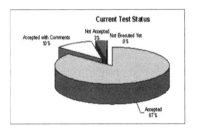

3.6.2.3 Check Sheets

Check sheets are a good way to give a quick overview of status. They can be used to show progress compared to plan, for example, for planned test cases, planned test areas, or defined risks.

Check sheets can be presented as colorful graphics or expressed as lists or hierarchies. They are usually easy to produce and easy to understand. Some organizations make wall-size check sheets and stick them in the meeting room or the corridor. This way everyone has easy access to the information about the progress of the testing.

A few examples of check sheets are shown below.

The first is an extract of the check sheet presented on Systematic's intranet. It is updated every day. Even though the text has been deliberately blurred and the extract is small, it gives an impression of things going well. There are no black or white fields in the status column.

Status for project: ksdf				
Area	Remain	% Complete	Status	Comment
agfdg	8	56		
gstyk	0	100		
jl,flli	0	100		
dsrahjtdulk	1	80		
ths	2	56		
jdvw	0	100		
yjdtek	0	100		
	0	87		

Legend
Completed
In progress
Blocked (see comment)
Not started

The next is a dashboard suggested by James Bach.

Area	Test Effort	Coverage planned	Coverage achieved	Quality	Comments
Startup	High	>80%	27%	☺	ER 52
Discount	Low	>40% <70%	53%	☺	
Pricing	**Blocked**	>40% <70%	14%	☹	**ER 86**

James Bach's recommendations or the presentation are to draw it on the wall, make it huge, and update it every day.

The last example here is a tiny extract of a hierarchical check sheet showing the progress of a component test for a system.

The marked components have been successfully component tested and are ready for integration.

The integration testing has not yet started—no interfaces are marked as having been successfully tested. It is however easy to see which interfaces we can test now.

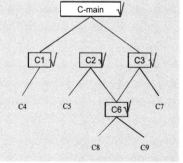

3.6.2.4 Risk-Based Reporting

If our test approach is based on identified and analyzed risks, it is appropriate to report on the test progress in terms of these risks.

The purpose of this test is to eliminate the risk, so the reporting must be in terms of eliminated risks. The open risks at the test start could be illustrated like this:

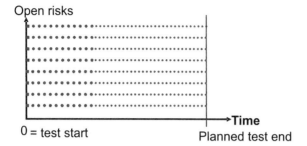

At any point in time, we must make it possible to see from the updated progress graph which risks are still open, if any. The risks with the small vertical line across them are eliminated and hence no longer present any threat to the system!

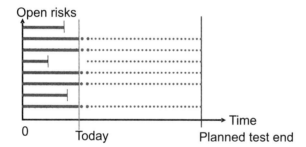

3.6.2.5 Statistical Reporting

The way a process is performed is different from project to project and over time, because processes are performed by people, not machines.

Statistics is the science of patterns in a variable world. We can say that statistics make the invisible visible. This means that statistical methods can be used to help us:

▶ Understand the past;
▶ Control the present;
▶ Predict the future.

Statistics also include handling of "fortuitousness," that is, happenings that are out of the ordinary.

When we have to deal with many happenings assumed to be "alike," we need to find out what "alike" means. To do that we must find out what the norm is, and what variances are allowed to still call things "normal."

Norm and variation vary. In our family the norm is that we are friendly and talk to each other in nice, calm tones of voices. I, however, have a short temper, and sometimes raise my voice without anything being really out of the normal. If, on the other hand, I keep quiet, then my mood is not within the norm. My husband is different: if he raises his voice just a little bit, he is sure to be in a very bad mood.

The norm in statistics can be calculated in three much used ways: the mean—the arithmetic average; the median—the value that splits the group in the middle, and the modus—the most frequent value.

But how far from the "normal" value can a given value be and still be considered within the norm? This can be calculated as the "upper control level" and the "lower control level."

All this can be illustrated in a control sheet.

An example of a control sheet is shown here. The values are ratings for a course. Every week 10 evaluations are randomly sampled and the average is plotted in the graphs. The graph shows the upper and lower control levels (UCL and LCL, respectively) for the series of ratings.

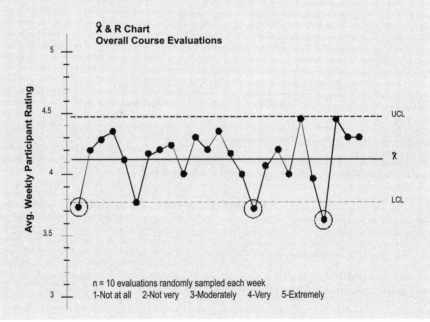

The values here are indicators for the course performance. We can choose other values that can act as indicator values for our processes if we want to control how they are performed.

An indication value may be, for example, the average time it takes per requirement to produce test cases.

When we examine the control sheet, we should be looking for warnings of something being outside the borders of the norm. Such warnings might include:

◗ One value outside either control level (CL);
◗ Two out of three values on the same side of the mean;
◗ Six values in a row either up or down;
◗ Four values in a row alternately up and down.

Many tools can assist in the necessary statistical calculations. The use of control sheets and statistics is rather advanced process control—belonging to CMMI maturity level 4—and we will not go into further depth here.

3.6.3   Stay in Control

No matter which way the progress is measured and presented, the test manager must analyze the measurements. If something seems to not be going as expected, further analysis must be made to determine what may be wrong.

Sometimes we need to take action to stay in control.

Keeping the triangle of test quality in mind, you have three aspects that can change—and at least two must be changed at a time to keep the balance. The aspects are:

◗ The resources available for the activity;
◗ The time available for the activity;
◗ The quality of the work to be performed.

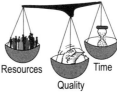

Usually when things are getting out of control it is because we are behind schedule or because our time frame has been squeezed. To compensate for this we must try to obtain additional resources and/or change the quality of the testing. The latter can be done by changing the test completion criteria and/or changing the amount or depths of the tests to be performed.

Any change you make must be reflected in the plan. The plan must be updated with the new decisions based on the new information. The new plan must be reviewed and approved, just like the first one, and it must be communicated to all relevant stakeholders.

Remember that *it is not a virtue to comply with the plan at any cost—the virtue lies in the plan complying with reality.*

Examples of things not being as they should be are:

▶ The delivered software is not ready for testing.
▶ The easy test cases have been run first.
▶ The test cases are not sufficiently specified.
▶ The test cases do not give the right coverage.
▶ General defects have widespread effects.
▶ Defect correction is too slow.
▶ Defect correction is not sufficiently effective.

Based on this analysis the test manager must identify what can be done to remedy or mitigate the problems.

Possible actions might include:

▶ Tighten entry criteria.
▶ Cancel the project.
▶ Improve the test specifications.
▶ Improve the incident reporting.
▶ Perform a new risk analysis and replan.
▶ Do more regression testing.

The important message to the test manager is that he or she must intervene as soon as deviations appear!

As mentioned before:

If you do not control the test, it will control you!

To sum up, we can say that as test managers we must set out the destination and plan how to get there; collect data as we go along; analyze data to obtain information; and act on the information and change destination and plan as appropriate.

Questions

1. What are the three main activities in the test management process?
2. What does it mean that a test plan should be SMART?
3. How does a test management process interact with an IT project management process?

4. What is the relation between test project management and test subprocess management?

5. What is the relation between test subprocess management and dynamic testing?

6. How may planning be "invisible" work?

7. What are the three things that should guide monitoring?

8. How may lessons learned be collected?

9. What types of documentation are produced from a test management process?

10. What information should be present for any document?

11. What might the test item for a test be?

12. What is the relationship between the test item and features to be tested?

13. What is a stakeholder?

14. What are the two risk types that should be handled in a test plan?

15. What might test criteria include?

16. What is regression testing?

17. What might cause a pause in the test execution?

18. How can you illustrate who carries which responsibilities?

19. In which part of the test plan do the testing tasks, the estimates, and the people come together?

20. What guides when a test status report is issued?

21. What topics should be covered in a test status report?

22. What topics should be covered in a test completion report?

23. What questions can you ask to identify stakeholders?

24. What stakeholders could we have from the business?

25. What information may be collected about a stakeholder?

26. What is the purpose of a communication plan?

27. What is the golden rule of testing?

28. What is a risk?

29. What is the risk level?

30. What is a process risk?

31. What is a project risk?

32. What might a project risk be?

33. What is a product risk?

34. What type of risk is testing useful for?

35. What are the activities in risk management?

36. Which risk identification techniques could we use?

37. What is a risk checklist used for?

38. What is the main rule for brainstorming?

39. How must an expert interview be prepared?

40. What is risk analysis?
41. What information might be collected for a risk register?
42. How might the viewpoints of risk differ for different roles?
43. What kinds of scales can be used for risk analysis?
44. What is the effect of a risk?
45. What is a composite effect analysis?
46. How do you calculate the final effect?
47. What is risk probability?
48. What is the result of a risk analysis used for?
49. How many times should a risk analysis be performed and why?
50. What is mitigation?
51. What actions can be taken as a result of a risk analysis?
52. Which action is most appropriate for product risks?
53. How is formality of testing and risk levels related?
54. How can you prioritize the testing for risks?
55. How can you use risk level to distribute testing resources?
56. What can you do if testing time is cut?
57. What is estimation, and what is not estimation?
58. How precise can an estimate be?
59. How is test estimation different from ordinary project estimation?
60. What are the six steps in the estimation process?
61. What are the three estimation technique types?
62. What is the analogy technique based on?
63. What are the steps in the Delphi technique?
64. What three estimates do we need for the successive calculation estimation technique?
65. What is the estimation based on in the successive calculation estimation technique?
66. What are the five things you count for function point calculation?
67. Which test estimation technique is based on function points?
68. What is the difference between all other techniques and the percentage distribution technique?
69. What must be taken into account when defining the finish date for a task?
70. What is the difference between direct and indirect measurements?
71. How can subjective measurements be used?
72. What should be noted about the measurements we collect?
73. How can we present measurements?
74. What is the ink-factor?

75. What is the principle in S-curves?
76. What is a check sheet?
77. What is risk-based reporting?
78. Why should we use statistical reporting for process performance?
79. What must we do to stay in control?
80. What happens if we don't control the test project?

Static Testing (Review)

Static testing—or review—in the sense of having a second pair of eyes looking at something one has produced has probably been practiced since the first cave men painted the walls of the caves.

In software the static testing type was formally introduced in the 1970s. Since then a large volume of articles and a few books and comprehensive studies about static testing have been published.

Despite this there is still some confusion about terminology. Are we talking about reviews or static testing?

In this book the term "static testing" is chosen as the overall term for any testing that is not dynamic (i.e., testing in which the test item is not executed (is not "running" and hence is "static").

The economic benefits from performing static testing can be quite significant.

4.1 Introduction to Static Testing

4.1.1 History of Static Testing

In the software industry static testing was first officially introduced by Michael Fagan in the early 1970s. He wrote: "We had a number of projects coming in late in a number of departments. I knew I had to take some action to reverse this trend, so I worked with several of my colleagues to perform some analyses of what was happening and we found that there were defects in some of our designs that were causing the delays. In some cases we were twelve weeks behind schedule and way over budget. So we designed and implemented an organized process to search for design defects at a very early point in the development process and eliminated them before they could become a problem and cause delays and budget overruns." Static testing as we know it today was born.

4.1.2   Static Testing Definition

Dynamic testing is testing of software where the test item, the code, is being executed on a computer. Dynamic testing requires something that is executable and a more or less elaborate test environment.

The ISTQB vocabulary defines static testing as "Testing of a software development artifact, e.g., requirements, design or code, without execution of these artifacts, e.g., reviews or static analysis."

The IEEE 1028 Standard for Software Review and Audits provides a thorough definition and description of review and audit techniques. It defines *review* as "An evaluation of software element(s) or project status to ascertain discrepancies from planned results or to recommend improvement. This evaluation follows a formal process (for example, management review, technical review, software inspection or walk-through)."

The ISO 29119 Standard for Software Testing does not include static testing, but it does define it as "Testing in which a test item is examined against a set of quality or other criteria without code being executed. Examples are reviews and static analysis."

The primary objective of any static testing is to find defects in the test item and hence provide information about the quality of what has been produced. When we perform static testing we look directly at the written or drawn work products. This means that we are looking for defects directly— those that the producer happened to place there as the result of a human mistake.

4.1.3   Static Testing Cost/Benefit

There are costs associated with static testing, mainly because it takes time to perform.

A rule of thumb says that 15% of the development budget should be reserved for all of the static testing activities. These include:

- ❯ Description of the static testing processes in general;
- ❯ Performance of static testing;
- ❯ Collection and analysis of metrics;
- ❯ Improvement of the static testing processes.

To offset those costs, however, note that the benefits of static testing are plenty.

First of all, the benefit lies in the *early defect detection*. We can save a lot of money by finding the defects close to the time of their introduction.

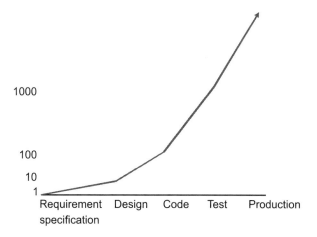

1000

100

10

1

Requirement   Design   Code   Test   Production
specification

Original from Grove
Consultants; also
inspired by IBM.

The graph above (also presented in Chapter I) shows that the cost of correction of a defect grows by a factor 10 or more for each development phase it "survives." If a defect is introduced in the requirements phase and found and corrected in that phase, we can say that this costs us 1 unit. If the defect is overlooked and not found until the design phase, it will cost us 10 units to correct, and so on, during the course of the development life cycle.

If we add the fact that research shows that more than half of the defects found in a product's life cycle—from requirements to disposal—can be traced back to defects in the requirements, it is clear that there is money to be saved by performing static testing from the very start of a development project.

Another contribution to the benefit of static testing is that we find the actual defects. Part of the cost involved in defect correction is the time it takes to actually locate the defect. In dynamic testing we see the failures caused by the underlying defects, but rarely the actual defects. Hence, it is faster to identify what is wrong and what should be changed when we use static testing.

The last benefit to be mentioned here is the fact that static testing is *cheap and easy* to perform. Unlike dynamic testing, it does not require sometimes elaborate and expensive test environments. Static testing can be performed on anything that can be read or otherwise looked at throughout the product life cycle, and it requires no special investments other than a desk and either paper or pencil, or the PC that the reviewer would have anyway.

Performance of timely static testing provides other benefits to the organization, including the following:

▸ Management gains earlier insight into the quality of what is being produced if we report information about our early findings.

▶ We get better productivity during development and an overall increase in efficiency, partly because defects are found early, partly because static testing gives better insight into what is to be produced.

▶ Our dynamic testing time is decreased because we have fewer defects to deal with.

▶ Performance of static testing also means that fewer defects are sent out to the customer, leading to higher trustworthiness and reduced maintenance.

▶ On the softer side static testing can spring off new ideas about how to do things better, because knowledge sharing is an important part of static testing.

▶ A better esprit de corps can be promoted since more stakeholders are involved in getting the best quality of the product from the beginning—we did this together!

▶ In more mature organizations, data collected from static testing, especially inspections, can be used to improve the static testing process and any other process as well.

4.1.4 Static Testing Items

Everything that can be read or otherwise looked at can be a test item for static testing. If we look at what is being produced during the development and maintenance of a product, there are test items for static testing in every phase from the earliest conception of the product to its disposal. Also documents produced by the organization and the supporting process areas can, and should, be items for static testing.

A few examples of documents that can be test items in static testing are listed below. The list is by no means exhaustive and should only be used as inspiration for identifying possible static test items in your organization.

▶ Organizational documents, such as policies, strategies, plans, reports, contracts, sales and marketing materials, and supplier agreements;

▶ Plans for products, projects, quality assurance, testing, configuration management, and customer communication;

▶ Requirement specifications from the business and from the users, and for software, hardware, data, network, and services;

▶ Design for products, architecture, and detailed components;

▶ The actual product, such as code, data, hardware, installation guides, manuals, and educational material;

▶ Test specifications and test reports for all test subprocesses, such as component testing, integration testing, system testing, and performance testing;

▶ Process descriptions, templates, examples, and technique descriptions.

4.1.5 Overview of Static Testing Types

There are a number of ways in which static testing can be performed. The static testing types described in this book fall in two groups:

▶ Static testing performed by people;
▶ Static testing performed with the assistance of a tool.

The types in the first group can be performed on anything written or otherwise documented. They have a different level of formality, and they include, listed in order of increasing formality:

▶ Informal review;
▶ Walk-through;
▶ Technical review;
▶ Management review;
▶ Inspection;
▶ Audit.

An audit is not necessarily more formal than an inspection, in terms of strictly following a specific procedure. Audit is, however, listed here as most formal because it is always performed by a third party in relation to the project for which it takes place.

The term "Peer review" is sometimes used in connection with static testing. ISTQB states that all of the above static testing types can be performed within a peer group, in which case it is called a peer review. Hence, a peer review is not a specific static testing type.

The types performed with the assistance of a tool are:

▶ Static analysis;
▶ Dynamic analysis.

Static analysis is performed on written code (i.e., the code is not being executed and the test is hence static). Dynamic analysis is performed on running code, so it is debatable if this is a static testing type. The reason for placing that type here is that it is not the implemented functionality that is being tested, but the effects of possible defects in the code.

Note that the ISTQB syllabi categorize these test types as analytical, rather than static.

Each of the types is described in detail in Section 4.3 below.

The choice of the static testing type to use in any given situation can be based on a number of aspects, including risk and purpose. This is further described in Section 4.3.8 below.

4.1.6   Psychological Aspects of Static Testing

We must be aware that static testing may end in frustration both for the author and the other participants when static testing is introduced and even when it is performed on a regular basis.

The author has done his or her best and is perhaps expecting to be praised for the good work during the static testing feedback period. This will, however, rarely happen. The reviewers are, as they should be, looking for shortcomings and defects, and even if the work is in fact excellent there will always be something to find that should be brought forward. The reviewers do not expect the author to be personally offended by the static testing feedback process; they may even expect to be praised for doing a good job finding defects.

Both parties need to keep in mind that static testing is a necessary and effective activity, and that it is performed to help increase the quality of the work. There is nothing wrong with making mistakes—everybody does that. And there is nothing wrong with pointing out mistakes, as long as the reviewers keep the static testing objective and the reporting matter of fact.

The static testing manager should be attentive to the fact that he or she can enhance the team spirit by using static tests in a constructive way and instill the understanding in all participants that static tests give better understanding of the product, the processes, the colleagues, and one's own capability, and that static tests help increase the maturity level in the organization.

All participants in static testing, as in all kinds of testing, should learn to give and receive criticism in a constructive way, as described in Section 8.5.

4.1.7   Static Testing in the Life Cycle

Static testing can, and should, start when something is written down or otherwise documented in the product life cycle. It is particularly important to perform static testing before others are going to use what is being produced to reduce the risk of further work taking more time and hence being more expensive than necessary (see the figure in Section 4.1.3).

In agile development informal static testing is constantly being performed, because the people in the team work so closely together. There may, however, be a need for more formal static testing of major products from time to time, but that depends of the nature of the product.

In more formal development models, each development phase usually ends with a milestone with a specified outcome. The example below shows some planned milestones for a product of relatively high safety criticality.

An example of milestones with associated deliverables for a project following a waterfall model is:

> ▶ Closing of contract;
> ▶ Closing of requirements specification;
> ▶ Closing of architectural design;
> ▶ Closing of detailed design;
> ▶ Acceptance/qualification of complete product;
> ▶ Final delivery/operational readiness.

Appropriate static testing should be performed on the deliverables for the milestones as part of the approval of the milestone; but these should not be the only static testing performed during the development life cycle; the more the better within reason related to the risk.

4.2   Static Testing Process

Even though the static testing types are different from each other in some ways, they should all be performed within the framework of the generic static testing process.

The current version of ISO 29119 does not include a static testing process. Had it done, it might have included the following activities:

> ▶ Preparation of rules and/or check lists;
> ▶ Performance of the static test;
> ▶ Debriefing and/or reporting.

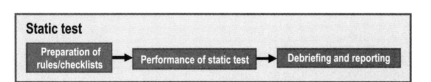

The static testing process does not directly include iterations; if a static test is not performed as expected or if the test item is not accepted, a new static test should be planned.

4.2.1   Interaction with Other Test Processes

Static testing is performed within the framework of a test sub-process, and will only directly interact with the test sub-process management, as illustrated in the figure below.

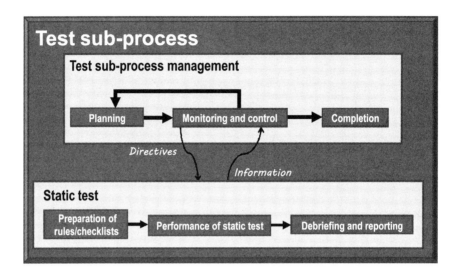

Directives will be issued from the test sub-process management to the static testing process to initiate or stop action during the course of the static test. This may be, for example, relaying a directive for preparing a checklist.

Information will go the other way from the static testing process to the test sub-process management to keep the test project manager aware of progress and/or problems of the actual testing. This information may be further relayed and used to update appropriate plans.

When a static test is completed this must be communicated to the test sub-process.

4.2.2   Detailed Activities

The static testing process is fairly simple; the involved activities are described below.

4.2.2.1   Preparation of Rules/Checklists

The first activity is the preparation of the test basis. This is not the planning, which is done in the management process, but more technical preparation, such as defining which rules should be used for the static test or finding or writing more detailed checklists.

Rules may be internal rules or standards in an organization, for example, a design guide for the user interface, or it may be external standards, for example, IEC/ISO 61508, Functional Security for Electric/Electronic Programmable Safety-Related Systems.

Checklists are a valuable asset in an organization and they should be maintained with care. Once a checklist has been produced, it should be updated based on the experience gained by each use. Entries may be added, changed, or removed in order to keep the checklist "sharp" and useful. An example of a checklist is presented in Section 4.2.3.

4.2.2.2   Performance of Static Testing

The actual performance of the static test depends very much on the chosen type of test.

In general though we can say that the checking performed in static testing can be done in three directions relative to the document under test:

> ▶ Backward
>   Here we check if the document corresponds to its basis documentation and other related documents.

> ▶ Internal
>   Here we check if the document is kept within the bounds of its purpose and scope, conforms to the template or standard on which it is built, is understandable, and is free of spelling mistakes, incomprehensive language and unexplained abbreviations.

> ▶ Forward
>   Here we check if the document is useful as the basis for further (development) work.

Like dynamic testing, static testing requires the existence of basis documentation specifying the expectations for the document under test. Basis documentation may be other documents in the life cycle, checklists, or standards. Standards can be project specific, company specific, and/or public.

If basis documentation is not available, we can only check the document internally, that is, check the document against itself, for example, for inconsistencies.

Without basis documentation our testing will be based on assumptions, experience, and "feelings."

The static testing types are described in detail in Section 4.3 below.

4.2.2.3   Debriefing and Reporting

When the actual checking of the document is performed, the results must be reported, registered, and managed. The reporting and registration often take place at a meeting where thc identified defects are described and possibly officially registered.

The form and formality of the meeting depends on the type of the static testing being performed as described in Section 4.3 below.

Depending on the formality of the project as a whole, registered defects from a static test may go through the same incident life cycle as incidents identified in a dynamic test; this is described in Section 8.2.

In general, we can say that a static test on a particular document will have one of three possible outcomes: (1) accepted, (2) accepted with rework, or (3) rejected.

1. If everything is fine and no (serious) defects are found, the document can be accepted as it is. No further work is necessary before the document can be used as the basis for further work and/or become the basis document for other static or dynamic tests.

2. It may, on the other hand, happen that a number of (serious) defects are found. If the defects are not too many and not too serious compared with the quality criteria, it may be decided that some rework is needed before the document can be used further, but that a repeat of the static testing is not required. The document is accepted on the understanding that the necessary rework will be done before the document is released.

3. In the case where the defects found are too numerous and/or too serious in view of the quality criteria, the document can be rejected. This means that it is returned to development for further work before it may be presented for static testing again.

4.2.3   Produced Documentation

The tangible outcomes of the performance of a static testing process are, in principle, a reference to or list of rules or a checklist and a registration of the findings (i.e., the identified defects).

Rules or checklists or indeed registration of findings are not always used or made for static testing, however. Static testing will still provide value, but not as much as it could have done in a bigger perspective.

The contents of the documents are described below.

4.2.3.1   Static Testing Checklist

A checklist is a very simple document. It may be the result of interpretation of a set of rules or a standard and/or based on people's experience. Documents like these may be used for activities other than static testing, for example, for preparation of the document; it all depends on the actual contents.

4.2.3.1.1   Checklist Contents

All documents should include some document-specific information. This should adhere to the organization's convention for document identification, if there is one; see Section 3.1.4.1.1 for an example.

Inspired by ISO 29119 the following table of contents for a static testing checklist is suggested. This may of course be tailored to the individual situation.

1.1   Checking Elements
2.1   Unique Identifier
3.1   Checking Element

There may be only one list of checking elements in a checklist document or there may be a number of lists of different categories. The example below shows a document with several small checklists.

4.2.3.1.2   Checklist Contents Example

The table below provides an example of a checklist document with checklists categorized according to quality requirements for a requirements specification document. The example is an extract of a longer checklist.

Requirements document checklist	
1. The requirement specification must be *clearly structured*.	
1.1	Is there a table of contents?
1.2	Does the order of sections and subsections seem logical?
1.3	Is there a "Reader's guide" section?
1.4	Are appendices and/or references used for large amounts of information?
2. The requirement specification must be unambiguous.	
2.1	Is there a glossary?
2.2	Does it appear to be sufficient?
2.3	Are all words that you would expect to see in the glossary present?
3. The requirement specification must be *traceable*.	
3.1	Does the specification have a unique ID?
3.2	Is the unique ID relatively short?
3.3	Does the number include a version number?

4.2.3.2   Static Testing Defect List

The defects identified during the performance of a static test may be registered in a more or less formal way, depending on the static testing type and the general risk exposure of the product. Sometimes the defects are informally noted directly in the document under test, in other situations a formal defect registration must be produced.

A formal defect registration form is described below.

4.2.3.2.1 Static Testing Defects List Contents

All documents should include some document-specific information. This should adhere to the organization's convention for document identification, if there is one; see Section 3.1.4.1.1 for an example.

Inspired by ISO 29119 the following table of contents for a static testing defect list is suggested.

1. **Static Testing Defect Elements**

    1.1 **Unique identifier**

    This section should provide a unique, short identification of the defect. This is usually in the form of a number, possibly with a prefix to ensure uniqueness across test sub-processes in a test project.

    1.2 **Source**

    This section should provide information about the stakeholder, who has identified the defect.

    1.3 **Category**

    This section should provide a categorization of the defect regarding its importance to facilitate the most effective handling of defects. The organization should agree on one or more useful categorization schemes.

    1.4 **Position details**

    This section should provide detailed information about where in the document the defect was found, in order for the person responsible for handling the defect to quickly and reliably be able to find the defect.

    This may sound trivial, but experience shows that if this information is not carefully worded, time will be wasted finding the exact position of the observed defect.

    The structure of the position details should be fixed to enable sorting.

    1.5 **Description**

    This section should provide details about the defect. The quality of this description may have an impact on the time it takes to handle a defect and decide if it is a defect or not. An extra few minutes spent on the description may save more time for the person responsible for handling the defect.

1.6 Rationale

This section should provide an explanation for raising the defect if this is not evident from the comment.

1.7 Proposed new text

This section should provide suggestions for rewording and/or other changes to be made to the document under static testing to remedy the defect.

In very formal static test, except inspection, defects are automatically rejected if no new text is proposed.

1.8 Status

This section should provide the current state of the defect in relation to the defect life cycle. For example, the state may be:

▶ Open;

▶ Accepted;

▶ Accepted in principle;

▶ Not accepted;

▶ Duplicate;

▶ Implemented.

1.9 Comment

This section should provide any information that the person responsible for the handling of the defect may like to convey to the source of the defect regarding the decision made about the defect.

4.2.3.2.2 *Static Testing Defect Contents Example*

The table below provides a small excerpt of a very formal static testing defect list (used during development of ISO standards).

Document:	XX Document						
S.	**No.**	**Cat.**	**Clause, Sub-clause**	**Description and rationale**	**Proposed new text**	**Status**	**Comment**
	...						
ES	3	GE	5.2.1, 5.3.1, 6.2.1, etc.	The second sentence does not provide an example for the first sentence in the paragraph.	Suppress "For example,"	Accepted	Text removed
ES	4	E	5.2.3.2	"The details of activities in the test process may be described in more detailed test processes" Probably they would be described	"The details of activities in the test process may be described in more detailed test documents"	Accepted in principle	text changed to "..detailed test process documents."
FR	8	TE	6.2.12	This section should be a part of 6.2.6, where test strategy for the project is defined.	Suppress 6.2.12 and make it explicitly a section of 6.2.6.	Not accepted	The plan may deviate in more areas than those in the 6.2.6
	...						

4.3   Static Testing Types

4.3.1   Overview of Static Testing Types

As can be seen from the different definitions of static testing in Section 4.1.2, a number of static testing types, or techniques, have been defined. The types to be discussed here are, in order of formality:

- ▶ Informal review;
- ▶ Walk-through;
- ▶ Technical review;
- ▶ Management review;
- ▶ Inspection;
- ▶ Audit.

	Walk-Through	Technical Review	Management Review	Inspection
Primary purpose	Finding defects	Finding defects	Monitoring progress	Finding defects
Secondary purpose	Sharing knowledge	Making decisions	Finding defects	Process improvement
Preparation	Usually none	Get and/or prepare rules/checklists Familiarization	Preparation	Formal preparation
Use of test basis	Rarely	Maybe	Maybe	Always
Leadership of meeting	Author	As appropriate	As appropriate	Trained moderator
Recommended group size	3–7	3–9	3–9	3–6
Formal procedure	Usually not	Sometimes	Sometimes	Always
Volume of material	Relatively low	Moderate to high	Moderate to high	Relatively low
Collection of metrics	Usually not	Sometimes	Sometimes	Always
Output	Sometimes an informal report	Defect list More or less formal report	Defect list More or less formal report	Defect list, measurements, and formal report.

An overview of the similarities and differences in these, except informal review and audit as the "outliers" in formality, is shown in the table above.

All of the static testing types are described in details in the following sections.

The descriptions are on the ceremonious side, outlining the principle for each type of static test. This does not mean that static testing can only and should only be performed as described here; static testing is valuable, even if it is not performed completely "according to the book." The descriptions should be seen as inspiration, not rules; and the performance of static testing should always be tailored to the situation.

4.3.2   Informal Review

The informal review is, as the name indicates, the least formal type of static test. This is what we all do from time to time, mostly without thinking about it as a static test: asking a colleague or a friend to look at something we have produced and to give us feedback.

Informal reviews may be performed for any type of document or other written or drawn material produced in an organization.

The objectives of informal reviews are very individual, depending on the author's needs. It could be everything from finding spelling and grammar mistakes, finding problems in the structure of the products to defects in the actual contents from a professional point of view.

An informal review follows no formal documented process. The participants are normally just the author and one or two reviewers. The reviewer(s) are usually chosen by the author. Most people have a network of reviewers to choose from, depending on the document to be reviewed and the review objective.

I have a number of reviewers for special objectives: one for spelling and grammar, one for formalities and references, and a couple of trusted colleagues for contents.

This type of static testing can be performed on any document at any state during its production. The author decides when he or she would like an informal review to take place. It could be on an early draft to make sure the structure and level are correct, or it could be on the final draft to iron out the last tiny crinkles before the document is released.

The reviewer reviews the document when it fits into his or her schedule after agreement with the author. Basis documents are rarely used; the review is done according to the reviewer's perception.

The author typically gets feedback in either pure verbal form or in the form of notes scribbled in the document under test.

Even though informal reviews rarely involve meetings as such, it is always a good idea to go through the notes with the reviewer(s). Notes may be unreadable and they may be difficult to understand for the author.

The result of an informal review varies, and is very much dependent on the review skills of the chosen reviewer(s).

The author decides when the review is over. He or she may correct the document as he or she sees fit; there are no obligations following an informal review.

Informal reviews have a few disadvantages. One is the dependency on the reviewers' reviewing skills, but that can easily be overcome by finding the right reviewers for the job. Another disadvantage is that usually no records are kept of the reviews and hence no data are available for calculation of effectiveness.

The benefits of informal reviews should, however, not be underestimated. Even though the reviews are informal they can be very useful. In most companies material must not be delivered to others without having at least been through an informal review.

4.3.3 Walk-Through

A walk-through is a step-by-step presentation of a document by the author at a walk-through meeting. The primary objective is to find defects. Quite often the author discovers defects him- or herself just by going through the document, as I suspect most of us have experienced.

The secondary objective is to create a common understanding of the contents of the document under test. This is in fact often regarded as the primary objective. It is not necessarily just a question of the participants understanding what the author has thought; it can be a question of the author getting an understanding of where the participants want to go.

Because of the secondary objective of walk-throughs, these are particularly useful for documents that are going to be used as a basis for further work. Such documents may be:

▶ Plans;

▶ Requirements specifications;

▶ Design specifications;

▶ Test procedures.

Walk-throughs are usually planned to take place at specific points in the course of a development or maintenance project. It can be early in the production process for a document to make sure the author is going in the right direction, or it may be as part of a handover of the objects to those who are going to use the document as the basis for their work.

Any document may be the object of a walk-through. The object is, however, most often code or design since a common understanding of the contents is most important here.

The process for walk-throughs is usually not very formal. When the document is in a state corresponding to the defined entry criteria, the walk-through is scheduled and the participants, usually three to seven people, are invited. The reviewers may get the document in advance to familiarize themselves with it, but no formal preparation is required.

A walk-through meeting is always part of the process. The author acts as the presenter of the document and the only other role represented is that of the reviewers (listeners). In cases of potential conflict a neutral facilitator may be present.

At the meeting the author "walks through" the object. This may be in the form of a dry run of the design or the code, maybe using scenarios or use cases, or a step-by-step presentation of the contents. In the course of this presentation, the defects, omissions, possible changes, improvement ideas, style issues, and alternatives that pop up are noted and discussed.

Walk-through meetings should not last longer than 1 or 2 hours, so the volume that can be the "walked through" cannot be too high. If the full volume of the document is too high, representative samples must be selected, and the information gathered may be applied to the rest of the document during rework.

After the walk-through meeting a more or less formal test completion report should be produced summarizing the test performance and the findings.

The exit criteria for a walk-through are usually that the meeting has been held and the report approved. Corrections to the document under test are made at the author's discretion.

The only slight disadvantage of walk-throughs is that the benefit depends on the author's ability to present the item. Some people find it extremely hard to express themselves verbally in front of an audience and that may jeopardize the benefit of a walk-through. It is said that practice makes perfect, and this also applies to walk-throughs. If the author finds it hard, then start with a very small audience, maybe only one person, and practice the technique.

Walk-throughs are well worth the effort. The defect finding is an important benefit, but the transfer and sharing of knowledge and understanding is even more important and useful in an organization. This is valid for groups of experienced people, groups of people with varied experience, and for groups with newcomers who are being trained.

4.3.4   Technical Review

A technical review is a group discussion activity, usually among peers, that focuses on achieving consensus on an approach to be taken for the item under test.

Any document can be the object of a technical review. Despite the name, managerial documents such as plans may also be the object of technical reviews. Basis material in the form of preceding documents, requirements for the object, and/or standards and checklists should be used.

The primary objective is of course to find defects. The secondary objective is to make decisions, technical or managerial as the case might be, and reach consensus about the approach to the work.

Technical reviews are usually planned to take place at certain points in time in the development life cycle.

Technical reviews must be managed by somebody other than the author.

Roles are defined for technical reviews. The roles are a chairperson for the review meeting, a presenter, the reviewers, the author, and a recorder. The chair and presenter roles are often filled by the same person. The total number of participants should be three to nine people.

It is important for the participants in a technical review to be at more or less the same level in the organization. A manager should not participate in a technical review, because this might make the author and perhaps other participants uneasy and will lower the technical benefits of the review.

The manager schedules the preparation and the review meeting and presents the material to the reviewers. The reviewers are usually expected to examine the material for defects and other issues before the review meeting is held.

At the review meeting the chair provides an overview of what is going to happen. The document is leafed through page by page and defects are registered and may be discussed. Conclusions about what should be changed and what should not should be reached before the end of the meeting.

The author is present, but in contrast to his or her role in a walk-through, the author should stay silent and listen during a review meeting. Clarifying questions may be asked and answered, but the author should not try to "defend" or explain what is written in the document.

A defect list should be collected during the meeting; and a test completion report may be written after the review meeting summarizing the findings and the conclusions. In some cases measurements related to the time and defect finding are reported.

If the document is rejected and a new review is to be performed, this must be scheduled by the review manager.

If the document needs rework before it can be approved, this will take place after the meeting and is usually done by the original author.

The disadvantages of technical (and management) reviews are few. The outcome depends on the reviewers, but these can be selected carefully to get the best results. If reporting of measurements is not imposed, it is difficult to calculate the effectiveness of the technical reviews, but the measurements are not difficult to obtain, if they are wanted.

The benefits of technical reviews are even greater than those for informal reviews, and they are generally also more effective. Defects are found early and cheaply, information about the quality of the produced items is gathered, and the participants learn from each other.

4.3.5   Management Review

A management review is a managerial group activity that focuses on check-ing of progress of the work related to the plan under review. Any type of plan may be reviewed, including:

Project-Related Plans:

- ❯ Project management plans, including schedule and resources;
- ❯ Quality assurance plans;
- ❯ Test plans;
- ❯ Configuration management plans;
- ❯ Risk management plans;
- ❯ Contingency plans.

Plans Pertaining to the Product:

- ❯ Safety plans;
- ❯ Installation plans;
- ❯ Maintenance plans;
- ❯ Backup and recovery plans;
- ❯ Disaster plans.

Reports:

- ❯ Test status reports;
- ❯ Test completion reports.

The objective is to find defects in the document under static test, but this is usually the secondary objective for management reviews, while the pri-mary objective is to monitor progress according to the current plan, to assess status, to perform a new risk analysis in light of the present situation, and to make necessary decisions. These decisions may include changes in activities, resources, schedule, and/or scope and quality goals. After the review the plan must be updating accordingly.

Management reviews are usually planned to take place at certain times in the development life cycle, typically in connection with defined mile-stones; that is, transfer from one development phase to the next.

There is usually no basis material as such unless a document is reviewed in relation to a document standard or the like. On the other hand, a man-agement review is performed using all appropriate information about the status of the project and the product, like status reports concerning both technical and financial aspects, and defect reports.

The roles that should be filled for a management review are a decision maker (usually the owner of the plan), a leader, reviewers, and a recorder. The reviewers are relevant stakeholders and should include management and technical staff involved in the execution of the planned activities.

 For a formal management review of a test plan, the reviewers should include the test manager, the project manager (higher management), and the people responsible for the detailed testing activities.

The total number of participants in a management review should be about three to ten people.

 The management review process is usually fairly formal. The leader schedules the preparation and the review meeting and presents the plan and any other information to the reviewers. The reviewers are usually expected to be prepared by having read the plan and any deviations from the previous plan before the review meeting is held.

At the review meeting the plan is checked for compliance with other plans and consistency with reality. Conclusions about what should be changed in the plan and what should not should be reached before the end of the meeting.

 A sprint planning meeting in agile development using SCRUM is an example of a management review that is far less formal and where all participants share the roles. The purpose is, however, the same.

The disadvantages of management reviews are few. The outcome depends on the reviewers, but these are usually sufficiently committed.

The benefits of management reviews are many. A plan that is agreed on by all relevant stakeholders has a higher probability of being followed than a plan without such an agreement.

4.3.6 Inspection

Inspection is a formal and well-defined type of static test. Inspections were first introduced in 1972 at IBM by Michael Fagan, and since then the inspection process has evolved through use in regular development and experimentation.

Fagan inspections have a number of specific characteristics, which must all be observed before a static testing activity may indeed be called an inspection. The characteristics are:

- ▶ The process followed must be the formally defined process.
- ▶ The roles must be the defined inspection roles.
- ▶ Source material (basis documentation) must always be used.

▶ The inspectors must look for specific kinds of issues.
▶ Metrics must be defined and collected.
▶ Process improvement is an integrated part of the process.
▶ The moderator and the inspectors must be trained.

Inspections have two official purposes:

▶ Product improvement;
▶ Process improvement.

As for the other static testing types, the main objective of inspections is to find defects and thereby contribute to the improvement of the product.

The secondary and almost as important objective of inspections is contribution to process improvement. This is primarily aimed at improvements to the inspection process itself, but other processes may also benefit from the results of inspections. The process improvement objective is supported by collection and analysis of measurements for all inspections.

The formally described Fagan inspection process consists of the activities:

▶ Planning;
▶ Overview;
▶ Preparation;
▶ Meeting;
▶ Rework;
▶ Follow-up.

The roles in play in these inspections are:

▶ Inspection leader;
▶ Author;
▶ Inspectors;
▶ Moderator (meeting chair);
▶ Recorder.

Some of the important aspects of Fagan inspections are described below.

4.3.6.1   Inspection Planning
The inspection leader is the same role as the test subprocess manager. The responsibilities are those related to the test management process, that is,

the planning activity regarding the document to be inspected, the people involved, the metrics to collect, and the schedule and logistics.

An inspection leader should be trained in the inspection process, in the metric plan in the organization, in general process improvement, in statistical improvement methods, and in the organization's inspection policy.

The planning must take the nature of the document to be inspected into account, and the *optimal checking rate* must be determined. The checking rate is the number of units, typically pages, to be inspected per time unit, typically hours. Measurements collected for inspections should be used to determine the optimal checking rate for the various types of items in an organization.

Inspection is an intensive static testing type and it is usually not possible to inspect an entire document in one single inspection cycle The test manager must decide to use either chunking or sampling.

Chunking means that the document is divided into segments of a few pages (or other units as appropriate) at a time. All relevant parts of the document are checked in a number of cycles. This technique has the very useful side effect that defects found in one chunk can be corrected in other chunks before these are subjected to the inspection.

Sampling means that only a selected part(s) of the document is to be inspected. Based on the results of the inspection of the sample, defect densities for the uninspected parts can be calculated. Sampling is a cheaper alternative to checking the entire document, and it can be used to provide a firsthand measure of quality, to train the inspectors, and to gain insight into defect patterns. The underlying idea of sampling is that defects in one part of a document often exist in other parts as well.

In addition to this an inspection leader should also make sure that:

▶ The entry criteria for the inspection are met.
▶ The exit criteria are met.
▶ Process improvement of the inspection process and other processes is supported by the findings from the inspection.

Planning is also concerned with defining and allocating the roles in the inspection. The most important role is that of inspector; inspectors may be selected according to specific skills, technical or domain knowledge, and/or availability. Inspectors may have individual inspector roles; that is sub-roles related to the inspector role. The concept of inspector roles is described below.

It is quite often seen that the inspection leader also fills the role of moderator and takes part in the inspection meeting in that capacity.

4.3.6.1.1   Inspection Entry and Exit Criteria

Entry and exit criteria must always be defined and adhered to for an inspection.

The purpose of the entry criteria is to make sure that time is not wasted by starting the inspection process too early. The document to test must be in a reasonable state, so that any issues can be easily handled and corrected.

Entry criteria may be:

- ▶ Relevant checklists are available.
- ▶ Basis documents have exited their inspections with a known and acceptable remaining defect level.
- ▶ In 10 minutes of trial examination not more than 1 major defect is found.
- ▶ The document has gone through spell checking, indexing, and grammar checking as appropriate.

Exit criteria must be met in order for the document to be approved and the inspection to be officially finished. Exit criteria are therefore defined both for the document and for the inspection process.

Exit criteria for the document being inspected may be that the entry criteria are still met, that any necessary rework has been performed, and that this rework has been verified by the inspection leader.

For the inspection as such, the exit criteria may be that the checking and logging rates were within the prescribed limits and that the estimate for remaining defects in the document is below an acceptable limit.

4.3.6.1.2   Inspector Roles

The inspectors are the people doing the actual checking of the document in the preparation activity.

The inspectors must be people who like to find defects. It may sound stupid, but many people are uneasy about finding defects in other people's work and this attitude may jeopardize the effectiveness of the inspection, and make it a very unpleasant experience for the inspectors.

During the preparation the inspectors must keep to the checking rate they have been given. They must make sure that they have finished the checking in time for the meeting, or they must give notice of problems to the inspection leader as soon as they occur.

The inspectors must also adhere to the inspector role they may have been assigned.

The concept of inspector roles is based on the facts that we tend to see what we are looking for and that we are usually only able to keep focus on one or two things at the time.

What do you see if you are asked to inspect the flowers in the drawing shown here?

If you are not asked to look for something in specific you may count the flowers, note the color of the flowers, count the number of leaves, see if there are more buds than open flowers, maybe note the band and its bow, and check if the number of stems correspond to the number of flowers and leaves.

That is all fine, but what about the faces hidden in the bouquet? Did you see them? If not, look again before you turn to the solution in Appendix 4.A.

The inspectors may be given specific inspector roles to make each of them focus on just what they are supposed to look for and hence make sure that all important aspects are given first priority by at least one inspector.

Note: The concept of specific focus points for reviewers may be useful in any type of static test.

Inspector roles may be chosen among the following (ordered alphabetically) or others that may be relevant in the context:

Checklist: The inspector must inspect the document in relation to specific or generic checklists. Checklists may summarize rules, previously experienced problems, usability, or any other imaginable aspect of the particular object.

Documents: The inspector must inspect the consistency between the document and one or more other documents.

Focus: The inspector must inspect the document looking for a specific kind of problems. The focus could be on usability, system implications, financial aspects, readability, grammar, cross-references, domain terms use, or perspective (for videogames or the like). This inspector role may be somewhat less objective than the others unless specific criteria have been defined.

Perspective: The inspector must inspect the document using a more active approach. The perspective is intended to represent or mimic a specific role in terms of who will be a future user of the object. This could be a designer, a tester, a programmer, or a user. It is important that the inspector having a perspective role either normally fills this role or understands it fully. The perspective role is less specific than the scenario role.

Procedural: The inspector must inspect the document following a specific procedure, for example, reading the document backwards.

Scenario: The inspector must inspect the document following a specific work procedure for a specific role. This inspector role is therefore more specific than the perspective role. Scenarios with accompanying questions must be created. This can be a significant task, but can on the other hand help avoid duplication of inspection efforts.

Standard: The inspector must inspect the document against external standards, for example IEEE, BS, or ISO standards, or internal standards such as company, organizational, business, project, or phase specific standards.

Viewpoint: The inspector must inspect the document as, for example, a user, an analyst, a tester, or a designer. This role is very similar to the perspective, but relevant base documents are also used.

No matter which inspector role an inspector is to follow, issues falling under another role may still be found and these should, of course, also be noted and logged during the inspection meeting. So should any issue identified in the base documents.

4.3.6.2   Inspection Overview
The overview is the kick-off of the inspection. The overview should include:

▶ Group education of inspectors;
▶ Assignment of inspector roles;
▶ Distribution of material.

The group education of the participants has two goals: education about the inspection process to be used in this particular inspection and about the material to be inspected. The plan for the inspection, not least the time assigned for each individual to prepare, should be presented. Information about the current state of inspections in the organization, including relevant statistics and future plans, should be given. This may set this particular inspection in perspective and may be a good motivational factor.

The overview ends with the assignment of specific inspector roles and handout of the test item and base material. It is important for the inspection leader to make sure everybody understands his or her role and is happy with it, and that everybody knows what the other roles are covering.

4.3.6.3   Inspection Preparation
The preparation activity is the core activity of the inspection. This is the execution of the testing.

During the preparation each of the inspectors performs individual checking of the object according to his or her assigned inspector role using the time allocated.

Each inspector performs the preparation when and where it suits him or her. The inspectors should make sure that they can sit undisturbed for the entire preparation time to be used, and that they perform the preparation before the inspection meeting is to take place.

The inspectors must follow the standard requirements for inspection preparations:

- ▶ Note starting time.
- ▶ Note down or mark identified defects.
- ▶ Focus on majors, at least in the beginning.
- ▶ Use the given time (no more, no less) to respect the checking rate.
- ▶ Count the number of defects per classification.

The classifications of defects used in inspections are usually:

- ▶ Major: The defect seems to concern more than the inspected item and/or will cause further damage.
- ▶ minor: The defect is not likely to cause damage to anything beyond the inspected item.
- ▶ ?: The defect needs to be clarified by the author; it may not be a defect after all.

Note that defects may be found in the base documents as well as in the inspection item. These should, of course, also be noted and reported.

4.3.6.4   Inspection Meeting

The purpose of the inspection meeting is to log the defects found during the preparation. It may seem unnecessary to have a meeting if all issues are noted down; however, experience shows that about 10% to 20% more defects will be found at the meeting. The meeting therefore enhances the effectiveness of the inspection.

The moderator chairs the meeting. He or she must be neutral with respect to the document being inspected and any base documents used. The moderator should be trained in conducting inspection meetings and know the rules. Being a good moderator requires good training, good people skills, and a good sense of judgment.

The moderator must:

- ▶ Cancel the meeting if anybody is unprepared.
- ▶ Be strict and diplomatic.

- Ensure that the logging rate is kept.
- Not allow discussions to evolve.
- Ensure that defects are aimed at the product, not the author.
- Keep solution-oriented statements to a minimum.
- Be able to make unpopular decisions like evicting someone or stopping the meeting.
- Keep participants with strong technical skills but low social skills from "killing" each other.

It may sound as if an inspection meeting is a terrible ordeal, and it may indeed be if care is not taken to make it the productive and inspiring activity it is supposed to be.

The moderator goes through the inspected document line by line, section by section, or using any other unit of the document that is relevant. For each unit the inspectors report their findings in turn, and the recorder logs the issues.

The reporting should concentrate on majors and questions. Minors can be given to the recorder later, as long as the relevant measurements are collected and registered.

When new defects are encountered during the meeting, these must be recorded as well, and they must be marked so that it is possible to see how many new defects an inspection meeting spurred.

A logging form may look like this:

Issue no.	M, m, o, n	Descr.	Doc. Systestplan	Page/Line
1.	M, o	No. scheme is unclear	—	p. 3,14.3 (17)
2.	M, o	Testgroup missing no. (CLL)	Systestplan	p. 5-6
3.	M, o	Heading 'User setup' not found in testplan	Systestplan	p. 5
4.	m, o	Term 'testing fields' meaning unlcear	—	p.3
5.	m, o	Term, 'setup user screen' not appropiate	—	p. 3
6.	m, o	Numbers not ordered	—	p. 3, purpose
7.	m, o	'validations' meaning unclear	—	p. 3 purpose
8.	M, o	71, 72, 77, 65 is headings, not	—	p. 3 purpose

In the second column *M* and m mean "Major" and "minor," respectively, as explained above; *o* means "old—defect found during preparation," and n means "new—defect found during the inspection meeting."

The recorder should be able to keep up with the logging rate and that should be kept as high as possible. As a rule of thumb one to two issues should be recorded per minute.

No solutions must be suggested or other discussions started during the recording. If needed, a solution-finding meeting may be scheduled to take place later.

An inspection meeting should not last longer than 1 hour. This is important in order to keep the logging rate high and focused. Breaks can, however, be used to smooth feathers, console the author, or keep people in line.

At the end of the inspection meeting, a conclusion must be reached as to whether the document is accepted, accepted with rework, or rejected.

4.3.6.5   Inspection Follow-Up

The inspection process cannot be finished before the exit criteria have been met. If a document has been accepted with rework, the inspection leader must make sure that the document has been corrected, and that this correction has not resulted in too many additional defects, before the inspection can be seen as completed.

The document should now be ready for others to use and to be placed under configuration management as ready according to the project plan.

The follow-up activity includes collecting the final measurements and ensuring that measurement analysis has been performed. Timing measurements must be collected for rework and follow-up, possibly distributed on individual activities such as edit time, time used to write defect reports, approval time, and analysis time.

Based on the measurements and other experience data, the number of remaining defects can be estimated, as can the cost saved by finding the defects now rather than later.

Any ideas for process improvements must be registered as appropriate.

4.3.6.6   Inspection-Based Process Improvement

The process improvement originating from inspections is based on analysis of the collected measurements. From the first pilot of inspections in an organization, measures must be collected to show the value of the inspection, calculating all of the time saved by finding defects earlier than normal. It is very important for the success of inspections that everybody involved understands the reason for the rigorous formality and is prepared to adhere to the rules.

Improvement of the inspection process in the organization should be ongoing in order for it to be adapted to the best use. Each organization must establish its own numbers for aspects such as:

- ❱ Optimal checking rate;
- ❱ Optimal logging rate;
- ❱ Optimal pages and/or participants per inspection.

Such measurements make it possible to create evidence of the benefits, efficiency, and effectiveness of formal inspections.

The practice of inspections in an organization should only continue if it is cost effective compared to other test methods.

Information gathered from inspections can also be used in process improvement initiatives beyond the inspection process. Root cause analysis of defects found, both defects in the inspected document and in the basis documents, can lead to processes in need of improvement.

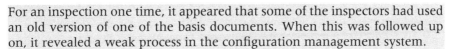 For an inspection one time, it appeared that some of the inspectors had used an old version of one of the basis documents. When this was followed up on, it revealed a weak process in the configuration management system.

4.3.7 Auditing

Auditing is the most formal static testing technique. Audits are performed by one or more auditors. Auditors must have a special education and certification to perform official audits.

Audits are usually performed late in the development life cycle, just before release of the product and/or close down of the project. Smaller audits may be performed in connection with other important milestones, or as "dress rehearsals" for official audits.

The primary objective of an audit is to provide an independent evaluation of an activity's compliance to applicable process descriptions, contracts, regulations, and/or standards.

Audits may be either internal or external. Internal audits are performed by auditors from the organization, but external to the project under audit. External audits are performed by auditors entirely external to the organization, usually from some sort of authority organization.

An internal audit may be conducted by certified auditors from the organization's method department to evaluate if CMMI-compliant processes for system and acceptance testing have been applied correctly.

An external audit may be performed by certified auditors from the U.S. Food and Drug Administration (FDA) to evaluate whether FDA regulations have been followed during the entire development life cycle of a product for use in connection with patient treatment at hospitals, and thereby determine if the product can be allowed into the American market.

Any document, technical as well as managerial, can be included in an audit. In an audit some, if not all, documents will usually be evaluated and their consistency as well as their collective compliance to the basis material checked.

A lead auditor is responsible for the audit, and he or she also acts as moderator. The lead auditor and any other participating auditors collect evidence of compliance through document examination, interviews, and walkthroughs of documents of special interest.

The audit leader decides when the audit should take place, and the documents will be audited in the state they are in at the time of the audit. Usually a fair warning is given and organizations may rehearse the audit to patch up any obvious defects in time.

The result of an audit is a report in which the findings are summarized in the form of lists of observations, deviations, recommendations, and corrective actions to be taken, as well as a pass/fail statement.

The disadvantages of audits are that they are expensive and the least effective static testing type. On the other hand, audits are usually performed because they are mandatory in some context and therefore serve a different purpose than pure defect finding, such as official approval of the product or process improvement.

4.3.8   Static Testing Type Selection

The static testing types have their individual strengths and weaknesses. In each particular case we have to select the most suitable type(s) to use.

The selection can be based on a number of aspects, including:

▶ Risk analysis

The higher the product risk is, the more formal the static testing type used should be.

▶ Objectives

Each type of static testing has a set of primary and secondary objectives, and these could also be used as the selection criteria.

▶ Development phase

The earlier we are in the development lifecycle, the more formal the static testing should be to make sure that we catch as many defects as possible here, before they grow more serious. We should also ensure that we are generally on the right track from the beginning. Then formality could be loosened in the later phases.

Static testing types may be mixed. Using one static testing type is far better than none, and using several static testing types makes the static testing even stronger.

Note that inspection should never be the first static testing type to apply, because this will jeopardize the effectiveness of the inspection.

Here are some examples of how static testing types may be mixed:

Informal review → Inspection

This order ensures that the trivial defects have been removed before the inspection so that the inspection can be focused on major issues.

Technical Review → Inspection → Walk-through

This order ensures that the document is as defect free as we may expect and that it is ready for transfer to another group of people for further development. This other group gets the best starting point by being introduced to the document by the author.

Technical review → Walk-through

This sequence of static testing types is less formal than the one above, but the objectives are the same.

Walk-through → Inspection → Informal review

This order ensures that the author is on the right track and can carry on working on the document until it is ready for inspection. After the inspection any minor spelling, grammar, and formatting issues will be caught before the document is released.

Informal review → Technical review → Inspection

This sequence is the most formal, and it ensures that the document doesn't have minor defects before the technical review and that the document is as defect free as we may expect both from a technical and a more formalistic point of view.

4.4   Static Analysis

Static analysis is a static test type usually performed using tool(s), but the only thing being executed during static analysis is the tool. Static testing tools are discussed in Section 9.1.3.1.

Traditionally, static analysis has been performed on code, but it may also be performed on requirements and architecture.

4.4.1   Static Analysis of Code

Many tools dedicated to static analysis are available on the market or as open source systems. Their capabilities vary a lot and depend very much on the coding language. Some standard development tools, such as compilers or linkers, are able to perform limited static analysis.

The static analysis techniques for code discussed here are:

- ◗ Control flow analysis;
- ◗ Data flow analysis;
- ◗ Compliance to standards;
- ◗ Calculation of code metrics.

4.4.1.1 Control Flow Analysis

A *control flow* is an abstract representation of all possible sequences of events—or paths—in the execution of a component or a system. The control flow is the basis for many of the structure-based test case design techniques described in Chapter 6.

A control flow goes from the starting point of the component or system and is transferred from one basic block to another to the end. A basic block (or node) is a bit of code that is executed as an entity with an entry point in the beginning of the block and only there, and with an exit point in the end of the block and only there.

It can be very useful to draw a control flow graph of the code. It gives an overview of the decision points, branches, and paths in a piece of code and its inherit complexity.

Two simple extracts of control flow graphs are shown below:

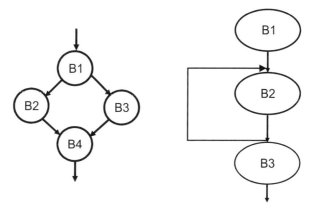

Basic blocks in parallel   Basic blocks with loop

Static analysis tools may be used to draw control flow graphs of larger pieces of code. It is, however, a good idea to train yourself to draw these by hand, because that gives a good understanding of how the code is structured.

A control flow graph does not necessarily give any idea of what the code is actually doing, but that is not important in this context.

Static analysis tools can find defects in the control flow, typically defects like:

▶ "Dead" code, i.e., code that cannot be reached during execution;
▶ Uncalled functions and procedures.

Both "dead" code and uncalled functions are quite often found in legacy systems. Undocumented changes and corrections have caused some code to be circumvented, but not removed. The cause of the change is since forgotten, but nobody maintaining the code has had the courage (or initiative) to get the unused code removed.

Such unused areas do not present direct risks. They do however disturb maintenance and they may unintentionally be re-invoked with unknown consequences.

4.4.1.2 Compliance to Coding Standard

A coding standard is a guideline for the standard style (layout) of the code being written in an organization.

Most static analysis tools can check for standard coding style violations, for example, missing indentations in IF statements. Some of the more sophisticated tools allow the definition of specific coding standards to be checked for.

It may seem trivial that coding standards should be defined and adhered to, but experience shows that it has several advantages, such as:

▶ Fewer faults in the code, because a good code layout enables the programmer to keep an overview of what he is writing;

▶ Easier component testing, because a well-structured code is easier to define test cases for when using white box techniques;

▶ Easier maintenance, because it is faster for others to take over code if all code is written in an identical style.

There are no disadvantages in requiring adherence to a coding standard, other than the programmers having to get used to it; but be aware of the quality of the coding standard considered—some are out-of-date or inappropriate. It is possible to get tools to format "rough" code according to coding standards.

4.4.1.3 Calculation of Code Metrics

Static analysis tools can provide measurements of different aspects of the code such as:

▶ Size measures—number of lines of code, number of comments;

▶ Complexity;

▶ Number of nested levels;

▶ Number of function calls—fan out.

Number of lines of code (LOC) can be reported as can number of lines of document (LOD). The ratio between these may be calculated as a derived measurement.

Measurements related to code lines may be difficult to work with. The sheer definition of a "code line" is not always as simple as it may sound. Numbers of code lines may also easily be manipulated by the programmers, if the measurements are used to quantify their efficiency.

Code complexity is a measure for how "tangled" the code is. The complexity is related to the number and types of decisions in the code. It is interesting from a testing point of view because it has an impact on the test effort: the higher the complexity, the larger the number of test cases required to achieve high decision and condition coverage.

The most commonly used complexity measure is McCabe's Cyclomatic Complexity (MCC). It was introduced by Thomas McCabe in 1976, and is often simply referred to as complexity, as CC, or as McCabe's complexity.

McCabe's Cyclomatic Complexity is a measure—a single ordinal number—of soundness of components. It measures the number of linearly independent paths through a code. It is intended to be independent of language and language formats.

The original definition of McCabe's Cyclomatic Complexity is:

$$MCC = (L - N) + 2*B$$

where

L = number of branches (lines in the flow graph).

N = number of sequential blocks (basis blocks or nodes).

B = number of broken sequences (this is used when we measure for more than one component. This is very rarely done, so B is usually = 1).

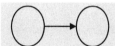
In this simple flow graph we have L = 1, N = 2, and B = 1 and therefore MCC = $(1 - 2) + 2 \times 1 = 1$

For this flow graph

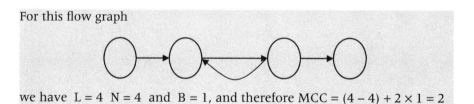

we have L = 4 N = 4 and B = 1, and therefore MCC = $(4 - 4) + 2 \times 1 = 2$

There are more simple ways of calculating McCabe's Cyclomatic Complexity. One way is based on a count of decisions and decision outcomes. It could be expressed like this

MCC = (SUM (*branches* – 1) for all decisions) + 1

IF statements always have two branches, so if we only have IF statements in the code we are looking at, we'll get

MCC = SUM(1) for all IF statements)) +1 = number of
IF statements +1

Constructions like CASE have more branches, so if we have a piece of code with two IF statements and 1 CASE statements with 10 possible outcomes, we would have MCC = 1 + 1 + 9 + 1.

Another way of calculating McCabe's Cyclomatic Complexity is by counting so-called regions in the code. A region is a closed area found in the flow graph.

The expression is

MCC = number of regions + 1

In the flow graph shown here, we have one region and we therefore have MCC = 2.

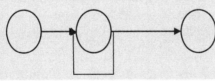

The graph shown below is created by a static analysis tool. The tool has calculated the MCC for the component to be 9.

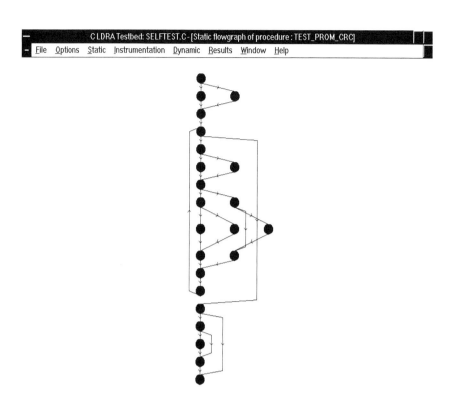

McCabe's Cyclomatic Complexity is a good indicator of test effort. Mathematical analysis has shown that it gives the exact number of tests needed to test every decision point in a program for each decision outcome.

Some testers have experienced a positive linear connection between the number of faults and the MCC (i.e., that the higher the CC, the higher the number of faults). Others have found that the connection is rather that a low CC and a high CC indicate relatively fewer faults, while more faults are found in the areas where the CC is around average. Try to get your own measurements for this.

A rule of thumb says that the MCC should not be more than 10. If we find a higher CC in a component, it should be revisited—maybe it could be restructured or divided. McCabe's CC measures, however, have been seen up to more than 3,000, so we should also use visual judgment of the control flow graphs to determine the test effort.

Cyclomatic complexity can be used for purposes other than test planning, for example, in risk analysis related to:

▶ Code development;
▶ Implementation of changes in maintenance;
▶ Reengineering of existing systems.

Complexity measures other than McCabe's exist; however, they are rarely used, except perhaps for Halstead's Complexity Measure, an algorithmic complexity measure.

4.4.2   Static Analysis of Architecture

In the recent testing literature, the static analysis object has been expanded to include the architecture of the product as well as the classic code object.

The code has a structure that can be analyzed, and so has the product or system as a whole. This may, for example, be:

▶ Structure of components in the product calling/using each other;
▶ Menu structure of a graphical user interface for a product;
▶ Structure of pages and other features in a web product.

4.4.2.1   Static Analysis of a Website

A website is a hierarchical structure composed of web pages with elements such as tables, text, pictures, and links to other pages, both internally to the website itself and to external websites. The structure of a website is described in HTML: Hyper Text Markup Language.

Many tools exist to analyze the HTML code and the structure and detailed composition of websites; that is, to perform static analysis of websites.

The stakeholders for the static analysis information are both analysts, designers, testers, and those in charge of the maintenance of the websites, the webmasters.

One of the results of such an analysis is a graph showing the structure of the website. A graph can provide an overview of the tree structure or hierarchy of the site and show the depth, complexity, and balance of the structure.

A very simple website is shown here. The R is the root, a T illustrates a non-link tag, for example a table, and an L illustrates a link.

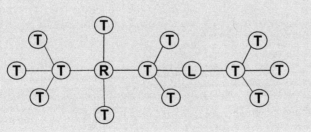

The graphs can be very colorful and look like the most amazing fireworks. The information extracted from the graphs can be used to:

> ▶ Test whether requirements for the website, for example, depth and balance, have been fulfilled, or whether the website needs to be restructured.
> ▶ Estimate test effort.
> ▶ Assess usability.
> ▶ Assess maintainability.

A rule of thumb is that the more balanced the website tree is, the lower the test and maintenance efforts are going to be and the higher the usability—and vice versa.

Websites are extremely dynamic products. The static analysis of a site prior to its release is only the tip of the iceberg of testing and monitoring a website. Dynamic analysis of the behavior of a site should be performed on a regular basis to identify problems such as:

> ▶ Broken links;
> ▶ Incomplete downloads;
> ▶ Deteriorating performance;
> ▶ Orphaned files.

Furthermore, information may be obtained about:

> ▶ Access patterns (where do users start and where do they end their visits);
> ▶ Navigation patterns;
> ▶ Activity over time;
> ▶ General performance;
> ▶ Page loading speed.

The website structure should also be monitored on a regular basis, because websites are likely to grow and change structure in an ad hoc manner.

4.4.2.2 Call Graphs

The analysis of the architectural structure of a product is on the borderline between design and testing. In the architectural design the product is decomposed into smaller and smaller components. Components call subroutines or functions in other components; in object-oriented design we say that classes provide methods for other classes to use. These dependencies or couplings can be illustrated in call graphs produced by tools.

Static architecture analysis tools can also provide measurements related to the coupling, such as:

- ▶ Fan-in: number of calls or uses of a specific function or methods made from other functions or methods (or the main program);
- ▶ Fan-out: number of calls or uses of functions or methods made from a specific component;
- ▶ Henry and Kafura metrics: coupling between modules;
- ▶ Bowles metrics: module and system complexity;
- ▶ Troy and Zweben metrics: modularity or coupling; complexity of structure;
- ▶ Ligier metrics: modularity of the structure chart.

These metrics may be more detailed and specific depending on the architectural paradigm.

Both the call graphs and the corresponding measurements provide valuable information for test planning. This information may be used to:

- ▶ Determine integration high-risk areas (high fan-out and/or fan-in);
- ▶ Determine a detailed integration testing sequence;
- ▶ Determine the intercomponent testing approach.

Especially in object-oriented architecture, it is also relevant to know the dynamic dependencies; that is how often a method is used during execution of the product. This information can be combined with the static architectural information to strengthen the test planning even more.

4.5 Dynamic Analysis

Dynamic analysis is the process of evaluating a system or a component based on its behavior during execution.

The two aspects of dynamic analysis are:

- ▶ Dynamic—code is being executed;
- ▶ Analysis—finding out about the nature of the object and its behavior.

Dynamic analysis cannot be done without tool support. Chapter 9 discusses the testing tool types.

Some dynamic analysis tools instrument the code in order to catch the relevant run-time information. This means that extra code is added to the code written by the developer. The effect of this is that it is not strictly the "real" code we are analyzing. In most cases this is without any importance.

The instrumentation may, however, have an adverse impact on performance, and that can pose problems if we are testing time-sensitive real-time software.

A component or larger object is executed when it has been instrumented. This execution may be execution of test cases for other test purposes or it may be execution of specific scripts produced for the analysis.

The great advantages of dynamic analysis are that it:

▶ Provides run-time information otherwise difficult to obtain.

▶ Provides information as a "by-product" of dynamic testing.

▶ Finds faults that it is almost impossible to find in other ways.

The dynamic analysis tool reports on what is going on during execution: It provides run-time information about the behavior and state of software while it is being executed. The information we can get from this covers:

▶ Memory handling and memory leaks;

▶ Pointer handling;

▶ Coverage analysis;

▶ Performance analysis.

4.5.1   Memory Handling and Memory Leaks

Memory handling is concerned with allocation, usage, and deallocation of memory.

The tools can detect memory leaks, where memory is gradually being filled up during extended use. This happens if we keep allocating memory and forget to deallocate it (or only deallocate a part of it) when it is no longer needed. If a system with a memory leak keeps on running we can end up with no more available memory. This will cause a failure, if it is not handled correctly in the code.

Memory is automatically deallocated when the execution stops; this is one of the reasons why memory leaks are not always detected during dynamic testing. When we test we rarely execute the software continuously for long periods, as it might be run in real life.

The advantage of dynamic analysis in connection with memory leaks is that the analysis can detect the possibility of memory leaks long before they actually happen.

4.5.2   Pointer Handling

Pointers are used to handle dynamic allocation of memory. Instead of working with a fixed name or address of a variable, we let the system find out where the actual location is, and we use a pointer to point to this location in the program.

The usage of pointers can go wrong in a number of ways. Pointers can, for example, be unassigned when used, lose their object, or point to a place in memory to which it is not supposed to point, say, beyond an array border or into some protected part of memory. A wrong pointer can cause part of the program or data stored in memory to be overwritten.

It may be very difficult to find the defects underlying failures caused by wrong pointer handling. These failures have a tendency to be periodic; that is, the program may run for a long time and then suddenly start to give wrong results or even crash.

Dynamic analysis tools can identify unassigned pointers and they can also detect defects in pointer arithmetic that can occur when, for example, the addition of two pointers results in a pointer that points to an invalid place in memory.

4.5.3   Coverage Analysis

The coverage obtained in an executed test can be measured by analysis tools. These tools provide objective measurement for some structural or white-box test coverage metrics, for example:

- ▶ Statement coverage;
- ▶ Branch coverage.

The tools provide measurements to be used in the checking against test completion criteria in a fast and reliable way.

Some tools can also deliver reports about uncovered areas. The more fancy ones produce colored reports where covered code is shown in one color and uncovered code in another. This is a great help when more test cases must be designed to obtain higher coverage.

4.5.4   Performance Analysis

All too many products have no or insufficient performance requirements and turn out to be unable to cope with real-world volumes and loads. Performance analysis aims at measuring the performance of a product under controlled circumstances before the product is released.

It is much better to test these aspects before the product breaks down when the first set of users starts using it. Tools may be used to measure what the performance is under given circumstances.

The performance testing tools can provide very useful reports based on collected information, often in graphical form. The tools can, relatively inexpensively, provide information about "bottleneck" areas.

Some companies have specialized in performance testing and offer to test products using their tools. This is a very useful alternative to investing in the tools yourself.

Questions

1. When was the concept of static testing first introduced in the software industry?
2. How much of a development budget should be used on static testing?
3. How much does the cost of defect correction increase for each phase a defect "survives"?
4. What are the benefit of static testing?
5. What types of items can be subjected to static testing?
6. What are the static testing types described in this chapter?
7. Why might static testing be a frustrating activity?
8. What are some of the development milestones where static testing may be used?
9. What are the activities in the static testing process?
10. How does the static testing process communicate with the test sub-process management process?
11. What are the three checking directions to be used in static testing?
12. What are the three possible outcomes of a static test?
13. Why are checklists useful in an organization?
14. How should observations from static testing be registered?
15. What are some of the pieces of information to collect for observations?
16. Which states can an observation have?
17. What characterizes an informal review?
18. What characterizes a walk-through?
19. What is the secondary purpose of walk-throughs?
20. What can jeopardize the effectiveness of a walk-through?
21. What are technical reviews also called?
22. Who should participate in a technical review?
23. What is the secondary purpose of technical reviews?
24. What is the test item in management reviews?
25. What is usually the main benefit of management reviews?
26. What characterizes an inspection?
27. What are the two official purposes for an inspection?

28. What are the six activities in an inspection?
29. What are the roles involved in inspections?
30. What is chunking and what is sampling?
31. Why are entry criteria defined for inspection?
32. Why may inspectors be given specific inspector roles?
33. Are inspector roles only useful for inspections?
34. What happens during the overview activity in inspections?
35. What must happen during preparation in inspections?
36. What characterizes a major defect in inspections?
37. What happens during the inspection meeting?
38. What should happen to new issues found during the inspection meeting?
39. What must happen to issues found in basis documents?
40. What are the two main activities in the follow-up?
41. How can inspections contribute to process improvement?
42. Who may perform audits?
43. How should the static testing types to use be selected?
44. Which rule applies when static testing types are mixed?
45. What is static analysis?
46. What is a control flow graph?
47. What can control flow analysis find?
48. What are the advantages of coding standards?
49. What are complexity measures used for?
50. What is the name and the definition of the most used complexity measure?
51. When should we look at the code as perhaps being too complex?
52. How can we get an overview of a website?
53 How is the test effort connected to the "shape" of a website?
54. When can we stop monitoring websites?
55. What are fan-in and fan-out?
56. What is dynamic analysis?
57. What is a memory leak?
58. What can go wrong with pointers?
59. What is coverage?
60. How can a performance problem be reported?

Appendix 4.A   Solution to the Flower Drawing

The drawing shown in Section 4.3.6.1.2 shows the faces of Napoleon, his wife Josephine, and his son Napoleon Jr. as indicated here.

It is a postcard from France from the period when Napoleon was not popular and it was dangerous to support Napoleon openly.

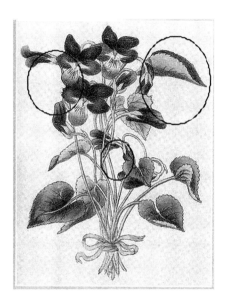

Dynamic Testing

Dynamic testing is the "classic" testing of software in which the test item, the code, is being executed on a computer. Dynamic testing requires something that is executable and a more or less elaborate test environment and is therefore more expensive to perform than static testing. It also usually requires more preparations in the form of the definition of test cases and/or test procedures.

But dynamic testing is indispensable and complements any static testing performed on the basis documentation and the code. *Dynamic testing is the moment of truth*. This is the point at which the actual software product is executed in a way that is as similar as possible to the actual execution that will be required of it when the real users are using it—does it work or does it not work?

The dynamic testing process consists of preparation where the test procedures are gradually derived from the test bases, and the execution of these test procedures. The principles are the same for all types of development from waterfall to agile, though the way to arrange the work and the level of documentation are different.

Don't be put off by the seeming formality of the dynamic testing process as it is described here. The process, that is, the way you perform the test, should always be tailored to the context in which the testing exists. If you do not have to comply with a standard, then you may still use the standard as a source of inspiration and pick the bits you find useful and skip the others.

Test procedures are always based on the expectations for the product, or as we usually say: the requirements. Therefore, this chapter includes a short introduction to requirements and also an introduction to the concept of traceability—the glue that holds the entire development and test effort together.

5.1   Introduction to Dynamic Testing

5.1.1   Dynamic Testing Definition

The ISTQB vocabulary defines dynamic testing as "Testing that involves the execution of the software of a component or system."

The ISO 29119 Standard for Software Testing defines it as "Testing that requires the execution of the test item."

There is, hence, agreement that it is the execution of the software test item that defines dynamic testing.

When we execute the software for dynamic testing, we provide some input, typically in the form of actions and/or data, and we observe how the software reacts. *The system's reaction is the actual result of the test.* If that result is different from the expected result, which we should have determined in advance, then the software has failed—and we say that the *test result* is that the test has failed. When the actual test result is identical to the expected result, then the test result is that the test has passed. This is illustrated in the figure below.

Test Case   **Test execution**

			Expected result
			2

Actual result

Actual result = Expected result => Test result = Passed

Actual result ≠ Expected result => Test result = Failed

The inspiration for what to use as input is derived from the test basis; this is described below.

Dynamic testing should provoke failures so that underlying defects are unveiled. The defects are there when the test item is delivered for testing; dynamic testing does not create the defects; it merely unveils them. The more failures a dynamic test provokes the more successful it is.

A failure is a sign of a defect somewhere in the software. Sometimes it is obvious what the defect is, sometimes it may take a long time to determine what it is; and sometimes the defect may indeed never be found.

5.1.2   Dynamic Test Items

Everything that can be executed on a computer can be a test item for dynamic testing. It may be, for example:

▸ A small piece of code or a script (a component) that is either compiled and executable or directly executable without compilation;

▸ A subsystem made up of components;

◗ A complete system made up of subsystems;

◗ A system-of-systems made up of systems;

◗ An interface and/or coexistence of two components, subsystems, or systems.

Dynamic testing can, and should, start when some executable software has been produced in the product life cycle. The smaller the test item is, the easier it is to determine any defects underlying a failure. It is therefore a good investment to start dynamic testing on the smallest items rather than waiting until larger test items—made up of the smaller ones—are available.

All too often time is spent on finding defects that cause failures during the dynamic testing of a complete system, when the failures could have been provoked in a dynamic test of a component and the defect more easily found.

5.1.3   Dynamic Testing Basis

Testing is comparing what you have to what you expected to get. Hence, one of the activities in dynamic testing is to derive test cases with input (action and/or data) to use, and the associated expected result, so that we can compare the expected result to the actual result we get from the product when we execute a test case.

We therefore need to know what to expect; we need a test basis to test against. Unless we are producing a system just for ourselves, other people will have a stake in the final project and hence some expectations for it.

These expectations are the most important part of the test basis, and they are in principle expressed as requirements. In principle, because expectations may in fact be expressed in many different ways.

In traditional projects expectations are usually expressed as more or less formal requirements, in the form of text and/or graphically.

In agile projects—at least those using Scrum as the management paradigm—expectations are expressed in the project backlog and refined in the sprint backlog. These expectations are usually expressed as user stories or other similar formats.

The expected result for a test case must always be determined from the requirements, in whatever form or shape they exist.

Section 5.3 below provides a very short introduction to requirements.

The inspiration for the input in a test case can come from various sources. It may come from the expectations, or it may come from checklists, the testers' experience, or the source code, depending on which test case design technique we use. Test case design techniques are used to facilitate the determination of which input to use to make the dynamic testing process effective and efficient.

And again, the expectations must be used to determine what the expected result is based on the given input.

5.1.4 Overview of Test Case Design Techniques

A number of test case design techniques been developed over the years to facilitate the derivation of test cases.

The most used test case design techniques are listed here, and described in detail in Chapter 6.

Specification-Based Techniques:

▶ Equivalence partitioning;
▶ Classification tree method;
▶ Boundary value analysis;
▶ Domain analysis;
▶ Syntax testing;
▶ Combinatorial testing;
▶ Decision tables;
▶ Cause-effect graph;
▶ State transition testing;
▶ Scenario testing;
▶ Random testing.

Structure-Based Techniques:

▶ Statement testing;
▶ Decision testing;
▶ Condition testing;
▶ Decision condition;
▶ Modified condition decision testing;
▶ Multiple condition testing;
▶ Path testing;
▶ Intercomponent testing.

Experience-Based Testing Techniques:

▶ Error guessing;
▶ Checklist-based;
▶ Exploratory testing;
▶ Attacks.

Defect-Based Techniques:

▶ Taxonomies;
▶ Fault injection and mutation.

5.2 Dynamic Testing Process

The dynamic testing process includes the following activities:

▶ Test design and implementation;
▶ Test environment setup;
▶ Test execution.

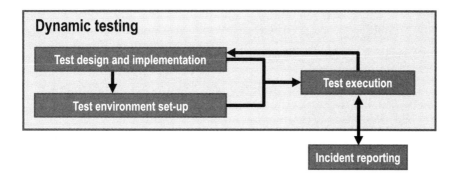

The dynamic testing process has iterations when monitoring of the test execution will show that the completion criteria defined in the pertinent test sub-process plan have not been met. In that case the directives may, for example, be to design some more test cases to obtain higher coverage.

In ISO 29119 the incident reporting activity is included in the dynamic test process to make it clear that incident reporting is a mandatory activity in connection with dynamic testing. In other process models incident reporting is an activity in configuration management, because it is an activity that can be used in connection with almost any other activity during development or maintenance of a product. In this book incident management, including incident reporting, is described in Chapter 8.

5.2.1 Interaction with Other Test Processes

Dynamic testing is performed within the framework of a test sub-process, and will only directly interact with the test sub-process management, as illustrated in the figure below.

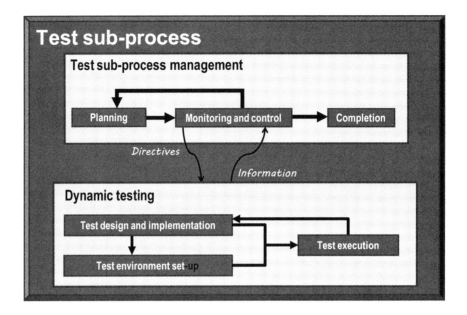

Directives will be issued from the test sub-process management to the dynamic testing process to initiate or stop action during the course of the dynamic test. This may require, for example, relaying a directive for starting the test design.

Information will go the other way from the dynamic testing process to the test sub-process management to keep the test project manager aware of progress and/or problems with the activities. This information may be further relayed and used to update appropriate plans.

When a dynamic test is completed, this must be communicated to the test sub-process.

5.2.2   Detailed Activities

The dynamic test process shown above has three activities, as described below.

5.2.2.1   Test Design and Implementation

The idea in scripted and structured testing is that the way the test is going to be executed is specified in more or less detail before the execution takes place.

The test design and implementation activity can start when the basis documentation is under preparation. A side effect of this is that we get an *extra review* of the basis documentation. Don't forget to feed any incident back through the correct channels.

The activity aims at designing test procedures that provide the required coverage as expressed in the test plan. This is where test case design techniques are a great help.

The test design and implementation activity includes the following subactivities:

- ◗ Identification of feature sets;
- ◗ Derivation of test conditions;
- ◗ Derivation of test coverage items;
- ◗ Derivation of test cases;
- ◗ Assembling of test sets;
- ◗ Derivation of test procedures.

The work is usually highly iterative; it can be quite a puzzle to design the best possible test cases and order those that should be executed in efficient test procedures.

5.2.2.1.1   *Identification of Feature Sets*

A feature set is a logical subset of the test item for a test sub-process, and it should be possible to treat any feature set independently of other feature sets in the subsequent test design work.

At the start of test design, the work is divided into a number of feature sets. The feature sets usually reflect the architecture of the test item and may be seen as the architecture of the test design.

The feature sets identified for a test item must cover the entire test item.

Working with feature sets makes the rest of the test design and implementation process easier to cope with, especially for larger test sub-processes like system tests or acceptance tests.

Test feature sets may also be known as test groups, test topics, or test areas.

The number of test feature sets we can identify depends on the test sub-process and the nature, size, and architecture of the test object:

- ◗ In a component test sub-process we usually have one test feature set per component.
- ◗ For integration testing we may have one or more feature sets per interface, depending on the complexity of the interface, and possibly one or more feature sets for any coexisting test.
- ◗ For system and acceptance test sub-processes, we typically have many tcst feature sets, depending on the size and complexity of the product.

A few examples of useful test feature sets defined for a system test sub-process are:

- ❯ Start and stop of the system;
- ❯ Functionality x;
- ❯ Functionality y;
- ❯ Usability;
- ❯ Performance;
- ❯ Error handling.

5.2.2.1.2   Derivation of Test Conditions

A test condition is a testable aspect of a test item such as a verifiable function, transaction, feature, quality attribute, or structural element identified as a basis for testing.

Test conditions are derived for each of the identified feature sets. They form the contents of a feature set.

The definition of a test condition is rather broad and it may be difficult to find out exactly what the test conditions are. A number of aspects need to be taken into account, including the test sub-process we are dealing with and the formality of the documentation.

Formal documentation makes it easier to derive test conditions. A formal requirement is a good candidate if we are working on a system test, as is a formal detailed design diagram if we are working on a component test. And even though agile development in principle does not produce formal documentation, a user story is also a good candidate for a test condition for a show case test.

With less formal documentation, we may have to extract bits of text from, for example, a functional description for a system test; or we may have to construct a flow diagram based on the actual code we are going to test in a component test.

The important point in derivation of test conditions is that the relevant stakeholders agree on the result and that everything that belongs to a feature set has been identified as a test condition.

Example 1: Test conditions for a system test of the EuroBonus scheme of StarAlliance.

This short description is taken from the SAS website, and could well be from the functional description available to the testers:

"There are 3 member levels: Basis, Silver, Gold. Your member level is determined by the number of Basis Points you earn within your personal 12 month period. You will automatically be upgraded to Silver Member if you earn 20.000 Basis Points during your earning period. If you earn 50.000 Basis Points in the period you a become Gold Member. The earning period runs for 12 month from the first day of joining."

From this we can derive the following test conditions:

TC1.1: A member starts as a Basis member.

TC1.2: A member will automatically be upgraded to Silver Member if he/she earns 20.000 Basis Points during an earning period. If he/she earns 50.000 Basis Points in a period he/she becomes Gold Member.

TC1.3: An earning period is 12 months. The start of a period is the date a member joins.

Note that the text is not copied word for word, but slightly rephrased. We'll have to make sure that the rephrasing is acceptable for the stakeholders.

Example 2: Test condition for a piece of code.
The following piece of code is what we want to test.

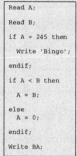

```
Read A;
Read B;
if A = 245 then
    Write 'Bingo';
endif;
if A < B then
    A = B;
else
    A = 0;
endif;
Write BA;
```

To make further test design easier (and as a control of the code), we have drawn a flow diagram based on the code. This is now our test condition:
TC2.1

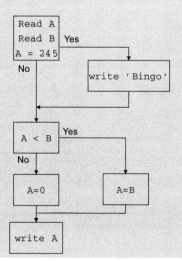

If it is not possible to derive clear and complete test conditions from the test basis, we'll have to ask the stakeholders for clarification—*never guess*.

Even though ISO 29119 is quite specific in its requirements for the contents of a test specification, test conditions are not very often formally documented. They are usually sketched out during the analysis and design work or documented using labeling of requirements or other expressions of expectations.

On the other hand, test conditions may be the way expectations are documented, if they are not otherwise documented.

The decision about how much documentation of test conditions is needed should be based on the strategy and the risks involved.

5.2.2.1.3 Derivation of Test Coverage Items

From ISO 29119: A test coverage item is an attribute or combination of attributes that is derived from one or more test conditions by using a test design technique that enables the measurement of the thoroughness of the test execution.

This definition tells us that we now have to examine the test conditions and decide which test case design technique to use for each. The choice of test case design technique depends on the nature of the test condition and the risk profile for the product. Test case design techniques are described in detail in Chapter 6.

Each test case design technique creates its own type of coverage element. For equivalence partitioning, for example, the coverage element is partition, and for statement testing the coverage element is statement. We will therefore get different types of coverage elements depending on the test case design techniques we use.

Example 1 has the test conditions listed above.

Based on the first two we can derive the following coverage items using equivalence partitioning:

P1: 0–20.000 points earned in a period = Basis Member

P2: 20.001–50.000 points earned in a period = Silver Member

P3: 50.001 or more points earned in a period = Gold Member

Some assumptions have been made here, and there are also things we need to ask the stakeholders, for example: What is the lowest amount of points you earn for a flight, and is there a limit to the number of points you can have?

If we use the boundary value analysis technique on the equivalence partitions, we can derive boundary coverage elements.

Example 2 has the graphical test condition shown above.

If we use the statement test case design technique and directly see the statements in the diagram, we get:

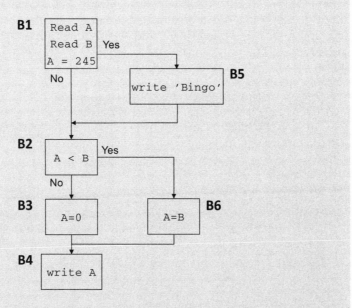

We could also consider each basic block a coverage item; that gives the same result in the end.

5.2.2.1.4   Derivation of Test Cases

A test case is a set of test case preconditions, inputs (including actions, where applicable), and expected results, developed to drive the execution of a test item to meet test objectives, including correct implementation, error identification, checking quality, and other valued information.

Based on the test coverage items, we can now derive test cases.

The test cases we derive should strike the best possible balance between being:

- Effective—having a reasonable probability of detecting errors;
- Exemplary—being practical and with a low redundancy;
- Economic—having a reasonable development cost and return on investment;
- Evolvable—being flexible, structured, and maintainable.

We can derive test cases in two phases; that is, we first derive high-level or logical test cases and then, if it turns out that we are actually going to execute a specific high-level test case, we derive the corresponding low-level (or concrete) test case.

A *high-level test case* is a test case where we don't go into too many details regarding preconditions and expected output, and maybe only sketch the input we are going to use. There are two reasons for this, both based on the fact that it may be difficult and time consuming to determine what an expected output is. One reason is that depending on the required coverage for a test, we may not have to execute all of the derived test cases, and we can save the effort until we know for sure which test cases have been selected for execution. The other reason is that we might be able to cover a number of test coverage items in one test case if we choose the input with care, and we can save the effort until we have determined precisely which to use for a given test case to make it cover more coverage items.

Example 1 has the coverage items listed above.

Based on these we could derive the following high-level test cases:

HTC 1: Check that an earned sum of Basis Points of 0–20.000 incl. for a given member in a period will make that member a Basis Member.

HTC 2: Check that an earned sum of Basis Points of 20.001–50.000 incl. for a given member in a period will make that member a Silver Member.

HTC 3: Check that an earned sum of Basis Points of 50.001–? incl. for a given member in a period will make that member a Gold Member.

From the high-level test cases, we go on to define the low-level test cases. Before we do that we might have created a test set (see below), so that we know which test cases we are going to execute. It is not always necessary to execute all of the test cases we have identified; the test cases to be executed must be selected based on the coverage requirements and the risk profile for the product.

A *low-level test case is* a test case with specific values defined for both the input and the expected result.

One low-level test case created from the list of high-level test cases above could be:

Test Case: 3.6 (17)

Objective: The purpose of the test case is to test that when the sum of earned points gets to 20.001 or more during a period for a member, then the member status will be augmented to Silver Member.	
Priority: 1	**Traceability:** TC1.2; P2
Precondition: The current sum of Basis Point for Mrs. Hass is 14.300. Mrs. Hass' member status is Basis Member. The system is ready for entry of newly earned Basis Points for Mrs. Hass.	
Input: Enter 6.500 and press [OK].	
Expected result: The sum of points is now shown as 20.800, and Mrs. Hass' member status is shown as Silver Member.	

The expected result must be determined from the basis documentation where the expectations for the coverage item(s) are described.

The expected results should be provided in full, including not only visible outputs but also the final state of the software under test and its environment. This may include a new current form on the screen, changed stored data, printed reports, etc.

We may, for example, have the following test cases, where the first gives a visible output and the second does not give a visible output, but makes a new form current.

Case	Input	Expected result
1.	Enter "2" in the field "Number of journeys:"	The value in the field "Total points:" is the value in field "Points per journey:" x 2.
2.	Try to enter "10" in the field "Number of journeys:"	The value in the field "Total points:" is unchanged. An error message pop-up is current and showing error message no. 314.

There are two rules concerning the determination of the expected result:

1. *The expected result must never, ever be derived from the code,* only from the expectations (otherwise you are testing that the code works as it works).

2. If it turns out that it is not possible to identify the expected result from the test basis, you must *never, ever just guess or assume—ask for clarification.*

Sometimes it can be difficult to determine the expected result from the basis documentation. In such cases an oracle may be used. Oracles are discussed under tools in Section 9.3.2.

It cannot be pointed out strongly enough that if you guess or assume what the expected result may be, *you are wasting everybody's time.* The chance of your getting it wrong is much higher that your chance of getting it right.

You also prevent your organization from getting better, because the people responsible for the documentation of the expectations will never know that they should and could do a better job. Go and talk to the people: Point out what you need to be able to test, make suggestions based on your test experience, use some of the test case design techniques to express the expectations, for example decision tables, and help make the basis documentation better. It is worth it.

As you work with the test cases, it should become clear which *test environment and test data* you need to be able to execute the test cases. The test environment and test data requirements should be identified and communicated to those responsible for establishing the test environment and test data, respectively.

The requirements for the test environment and test data must be as specific as possible in order to get the right test environment established at the right time (and at the right cost). Beware—*the setting up of this is often a bottleneck* in the dynamic testing process, mostly because the requirements are insufficiently described, underestimated, and/or not taken seriously enough. Either the environment and test data are not established in time for the actual test execution to begin and/or they are not established according to the requirements. If the test environment and test data are not ready when the test item is ready for the test to be executed, *it jeopardizes the test schedule.* If it is not correct *it jeopardizes the validity of the test.*

The test environment and test data requirements should be specified as part of the activity of deriving test cases—or at the latest when the test procedures are derived as described below, and in time for them to be ready, when they are needed for execution of the test.

The test environment could, for example, include:

- Hardware—to run on and/or to interface with;
- Software—on the test platform and other applications to interface with;
- Peripherals (printers including correct paper, fax, CD reader/burner);
- Network—provider agreements, access, hardware, and software;
- Tools and utilities;
- Data—actual test data, anonymization, security, and roll-back facilities;
- Other aspects—security, load patterns, timing, and availability;
- Physical environment (room, furniture, conditions);
- Communication (phones, Internet, paper forms, paper, word processor or the like);
- Sundry (paper, pencils, coffee, candy, fruit, water).

It is not possible to provide general guidelines for test data; that depends entirely on the expectations for the product.

5.2.2.1.5   Assembling of Test Sets

A test set is a collection of test cases selected for execution for a specific purpose or for another reason, for example, that they require the same specific test environment. Assembling test cases is the first activity in the test implementation phase.

The objective may be, for example, to execute enough test cases to reach the coverage required in the test plan for a specific test sub-process, for example, a system test. The test cases are selected from the derived test cases based on the required coverage, the risk profile, and/or the priority of the test cases.

At a later point in time, the objective may be, for example, to execute a retest and associated regression test following defect corrections. In this case it is likely that fewer test cases will be selected than for the first execution.

The assembling of test cases to form a specific test set is done by pointing out the desired test cases among all of the derived test cases. In practice, the assembling of a test set may be done by labeling the selected test cases kept in, for example, a database or a spreadsheet.

The completion criteria for a component test could include a demand for 85% decision coverage.

5.2.2.1.6 Derivation of Test Procedures

A test procedure is a recipe for the execution of the test cases in a test set.

The test cases selected in a test set are ordered in a reasonable order, so that the execution of one test case establishes the precondition(s) for the next test case.

A test procedure is initiated with any actions that are necessary to establish the preconditions for the first test case in the procedure.

It may be necessary to include actions to wrap up after the execution of the last test case in the procedure.

During the derivation of the test procedures for a specific test, the requirements for the test environment and test data may be refined.

5.2.2.2 Test Environment Setup

The test environment, here considered to include the test data, is a necessary prerequisite for test execution—without a correct environment the test is either not executable at all or the results will be open to doubt.

The environment requirements are outlined in the test plan based on the strategy. The test plan also describes by whom and when the test environment is to be created and maintained. Additional requirements for the environment are identified during the test analysis and implementation activity and documented as test environment and test data requirements. The exact requirements for test data needed to execute test procedures may only be determined quite close to the actual execution, and it is therefore important that planning and facilities for setting up specific test data are well prepared in advance of the execution.

Problems with the test environment may force testing to be executed in other less suitable environments. The testing could be executed in inappropriate

competition with other teams and projects. If we test in the development environment, test results can be unpredictable for inexplicable reasons due to the instability of this environment. In the worst case, testing is executed in the production environment, where the risk to the business can be significant.

The specific requirements for the test environment differ from test sub-process to test sub-process. In any case the test environment should resemble the future production environment as much as possible and feasible.

In some cases it may be *too expensive, dangerous,* or *time consuming* to establish such a test environment, for example, for products that are required to destroy something under certain circumstances. If this is the case dynamic testing may be unexecutable and other test methods, such as inspection of the code, might need to be used to verify the product.

The people responsible for establishing the test environment should do so based on the requirements and report back to the test management when they are ready. The established test environment, including test data, should be verified before the actual test execution starts.

As the test execution progresses, the test environment, including test data, must be maintained so that it is always valid according to the test plan. This is due to the facts that the execution of test procedures will change the initial environment and that the different test procedures may have a different test environment and test data requirements. The maintenance may include resetting or changing database contents, adding or removing peripherals and/or tools, and changing available interfaces.

5.2.2.3   Test Execution
5.2.2.3.1   Executing Test Procedures
Test execution can begin when the time is right according to the plan and when everything is ready, that is, when the given entry criteria for the test executions are fulfilled. Entry criteria may include:

- ▶ The test item is ready, having passed earlier tests.
- ▶ The test specification is ready and approved by the stakeholders.
- ▶ The people scheduled to participate in the test execution are available and properly trained and briefed.
- ▶ The production is ready to support the execution, if needed.
- ▶ Support processes, not least configuration management including incident management, are in place. Support processes are discussed in Chapter 1.

The actual execution of the test procedures is what everybody has been waiting for: The moment of truth! But even though we are eager to start the test execution, we should *not be tempted to make a false start.* We need to make sure that the execution entry criteria have been fulfilled.

If the test object has not passed the entry criteria defined for it, do not start the test execution. You will waste your time, and you risk teaching the developers and others that they don't need to take the entry criteria seriously.

In structured testing, in principle all that the testers have to do during test execution is to follow the test specification and register all incidents along the way. If the execution is done by a tool, this is exactly what will happen.

We have taken great care in writing the test procedures, and it is important to follow them. There are several reasons for this:

▶ We need to be able to collect actual time spent and compare this with the estimates to improve our estimation techniques.

▶ We need to be able to compare the progress with the plan.

▶ We need to be able to repeat the tests exactly as they were executed before for the sake of retesting and regression testing.

▶ In some cases it should be possible to make a complete audit of the test.

None of this is possible if we don't follow the specification, but omit or add activities as we please.

There is nothing wrong with getting new ideas for additional test cases to improve the test specification during the execution. In fact, we neither can—nor should—avoid it. But in structured testing such new ideas should be treated as incidents (enhancement requests) for the test. If we are performing more free test execution, for example, using experienced-based testing, then we are of course free to follow any new idea.

5.2.2.3.2 Identifying Failures

For each test case we execute, the actual result should be logged and compared to the expected result, defined as part of the test case, and the test result (pass or fail) should be determined and logged. This can be done in various ways depending on the formality of the test. For fairly informal testing a tick mark, √, is sufficient to indicate when the actual result matched the expected result (a pass). For more formal testing, for example, for safety critical software, the authorities require that the actual result be recorded explicitly. This could be in the form of screen dumps, included reports, or simply writing the actual result in the log. This type of logging may also serve as part of the proof that the test has actually been executed.

We need to be very careful when we compare the expected result with the actual result, in order not to miss failures (called false-positives) or report correct behavior as failures (called false-negatives).

(Note that the ISTQB definitions are the inverse:

▶ False-positive result = false-fail result: A test result in which a defect is reported although no such defect actually exists in the test object.

▶ False-negative result = false-pass result: A test result that fails to identify the presence of a defect that is actually present in the test object.

You may use the definitions you are comfortable with as long as they are agreed on within your organization.)

If the actual outcome does not comply with the expected outcome, we have a failure on our hands. Any failure must be reported in the incident management system. The reported incident will then follow the defined incident life cycle. Incident reporting and handling are discussed in Chapter 8.

It is worth spending sufficient time reporting the incident we get. Too little time spent on reporting an incident may result in wasted time during the analysis of the incident. In the worst case it may be impossible to reproduce the failure if we are not specific enough in reporting the circumstances and the symptoms.

Don't forget that the failure may be a symptom of a defect in the work products, like the test environment, the test data, the prerequisites, the expected result, and/or the way the execution was carried out. Such failures should also be reported in order to get the defect corrected, and gather information for process improvement.

5.2.2.3.3   Test Execution Logging

As we execute, manually or by the use of a tool, we must log what is going on. We must record the precise identification of the test item, the test environment, and test procedures we use. We must also log the result of the checking, as discussed above. Last but not least we must log any significant events that have an effect on the testing.

The recording of this information serves a number of purposes. It is indispensable in a professional and well-performed test.

The test execution may be logged in many different ways and is often supported by a test management tool. Sometimes the event registration is kept separate in a test journal or diary.

It is handy and efficient if the test procedure has built-in logging facilities that allow us to use it for test logging as we follow it for test execution. An example of this is shown below.

Test procedure: P11 (3)

Objective: This test procedure tests …	
Priority: 2	
Start-Up: The form F1 must be current.	
Relationships to Other: None	
Expected Duration: 15 min.	
Execution Time: *Log when* **Initials:** *Log who*	
System: *Identify item etc.* **Result:** *Log overall test result*	

Case	Input	Expected Output	Actual Output
3.6 (17)	Enter…	The sum …	*Log result*
3.8 (18)	Enter…	The value..	

Stop and Wrap Up: Run the "Clean 1" script.

The information about which test procedures have been executed and with what overall results should be available at any given time. This information is used to monitor the progress of the testing.

The identification of the test item and the test procedure may be used to ensure that possible retesting after defect correction is done on the correct version of the test item (the new version) using the correct version of the test procedure (the old or a new version as the case might be).

The rationale—the tracing to the coverage items—can be used to calculate test coverage measures. These are used in the subsequent checking for test completion.

Information about who executed the test may be useful in connection with defect finding, for example, if it turns out to be difficult for the developer to reproduce a failure or understand a defect report.

5.2.3   Produced Documentation
The tangible outcomes of the performance of a dynamic test process are:

▶ Test specification, split into:
  ▶ Test design specification;

- ▶ Test case specification;
- ▶ Test procedure specification.
- ▶ Test environment requirement;
- ▶ Test data requirement;
- ▶ Test environment readiness report;
- ▶ Test data readiness report;
- ▶ Test execution documentation, split into:
  - ▶ Actual results;
  - ▶ Test results;
  - ▶ Test execution log.

The contents of the documents may be as described below.

5.2.3.1   Test Specification

A test specification is created to document the decisions made during the test design and implementation and to facilitate the execution.

The test specification may be split into three chapters or individual documents:

- ▶ Test Design Specification;
- ▶ Test Case Specification;
- ▶ Test Procedure Specification.

This will make it easier to handle a potentially large test specification, and may also facilitate parallel design and implementation work, if needed.

5.2.3.1.1   Test Specification Contents

All documents should include some document-specific information. This should adhere to the organization's convention for document identification if there is one; see Section 3.1.4.1.1 for an example.

5.2.3.1.2   Test Design Specification

5.2.3.1.2.1   Test Design Specification Contents

Inspired by ISO 29119 the following table of contents for a test design specification is suggested. This may, of course, be tailored to the individual situation.

Note that Section 5.2.3.1.2.2 below provides example of the contents of a test design specification; you might want to look at this as you read the description of the contents.

1. Feature set

    1.1   Unique identifier

    This section should provide a unique, short identification of the feature set. This is usually in the form of a number, possibly with a prefix to ensure uniqueness across test sub-processes in a test project.

    1.2   Objective

    This section should provide a description of the feature set. It usually has the form of a meaningful title.

    1.3   Priority

    This section should provide a priority for the feature set based on an agreed scale for feature set priority.

    1.4   Specific strategy

    This section should provide any specific guidelines for handling the testing of the feature set based on the relevant test strategy.

    1.5   Traceability

    This section should provide references to the expectations. This is usually not very detailed, because the more detailed traceability will be provided for test conditions, test coverage items, and/or test cases.

2. Test condition

    2.1   Unique identifier

    This section should provide a unique, short identification of the test condition. This is usually in the form of a number, possibly with a prefix to ensure uniqueness across the feature sets for the test sub-process.

    2.2   Description

    This section should provide either the test conditions or a reference to where it is defined in the test basis. The test conditions may be expressed in text or graphically.

    2.3   Priority

    This section should provide a priority for the test condition based on an agreed-on scale for test condition priority.

    2.4   Traceability

    This section should provide references to the expectations.

5.2.3.1.2.2   Test Design Specification Example

The table below provides an example of some feature sets identified for the system test of the EuroBonus scheme of StarAlliance, used in the example above. The example here is rather short, but I hope it may serve as inspiration.

Feature Sets				
ID	**Objective**	**P**	**Specific Strategy**	**Trace**
S1 (1)	This feature set covers creation and maintenance of member information.	2	None	Req. 67—115
S5 (2)	This feature set covers calculation of earned points and handling of member status.	1	Classification tree method must be used to derive coverage items for period handling.	Req. 22—53 + 67—81
S6 (3)	This feature set covers handling of special offers to members.	3	None	Req. 318—336

The table below provides an example of some test conditions derived from the feature sets for the EuroBonus scheme of StarAlliance. Again the example is rather short, but hopefully inspirational.

Test Conditions for Feature Set S1			
ID	**Description**	**P**	**Trace**
S1.4 (1)	Creating new member	1	Req. 67—71
S1.5 (2)	Changing personal member information	2	Req. 72—93
S1.1 (3)	Manual change of earned points	1	Req. 104—111
S1.2 (4)	Deleting members		Req. 112—115

Note that it is not very common to document the test design as thoroughly as described here. Often a list of feature sets with a short purpose description and list of the test conditions for each is sufficient.

The *unique identification* is the number in brackets, for example (4). The number before the unique identifier is the sorting order, for example 2.1, to ensure that the feature sets and test conditions are presented in a logical order independently of the unique number. The "disorder" of the unique identification is a sign of the iterative way in which they have been designed. Often, a running number, that changes as, for example, the feature sets are changed around, is used as the unique identifier; this is a very bad idea and may cause a lot of trouble during the creation of the test design specification.

5.2.3.1.2.3   Test Design Specification Mapping ISTQB/ISO 29119

There is no explicit equivalence to the ISO 29119 test design specification in the ISTQB syllabi. The division of the work into feature sets or the like is not mentioned. Test conditions are mentioned, but not explicitly defined in this context (but in the context of structure-based test case design techniques).

IEEE 829:1998 operates with the concept of a test design, which resembles a feature set.

The table below therefore presents a mapping between the IEEE description of the contents of a test design plan and the table of contents for a feature set and a test condition provided in ISO 29119. A blank entry means that there is no equivalence.

Note that IEEE 829 is superseded by ISO 29119.

ISTQB (IEEE 829–1998)	ISO 29119:2013
Features to be tested (test conditions)	Feature set: Traceability
Approach refinement	Feature set: Specific strategy
List of high-level test cases	All test conditions
List of expected test procedures	
Feature pass/fail criteria	
Test design specification approvals	

5.2.3.1.3   *Test Case Specification*

5.2.3.1.3.1   Test Case Specification Contents

Inspired by ISO 29119 the following table of contents for a test case specification is suggested. This may, of course, be tailored to the individual situation.

Note that Section 5.2.2.1.4 above provides an example of test coverage items and an example of a test case.

1. **Test coverage item**

    1.1   **Unique identifier**

    This section should provide a unique, short identification of the test coverage item. This is usually in the form of a number, possibly with a prefix to ensure uniqueness across the feature sets for the test sub-process.

    1.2   **Description**

    This section should provide either the test coverage item or a reference to where it is defined in the test basis. The test coverage item may be expressed in text or graphically.

    1.3   **Priority**

    This section should provide a priority for the coverage item based on an agreed-on scale for coverage item priority.

1.4 Traceability
This section should provide references to the test basis.

2. Test case

2.1 Unique identifier
This section should provide a unique, short identification of the test case. This is usually in the form of a number, possibly with a prefix to ensure uniqueness across test sub-processes in a test project.

2.2 Objective
This section should provide a description of the purpose of the test case. This may be in the form of a paraphrasing of the requirements that the test case covers or a meaningful title.

2.3 Priority
This section should provide a priority for the test case based on an agreed-on scale for test case priority.

2.4 Traceability
This section should provide detailed references to the test basis.

2.5 Preconditions
This section should provide a comprehensive description of the state of the test item and the test environment, including the state that the test data must be in before the execution of the test case can begin.

2.6 Input
This section should provide a comprehensive description of the actions and/or data that must be given to the test item to make it react as expected.

2.7 Expected results
This section should provide a detailed description of the expected reaction of the test item as a result of giving the input to it.

2.8 Actual results and test result
These sections may be included in the test case as placeholders for logging the actual result and the test result obtained during execution of the test case.

5.2.3.1.3.2 Test Case Specification Example
Section 5.2.2.1.4 above provides an example of test coverage items and an example of a test case.

Test Case Specification Mapping ISTQB/ISO 29119

ISTQB defines a coverage item as "An entity or property used as a basis for test coverage, e.g., equivalence partitions or code statements"; but does not use it. IEEE 829–1998 has no clear concept of test coverage. Both, however, describe the concept of a test case.

The table below therefore only presents a mapping between the IEEE description of the contents of a test case. A blank entry means that there is no equivalence.

Note that IEEE 829 is superseded by ISO 29119.

ISTQB (IEEE 829–1998)	ISO 29119:2013
	Unique identifier
Objective	Objective
	Priority
	Traceability
Preconditions	Preconditions
Test data requirements	Input
Expected results	Expected results
Postconditions	

5.2.3.1.4 Test Procedure Specification

5.2.3.1.4.1 Test Procedure Specification Contents

Inspired by ISO 29119 the following table of contents for a test procedure specification is suggested. This may, of course, be tailored to the individual situation.

1. **Test set**

   1.1 **Unique identifier**
   This section should provide a unique, short identification of the test set. This is usually in the form of a number, possibly with a prefix to ensure uniqueness across test sub-processes in a test project.

   1.2 **Objective**
   This section should provide a description of the test set. It usually has the form of a meaningful title.

   1.3 **Priority**
   This section should provide a priority for the test set based on an agreed-on scale for test set priority.

   1.4 **Contents (Traceability)**
   This section should provide references to the test basis.

2. Test procedures

2.1 Unique identifier

This section should provide a unique, short identification of the test procedure. This is usually in the form of a number, possibly with a prefix to ensure uniqueness across test sub-processes in a test project.

2.2 Objective

This section should provide a description of the test procedure. It usually has the form of a meaningful title.

2.3 Priority

This section should provide a priority for the test procedure based on an agreed-on scale for test procedure priority.

2.4 Start-up

This section should provide the necessary actions to get the test environment ready for execution of the test procedure. This is usually derived from the preconditions for the first test case in the test procedure.

2.5 Test cases to be executed (traceability)

This section should provide a list of the test cases that form the test procedure, in execution order. It may be in the form of the full test cases, or references (traceability) to the test cases described in details elsewhere, for example, in a tool.

2.6 Relationship to other procedures

This section should provide information about any relationships that this test procedure may have to others. It may be, for example, that another test procedure should always be executed before this (or the environment be set up as if it had).

2.7 Stop and wrap-up

This section should provide any information needed to bring the execution to a graceful stop, and facilitate the start of executions of other test procedures, for example, resetting of the test data.

5.2.3.1.4.2 Test Procedure Specification Example

The table below provides an example of a test set.

Test set: 1.3 (4)
Objective: Test of Member Status determination
Priority: 2
Contents: Test case 15—23, 54—89, 218

Note that the unique identification of the test cases is used to point to the test cases in the test set.

Section 5.2.2.3.3 above provides an example of a test procedure. Note that this example shows a test procedure aimed at manual execution. Test procedures can of course also be produced using a tool and/or aimed for automated execution. An automatically executable test procedure is often referred to as a test script, and it may come in many different forms depending on the tool used.

5.2.3.1.4.3 Test Procedure Specification Mapping

Even though ISTQB syllabi include a process called Test Implementation, it is not explicit concerning the concepts of test sets and test procedures.

IEEE 829 does not cover the concept of a test set either. It does provide a test procedure example, but that is very elaborate and does not seem to correspond to the test procedure defined in ISO 29119.

There is hence no mapping possible for the ISO 29119 test procedure specification to either ISTQB or IEEE 829.

5.2.3.2   Test Environment Requirements

The test environments requirements are specified to *document the needs for the test environment* identified during derivation of test cases and derivation of test procedures.

As mentioned above test environment requirements should be documented thoroughly to ensure that the right environment is present when test execution starts.

5.2.3.2.1   Test Environment Requirements Contents

All documents should include some document-specific information. This should adhere to the organization's convention for document identification if there is one; see Section 3.1.4.1.1 for an example.

Inspired by ISO 29119 the following table of contents for test environment requirements is suggested. This may, of course, be tailored to the individual situation.

1. **Test environment requirements**
   1.1   **Unique identifier**
   This section should provide a unique, short identification of each test environment requirement. This is usually in the form of a number, possibly with a prefix to ensure uniqueness across test sub-processes in a test project.

1.2 Description

This section should provide detailed information about the specific piece of environment needed.

1.3 Responsibility

This section should provide information about the organizational unit or person responsible for providing the specified piece of environment.

1.4 Period needed

This section should provide detailed information about when the described piece of test environment is needed. It is especially important to specify when the piece of environment is first needed

5.2.3.2.2 Test Environment Requirements Example

The table and text below provide a small excerpt of test environment requirements.

Detailed Test Environment Requirements		
ID	**Description**	**Responsible**
ER1	Hardware: Three PCs	Production
ER2	Software: MS Windows 7 or later	Production
...		
ERn	Security controls are identified in the Corporation Security Protocol.	Security manager
ERm	Refer to the Test Plan for relevant testing tools.	Production and development.
...		

Note that all data are needed for the entire system testing period; please refer to the system test plan [PTP].

5.2.3.2.2.1 Test Environment Requirements Mapping

There is no corresponding information item to map to.

5.2.3.3 Test Data Requirements

The test data requirements are specified to *document the need for test data* identified during derivation of test cases and derivation of test procedures.

As mentioned above test data requirements should be documented thoroughly to ensure that the right data are present when test execution starts.

5.2.3.3.1 Test Data Requirements Contents

All documents should include some document-specific information. This should adhere to the organization's convention for document identification if there is one; see Section 3.1.4.1.1 for an example.

Inspired by ISO 29119 the following table of contents for test data requirements is suggested. This may, of course, be tailored to the individual situation.

1. Test data requirements

   1.1 Unique identifier
   This section should provide a unique, short identification of the test data requirement. This is usually in the form of a number, possibly with a prefix to ensure uniqueness across test sub-processes in a test project.

   1.2 Description
   This section should provide detailed information about the test data that is required. The more detailed the better the chance of getting the test data that is needed.

   1.3 Responsibility
   This section should provide information about the organizational unit or person responsible for providing the specified test data.

   1.4 Period needed
   This section should provide detailed information about when the described test data is needed. It is especially important to specify when the data is first needed.

   1.5 Resetting needs
   This section should provide details about when the specified data should be restored. Data is usually changed during execution of test procedures, so test data might need to be restored to be available for further execution of test procedures.

   1.6 Archiving or disposal
   This section should provide details of what is going to happen to test data when is has been used during execution of test procedure(s) and is no longer immediately needed for the present test. Maybe the data should be archived for future use, maybe it should be disposed of, for example if it is confidential.

5.2.3.3.2 Test Data Requirements Example

The table and text below provide a small example of test data requirements.

Detailed Test Data Requirements				
ID	Description	Responsible	Reset	A/D
DR1	At least 20 members for various countries in the database.	Production	Yes	A
DR2	An ordinary user and a system administration user.	Production	N/A	D
...				
DRn	Table with 5 different trips with different points.	Production	N/A	A
DRm	Table with membership status and necessary point to obtain each.	Production	NA	A
...				

All data is needed for the entire system testing period; please refer to the system test plan [PTP].

Resetting "Yes" means that the IT department has to be able to restore the original database on request.

5.2.3.3.2.1 Test Data Requirements Mapping
There is no corresponding information item to map to.

5.2.3.4 Test Environment or Data Readiness Report
A test environment report and a test data readiness report are identical in structure, and are therefore described as one here.

5.2.3.4.1 Test Environment or Data Readiness Report Contents
The two reports are identical in structure and the contents are therefore presented once here.

All documents should include some document-specific information. This should adhere to the organization's convention for document identification if there is one; see Section 3.1.4.1.1 for an example.

Inspired by ISO 29119 the following table of contents for an environment readiness report or a data readiness report is suggested. This may, of course, be tailored to the individual situation.

1. Test environment/data readiness report
    1.1 Unique identifier
    This section should provide a unique, short identification of the test data requirement or test environment requirement that is being reported, respectively.

    1.2 Description of status
    This section should provide the status of the test data or test environment item status.

5.2.3.4.2 Test Environment or Data Readiness Report Contents Example

The table below provides an example of a readiness report that may be for either a test environment or test data.

Requirement	Status	Comments
DR1	Delayed	Due to database maintenance, the data migration to the test environment will be complete by March 22, 2008.
...		
DRn	Ready	
DRn+1	Ready	
...		

5.2.3.4.2.1 Test Environment or Data Readiness Report Mapping

There is no corresponding information item to map to.

5.2.3.5 Test Execution Log

In the test execution log larger events happening during the execution of the test are logged. This information may be useful when the course of the test is analyzed.

5.2.3.5.1 Test Execution Log Contents

All documents should include some document-specific information. This should adhere to the organization's convention for document identification if there is one; see Section 3.1.4.1.1 for an example.

Inspired by ISO 29119 the following table of contents for a test execution log is suggested. This may, of course, be tailored to the individual situation.

1. Event

   1.1 Unique identifier

This section should provide a unique, short identification of the event.

   1.2 Time

This section should provide the precise time when the event occurred. It might not need to be down to seconds, but still precise enough to be useful.

   1.3 Description

This section should provide a precise description of what happened.

1.4   Impact

This section should provide a specification of the impact the event has had or might have on the test in question.

5.2.3.5.2   Test Execution Log Contents Example

The table below provides an example of a test execution log. The example is an extract of a longer log.

ID	Time	Description	Impact
L1	09:50	No connection to external system CAV	Will return
L2	11:10	No more paper in the printer	30 min. delay
...			
Ln	15:40	User representative had to leave	Only one witness
...			

5.2.3.5.2.1   Test Execution Log Mapping ISTQB / ISO 29119

The table below presents a mapping between the IEEE 829 description of a test log and the ISO Test Execution Log. A blank entry means that there is no equivalence.

Note that IEEE 829 is superseded by ISO 29119.

ISTQB (IEEE 829–1998)	ISO 29119:2013
Log identifier	Unique identifier
	Time
Description of the test	
Activity and event entries	Description
	Impact

5.2.3.6   Incident Report

The contents of an incident report are covered in Chapter 8.

5.3   Short Introduction to Requirements

This book is about testing, not requirements. A short introduction to requirements is, however, given in this section. The purpose is to make testers understand requirements better, and equip them to take part in the work with the requirements and help to get the requirements expressed in a way that facilitates their use as a basis for all testing.

All product development starts with the definition of expectations or requirements for the product. These expectations are the ultimate basis for all testing related to the specific product, as described above.

5.3.1 Requirement Levels

Requirements are usually defined at different levels, for example:

▶ Business requirements;
▶ User requirements;
▶ System requirements.

Requirements come from different stakeholders. Different stakeholders speak different "languages" and the requirements must be expressed in ways that allow the appropriate stakeholders to understand, approve, and use them.

The organization and top management "speak" money—they express business requirements. Business requirements may be tested, but most often they are not tested explicitly, but are instead evaluated after implementation of the product.

The users say "support of my work procedures"—they express user requirements. User requirements are usually tested in the acceptance testing.

Following a possible product design, where the product is split up into , for example, a software system and a hardware system, we must express the system requirements. The software requirements are used by the software developers and testers and they are tested in the system testing, and used as basis in other test sub-processes, for example, component testing.

5.3.2 Requirement Types

The requirement specification at each level must cover all types of requirements.

The most obvious requirements type is the functional requirements. No functionality => no system. But as important as it may be, functionality is not enough.

We must have some requirements expressing how the functionality should behave and present itself. These requirements are usually known as nonfunctional requirements. We could also call them functionality-enhancement requirements, because they express how the functionality

should be enhanced by, for example, a reasonable performance and/or a high level of usability. These requirements are discussed in detail in Chapter 7.

The functional and nonfunctional requirements together form the product quality requirements.

On top of this we may have environment requirements. These are requirements that are given from the environment (in the greatest meaning of the word) the system is going to work in, and these requirements are not open to discussion. They can come both from inside and outside of the organization, and can be derived from standards or other given circumstances. Environment requirements may define the browser(s) a Web system must be able to work on, or a specific standard to be complied with, for example.

To make the requirements tower balance, we need to have project requirements (or constraints) to carry the other requirements. These are cost, resources, and time related, and the concern of project management.

5.3.3 Requirement Styles

Requirements can be expressed in many ways. Typical styles are statements and models, including tables and graphic models.

The most common style is perhaps the statement style. Here each requirement is expressed as a single (or very few) sentences in natural language. The template shown below is very useful when writing requirements.

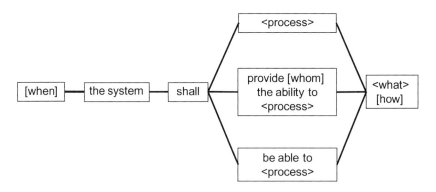

If there is no "when" condition, start the requirement with:

"The system shall ..."—to keep focus on the product or system.

Then proceed to how the system shall act (i.e., do automatically, provide a user the ability to do, or be able to do) and end with what and possibly how.

An example of such a requirement is:

"The system shall provide the administrator the ability to change a selected customer's telephone number."

Other rules for good requirements include:

- ◗ Avoid synonyms—stick to a defined vocabulary.
- ◗ Avoid subjective words (useful, high, easy)—requirements must be testable.
- ◗ Avoid generalities like "etc." and "and so on"—this is impolite; think the issue through.
- ◗ Be aware of "and" and "or"—is this really two or more requirements?

To make statement requirements more precise and testable, we can use metrics and include information such as the scale to use, the way to measure, the target, and maybe acceptable limits. This is especially important for nonfunctional requirements!

Examples of such requirements are:

[56] The system shall ensure that the maximum response time for showing the results of the calculation described in requirements 65 shall be 5 milliseconds in 95% of at least 50 measurements made with 10 simultaneous users on the system.

[UR.73] The system shall ensure that it takes a representative user (a registered nurse) no more than 30 minutes to perform the task described in use case 134 the first time.

A *task* is a series of actions designed to achieve a goal. Task styles may be stories, a scenario, a task list, or a use case. Requirements expressed in these ways are easy to understand, and they are typically used to express user requirements. They are easy to derive high-level test cases and procedures from.

A *model* is a small representation of an existing or planned object. Model can be domain models, prototypes, data models, or state machines.

A *table* is a compact collection and arrangement of related information. Tables may be used for parameter values, decision rules, or details for models.

The styles may be mixed within each of the requirement specifications so that the most appropriate style is always chosen for a requirement.

5.3.4 Requirements for Requirements

Requirements need to conform to certain quality criteria. The quality criteria may include that the requirements are:

- ◗ Harmonized—at the same level of abstraction;
- ◗ Prioritized—marked regarding importance;
- ◗ Unambiguous—have only one possible interpretation;

‣ Valid and current—reflect a true need;

‣ Correct—reflect the stakeholders' needs;

‣ Consistent—in agreement with each other;

‣ Verifiable (testable)—possible to determine fulfillment;

‣ Implementable—possible to fulfill;

‣ Traceable—both individually and as a set;

‣ Complete—full sentences or models without holes;

‣ Understandable—making sense to stakeholders.

5.4   Traceability

References are an important part of the information to be documented in the test specification. A few words are needed about these.

There are two sets of references:

‣ References between test specification elements;

‣ References from test specification elements to basis documentation.

The first set of references describes the structure of the elements in the test specification. These may be quite complex with, for example, test cases belonging to more test procedures and more test groups.

The references to the basis documentation enable traceability between what we are testing and how we are testing it. This is very important information. Ultimately traceability should be possible between test cases and coverage items in the basis documentation.

You should be able to see the traces from the test cases to the coverage items. This will help you identify if there are test cases that do not trace to any coverage item—in which case the test case is superfluous, and should be removed (or maybe a specification like a requirement or two should be added!). This "backward" trace is also very helpful if you need to identify which coverage item(s) a test case is covering, for example, if the execution of the test case provokes a failure.

You should also be able to see the traces from the coverage items to the test cases. This can be used to show if a coverage item has no trace, and hence is not covered by a test case (yet!). This "forward" trace will also make it possible to quickly identify the test case(s) that may be affected if a coverage item, say, a requirement, is changed.

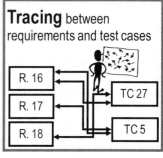

If the coverage items and the test cases are uniquely identified, preferably with a short identifier, it is easy to register and use the trace information.

Instead of writing the trace(s) to the coverage item(s) for each test case, it is a good idea to collect the trace information in trace tables. This can be done using a typical office automation system, such as in a Word table, Excel, or (best) a relational database.

The example below is an extract of two tables, showing the "forward" and the "backward" traces between test cases and requirements, respectively.

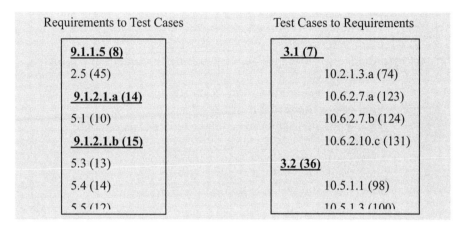

Requirements to Test Cases	Test Cases to Requirements
9.1.1.5 (8)	**3.1 (7)**
2.5 (45)	10.2.1.3.a (74)
9.1.2.1.a (14)	10.6.2.7.a (123)
5.1 (10)	10.6.2.7.b (124)
9.1.2.1.b (15)	10.6.2.10.c (131)
5.3 (13)	**3.2 (36)**
5.4 (14)	10.5.1.1 (98)
5.5 (12)	10.5.1.3 (100)

Questions

1. Why is dynamic testing called "dynamic"?
2. What are the concepts of expected result, actual result, and test result?
3. From where must the expected result be derived?
4. What are test case design techniques used for?
5. What are the activities in the process of dynamic testing?
6. How does the dynamic testing process communicate with the test sub-process management?
7. What are the subactivities in the test design and implementation activity?
8. What is a feature set?
9. What is a test condition?
10. What is a coverage item?
11. What is a test case?
12. What is the difference between a high-level and a low-level test case?
13. What are the two rules for an expected result?
14. What might the test environment include?

15.   What is a test set?
16.   What is a test procedure?
17.   What might render it impossible to establish a test environment?
18.   Why should test procedures be followed during execution?
19.   What do we get if the actual result of execution is different from the expected result?
20.   Why is it interesting to know who executed a specific test procedure?
21.   How might a test specification be split into smaller documents?
22.   What do you need to set a priority?
23.   How is a test condition be expressed?
24.   What is the difference between a unique number and a sorting number?
25.   What are preconditions for a test case?
26.   What might input to a test case consist of?
27.   What is the main difference between a test set and a test procedure?
28.   What relationships exist between test procedures?
29.   What should be defined for test environment requirements?
30.   What should be defined for test data requirements?
31.   What should be written when test environment and/or test data requirements are fulfilled?
32.   What should be kept during test execution?
33.   What are the most common requirement levels?
34.   What are the classic requirement types?
35.   How should a requirement start?
36.   What is a "task" requirement?
37.   What are the requirements for requirements?
38.   What can "backward" tracing be used for?
39.   What can "forward" tracing be used for?
40.   What is a precondition for easy registration of traces?

Test Case Design Techniques

Designing test cases is about finding the input to be able to test a test condition, that is, to derive the input part of a test case. The techniques cannot be used to derive the expected output; this must be derived from the specification for the product to be produced.

Test case design techniques support systematic test design, and can assist us in making a test specification effective and efficient.

The full test design process is described in Section 5.2.2.1, where the test design from identification of the test feature set, to derivation of test conditions and test coverage items, to derivation of test cases, and its documentation are explained in detail.

Test case design techniques are the synthesis of "best practice"—not necessarily scientifically based, but based on many testers' experiences.

The advantages of using test case design techniques include that the design of the test cases may be repeated by others, and that it is possible to explain how test cases have been designed using a specific technique. This makes the test cases much more trustworthy than test cases "picked out of the air."

Test case design techniques also have, despite all their advantages, a few pitfalls, which we need to be aware of. Even if we could obtain 100% coverage of what we set out to cover, faults could still remain after testing, simply because the code does not properly reflect what the users and customers want. Validation of the requirements before we start the dynamic testing process can mitigate this risk.

There is also a pitfall in relation to value sensitivity. Even if we use an input value that gives us the coverage we want, it may be a value for which incidental correctness applies. An example of this is the fact that 2 + 2 equals 2 * 2; but 3 + 3 does not equal 3 * 3, so if the programmer accidentally has written "+" instead of "*" in the

Contents

code, the test will pass if we choose "2" as the input, and fail if we choose "3." Different techniques may be used on the same test item to mitigate this risk; for example, the use of structure-based techniques could be supplemented by experience-based techniques.

6.1   Test Coverage

Coverage is one of the most important ways to express how much we test; this is a way to express the quality of the test.

The test case design techniques are all based on models of the system, typically in the form of requirements or design, and *a coverage element is therefore identifiable for almost all techniques*. This allows us to calculate the coverage we obtain using input values based on the various test design techniques.

If we use the equivalence partitioning technique, the coverage element is the equivalence partition, and the coverage can be calculated as the percentage of the total number of identified equivalence partitions that have been exercised by a test:

Coverage = (no. of exercised partitions * 100)/total no. of partitions

It is worth noticing that coverage is always expressed in terms related to a specific test design technique. Having achieved a high coverage using one technique only says something about the testing based on that technique, not the complete testing possible for a given test item.

6.2   Specification-Based Techniques

The specification-based test case design techniques are used to design test cases based on an analysis of the description or model of the product without reference to its internal workings. These techniques are also known as black-box test techniques.

The specification-based techniques are dependent on descriptions of the expectations of the product. This could be in the form of requirements specifications, but may also be in the form of user manuals and/or process descriptions. If we are lucky we get the requirements expressed in ways corresponding directly to the techniques; if not, we will have to analyze and rephrase the descriptions during test design.

The specification-based techniques can be used in all test sub-processes. They are ideal for system and acceptance tests, and they can be used as a starting point in, for example, component testing and integration testing, where a first set of test cases can be designed directly from the requirements. These test cases can then be supplied with test cases derived using structure-based test case design techniques to obtain adequate coverage.

The specification-based techniques have associated coverage measures, and the application of these techniques refines the coverage from requirements coverage to specific coverage items for the techniques.

The specification-based test case design techniques covered in this book are:

▶ Equivalence partitioning;
▶ Classification tree method;
▶ Boundary value analysis;
▶ Domain analysis;
▶ Syntax testing;
▶ Combinatorial testing;
▶ Decision table;
▶ Cause-effect graph;
▶ State transition testing;
▶ Scenario testing;
▶ Random testing.

The covered techniques are those described in ISO 29119 and ordered in the same way. This means that the techniques described here are slightly different from those specified in ISTQB, where the syntax testing technique is not included, but where, on the other hand, user story testing is. This is my personal choice, because I find syntax testing very useful, and user stories in terms of the application of the test techniques principle not distinguishable from other types of requirements expressed in a natural language.

6.2.1 Equivalence Partitioning

Designing test cases is about finding the input to cover something we want to test. If we consider the number of different inputs that we can give to a product we can have anything from very few to a huge amount of possibilities.

A product may have only on button and it can be either on or off = two possibilities.

A field must be filled in with the name of a valid postal district = hundreds if not thousands of possibilities.

It can be very difficult to figure out which input to choose for our test cases. The equivalence partitioning test technique can help us handle situations with many input possibilities without getting many test cases essentially testing the same thing.

6.2.1.1 Equivalence Partitioning Description

The basic idea of the equivalence partitioning technique is that we can partition the input or output domain into equivalence partitions, where the assumption is that all the members in a partition cause the software to behave in the same way. This assumption is based on the specification of the product's expected behavior, and it means that all members in an equivalence partition will either fail or pass the same test. One single member of a partition will therefore represent all members, and we only need to deal with one member instead of many or all.

Equivalence partitions should be defined in such a way that all members of the domain belong to exactly one partition—no member belongs to more than one partition and no member falls outside the partitions.

The most common types of equivalence class partitions are intervals and sets of possibilities (unordered or ordered lists).

When we partition a domain into equivalence partitions, we will usually get both valid and invalid partitions. In my opinion an invalid partition is one where we cannot tell from the specification how the product should react to input from that partition. Other people define invalid partitions as those where the system is supposed to reject the input somehow; but I think this is misleading, because the system's reaction is sometimes specified, sometimes not. All reasonable partitions where the system's reaction is unspecified should make the tester alert and ask stakeholders what the reaction should be, rather than guess.

6.2.1.2 Equivalence Partitioning Examples

Equivalence partitioning for intervals may be illustrated by a requirement stating:

Income in €	Tax Percentage
Up to and including 500	0
More than 500, but less than 1,300	30
1,300 or more, but less than 5000	40

If this is all we know, we have:

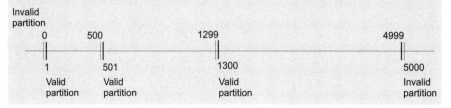

The invalid partitions in the example above are two of many possibilities. When we identify invalid partitions we must think about the product risk profile and the possible input the future users may provide.

Examples of other invalid equivalence partitions for the above example may be input containing letters, containing other characters (for example, a comma or a period), or containing nothing.

We could avoid invalid partitions by covering all possible input, within reason, in the requirements.

Adding a requirement like the following would eliminate invalid partitions in the above example:
"The system shall give a warning for all input different from numbers between and including 1 to 4999, saying that the input is illegal, and clear the input from the field."

An example illustrating an unordered list is a product that can suggest an appropriate dye for blond, brown, black, red, or gray hair colors, but no other colors. The only valid equivalence partition is the list of values from which we can pick one for our test; all other values belong to invalid partitions (unless we specify how the system should react to them).

6.2.1.3 Equivalence Partitioning Coverage

The coverage element for the equivalence partitioning test case design technique is an equivalence partition.

The equivalence partition coverage is measured as the percentage of the total number of identified equivalence partitions that have been exercised by a test:

Coverage = (no. of exercised partitions * 100)/total no. of partitions

To exercise an equivalence class, we need to pick one value in the equivalence partition and make a test case for this. For intervals we could pick a value near the middle of an equivalence partition, but any value will do.

For test cases for the tax percentage example above, with the added requirement, we could, for example, choose the input values 234, 810, 2207, and 6003. This will give a coverage of 100%.

For the hair colors we could choose the colors "black" and "green" as examples of input for the valid and invalid partitions, respectively. This will also give a coverage of 100%.

6.2.2   Classification Tree Method

The classification tree method supports design of test cases by having us look at the input domain of the test object from various aspects and form disjoint and complete classifications based on the requirements.

The method has a number of characteristics:

> ◗ The classification tree method is supported by a graphical representation of the classifications in the form of a tree (upside down). An example is shown below; don't worry if you cannot read the text, it is not relevant.

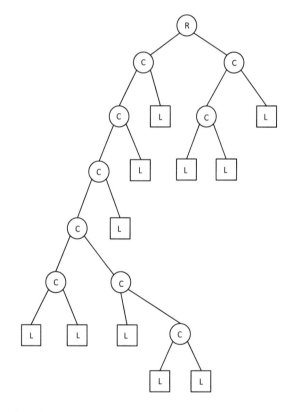

> ◗ In the classification tree method, the partitions (i.e., the classifications and classes) must be completely disjoint (nonoverlapping). (In equivalence partitioning, they could overlap depending on how the technique is used.)

> ◗ The classification tree supports combinations of classes when the test cases are designed. This is illustrated below, where the dots on

the horizontal line from a test case, for example, T1, show which classes are represented in the specific test case.

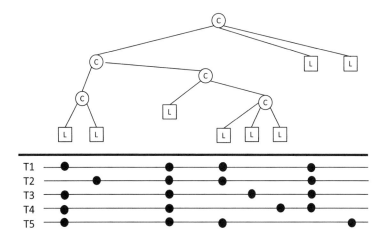

The classification tree method is very similar to equivalence partitioning, and it is a matter of personal taste which you like best. For what it is worth, my personal preference is the classification tree method.

6.2.2.1 Classification Tree Method Description

The idea in the classification tree method is that we can partition a domain related to the product, for example, an input domain, in several ways and that we can refine the partitions in a stepwise fashion. Each refinement is guided by a specific aspect or viewpoint on the domain at hand, based on the relevant requirements.

The result is a classification tree, the principle of which is shown in the figure below.

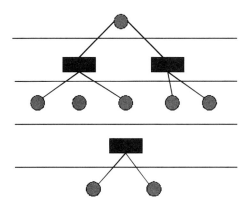

There are two types of nodes in the tree

▶ (sub) domain nodes;

▶ aspect nodes.

The two types must always alternate in the tree.

The root domain (which is highest in the graph!) may be the complete collection of all possible inputs, outputs, and states for a selection of related requirements. Note that "state" is a broad term here; it means anything that characterizes the system at a given point in time and includes for example which window is current, which field is current, and all data relevant for the behavior both present on the screen and stored "behind the screen."

The aspect is the point of view you use when you are performing a particular partitioning of the domain at which you are looking.

It is important to be aware that it is possible to look at the same domain in different ways (with different aspects) and get different subdomains as the result. This is why there can be more aspects at the same level in the classification tree and more subdomains at the same level (under the aspects) as well.

When we create a classification tree we start at the root domain. We must then:

▶ Look at the domain and decide on the views or aspects we want to use on the domain;

▶ For each of these aspects:

　▶ Partition the full root domain into classes; each class is a subdomain;

　▶ For each subdomain (now a full domain in its own right):

　　▶ Decide aspects that will result in a new partitioning;

　　▶ For each aspect:

　　　▶ And so on .....

At a certain point it is no longer possible or sensible to apply aspects to a domain. This means that we have reached a *leaf of the tree.* The tree is finished when all our subdomains are leaves (the lowest in the graph!).

Leaves can be reached at different levels in the classification tree. The tree does not have to be symmetric or in any other way have a predictable shape.

A leaf in a classification tree is similar to a partition in equivalence partitioning: We only need to test one member, because all members are assumed to behave in the same way.

We should remember to check the tree as we go on: *Any* member of a domain must fit into one and only one subdomain.

When the tree is complete, we can use it to derive test cases by identifying an input representative for each input leaf; output leaves are used to indirectly identify input by going backward from the output to the input that should create it. State leaves are used to define necessary test data.

A classification tree may be presented as a tree graph as shown above; many tools support this presentation. It is also possible to present a classification tree in a table using, for example, Excel; this is the method used in the example below.

6.2.2.2 Classification Tree Method Examples

In this example we are going to test the following requirements for a small telephone list system:

(1) A person can have more than one phone number.
(2) More than one person can have the same phone number.
(3) There is one input field where you can type either:
    ▶ phone number;
    ▶ a full name;
    ▶ part of a full name.
(4) A person shall be found if one or more names match.
(5) One or more people shall be found if the phone number matches.
(6) The output shall be either:
    ▶ an entry for each person that is found;
    ▶ an error message: no person found.

The result of the analysis is the classification tree shown below, where domains are shown in noncursive and aspects are shown in cursive. Leaf domains are shown in bold.

Full domain					
	state of list				
		empty			
		not empty			
			people with their own telephone nos.		
				some people with 1 telephone no.	
				some people with more telephone nos.	
			some people with shared telephone no.		
				some people sharing 1 telephone no. with 1 other	
				some people sharing 1 telephone no. with several others	
				some people sharing more telephone nos. with 1 other	
				some people sharing more telephone nos. with several others	
	input type				
		pure text			
		pure numbers			
		mixture			
		empty			
		including special characters			
	match type				
		none			
		some			
			no. of matches		
				1	
				more	
			type of match		
				full name	
				part of name	
				telephone no.	

Note that this is one way to construct the classification tree for the shown requirements, other people may construct their trees differently.

One of the test cases that could be designed from this classification tree is as follows:

ID: 3.6 (17)
Objective: To test how the system finds matches on part of a name and present the result for a person with more telephone numbers.
Priority: 2
Traceability: Requirements (1), (3), (4), (5) and (6)
Precondition: There exists a telephone list with a number of people with one or more telephone numbers. There must be an entry for "Tommy Bernard Smith" having more than one telephone number. No other entry must have names or parts of names identical to this.

Case	Input	Expected Output	Actual Output
3.6 (17)	Enter "Bernard"	Tommy Bernard Smith and the correct list of his telephone numbers.	

As you design the test cases, you may like to tick off the leaves that your test cases cover in the classification tree above to keep track of the coverage and the combinations your test cases cover.

Below is an example of the classification tree method applied for all possible dates. It may be used to derive test cases concerning handling of dates according to specific requirements.

It may be further expanded if a higher granularity is needed; the first leaf could for example be split into a leaf domain for all dates on the 28th of February and a leaf for all other dates from the 1st to the 28th in a month.

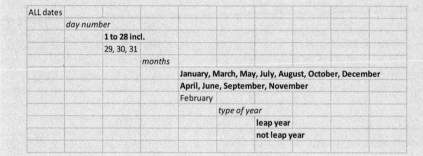

ALL dates				
	day number			
		1 to 28 incl.		
		29, 30, 31		
			months	
				January, March, May, July, August, October, December
				April, June, September, November
			February	
				type of year
				leap year
				not leap year

6.2.2.3 Classification Tree Method Coverage

The coverage element for the classification tree test case design technique is a *leaf.*

The classification tree method coverage is measured as the percentage of the total number of identified leaves that have been exercised by a test:

Coverage = (no. of exercised leaves * 100)/total no. of leaves

To exercise a leaf we need to pick one value in the leaf class and make a test case for this.

If we have a large tree with many domains, it is possible that one input will represent more leaves, so that we can reach a given coverage with fewer test cases. In areas of high risk we can also choose to test combinations of leaf classes mixing this test case design technique with a combinatorial test case design technique.

6.2.2.4   Classification Tree Method Hints

The classification tree method facilitates the test case design when it is too complex to make pure equivalence class partitioning.

This is mainly the case when input is composed of more parts, and the relations between the input parts rather than the individual parts determine the outcome. This is, for example, the case in forms where more input is given before the collection of input items is handled.

Remember that not only what is entered by the user as input determines the output. Lists, files, database tables, and other types of data used by the product determine the state of the product and should be considered, for example, in terms of preconditions for our test cases.

We should remember to check the tree as we construct it: *Any* member of a domain must fit into one and only one subdomain.

6.2.3   Boundary Value Analysis

A boundary value is the value on a boundary of an equivalence partition or a classification tree leaf based on intervals of values. Boundary value analysis is hence strongly related to these two other test case design techniques.

The boundary values require extra attention because defects are often found on or immediately around these.

6.2.3.1   Boundary Value Analysis Description

Boundary value analysis is the process of identifying the boundary values for an interval, and identifying possible test case inputs in relation to these boundary values.

For interval partitions or classes with precise boundaries, it is not difficult to identify the boundary values—they are the values at either end of the interval.

An equivalence partition specified as 0 <= income <= 500 has a clearly defined boundary value at either end of the interval, namely, the values "0" and "500."

If the boundaries are not precisely defined, we need to know what the increment is.

If the above interval had been specified as 0 <= income < 500, and the smallest increment was given as 1, we would have an equivalence class with the two boundaries "0" and "499."

Sometimes we'll experience equivalence partitions or classes with an open boundary in one end (or indeed in both ends), that is, a situation where a boundary is not specified and not immediately identifiable. This can happen, for example, in connection with people's income, because in theory there is no upper boundary for an income. This makes it difficult to identify a boundary value for testing purposes. In these cases we must first of all try to get the specification changed to set a boundary value. If that is not possible, we can look for information in other requirements, look for indirect or hidden boundaries, omit the testing of the nonexisting boundary value, or use a value defined by the underlying operating system or an "extreme" value.

Having identified the boundary values of a given interval, two different approaches are used for boundary value analysis (i.e., to identify input for testing):

1. *Two-value boundary testing:* The boundary value itself and the value that is one increment *outside* the boundary are the coverage elements.

2. *Three-value boundary testing:* The boundary value itself and the values one increment *on either side* of the boundary are the coverage items.

Some considerations are needed for both approaches concerning the value outside of the boundary. One is that the value outside the boundary may be the boundary value of an adjacent interval, whether this is valid or not. This means that there will either be an overlap in boundary values, or the value outside the boundary is a member of an invalid partition or class; this latter case will have to be handled as described above for invalid partitions.

The choice between the two-value boundary testing or three-value boundary testing should be governed by the risk profile for the product.

6.2.3.2 Boundary Value Analysis Example

In this example we use the following requirements:

[UR 631] The system shall allow shipments for which the price is less than or equal to 100 €.

We can identify the boundaries as:

Lower boundary = 0.00 €

Upper boundary = 100.00 €

where the confirmed assumptions are that the increment is 0.01 € and that a negative price is not possible.

The two-value boundary analysis gives us the following possible input values: –0.01, 0.00, 100.00, and 100.01 €.

The three-value boundary analysis gives us the following boundary values and hence possible input values: –0.01, 0.00, 0.01, 99.99, 100.00, and 100.01 €.

6.2.3.3   Boundary Value Analysis Coverage

As mentioned above, the coverage element for the boundary value analysis test case design technique depends on the approach.

For the two-value boundary testing, the coverage element is *the boundary value itself and the value that is one increment outside the boundary*.

For the three-value boundary testing, the coverage element is *the boundary value itself and the values one increment on either side of the boundary values*.

The boundary value coverage is measured as the percentage of coverage elements that have been exercised by a test; for example, for two-value boundary testing:

Coverage = (no. of exercised boundary values and values outside * 100) / total no. of values

To exercise a boundary value, we need to use the identified values as input to test cases.

If we take the example above, where we had the two-value boundary values: −0.01, 0.00, 100.00, and 100.01 €, and we use the values 0.00 and 100.00 for test cases we'll get a coverage of 50%.

6.2.4   Domain Analysis

Note: *This technique is not included in ISO 29119, but included here because it is included in the ISTQB Advanced Test Analyst Syllabus.*

In the equivalence partitioning and classification tree methods, we operate with one-dimensional partitions. The domain analysis test case design technique is used when our input partitions or classes are multidimensional, that is, when borders depend on combinations of aspects or variables. If two variables are involved, we have a two-dimensional domain; if three are involved, we have a three-dimensional domain, and so on.

It is difficult for people to picture more than three dimensions, but in theory there is no limit to the number of dimensions we may have to handle in domain analysis. We will use two-dimensional domains in this section; the principles are the same for any number of dimensions.

6.2.4.1   Domain Analysis Description

The domain analysis is best described using an example.

For equivalence partitioning we may think of an example of intervals of income groups, where 0.00 <= Income < 5,000.00 is tax free. This is a one-dimensional domain.

If people's capital also counts in the calculation, so that income is only tax free if it is also less than twice the capital held by the person in question, we have a two-dimensional domain.

The two-dimensional domain for tax free income is shown as the striped area in the figure below (assuming that the capital and the income are both ≥ 0.00):

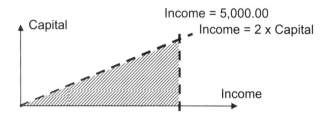

Borders may be either open or closed. A border is *open* if a value on the border does not belong to the domain at which we are looking. This is the case in the example where both the borders are open (income < 5,000.00 and income < 2 × capital).

A border is *closed* if a value on the border belongs to the domain at which we are looking.

If we change the border for tax-free income to become: income <= 2 × capital, we have a closed border. In this case our domain will look like this:

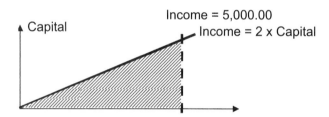

In equivalence partitioning we say that a value is in a particular equivalence class—and so we do in a way for domain analysis. Here, however, we operate with points relative to the borders:

▶ A point is an In point in the domain we are considering if it is inside and not on the border;

▶ A point is an Out point to the domain we are considering if it is outside and not on the border (it is then in another domain).

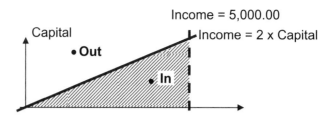

An In point and an Out point relative to the domain are illustrated here.

In the boundary value analysis related to equivalence partitioning described above, we operate with the boundary values on the boundary and one unit inside. In domain analysis we operate with On and Off points relative to each border.

We have:

▶ A point is an On point if it is on the border between partitions.
▶ A point is an Off point if it "slightly" off the border.

If the border of the domain we are looking at is closed, the Off point will be outside the domain. The "slightly" may be one unit relative to what measure we are using, so that the Off point lies on the border of the adjacent domain. This works for all practical purposes, as long as we are not working with a floating point where "one unit" is undeterminable; in this case the "slightly" will have to be far enough away from the border to ensure that the Off point is inside the adjacent domain.

For the closed border of income <= 2 × Capital, the border of the adjacent domain is shown here with an On and an Off point.

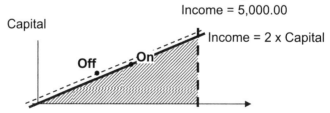

If the border of the domain we are looking at is open, the Off point will be "slightly" (or perhaps one unit) inside the domain, namely, outside (or on) the closed border of the adjacent domain.

In our case with the income < 5,000.00 an On point and an Off point may look like this:

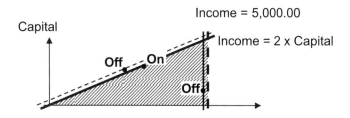

6.2.4.1.1 Domain Analysis Strategy

The number of test cases we can design based on a domain analysis depends on the domain analysis strategy we decide to follow. A strategy can be described as:

N-On * N-Off

where N-On is the number of On points we want to test for each border and N-Off correspondingly is the number of Off points we want to test for each border for the domains we have identified.

If we choose a 1 * 1 strategy we therefore set out to test one On point and one Off point for each border of the domains we have identified. This is what is illustrated above for the one domain we are looking at (not taking the capital >=0 border into account). If our strategy is 2 * 1, we set out to test two On points and one Off point for each of the borders for all the domains we have identified. In this case the On points will be the points where the borders cross each other, that is, the extremes of the borders.

In a 1 * 1 strategy we will get two test cases for each border. If we are testing adjacent domains, we will get equivalent test cases because an Off point in one domain is an In point in the adjacent domain. These test cases will have identical expected outcome if identical values are chosen for the low-level test cases. These duplicates need not be repeated in the test procedures for execution.

6.2.4.1.2 Domain Analysis Test Design Template

The design of the test conditions based on domain analysis and with the aim of getting On and Off point coverage can be captured in a table like this one.

Tag						
Border 1 condition	ON	OFF				
Border 2 condition			ON	OFF		
Border n condition					ON	OF

Table designed by Carsten Jørgensen.

The table is for one domain. It must be expanded both in length and width to accommodate all the borders our domain may have.

The rule is: divide and conquer.

For each of the borders involved we should:

- Test an On point.
- Test an Off point.

If we want In point and Out point coverage as well, we must include this explicitly in the table.

When we start to design test cases, we add a row for each variable to select values for. In a two-dimensional domain we will have to select values for two variables.

Tag						
Border 1 condition	ON	OFF				
Border 2 condition			ON	OFF		
Border n condition					ON	OF
Variable X						
Variable Y						

For each column we select a value that satisfies what we want. In the first column of values, we must select a value for X and a value for Y that gives us a point On border 1. We should aim at getting In points for the other borders in the column, though that is not always possible. For each of the borders, we should note which kind of point we get for the selected set of values.

This selection of values can be quite difficult, especially if we have high-dimensional domains. Creating the table in a spreadsheet helps a lot and other tools are also available to help.

6.2.4.1.3 Domain Analysis Example

In this example we test the following user requirement:

[UR 637] The system shall allow posting of envelopes where the longest side (l) is longer than or equal to 12 centimeters, but not longer than 75 centimeters. The smallest side (w) must be longer than or equal to 1 centimeter. The (length minus twice the width) must be greater than or equal to 10 centimeters. Measures are always rounded up to the nearest centimeter. All odd envelopes are to be handled by courier.

We can rewrite this requirement to read:

```
length >= 12
length < 75
width >= 1
length - (2 x width) >= 10
```

This can be entered into our template:

Tag	TC1	TC2	TC3	TC4	TC5	TC6	TC7	TC8
length >= 12	ON 12	OFF						
length < 75	12 in		ON	OFF				
width >= 1	1 in				ON	OF		
l − 2 × w >= 10	10 on						ON	OF
Length	12							
Width	1							

In the table shown above, we have entered values for the first test case, namely, length = 12, to get the On point for the first border condition. The simultaneous selection of width = 1 gives the points indicated for each border in minuscule under the number.

The table fully filled in may look like this:

Tag	TC1	TC2	TC3	TC4	TC5	TC6	TC7	TC8
length >= 12	ON 12	OFF 11	75 in	74 in	15 in	15 in	30 in	31 in
length < 75	12 in	11 in	ON 75	OFF 74	15 in	15 in	30 in	31 in
width >= 1	1 in	1 in	30 in	30 in	ON 1	OFF 0	10 in	11 in
l − 2 × w >= 10	10 on	9 out	15 in	14 in	13 in	15 in	ON 10	OFF 9
Length	12	11	75	74	15	15	30	31
Width	1	1	30	30	1	0	10	11

We now need to determine the expected results, and then we have our test cases ready.

6.2.4.1.4 Domain Analysis Coverage

It is possible to measure the coverage for domain analysis. The coverage elements for the identified domains are the In points and the Out points. The coverage is measured as the percentage of In points and Out points that have been exercised by a test. Do not count an In point in one partition being an Out point in another partition to be tested twice.

The coverage elements for the borders are the On points and Off points. The coverage is measured as the percentage of On points and Off points that have been exercised by a test relative to what the strategy determines as the number of points to test. Again do not count duplicate points twice.

6.2.5 Syntax Testing

Note: This technique is not part of the ISTQB syllabus, but included here because I find it useful.

Syntax is a set of rules where each defines the possible ways of producing a string of characters in terms of sequences of, iterations of, or selections among strings.

Many of the "strings" we are surrounded by in daily life are guided by syntax. For example:

▶ Web addresses: www.aaaaa.aa, aaaaa.aa

(note the difference in appearances! My word processer recognizes the first one, but not the second one, because the "www" is missing);

▶ CPR number: ddmmyy-nnnn

(Danish Central Person Registration number);

▶ Credit card number: nnnn nnnn nnnn nnnn

(my VISA card—some other cards have different syntaxes).

In the examples above the rules for the different strings are expressed using for example "n" to mean that a number should be at a specific place in the string or "dd" to indicate a day number in a month.

We can set up a list of rules, defining strings as building blocks and defining a notation to express the rules applied to the building blocks in a precise and compressed way. The building blocks are usually called the elements of the entire string.

The syntax rule for the string we are defining must be given a name.

The most commonly used notation form is the Backus-Naur form. This form defines the following notations:

""   elementary part, e.g.   "1" "-"

| alternative separator   "A" |"B"

[ ]   optional item(s)   [" "]

{}   max. repetition of item   {5}

These notations can be used to form elements and the entire string.

An example of a syntax rule for a string called pno. could be:

```
pno. = 2d [" "] 2d [" "] 2d [" "] 2d
```

Here we have defined the elements:

```
2d = dig dig
dig = "0" |"1" |"2" |"3" |"4" |"5" |"6" |"7" |"8" |"9"
```

This means that the pno. string must consist of four sets of two digits. The digits can range from 0 to 9. The sets of two digits can be separated by blanks, but they can also not be separated.

A valid string following this syntax is a Danish telephone no.: 39 62 36 48.

The way my father used to write his telephone number is, however, illegal according to this syntax: 45 940 941.

6.2.5.1   Syntax Testing Description

To derive test coverage items, we need to identify options in the syntax and test these independently. Options appear when we can choose between elementary parts or elements for a given element or for the entire string. Syntax testing does not include combinations of options as part of the technique.

We may also want to *test invalid syntax* as well as valid syntax. For this we operate with possible mutations. Examples of the most common mutations are:

▶ Invalid value is used for an element.

▶ One element is substituted with another defined element.

▶ A defined element is left out.

▶ An extra element is added.

As for other invalid tests we need to know how the system is expected to react, either by finding appropriate expectations or by asking stakeholders.

6.2.5.2   Syntax Testing Example
In this example we will test the input of a member number.

The syntax defined for the member number is

```
member no. = type" "no" "mm"-"yy
```

First we list the options derived from the entire string, the elements, and
the elementary parts.   **options**

```
member no. = type" "no" "mm"-"yy  none
type = "B"  |"S"  |"G"   3
no = dig dig dig  none
mm = "01"  |"02"  |..... |"11"  |"12"  12
yy = dig dig  none
dig = "0"  |"1"  |"2"  |... |"8"  |"9"  10
                                          25
```

We have 25 possible independent mutations. We can list them in the template like this:

Tag	Description
T1	"B" |"S" |"G"
M1	"01" |"02" |..... |"11" |"12"
D1	"0" |"1" |"2" |... |"8" |"9"

The table below shows a few of the 25 possible inputs to test cases that
we can identify; note how the values not being mutated are kept unchanged.
The tag references the tag of the possible mutations.

Tag	Input
T1	B 326 04-05
T1	S 326 04-05
M1	G 326 01-05
M1	G 326 02-05
M1	G 326 03-05
M1	G 326 12-05
M1	G 111 01-11
M1	G 222 01-22
M1	G 999 01-99
M1	G 000 01-00

To test *invalid syntax* we list the mutations we want to try. In this example these are:

Tag	Mutation Description
MU1	Invalid value—applicable to all positions in the string
MU2	Substitute—any two elements
MU3	Element missing—applicable to all elements
MU4	Extra element—anything, but may not be possible

There is an infinite number of possible test case inputs for the mutations. We list only a few here:

Tag	Input
MU1	F 456 02-99
MU1	B-326 02-99
MU1	B a26 02-99
MU1	B-326 02-9g
MU2	BB456 02-99
MU2	B B 02-99
MU3	B 02-99
MU3	B 456 -99
MU4	BB 456 02-99

6.2.5.3 Syntax Testing Coverage
There is no industry agreed-on approach to calculating coverage for syntax testing.

6.2.5.4 Syntax Testing Hints
The number of invalid strings to test depends on the risk related to invalid input wrongly being accepted.

It can be a bit tricky to work with mutations, because some may be indistinguishable from correctly formed input if elements are identical. Some mutations may also be indistinguishable from each other, in which case they should be treated as one.

It is possible to define more mutations than those listed above, depending on the nature of the syntax.

To get an even stricter test we can use combinations of mutations. Who knows; maybe two wrong elements at a time will cause the string to be accepted.

The number of test cases may be reduced by having a single test case cover several options. This may, however, increase the fault correction time, if failures are encountered, because it can be more difficult to locate the fault.

6.2.6 Combinatorial Testing

IT products are usually complicated and the inputs they require are often combinations of a number of single inputs. Consider the example below.

A product is designed with a form for entering different information about clients, both actual and potential. The following information must be supplied—the values in parentheses after the information type are the possible valid values from which to select:

▶ Size (small, medium, large);
▶ Business (private, civil administration, defense);
▶ Relevance (low, middle, high);
▶ Status (customer, lead, potential).

For this simple form, there are $3 \times 3 \times 3 \times 3 = 81$ possible combinations of input.

Combinatorial test case design techniques may be used to structure the way we identify inputs for test cases where more parameters each have a number of possible values. A parameter is a named piece of information, for example, "Size" and "Relevance." The possible values are those defined for the parameter, for example "small," "medium," and "large" for the "Size" parameter.

The combinatorial test techniques range from:

▶ All combinations testing, in which all possible combinations of all values for all parameters in question are identified (81 possibilities in the example above) to
▶ 1-wise testing—where all values for each parameter are identified in isolation (12 possibilities in the example above).

Note that the 1-wise testing is stronger than equivalence partitioning, because all values are considered coverage items, not only one value.

In some high-risk situations it may be possible and relevant to test all combinations; but in most situations it is not. An often-used choice is *pairwise testing*, which is described below.

6.2.6.1 Pair-Wise Testing Description

In the pair-wise test case design technique, we aim at testing all pairs of possible combinations of the values for the parameters. This reduces the number of test cases compared to testing all combinations, and experience shows that it is sufficiently effective in finding defects in most cases.

It is not always an easy task to identify all the possible pairs we can make from the combination possibilities. If there are many parameters and they each have many possible values, it can easily get out of hand.

The orthogonal arrays technique can help, as described below.

6.2.6.1.1 Orthogonal Arrays

Orthogonal arrays were first described by the Swiss mathematician Leonhard Euler, born in 1707. He introduced much of the modern terminology for mathematical analysis, including the notation for mathematical functions.

An orthogonal array is a two-dimensional array (a matrix) of values ordered in such a way that all pair-wise combinations of the values are present in any two columns of the arrays.

An example of the simplest possible orthogonal array is:

1	1	1
1	2	2
2	1	2
2	2	1

Select any two columns in the table and you will see that all the possible pairs of 1 and 2, namely, (1,1), (1,2), (2,1), and (2,2) are present.

An orthogonal array is called mixed if not all the columns have the same range of values. In the above table each column has only 1's and 2's, but we can also have an orthogonal array where one column only has 1's and 2's and other columns have 1's, 2's, and 3's, for example.

If we want to use an orthogonal array to assist us in finding pairs of values for pair-wise testing, we need to know which type of array we need. Here the description of the nature of orthogonal arrays can help us.

The size and contents of orthogonal arrays may be described in a general manner as follows:

$(N, s1^{k1} s2^{k2})$ where

N = number of rows;

s = number of levels = number of different values for a parameter;

k = number of factors = number of parameters with the same s.

The description is often ordered so that the s's are ordered in ascending order, though the actual columns in the array may be arranged differently.

The simple orthogonal array shown above can be described as (4, 2^3).

An orthogonal array described as (72, 2^5 3^3 4^1 6^7) is a mixed array with 72 rows, 5 columns (parameters) with 2 different values, 3 columns (parameters) with 3 different values, 1 column (parameter) with 4 different values, and 7 columns (parameters) with 6 different values, for a total of 16 columns. This is a large array.

Creating orthogonal arrays is not a simple task. Many people have contributed to libraries of orthogonal arrays and new arrays are still being created. A large number of arrays in all sizes and mixtures may be found on http://neilsloane.com/oadir.

When we want to use orthogonal arrays to help us identify all pairs of possible inputs that we want to test, all we need to do is find a suitable array and substitute the values in this with our values. We are then guaranteed to have identified all the possible pairs.

The process is the following:

 ◗ Identify the parameters that can be combined.
 ◗ For each of the parameters, count the possible values it can have, e.g., (P1;s=2), (P2;s=4), and so on.
 ◗ Find out how many parameters have each number of values, for example, 3 times s = 2, 1 time s = 4, and so on (this provides you with the needed sets of s^k, e.g., 2^3 4^1);
 ◗ Find an orthogonal array that has a description of at least what you need—if you cannot find a precise match, take a bigger array; this often happens, especially if we need a mixed array;

Substitute the possible values of each of the parameters with the values in the orthogonal array. If we had to choose an array that was too big, we can just fill in the superfluous cells with valid values chosen at random.

6.2.6.1.2 Orthogonal Array Example

This example covers the system with the input parameters and their corresponding valid values from above :

 ◗ Size (small, medium, large);
 ◗ Business (private, civil administration, defense);
 ◗ Relevance (low, middle, high);

▶ Status (customer, lead, potential).

There are four input possibilities, and each of them has three possibilities, so we need at least an array of (3^4). One such array can be found on the Internet, namely:

1	1	1	1
1	2	2	3
1	3	3	2
2	1	2	2
2	2	3	1
2	3	1	3
3	1	3	3
3	2	1	2
3	3	2	1

We will now assign the first column to Size, and substitute the values in the array with the possible values for size.

The array will look as shown below, where we have added an extra row to show which column represents which input:

Size			
small	1	1	1
small	2	2	3
small	3	3	2
medium	1	2	2
medium	2	3	1
medium	3	1	3
large	1	3	3
large	2	1	2
large	3	2	1

The fully substituted orthogonal array is shown below:

Size	Business	Relevance	Status
small	private	low	customer
small	civil administration	middle	potential
small	defense	high	lead
medium	private	middle	lead
medium	civil administration	high	customer
medium	defense	low	potential
large	private	high	potential
large	civil administration	low	lead
large	defense	middle	customer

From this table we can see that it takes nine rows to cover all pairs of input.

6.2.6.2 Pair-Wise Testing Coverage

The coverage element for pair-wise testing is pairs of input based on the values for the parameters in question.

The pair-wise testing coverage is measured as the percentage of the total number of pairs that have been exercised by a test:

Coverage = (no. of exercised pairs * 100)/total no. of pairs

The total number of all possible pairs of input is the number of rows in the orthogonal array used; 9 in the example above.

6.2.6.3 Pair-Wise Testing Hints

When we create pairs of values as described above, all the values have equal weight. This means that the orthogonal arrays do not take the distribution of the values and the risks associated with individual pairs into account.

It may well be that one particular value is much more common than any of the others—no doubt for example that there are many more private businesses than defense-related businesses around.

It may also be possible that a specific combination has a much larger risk level than the others, that is, that the effect of a defect not found for that combination is much higher than for all other combinations—it could for example be serious for our company if all defense leads were left out of a mail list with invitations to a special sales event, whereas it would hardly make any difference if small-private businesses were missed from a general mailing campaign.

To overcome this we should apply risk analysis to pair-wise testing and design more test cases around the combinations with a high-risk level.

In some cases the pairs we have established to test are not actually testable. One value of one input may be prohibitive for a specific value for another input. In this case there is nothing else to do other than leave that test case out and explain why a lower coverage than expected was achieved.

6.2.7 Decision Table

A decision table is a table showing the expected reactions of the product depending on certain combinations of input conditions.

Decision tables are often used to express rules and regulations for embedded systems and administrative systems. They seem to have gone a little out of fashion, and that is a shame. Decision tables are excellent for providing an overview of input conditions and also for determining if requirements are complete, that is, if requirements cover specification of all reactions to the input combinations.

It is often seen that what could have been expressed in a decision table is poorly explained in text. The text may be several paragraphs or even pages long and reformatting of the text into a decision table will make it much clearer what is going on, and also often reveal omissions in the requirements.

Decision tables are useful for providing an overview of combinations of input and the resulting output. The combinations are derived from the requirements; if we are lucky requirements are expressed directly in decision tables where appropriate.

6.2.7.1 Decision Table Description

The template to capture decision table test conditions and reactions is as shown below, where the top row indicates the numbered input combinations.

	C1	C2				Cn
Input condition 1						
Input condition ..						
Input condition n						
Reaction 1						
Reaction n						

Often input conditions and output conditions are expressed as something that is either true or false. An example input condition is "The BREW button has been pushed." Such decision tables always have $1+2^n$ columns, where n is the number of input conditions, because there are always 2^n combinations of true or false for n conditions. (The first column is the input condition and reaction texts.)

A decision table may also be extended; that is, it can be a table where more values than true or false are possible for input conditions and/or reactions. We could, for example, have an input condition where the possible values were "Skim milk," "Milk," or "Nothing." In this case the number of columns is 1+ the product of the number of possibilities for each condition. If we have, for example, the above choices for addition to a coffee and we can order coffee that is either "Normal" or "Extra," we would get 1 × 3 2 = 7 columns.

The number of rows in decision tables depends on the number of input conditions and the number of dependent reactions. There is one row for each condition and one row for each reaction.

A decision table with two true or false conditions and two reactions will look like this:

Input condition 1	T	T	F	F
Input condition 2	T	F	T	F
Reaction 1	T	T	F	F
Reaction 2	T	T	T	F

The table is read a column at the time. We can, for example, see in the above table that if both input conditions are true, then both reactions will be true (will happen).

The easiest way to fill out a decision table is to fill in the input condition rows first. For the first input condition, half of the cells in the rest of the row are filled with T for true, and the second half are filled with F for false. In the next row half of the cells under the Ts are filled with T and the other half with F, and likewise for the cells under the F's. Keep on like this until the T's and F's alternate for each cell in the last input condition row.

Note, that it is not a rule that the values for the conditions and reactions should be T or F; they could, for example be Yes or NO, or 1 or 0.

In an extended decision table, the possible values for the conditions are filled in instead of true and false. For each condition the possible values may have to be repeated to allow all combinations to be expressed.

An extended decision table with the above possibilities for the conditions will look like this (the reactions are not included for simplicity):

Input condition 1	S	M	N	S	M	N
Input condition 2	N	N	N	E	E	E

It takes more consideration to fill in the input conditions for an extended decision table, because it is not as mechanical and we need to take care that all combinations of values are represented.

A decision table is read a column at the time. We can, for example, see in the first example above that if both input conditions are true, then both reactions will be true (will happen).

The values for the resulting actions must be extracted from the requirements. These can in no way be filled in automatically.

6.2.7.2 Decision Table Example

In this example we are going to test the following requirements.

[76] The system shall only calculate a discount for members.

[77] The system shall calculate a discount of 5% if the value of the purchase is less than or equal to 100 €. Otherwise the discount is 10%.

[78] The system shall write the discount% on the invoice.

[79] The system shall write in the invoices to nonmembers that membership gives a discount.

Note that we are only going to test the calculation and printing on the invoice, not the correct calculation of the discount.

	TC1	TC2	TC3	TC4
Purchaser is member	T	T	F	F
Value <= 100 €	T	F	T	F
No discount calculated	F	F	T	T
5% discount calculated	T	F	F	F
10% discount calculated	F	T	F	F
Member message on invoice	F	F	T	T
Discount% on invoice	T	T	F	F

In the above example the reactions concerning the discount are in fact one reaction that has three possible values: 0%, 5%, and 10%. This means that the decision table could be rearranged as an extended decision table, as shown below.

	TC1	TC2	TC3	TC4
Purchaser is member	T	T	F	F
Value <= 100 €	T	F	T	F
Discount calculated	5	10	0	0
Member message on invoice	F	F	T	T
Discount% on invoice	T	T	F	F

6.2.7.3 Decision Table Coverage

The coverage element for decision tables is a combination of input conditions.

The decision table testing coverage is measured as the percentage of the total number of combinations that have been exercised by a test:

Coverage = (no. of exercised combinations * 100) / total no. of combinations

Sometimes it is not possible to obtain 100% combination coverage because it is impossible to execute a test case for a combination.

6.2.7.4 Collapsed Decision Table

Sometimes it seems evident in a decision table that some conditions are without effect because one condition decision is decisive. For example, if one condition is false a reaction is to be false no matter what the values are of all other conditions.

This could lead us to collapse the decision table, that is, reduce the number of combinations by only taking one of those where the rest will give the same result. This technique is related to the modified condition decision testing discussed in Section 6.3.5.

The decision to collapse a decision table should be based on a risk analysis.

6.2.8 Cause-Effect Graph

A cause-effect graph is a graphical way of showing inputs or stimuli (causes) with their associated outputs (effects). The graph is a result of an analysis of requirements or otherwise described expectations. Both input and expected results for test cases can be derived from a cause-effect graph.

The technique is a semiformal way of expressing requirements that are based on Boolean expressions.

In principle any functional requirement can be expressed as:

f(old state, input) $\rightarrow$ (new state, output)

This means that a specific treatment (f = a function) for a given input transforms an old state of the system to a new state and produces an output.

We can also express this in a more practical way as:

f(ops1, ops2,..., i1, i2,..i) (ns1, ns2,..,o1, o2..) ⬤———⬤

where the old state is split into a number of old partial states, and the input is split into a number of input items. The same is done for the new state and the output.

The causes in the graphs are characteristics of input items or old partial states. The effects in the graphs are characteristics of output items or new partial states.

Both causes and effects have to be statements that are either "True" or "False." True indicates that the characteristic is present; False indicates its absence.

The graph shows the connections and relationships between the causes and the effects.

6.2.8.1 Cause-Effect Graph Description

A cause-effect graph is constructed in the following way based on an analysis of selected suitable requirements:

- ◗ List and assign an ID to all causes.
- ◗ List and assign an ID to all effects.
- ◗ For each effect make a Boolean expression so that the effect is expressed in terms of relevant causes.
- ◗ Draw the cause-effect graph.

An example of the appearance of a cause-effect graph is shown below.

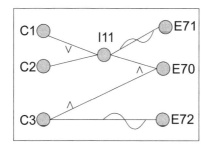

The graph is composed of some simple building blocks:

Identified cause or effect—must be labeled with the corresponding ID. It is a good idea to start the IDs of the causes with a C and those of the effects with an E. Intermediate causes may also be defined to make the graph simpler.

Connection between cause(s) and effect—the connection always goes from the left to the right.

This means that the causes are combined with AND, that is, all causes must be True for the effect to be True.

∨

This means that the causes are combined with OR, that is, only one cause needs to be True for the effect to be True.

This is a negation, meaning that a True should be understood as a False, and vice versa.

The arch shows that all the causes (to the left of the connections) must be combined with the Boolean operator—in this case the three causes must be "ANDed."

Test cases may be derived directly from the graph. The graph may also be converted into one or more decision tables, and the test cases derived from these.

Sometimes constraints may apply to the causes and these will have to be taken into consideration as well.

6.2.8.2   Cause-Effect Graph Example

In this example we are going to test a web page, on which it is possible to sign up for a course. The web page looks like this:

Sign up for course

Name:

Address:

Zip Code: City:

Course Number:

Submit

First we make a complete list of causes with identification. The causes are derived from a textual description of the form (not included here):

C1. Name field is filled in.

C2. Name contains only letters and spaces.

C3. Address field is filled in.

C4. Zip code is filled in.

C5. City is filled in.

C6. Course number is filled in.

C7. Course number exists in the system.

An intermediate Boolean may be introduced here, I30, meaning that all fields are filled in. This is expressed as:

I30 = and (C1, C3, C4, C5, C6)

The full list of effects with identification is:

E51. Registration of delegate made in the system.

E52. Message shown: All fields should be filled in.

E53. Message shown: Only letters and spaces in name.

E54. Message shown: Unknown course number.

E55. Message shown: You have been registered.

We must now express each effect as a Boolean expression based on the causes. They are:

E51 = and(I30, C2, C7)

E52 = not I30

E53 = and(I30, not C2)

E54 = and(I30, C2, not C7)

E55 = E51

Drawing the causes and the effects and their relationships gives us the cause-and-effect graph. Test cases can be designed directly from the graph.

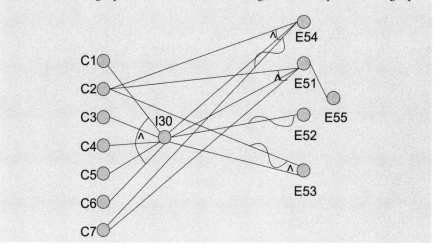

6.2.8.3 Cause-Effect Graph Testing Coverage

The coverage element for a cause-effect graph is one combination of input.

The cause-effect graph testing coverage is measured as the percentage of the total number of combinations that have been exercised by a test:

Coverage = (no. of exercised combinations * 100) / total no. of combinations

6.2.8.4 Cause-Effect Graph Hints

The cause-effect graph test case design technique is very suitable for people with a graphical mind.

For others it may be a help in the analysis phase and the basis for the construction of a decision table from which test cases can be described as discussed above.

Cause-effect graphs frequently become very large—and therefore difficult to work with. To avoid this, we can divide the specification into workable pieces of isolated functionality. We may also remove impossible combinations, or reduce the combinations by only keeping those that independently affect the outcome, as in modified condition decision testing, discussed in Section 6.3.5.

6.2.9 State Transition Testing

State transition testing is based on a state machine model of the test item. State machine modeling is a design technique most often used for embedded software, but most products can be modeled as one or more state machines, including modern graphical user interfaces where the user's next act is unpredictable.

If we are lucky we get the state machine model as part of the specification we are going to test against, if that is a suitable way of expressing the expectations. Otherwise it is a good idea to reformat the specifications to one or more state machine model(s).

The idea in a state machine model is that the system can be in a number of well-defined states. A state is the collection of all features of the system at a given point in time, including but not restricted to, all visible data, all stored data, and any current form and field.

The transition from one state to another is initiated by an event, the system just sits there doing nothing until an event happens. An event will cause an action from the system, and it will change into another state (or stay in the same state).

A transition = start state + event + action + end state

The principle in a state machine is illustrated next.

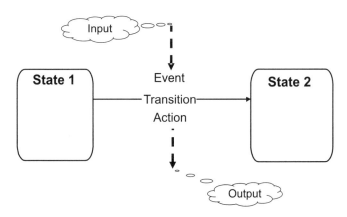

State machines can be depicted in many ways. The figure below shows a state machine presentation of a report printing menu, where the states are depicted as circles and the events and actions are written next to the transitions depicted as arrows.

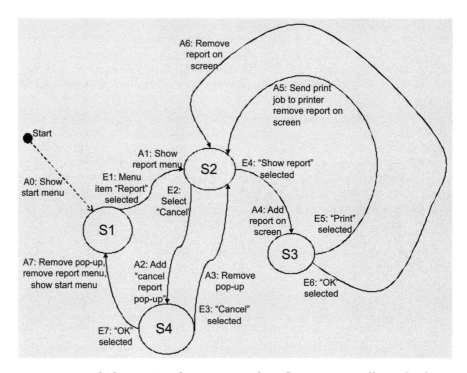

It is a good idea to give the states an identification, typically in the form of a number. The events, actions, and transitions should also be identified by name or number.

Note that the state machine in the example has a start state. This could be a transition from another state machine describing another part of the full system. In most cases a state machine will also have one or more exits, where control is transferred to another state machine or the system closes down.

6.2.9.1 State Transition Testing Coverage

State transitions can be performed in sequences. The smallest "sequence" is one transition at the time. The second smallest sequence is a sequence of two transitions in a row. Transition sequences can in theory be of any length.

The coverage element for state transition testing is measurable for different lengths of transition sequences. The state transition general coverage measure is:

Chows n-switch coverage

where n = sequential transitions − 1.

(We could also say that n = no. of "in-between-states.")

If we want to work with Chows 0-switch coverage, our coverage element would be a *single transition*, and the Chows 0-switch coverage would be the percentage of all single transitions being executed in the test.

For a *Chows 1-switch coverage* we could calculate:

Chows 1-switch Coverage = (no. of exercised two-transitions in sequence * 100)/(total no. of two-transitions in a sequence)

State transition testing coverage is measured for valid transitions only. Valid transitions are transitions described in the model. There may, however, also be invalid, or so-called null-transitions and these should be tested as well, as described below.

6.2.9.2   State Transition Testing Description

A number of tables are used to capture the test coverage items during the analysis of state transition machines.

To obtain Chows 0-switch coverage we need a table showing all single transitions. These transitions are test coverage items and can be used directly as a basis for deriving test cases. A simple transition table is shown below, where:

Transition: the identification of the transition;

Start state: the identification of the start state (for this transition);

Input: the identification or description of the event that triggers the transition;

Expected output: the identification or description of the action connected to the transition;

End state: the identification of the end state (for this transition).

Transition	T1		Tn
Start state*			
Input			
Expected output			
End state*			

The "start" and "end" states are for each specific transition only—not the state machine as a whole.

Testing to 100% Chows 0-switch coverage detects simple defects in transitions and outputs.

To achieve a higher Chows n-switch coverage, we need to describe the sequences of transitions of the desired length. A table to capture test conditions for Chows 1-switch coverage is shown below.

Transition Pair	TP1		TPn
Start state*			
Input			
Expected output			
Intermediate state*			
Input			
Expected output			
End state*			

Here we have to include the intermediate state and the input to cause the second transition in each sequence. Again we need a column for each set of two transitions in sequence.

If we want higher Chows n-switch coverage, we must describe test conditions for longer sequences of transitions.

As mentioned above we should also *test invalid transitions*. To identify these, we need to complete a so-called state table. A state table is a matrix showing the relationships between all states and events, and resulting states and outputs.

A template for a state table matrix is shown below. The matrix must have a row for each defined state and a column for each input (event). In the cross-cell the corresponding end state and outputs must be given.

An invalid transaction is defined as a start state where the end state and output are not defined for a specific event. This should result in the system staying in the start state of the transition and no output or a null-action being performed, but since it is not specified we cannot know for sure.

	Input	
Start State		
		End state/Action

The "End state/Action" for invalid transitions must be given as the identification of the start state/"N" or the like, so that it is clear which they are.

We should try to avoid invalid transitions by asking what the output should be.

If it is not practical to define all possible state and event combinations explicitly, we should encourage the designers to define a default for truly invalid situations. For example, it could be defined that all null-transitions should result in a warning.

6.2.9.3   State Transition Testing Example

In this example we are going to identify test coverage items and test case inputs for the state machine shown below.

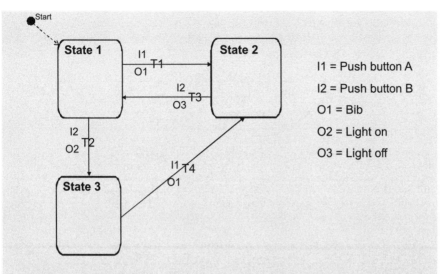

Don't worry about what the system is doing—that is not interesting from a testing point of view.

The drawing of the state machine shows the identification of the states, the events (inputs), the actions (outputs), and the transitions. The descriptions of the inputs and outputs are given to the right of the drawing.

First of all we have to define test conditions for all single transitions to get Chows 0-switch coverage.

Transition	T1	T2	T3	T4
Start state*	S1	S1	S2	S3
Input	I1	I2	I2	I1
Expected output	O1	O2	O3	O1
End state*	S2	S3	S1	S2

Identification of sequences of two transitions to achieve Chows 1-switch coverage results in the following table.

Transition Pair	T1/T3	T3/T1	T3/T2	T2/T4	T4/T3
Start state*	S1	S2	S2	S1	S3
Input	I1	I2	I2	I2	I1
Expected output	O1	O3	O3	O2	O1
Intermediate state*	S2	S1	S1	S3	S2
Input	I2	I1	I2	I1	I2
Expected output	O3	O1	O2	O1	O3
End state*	S1	S2	S3	S2	S1

We will not go further in sequences.

The next thing will be to identify invalid transitions. To do this we fill in the state table. The result is:

Input Start State	I1	I2	
S1	S2/O1	S3/O2	
S2	S2/**N**	S1/O3	
S3	S2/O1	S3/**N**	

We have two invalid transitions: State 2 + Input 1 and State 3 + Input 2.

The test cases to execute can now be created from these test coverage items.

TC	Input	Expected Output
1	Push button A	The system bibs + state 2
2	Reset to state 1 + push button B	The light is on + state 3
3	Push button B again	Nothing changes
4	Push button A	The system bibs + state 2
5	Push button A again	Nothing changes
6	Push button B	The light is off + state 1

6.2.9.4   State Transition Testing Hints

One of the difficulties of state machines is that they can become extremely complex faster and more often than you can imagine. State machines can be defined in several levels to keep the complexity down, but this is a design decision.

6.2.10   Scenario Testing

A scenario shows how the product is expected to interact with one or more actors. It may be defined as "A number of actions performed by the product as results of triggers from the actor(s)." An actor may be a user or another product with which the product in question has an interface.

The most well-known type of scenario is the concept of a use case that was first developed by Sweden's Ivar Jacobsen in 1992.

Use cases or other types of scenarios are much used to express user expectations at an early state in the development and they are therefore often used as a basis for acceptance testing (if they are kept up to date and still reflect the product as it has turned out in the end).

A scenario is usually expressed in a table and can, for example, provide the following information:

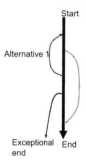

- ▶ A unique number and a name of the scenario;
- ▶ A short description of the purpose;
- ▶ Frequency;
- ▶ The actor(s);
- ▶ The start conditions and triggering event (if any);
- ▶ Rules to be applied (if any);
- ▶ The result and the postcondition;
- ▶ The scenarios or flows described in steps.

The first pieces of information are general information and useful for test design purposes, but the most interesting pieces of information are the scenarios or flows. This is where the product's expected reaction to the users' input is described and hence information to be used more or less directly in the test cases.

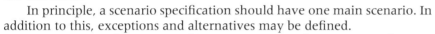

In principle, a scenario specification should have one main scenario. In addition to this, exceptions and alternatives may be defined.

A scenario can be structured in many ways, and it is up to each organization to define its own standard.

6.2.10.1 Scenario Testing Description

The testing of a scenario involves testing the main flow as specified in the steps in the scenario description. This means that test conditions should be derived from the scenario description.

This seems simple and it may be. But it is often seen that the "main flow" contains more or less hidden exceptions or alternatives. Go in search of expressions like "if," "in case of," or "while " to expose these.

Depending on the associated risks, it may also include testing the variants and exceptions. *Note:* Variants and exceptions may be difficult to test, if at all possible.

To get an overview of what a scenario description consists of, it is a very good idea to draw a flow diagram showing the main flow and all the alternatives and exceptions. This could be an eye-opening experience in terms of complexity.

As can be seen from the list above, a good use case provides useful information for testing purposes. We can get the identification of the use case for traceability purposes and the necessary preconditions directly from the description.

A use case description will rarely contain actual input values; these must be selected when we design our actual test cases. Based on the description, the postcondition(s), and possibly the rule(s), it should be possible to derive expected results for each test case based on selected input.

The information given for variants and exceptions, safety, frequency, and critical conditions can be used for risk analysis and decisions about which variants and exceptions to test and to what depths.

6.2.10.2 Scenario Testing Coverage

There are two ways to determine the coverage element for scenario testing:

▶ Full flow;

▶ Steps through a flow.

For full flow an entire flow, be it the main flow or an alternative or exceptional flow, is a coverage item. One test case is usually all that is needed to cover a flow, and the expected result is expressed in the scenario result and the postcondition, or the exception descriptions.

For the steps through a flow, each step is a coverage item, and at least one test case is needed to cover each step. The expected result is expressed as the system's reaction for each step. AM! The techniques for testing decision/branch testing described in Section 6.3.2 could be used to identify coverage items and achieved coverage.

In both cases it is theoretically possible for the number of coverage items to be unlimited; see the description of path testing in Section 6.3.6.

6.2.10.3 Scenario Testing Example

An example of a scenario is shown below.

2.1 Change Basis Data
Purpose: It must be possible for a subscriber to change his/her basis data, including create or remove a special delivery address.
Frequency: Rarely
Actor: Subscriber
Start conditions: The person acting as Subscriber is logged on to the system in accordance with the general requirements for "Log in."
Rule: A special delivery address is only valid for a period of not more than 3 weeks, and the period cannot overrun the period of the entire subscription period.
Post conditions: Subscriber has changed basis data and possibly created a special delivery address.

Main flow		
	Actor	**System**
Step 1	Chooses the function Change Basis Data.	Shows the input form for the function. Shows details for the subscriber, including a special delivery address if any.
Step 2	Name, address, and telephone number can be changed freely. If there is a delivery address, this can also be changed or deleted.	Registers changed basis data. Shows a message that a change of the e-mail address requires an application to the paper's service center.
Step 3	If a delivery address does not exist, it can be marked that a special delivery address is wanted.	The system makes it possible to enter a special delivery address, including the period that should be valid.
Step 4	If wanted: Enter a delivery address and the period it should be valid.	If wanted: Registers that a special delivery address exists, what it is, and the period it should be valid.
	[Period for delivery address is not valid]	
Step 5	Save changes.	Changes are saved.

Exceptions
Exception 1: Period for delivery address is not valid
The period is not valid, see rules. Informs about this. Allows the actor to try the step 3 again, or to return to the front page.

If we choose full flow coverage, the following test case covers the main flow:

TC	Input	Expected output
	Choose "Change Basis Data." Change the telephone number. Save changes.	The telephone number now has the changed value.

6.2.10.4 Scenario Testing Hints

Scenarios can be very deceptive, as can be seen from the above example, because a scenario may be seen as one requirement or a potentially large number of requirements describing complex flows.

When you work with scenarios you therefore need to be very careful that you understand to what depth the scenarios should be tested.

6.2.11   Random Testing

Random testing is a different technique from all the other specification-based techniques in that it is not directly based on the requirements. It is, however, based on a statistical model of the expected input pattern for one or more selected requirements.

6.2.11.1   Random Testing Description

The random testing technique can assist in generating input data based on a model of an input domain that defines all possible input values and their operational distribution for the requirement(s) that we set out to test.

Random input is not "out of the blue" random!

Expected input patterns can be estimated or may be known before deployment and that knowledge can be used in testing. There are many possible distributions, but the most common ones are the uniform distribution and the normal distribution.

In uniform distribution the probability of each value in the value domain is equal.

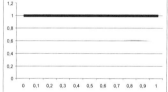

The outcome of throwing a die follows an equal distribution. The probability of getting a 6 is the same as that of getting any of the other values.

In the normal distribution there is an average value, which we have a high probability of getting. The further away from the average a value is, the lower is the possibility of getting that value.

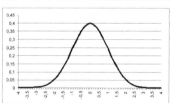

This is the case, for example, for the height of men in their forties. Most of these men are around 1.80 meters tall. Only a few men stand 2 meters tall, and likewise only a few reach no more than 1.6 meters.

For random testing we select input values for the test cases randomly from the input domain according to the input distribution. The selection of input is performed in a manner similar to that for a pools panel decision.

If the distribution is unknown, we can always use a uniform distribution.

Random testing can be used to generate input for test cases for specific requirements, in which case the expected results for the selected input values must be determined.

The technique can also be used if the objective is to generate a lot of input for, for example, reliability or performance testing, where the actual functional results of the test are not interesting in their own right.

The benefit of random input is that it is very cost effective, especially if automated; the input to many test cases in long sequences is cheap to develop (though the expected results may not be), the input requires little maintenance, and it gets around in the system in a trustworthy way.

Another benefit is that random input testing may find "unexpected" combinations and sequences and may detect initialization problems. It usually gives high code-related coverage. If automated it is very persistent testing, and long test runs may also find resource problems, such as memory leaks or list overflows.

6.2.11.2   Random Testing Coverage

There is no recognized coverage element for random testing, except for the case where the number of potential input values is known and can act as coverage items.

6.3   Structure-Based Techniques

The structural test case design techniques are used to design test cases based on an analysis of the internal structure of the test item. These techniques are also known as white-box test case design techniques.

Traditionally, the internal structure has been interpreted as the structure of the code. These techniques therefore focus on the testing of code and they are primarily used for component testing and low-level integration testing. In newer testing literature structural testing is also applied to architecture where the structure may be a call tree, a menu structure, or a web page structure.

Before we go any further, we need to define some white-box concepts. Below a small piece of code is shown to the left, and to the right the individual white-box concepts are identified; these are defined below.

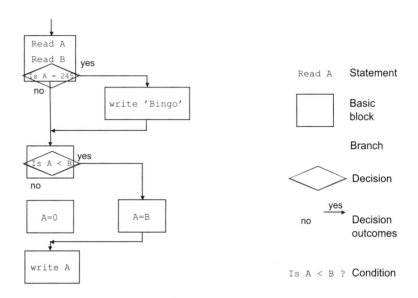

The first concept is that of a *statement*. An executable statement is defined as a noncomment or non–white space entity in a programming language; typically the smallest indivisible unit of execution.

A group of statements always executed together—or not at all—is called a *basic block*. A basic block can consist of only one statement or it can consist of many. There is no theoretical upper limit for the number of statements in a basic block.

The last statement in a basic block will always be a statement that leads to another basic block, or stops the execution of the component we are working with (e.g., return) or the entire software system (end).

A *branch* is a (virtual) connection between basic blocks. One or more branches will lead into a basic block (except to the first), and likewise there will be one or more branches leading out of a basic block (except the last).

Most basic blocks end in a *decision*; that is, a statement where the further flow depends on the outcome of the decision. Decision statements are for example IF … THEN …ELSE, FOR …, DO WHILE…, and CASE OF…

The branches out of a basic block are connected to the outcomes of the decision, also called *decision outcomes* or branch outcomes. Most decisions have two outcomes (true or false), but some have more, for example case statements.

The last concept is that of a *condition*. A condition is a logical expression that can be evaluated to be either true or false. A decision may consist of one simple condition, or a number of combined conditions.

Based on these definitions the structural test case design techniques covered in this book are:

- Statement testing;
- Decision testing;
- Branch condition testing;
- Branch condition combination testing;
- Modified condition decision testing;
- Path testing;
- Intercomponent testing.

There are differences in the naming of different structural test case design techniques; this is primarily due to personal preferences. Therefore, the table below maps the techniques named and described in this book to those named and described in ISO 29119 and by the ISTQB.

Structure-Based Test Case Design Techniques		
Described Here	**ISO 29119**	**ISTQB**
Statement testing	Statement testing	Statement testing
	Branch testing	
Decision testing	Decision testing	Decision testing
Branch condition testing	Branch condition testing	Condition testing
		Decision condition testing
Branch condition combination testing	Branch condition combination testing	Multiple condition testing
Modified condition decision coverage (MCDC) testing	Modified condition decision coverage (MCDC) testing	Modified condition/ decision coverage (MC/ DC) testing
	Data flow testing	Data flow testing
Path testing		Path testing
Intercomponent testing		API Testing

The structure-based test case design techniques all require the tester to understand the structure, that is, to have some knowledge of the coding language. The tester doesn't necessarily need to be able to write code. It is like with a foreign language: You may be able to understand what is being said, but find it difficult to express it yourself. This is usually not a problem anyway, because most structural testing of code is performed by programmers.

Structural testing is very often supported by tools, because the execution of components in isolation requires the use of stubs and drivers.

The techniques provide us with ideas for input. From where do we derive the expected output?

From the requirements—NEVER, ever from the code!

6.3.1   Statement Testing

Statement testing is a test case design technique in which test cases are designed to execute statements.

A statement is a unit of a given coding or scripting language executed in its entirety or not at all. The coding line:

```
b = 3 + a;
```

is one statement, whereas the coding line:

```
if a = 2 then b = 3 + a end if;
```

contains two statements.

The definition of a statement is independent of how the code is actually written and what language it is written in.

In statement testing we design test cases to get a specifically required *statement coverage*. Statement coverage is the percentage of executable statements (in a test item) that have been exercised in the test. Statement coverage is the weakest completion criterion of those described here.

The test item must be decomposed into the constituent statements, and we derive input for test cases from the code.

In the first example we have this small piece of code:

```
Read A;
Read B;
if A = 245 then
  Write 'Bingo';
endif;
Write B;
```

There are five statements (because "endif" doesn't count).
To get 100% statement coverage, we need one test case:

TC	Input	Expected output
TC1	A = 245	

Note: We have no means of finding out what the expected output is because the corresponding requirements or design is not included.

In the next example we will use this piece of code:

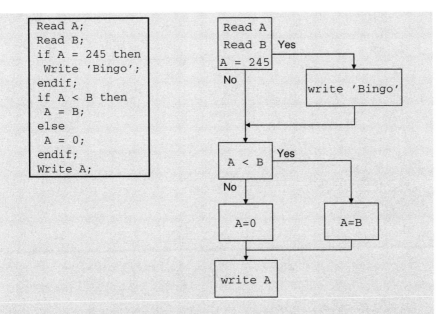

```
Read A;
Read B;
if A = 245 then
  Write 'Bingo';
endif;
if A < B then
  A = B;
else
  A = 0;
endif;
Write A;
```

Here we have eight statements. To get 100% statement coverage, we need two test cases:

TC	Input	Expected output
TC1	A = 245, B = 250	
TC2	A = 400, B = 250	

Again we don't know what the expected results should be.

6.3.2 Decision Testing

Decision testing is a test case design technique in which test cases are designed to execute decision outcomes.

Decision outcomes follow the branches of a basic block, and there is another described test case design technique called branch testing where test cases are designed to execute branches. Decision testing and branch testing are, however, very closely related and at 100% coverage, branch coverage and decision coverage give identical results. Hence, only decision testing is described here with references to branches where relevant.

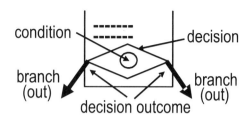

To define test cases for decision testing we have to:

▶ Divide the code into basic blocks.
▶ Identify the decisions (and hence the decision outcomes and the branches).
▶ Identify input to cover the decision outcomes (or branches).

In most cases a decision has two outcomes (true or false); but it is possible for a decision to have more outcomes, for example, in "case of ..." statements.

 Let us look at the Write 'Bingo' example again. We can see that this code has seven branches and four decision outcomes.

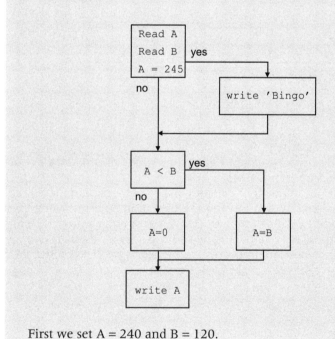

First we set A = 240 and B = 120.

This input covers three branches and we get branch coverage = 3/7 = 43%. It also covers two decision outcomes, and we get a decision outcome coverage of 2/4 = 50%.

Now we set A = 245 and B = 360.

This covers four more branches and two more decision outcomes, and we now have 100% branch coverage and 100% decision outcome coverage.

More test cases are often required to obtain 100% branch and decision outcome coverage than to obtain 100% statement coverage.

Decision coverage is usually measured using a software tool. Some tools can show the code and mark covered and uncovered decision outcomes by coloration of the code lines.

6.3.2.1   Other Decisions

Decisions may also be achieved by other statements than those using Boolean conditions, for example, "case," "switch," or "computed goto" statements, or counting loops (implemented by "for" or "do" loops). These should not go by untested. Two options are available for designing test cases for these:

▶ Assume that the decision is actually implemented as an equivalent set of Boolean conditions.

▶ Use a condition testing test case design technique as a supplement to decision testing.

6.3.3   Branch Condition Testing

A condition is a Boolean expression containing no Boolean operators (such as AND or OR) and that can be evaluated to be either TRUE or FALSE. An example is "a < c."

A statement like "X OR Y" is *not* a condition, because OR is a Boolean operator and X and Y Boolean operands. X and Y may in themselves be conditions.

Branch conditions are found in decision statements, that is, statements that will direct the flow into one branch or another.

Decision statements may have one condition like:

```
if (a < c) then …
```

They may also be composed of more conditions combined by Boolean operands, like:

```
if ((a=5) or ((c>d) and (c<f))) then …
```

or for short:

```
if (X or (Y and Z)) then …
```

The *branch condition outcome* is the evaluation of a branch condition to be either TRUE or FALSE. In branch condition testing we test condition outcomes.

The *branch condition coverage* is the percentage of branch condition outcomes in every decision (in a test item) that have been exercised by the test.

So to get 100% branch condition outcome coverage, we need to get each condition to be TRUE and FALSE, that is, we need two test cases.

In the first example with (a < c) we can design the test cases:

Test Case	a	c	(a < c)
1	5	7	True
2	6	2	False

In the next, more complex, example with (X or (Y and Z)) we also need to get each of the conditions to be TRUE and FALSE.

Without going into details about how to get X, Y, and Z to become TRUE and FALSE, we can see that we can still get 100% branch condition coverage with two test cases; for example:

Test Case	X	Y	Z
1	True	True	True
2	False	False	False

A 100% branch condition coverage for a decision can usually be obtained with two test cases regardless of the complexity of the decision statement.

In fact, 100% branch condition coverage may even be achieved without getting 100% decision outcome if the entire decision evaluates to the same for both cases. Branch condition testing may therefore be weaker than decision testing.

Note: Branch condition testing and the branch condition coverage test measurement are vulnerable to Boolean expressions that actually control decisions being placed outside of the actual decision statement.

Consider this example:

```
FLAG := A or (B and C);
if FLAG then
  do_something;
else   do_some thing_else;
  end if;
```

It may look as if we get 100% branch condition coverage by getting FLAG to evaluate to TRUE and FALSE, but in reality we need all of A, B, and C to evaluate to TRUE or FALSE.

To overcome this, we should design test cases for all Boolean expressions, not just those used directly in control flow decisions.

6.3.4   Branch Condition Combination Testing

With this test technique we test combinations of branch condition outcomes. To get 100% multiple branch condition coverage, we must test all combinations of outcomes of all branch conditions.

Because there are two possible outcomes for each branch condition (TRUE and FALSE), 2^n test cases, where n is the number of conditions, are required to get 100% coverage.

If we take the example from above:

```
    if (X or (Y and Z)) then ..
```

we have three conditions. We therefore need $2^3 = 8$ test cases to get 100% multiple branch condition coverage.

The test cases we need are:

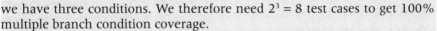

Test Case	X	Y	Z
	True	True	True
2	False	True	True
3	False	False	True
4	False	False	False
5	False	True	False
6	True	False	False
7	True	True	False
8	True	False	True

Note: The number of test cases grows exponentially with the number of conditions! This is a very thorough test, even though it may happen that some of the test cases are impossible to execute.

Sometimes the concept of "optimized expressions" jeopardizes the measurement of this test technique. Optimized expressions mean that a compiler short-circuits the evaluation of Boolean operators. For example, in the programming language C the Boolean AND is always short-circuited; the second operand will not be evaluated when the outcome can be determined from the first operand.

Short-circuits present no obstacle to branch condition coverage or modified condition decision coverage, but there may be situations where it is not possible to verify multiple branch condition coverage.

6.3.5 Modified Condition Decision Coverage (MCDC) Testing

Sometimes testing to 100% branch condition combination coverage would be to go overboard in relation to the risk associated with the component.

In these cases we can use the modified condition decision coverage testing technique. With this technique we should design test cases to execute branch condition outcomes that independently affect a decision outcome. This is a pragmatic compromise where we discard the conditions that do not affect the final outcome.

The number of test cases needed to achieve 100% modified condition decision coverage depends on how the conditions are combined in the decision statements:

▶ As a minimum we need n + 1 test cases;
▶ As a maximum we need 2n test cases,

where n is the number of conditions.

Still working with the same example as before:

```
if (X or (Y and Z)) then ..
```

we need the test cases listed in the table below.

Test Case	X	Y	Z	Result
1	True	-	-	True
2	False	True	True	True
3	False	False	-	False
4	False	True	False	False

An "-" means that it does not matter for the final outcome what the value of the condition is. In test case 1 the value of X is decisive, because there is an OR before the (Y and Z) condition. For the other test cases the value of (Y and Z) is decisive, again because of the OR.

We can hence get 100% modified condition decision coverage with just four test cases.

6.3.6   Path Testing

A path is a sequence of executable statements in a test item from an entry point to an exit point.

Path coverage is the percentage of paths in a component exercised by a specific test.

When you execute test cases based on any of the other structure-based techniques described above, you will inevitably execute paths through the code.

This example shows the four possible paths from beginning to end through the tiny bit of code.

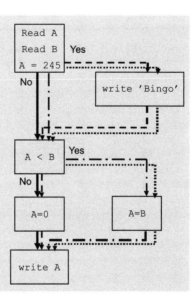

The number of possible paths through a test item is exponentially linked to the number of decisions, especially decisions involving loops.

The control flow diagram shown here for a bit of code includes a loop that may be exercised up to 20 times. Such a loop only gives

20 + 19 + ... + 1 possible different paths through the code.

In practice, it may easily become impossible to obtain 100% path coverage when loops are involved.

Path testing can be combined with a bit of error guessing. Experience shows that it can be useful to test the following types of paths:

- ▶ Minimum path;
- ▶ Path with no execution of any loop(s);
- ▶ Minimum path + 1 loop once;
- ▶ Path with 1 loop a number of times;
- ▶ Path with 1 loop the maximum number of times where possible.

6.3.7   Intercomponent Testing

Note: This technique is not included in ISO 29119, but included here because I find it very useful—especially since integration testing often is overseen and difficult to come to grips with.

The idea in structured design, object-oriented design, and most other design paradigms is that the functionality is distributed on a number of components and/or systems for ease of production and maintenance.

This means that interfaces exist between interacting components and systems. At the component level we say that components call functions in each other, or, as it is expressed in object-oriented design, use methods that other classes make available. At the system level other types of interfaces exist, for example, system to system using SOA, software to hardware integration, software to network integration, or software to manual procedure integration.

In the following, the concept of function calls will be used, but the idea is exactly the same for method usage and system interfaces.

The intercomponent testing technique is used in integration testing where the test items are these interfaces. The integration (testing) is performed after the component or system testing and assumes that logical and other types of defects in the body of the components or systems with interfaces have already been found.

Intercomponent testing is based on the design of the interfaces. For each function we should be able to find a design description of:

- ▶ Input: the input parameters required by the function;
- ▶ Functionality (which we are not interested in at this point);
- ▶ Output: the resulting output parameters produced by the function.

What we need to test are the calls to the functions, that is, the interfaces. The coverage element is calls, and the intercomponent coverage is the percentage of the total number of calls that we have covered in a specific integration test.

To identify the total number of calls made by all components or systems being integrated, we have to count, from the design, how many times each function is called. This is called fan-in: number of calls of a specific function from other functions (or the main program). This may be calculated using a static analysis tool (see Section 9.1.3.1). The sum of all the fan-ins provides the total number of calls.

For software components it is very difficult to say anything in general about the values for fan-ins. In system integration we normally have a very low fan-in, often only 1, for each system.

Test cases are designed to cover the calls.

We may combine the intercomponent testing with other techniques to get more thorough coverage of the input and/or output parameters, for example, equivalence partitioning and boundary value analysis for constraints on the parameters.

6.4 Experience-Based Testing Techniques

Defects are sly!

No matter how well we use the test case design techniques we cannot catch all of the defects. There are many reasons for this.

One is that not all failures occur every time the same action is performed. Sometimes a failure only occurs when we have performed the same action several times.

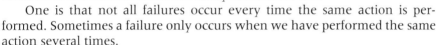

I use home-banking when I pay my bills. I enter the details for a bill, hit "OK," and then the details are presented in a form for my endorsement, and I can go on to the next bill. But—if I have more than eight bills to be paid at the same time, a failure occurs. For the ninth bill the endorsement form is blank! I endorse anyway, however, because the endorsement itself still works.

Another reason why we can miss defects is something called coincidental correctness. We may happen to choose input, for example, when choosing input in an equivalence partition that does not reveal a defect.

An illustration of this is a test of the formula n^n (n to the power of n). Unfortunately the programmer has misunderstood the formula and implemented it as "$n + n$." If we happen to choose the input value of 2, the expected result is 4 ($2 \times 2 = 4$)—but alas, $2 + 2$ also equals 4; this value does not reveal the defect, whereas the value 3 would have.

We also need to be aware that identical functionality may or may not be implemented identically. Many are the systems where, for example, date handling has been implemented by different implementation groups for different subsystems, and sometimes these implementations provide different implementations.

Furthermore, rare or fringe situations may be overlooked or deliberately left out in the specification of the structured test cases.

The sum of all this is that systematic testing is not enough! Because defects are sly we have to attack them in unpredictable ways.

This is where the nonsystematic testing techniques come in as a valuable supplement to structured testing techniques. The nonsystematic techniques discussed here are:

▶ Error guessing;
▶ Checklist based;
▶ Exploratory testing;
▶ Attacks.

These techniques may be used before the structural techniques to assess test readiness by uncovering "weak" areas. This can also be used as the input to initial risk analysis. The techniques may also be used after the structural testing as a final "mopping up"; hopefully providing extra confidence.

Nonsystematic testing techniques should NEVER be the only technique to be used.

6.4.1   Error Guessing

Error guessing is a test technique in which the experience of the tester is used to anticipate what defects might be present in the test object as a result of human errors made, and to design tests specifically to expose them.

This means that the tester uses his or her experience gained from the structured tests that have already been executed or from other test assignments to guess where defects may remain in the test object.

The tester has to think creatively—out of the box, over the borders, round the corners—both in relation to how the structured tests have been structured, how the test object has been produced, and the nature of the defects already found.

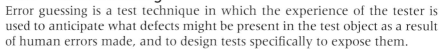

In relation to the testing approach, we could try to find alternative approaches, and ask ourselves:

▶ How could this be done differently?
▶ What would it be completely unlikely to do?
▶ What assumptions might the testers, who performed the structured tests, have made?

In relation to how the test object has been produced, we could ask ourselves:

▶ What assumptions might the analysts or the programmers have made?

> What happens if I use a value of 0 (both input and output)?
> What about cases of "none" and "one" in lists?
> What happens if I go over the limit?
> Are there any cases of "coincidence," for example, same value twice or same value for all?

The defects we have already found can be exploited to spur new ideas. We can for example ask ourselves:

> Are there other defects like this?
> Are there any reverse defects?
> Are there any perpendicular defects?

All of these questions and many more can be assembled and maintained in checklists.

The coverage for error guessing testing is related to the tester's experience base and not easily documented.

6.4.2 Checklist-Based Tests

Checklists can hold lists of possible defects that are known to escape the structured test. They are formed and maintained by experience—lessons learned from previous projects—and they are a valuable asset in an organization. Checklists may be used for designing both static and dynamic tests, and they can be used as a good starting point for, for example, risk identification or error guessing brainstorms.

Special checklists include defect taxonomies or rules derived from standards, for example, an internal standard for user interfaces.

Coverage for checklist-based testing is related to the contents of the checklists used. The coverage for a specific test may be calculated as the percentage of the items in the list(s) covered by the test.

An example of a checklist is the list shown below for CRUD testing. The abbreviation CRUD refers to the life cycle of data, namely:

> Create;
> Read;
> Update;
> Delete.

CRUD testing, that is, testing data entities according to their life cycles, is important.

The life cycles for data are usually not sufficiently specified in the data requirements. CRUD testing therefore starts with helping the analysts specifying sufficient requirements. The actual CRUD testing is sometimes on the verge of experience-based testing, because it may be based on previous experience of where CRUD defects appear and on related checklists.

The CRUD checklists provided below may be used as inspiration both for defining data requirements and for guiding CRUD testing.

CRUD checklist examples are shown here:
Concerning *creation of data* we may ask:

▶ Is it possible to create the first correctly?
▶ Is it possible to create a new correctly among existing?
▶ Is it possible to create the last (the highest number) correctly?
▶ Is it possible to create more than what is allowed?
▶ Is it possible to create if you are not allowed to create?

Concerning the *reading of data* we may ask:

▶ Is it possible to read data?
▶ Is it possible to find data in all the ways it is supposed to be found?
▶ Is it impossible to read data if you are not allowed?

Concerning the *updating of data* we may ask:

▶ Is it possible to change where it should be possible?
▶ Are changes saved correctly?
▶ Is a change reflected everywhere?
▶ Is it impossible to change in places where it should be impossible?

Concerning the *deletion of data* we may ask:

▶ Is it possible to delete where it should be possible?
▶ Is everything deleted?
▶ Do all deletes have the correct cascading effects?
▶ Is data that should not be deleted properly protected?

6.4.3   Exploratory Testing

Sometimes it is worthwhile to search in a structured way and use the results to decide on the future course as they come in. This is the philosophy used when people are looking for oil or landmines, and it is the philosophy in exploratory testing.

Exploratory testing is testing where the tester actively controls the design of the tests as those tests are performed and uses information gained while testing to design new and better tests. In other words exploratory testing is simultaneous:

- Learning;
- Test design;
- Test execution.

Exploratory testing is an important supplement to structured testing. As with all of the nonsystematic techniques, it may be used before the structured test is completely designed or when the structured test has stopped.

It is important for the course of the exploratory testing to be documented, so that we can recall what we have done. Imagine if drillings for oil were not documented; or if the search for landmines in a field were not documented—the exercises would be a waste of time and money. The idea in exploratory testing is not that it should not be documented, but that it should be documented as we go along.

Exploratory testing is not for kids!—nor for inexperienced testers.

Extensive testing experience and knowledge of testing techniques and typical defects are indispensable for performance of an effective exploratory test. It is also an advantage if the tester has some domain knowledge.

The exploratory tester needs to be able to analyze, reason, and make decisions on the fly, and at the same time have a systematic approach and be creative. The tester also needs some degree of independence in relation to the manufacturing of the system—the programmer of a system cannot perform exploratory testing on his or her "own" system.

Perhaps most importantly the exploratory tester must have an inclination toward destruction. Exploratory testing will not work if the tester is "afraid" of getting the system to fail.

6.4.3.1   Degrees of Exploratory Testing

One of the forerunners in exploratory testing is the American test guru James Bach. He has defined various degrees of exploration as illustrated in the figure below.

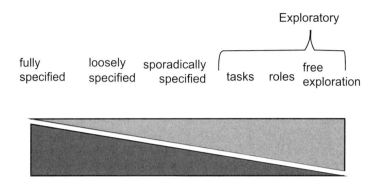

Furthest to the right we have the totally free exploration. The tester simply sits before the system and starts wherever he or she feels like it.

A step to the left we find the exploratory testing guided by roles. Here the tester attacks the system under test assuming a specific user role. This could be, for example, the role of an accountant, a nurse, a secretary, an executive manager, or any other role defined for usage of the system. This provides a starting point and a viewpoint for the testing that is exploratory within the framework of the role.

Further to the left is the exploratory testing guided by a specific task. Here the tester narrows the framework for the testing even more by testing within the viewpoint of a specific task defined for a specific role for the test item.

On the borderline between exploratory testing and structured testing we have the sporadically specified test. Here the tester has sketched the test beforehand and takes this as the starting point and guideline for the performance of the exploratory testing.

6.4.3.2 Performing Exploratory Testing

No matter which degree of exploration we use, we have to follow the principles in the general test process. We must plan and monitor; we must specify, execute, and record; and we must check for completion.

In the planning we consider what we are going to do and who is going to do it. We must choose the degree of exploration and describe the appropriate activities. The testing activities should be divided into 1-hour sessions. If the sessions are shorter we risk not getting an effective flow in the exploration; if they are longer we get tired and the effectiveness goes down.

It is important to make sure that the tester or testers are protected during the sessions. There should be no phones or other interruptions to disturb the flow of the testing.

The test specification, execution, and recording are done simultaneously during the exploratory testing session. Within the given degree of explo-

ration the tester should allow him- or herself to get distracted—you never
know what you may find.

The course of the testing session may be illustrated like this:

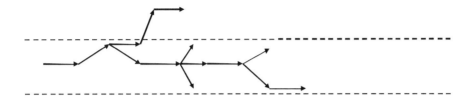

We must take stock from time to time to verify that we are on track.
For each session we must:

▶ Take extensive notes and attach data files, screen dumps, and/or
   other documentation as appropriate.

▶ Produce an overview of findings.

▶ Reprioritize the remaining activities.

The exploratory testing can stop when the purpose is fulfilled.

6.4.3.3 Exploratory Testing Hints

There are a few weaknesses in exploratory testing of which we need to be
aware. These weaknesses are part of the reasons why exploratory test must
be a supplement only to structured and specified testing.

The *weaknesses in exploratory testing* include:

▶ Exploratory testing does not support automated testing, and hence
   regression testing, very well.

▶ Because the exploratory testing is not specified in advance, it cannot
   provide feedback to design before the design is actually implemented.

▶ Even when accompanied by extensive notes, there is usually no
   firm documentation of test coverage for the exploratory testing.

▶ Exploratory testing can be very difficult to use for complex functionality—the main thread may easily be lost.

▶ Note taking is very difficult when working interactively.

The last weakness may be overcome by performing exploratory testing
as *pair testing*. This can work really well and it has a number of benefits. Pair

work sparks more ideas as the two testers inspire each other, and it enables mutual learning—even when the testers have different levels of experience.

Extroverted people get more energy from working together, and others are less likely to interrupt a pair.

The biggest benefit is perhaps that two testers can be focused on two tasks at a time: one can follow an idea, and the other can take notes. The focuses should switch between the two testers at regular intervals.

There are, of course, also *disadvantages of pair testing*. The main one is that a divided responsibility is no responsibility—if two people share a responsibility they carry 2% each.

Just as some people are extroverted, some people are introverted. Introverts get drained of energy when they work closely with others.

If the difference in experience is too large, it may cause "abandonment" by the less experienced tester because he or she may simply opt out. On the other hand, different opinions held by equally "strong" testers may block progress.

6.4.4   Attacks

The attack technique is a form of security testing; testing how resistant a product is to those who want to break into it in various ways and for various reasons, ranging from incidental mistakes, to "for fun," to serious crime.

Security testing is getting more and more powerful and sophisticated. As the market for e-commerce and e-business grows and more and more other applications get web access, the need for secure systems is growing. Even so, we are still constantly at least one step behind, and checklists of attacks are very valuable both to analysts defining requirements and to testers.

A product is vulnerable at the places where there is an opening into it; that is, where the product has interfaces. The interfaces a product can have include, but are not limited to:

- ▶ User interface;
- ▶ Operating system;
- ▶ API (application programming interface);
- ▶ Data storage (e.g., file system).

Attacks are used to find areas where the product will fail due to misuse or defects in these interfaces.

James Whittaker is one of the pioneers of attacks and he has created long lists of useful attacks. A few examples are listed here, grouped by type.

User Interface Attacks:
- ▶ Apply inputs that force all the error messages to occur.

- Apply inputs that force the software to establish default values.
- Explore allowable character sets and data types.
- Overflow input buffers.

Stored Data Attacks:

- Apply inputs using a variety of initial conditions.
- Force a data structure to store too many or too few values.
- Investigate alternate ways to modify internal data constraints.

Media-Based Attacks:

- Fill the file system to its capacity.
- Force the media to be busy or unavailable.
- Damage the media.

Other ways of attacking a product may be trying to cause unauthorized:

- Access to and control over resources, such as restricted files and data;
- Execution of programs or transactions;
- Access to and control over user accounts;
- Access to and control over privilege management;
- Access to and control over network management facilities.

The advantage of using attack-driven testing is that security holes can be closed before they are found by attackers. A pitfall is that this may create a false sense of security. There is no end to the imagination of those who want to do wrong, and we have to stay constantly alert to new weak spots. This is why checklists of any kind must be kept up to date with new experiences.

Security testing is discussed further in Section 7.3.5.

6.5   Defect-Based Techniques

In defect-based testing we are looking at the types of defects we might find in the test item. The techniques are therefore starting from previous experience, rather than the expected functionality or the structure of the test item.

The techniques may therefore be less systematic than the previously described techniques, since it is usually not possible to make an exhaustive collection of expected defects. The determination of defect-related coverage is hence also less comprehensive: Because there is no absolute amount of expected defects, only what we have chosen or selected as expected defects, the coverage is relative to that number.

The defect-based techniques covered here are:

▶ Taxonomies (not included in ISO 29119);
▶ Fault injection and mutation (not part of the ISTQB syllabus).

6.5.1 Taxonomies

A taxonomy is an ordered hierarchy of names for something. In this context it is an ordered hierarchy of possible defect types.

Such a taxonomy is a sort of checklist of defects to look for, and it is used to design test cases aimed at finding out if these defects are present in the product under test.

Many people have worked on defect taxonomies, starting with Beizer's Bug Taxonomy defined in the late 1980s. This taxonomy is quite comprehensive and lists possible defects in a four-level hierarchy with identification numbers. The first two levels are:

1   Requirements
        11 Requirements incorrect
        12 Requirements logic
        13 Requirements, completeness
        14 Verifiability
        15 Presentation, documentation
        16 Requirements changes
2   Features and Functionality
        21 Feature/function correctness
        22 Feature completeness
        23 Functional case completeness
        24 Domain bugs
        25 User messages and diagnostics
        26 Exception conditions mishandled
3   Structural Bugs
        31 Control flow and sequencing
        32 Processing
4   Data
        41 Data definition and structure
        42 Data access and handling
5   Implementation and Coding
        51 Coding and typographical
        52 Style and standards violation
        53 Documentation

6   Integration
        61 Internal interfaces
        62 External interfaces, timing, throughput

7   System and Software Architecture
        71 O/S call and use
        72 Software architecture
        73 Recovery and accountability
        74 Performance
        75 Incorrect diagnostics, exceptions
        76 Partitions, overlay
        77 Sysgen, environment

8   Test Definition and Execution
        81 Test design bugs
        82 Test execution bugs
        83 Test documentation
        84 Test case completeness

This taxonomy covers the entire development life cycle and may also be useful as a checklist for early static testing, for example, of requirements and design, as well as for static testing of the test specification.

Another defect taxonomy is given in IEEE 1044 in the categorization for incidents to be provided during the investigation phase of an incidents life cycle. This taxonomy has up to three levels, of which only the first is provided here with the corresponding codes:

IV310	Logical problem
IV320	Computation problem
IV330	Interface/timing problem
IV340	Data handling problem
IV350	Data problem
IV360	Documentation problem
IV380	Document quality problem
IV390	Enhancement
IV398	Failure caused by fix
IV399	Performance problem
IV400	Interoperability
IV401	Standards conformance
IV402	Other problem

Taxonomy testing is not a terribly effective test technique, especially not if the taxonomy used is a standard one that does not take the nature of the specific development process and product into account.

The taxonomies shown here, and others to be found in the testing literature are, however, very useful as starting points for making your own taxonomy or possible defects checklist.

The coverage element for taxonomy testing is the listed defects and the coverage is calculated as the percentage of these used in executed test cases.

6.5.2   Fault Injection and Mutation

Fault (or defect) injection and mutation are techniques in which the test item is changed in controlled ways and then tested. These techniques are used to assess the effectiveness of the prepared test cases, rather than actually looking for defects.

Fault injection is also known as fault seeding or "bebugging." In this technique defects are deliberately inserted into the source code, either by hand or by the use of tools.

The defects inserted may be inspired by a checklist or a defect taxonomy. The product is then tested and it is determined how many of the injected defects are found and how many other defects are found. These numbers are used to estimate how many real defects are still left in the product.

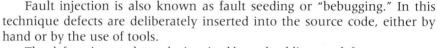

In a set of components 50 defects are injected prior to component testing. The component testing reveals

Injected defects: 26   and   New defects: 83

Based on this it is estimated that there remain 77 defects in the components and more tests should be designed, if this is not acceptable.

In mutation testing so-called one-token defects, such as "<" replaced with "<=", are made in the components. For each of these defects a new version of the affected components is created and tested to see if the prepared test cases reveal the defects. If they don't they will have to be examined and corrected to find the planted defects—and hopefully more real defects as well.

The coverage element for this type of testing technique is the injected defects and the coverage is calculated as the percentage of these found.

The drawback of the fault injection and mutation technique type is that the inserted defects are not necessarily realistic. It can also be a fairly big task to define and inject defects compared to the results to be gained.

Note also that even though the techniques help us identify more defects of the inserted types, there are a number of defects where it is of no use, for example, defects caused by omissions in the code or misunderstandings of the requirements.

Fault injection may also be applied to data, in the sense that data may be edited to be wrong compared to the correct data.

It is absolutely essential when using fault injection and mutation that a good configuration management system be in place. It must be clear what the "correct" code is and what code has been deliberately changed.

6.6 Choosing Test Techniques

The big question remaining after all of these descriptions of wonderful test case design techniques is: Which testing technique(s) should we use? The answer to that is: It depends!

There is no established consensus on which technique is the most effective. The choice depends on the circumstances, including the testers' experience and the nature of the test item.

With regard to the testers' experience, it is evident that a test case design technique that a tester knows well and has used many times on similar occasions is a good choice. All things being equal there is no need to throw old techniques overboard. Despite the general feeling that everything is changing fast, techniques do not usually change overnight. On the other hand, we need to be aware of new research and new techniques, both in development and testing becoming available from time to time.

A little more external to the testers' direct choice is the choice guided by risk analysis. Certain techniques are sufficient for low-risk products, whereas other techniques should be used for products or areas with a higher risk of exposure. This is especially the case when we are selecting between structural or white-box techniques. Testing and risk are discussed in Section 3.3.

Even further away from the testers, the choice of test techniques may be dictated by customer requirements, typically formulated in the contract. There is a tendency for these constraints being included in the contract for high-risk products. It may also be the case for development projects contracted between organizations with a higher level of maturity. In the case of test case techniques being stipulated in a contract, the tester responsible should have had the possibility of suggesting and accepting the choices.

Finally, the choice of test case design techniques can be guided or even dictated by applicable regulatory standards.

6.6.1 Subsumes Ordering of Techniques

It is possible to define a sort of hierarchy for the structural test case design techniques based on the thoroughness of the techniques at 100% coverage.

This hierarchy is called the subsumes ordering of the techniques. The verb "subsume" means "to include in a larger class." The subsumes ordering hence shows how the techniques relate to each other in terms of comprehensiveness. The ordering is shown here.

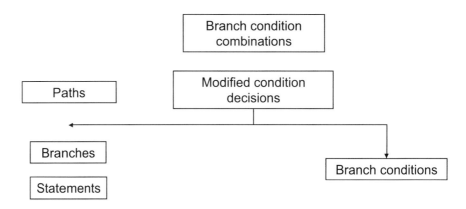

The ordering can only be read downward. We can see, for example, that modified condition decisions subsume branches. Paths also subsume branches, but we cannot say anything about the ordering of modified condition decisions in relation to paths.

Subsumes ordering does not tell us which technique to use, but it shows the techniques' relative thoroughness. It also shows that it does not make sense to require both a 100% branch and a 100% statement coverage for the same piece of software, because the latter will be superfluous.

6.6.2   Advise on Choosing Testing Techniques

No firm research conclusions exist about the rank in effectiveness of the functional or black-box techniques. Most of the research that has been performed is very academic and not terribly useful in the "real testing world."

One conclusion that seems to have been reached is: There is no "best" technique. The "best" depends on the nature of the product.

We do, however, know with certainty that the use of *some technique is better than none,* and that a combination of techniques is better than just one technique.

We also know that the techniques support systematic work and that techniques are good for finding possible defects. Using test case design techniques means that they may be repeated by others with approximately the same result, and that we are able to explain our test cases.

There is no excuse for not using some techniques.

In his book *The Art of Software Testing,* Glenford J. Meyers provides a strategy for applying techniques. He writes:

▶ If the specification contains combinations of input conditions, start with cause-effect graphing.

▶ Always use boundary value analysis (input and output).

◗ Supply with valid and invalid equivalence partitions (both for input and output).

◗ Round up using error guessing.

◗ Add sufficient test cases using white-box techniques if completion criteria have not yet been reached (providing it is possible).

As mentioned above some research is being made into the effectiveness of different test techniques.

Dr. Stuart Reid has made a study on the techniques of equivalence partitioning (EP), boundary value analysis (BVA), and random testing on real avionics code. Based on all input for the techniques he concluded that BVA was the most effective with 79% effectiveness, whereas EP only reached 33% effectiveness. Reid also concludes that some defects are difficult to find even with these techniques.

Questions

1. Why is it a good idea to use test techniques?
2. What is the other, perhaps more common, name for specification-based testing techniques?
3. What is the basic idea in equivalence partitioning?
4. Why might equivalence partitioning reduce the number of test cases?
5. How is equivalence partitioning coverage calculated?
6. What are the two types of nodes in a classification tree?
7. What are the two rules that must be observed when a classification tree is constructed?
8. With what does a classification tree end?
9. What is the coverage element for a classification tree?
10. What should be considered input in a classification tree?
11. What is boundary value analysis?
12. What are the two approaches to boundary value analysis?
13. What are the coverage elements for boundary value analysis?
14. What is syntax testing used for?
15. Who has defined a notation form for syntax?
16. How can you define invalid syntaxes?
17. What is combinatorial testing?
18. When can pair-wise testing be used?
19. What characterizes an orthogonal array?
20. How can an orthogonal array be described?
21. What is the weakness of pair-wise testing?

22. How many columns does a decision table have depending on the number of input conditions?
23. What is the coverage element for decision tables?
24. How can you fill in a decision table?
25. What is one of the main application areas for decision tables?
26. What is a cause-effect graph?
27. How is cause-effect graph coverage defined?
28. What are the building blocks of a cause-effect graph?
29. What does an arch mean in a cause-effect graph?
30. What does a transition consist of?
31. What is the coverage measure for state transition testing?
32. What is the lowest coverage level in state transition testing?
33. What is an invalid transition?
34. What is the main difficulty with state machines?
35. What is a scenario?
36. How can scenario testing coverage be measured?
37. What is random testing?
38. How can you measure coverage for random testing?
39. What is structure-based testing also known as?
40. What is a basis block?
41. From where must the expected results be derived in structural testing?
42. How does a basic block end?
43. What is a statement?
44. How is statement coverage defined?
45. What is a condition?
46. How is branch condition coverage defined?
47. How many test cases do we usually need to get 100% condition coverage for one decision?
48. How many test cases do we need to get 100% branch condition combination coverage for one decision?
49. What is done when designing test cases for modified condition decision testing?
50. What is a loop?
51. What are the main pitfalls when working with loops?
52. What is path testing?
53. What should be tested in path testing?
54. What causes path testing to be very difficult?
55. At which test level(s) is intercomponent testing used?
56. Why do we need experience-based testing?
57. What is error guessing?
58. What is a checklist?

59. What characterizes exploratory testing?
60. What are the degrees of exploratory testing?
61. What is important during exploratory testing?
62. What are the weaknesses in exploratory testing?
63. How can exploratory testing possibly be enhanced?
64. What are we looking for in attack testing?
65. What is a taxonomy?
66. Where can examples of defect taxonomies be found?
67. What can fault injection be used for?
68. What is important in connection with fault injection and mutation testing?
69. Which test technique is the best?
70. What is the subsumes order of test techniques?
71. Which test technique is better than none?
72. Which technique does G. J. Meyers recommend as the first test technique to use?

Testing of Quality Characteristics

A standard definition of the quality of a product is the degree to which the product fulfills the expectations of the customers and the users. We test to get information about the quality; that is, information about the fulfillment of the specified requirements and/or implied needs, the expectations.

The better the expectations are known, understood, and documented, the easier it is for the developers to produce a satisfactory product and the easier it is for testers to test it. This applies both for sequential, iterative, and agile development, even though the documentation takes on different forms.

This chapter is about software quality characteristics or quality attributes, as they are also called. Quality characteristics are a way of structuring and expressing the expectations for a product.

In a way this chapter is superfluous for testers because it is about expressing expectations. It is, however, a very good idea for testers to understand what quality characteristics are, and how they may be expressed. With this understanding testers can contribute to the quality of a product in a number of ways from the very start of the development life cycle, for example, by ensuring that expectations are expressed in a testable way and by preparing dynamic tests to cover all expectations.

The quality of a product should be measured both with regard to what the product shall do—the functional quality characteristic; and with regard to how the functionality shall present itself and behave—the often-called nonfunctional quality characteristics.

7.1 Quality Characteristics Overview

The ISO/IEC 25010 standard is the newest standard providing a quality model for products. It lists the following quality characteristics:

- Functional suitability;
- Performance efficiency;
- Compatibility;
- Usability;
- Reliability;
- Security;
- Maintainability;
- Portability.

This standard is used as the basis for this chapter and is the basis for the ISO 29119 standard as well.

The ISTQB syllabus is based in the ISO 9126, which has been superseded by ISO 25010. The following table provides a mapping between the two standards:

ISO 25010/ISO 29119	ISO 9126/ISTQB
Functional suitability	Functionality
Performance efficiency	
Compatibility	(at sublevcl)
Usability	Usability
Reliability	Reliability
Security	(at sublevel)
	Efficiency
Maintainability	Maintainability
Portability	Portability

There are also differences in the subcharacteristics, which are outlined in the subsections below.

In ISO 25010 language, the quality characteristics cover the existence of a set of functions and their specified properties in the product. The functions are those that satisfy stated or implied needs, from the point of view of a stated or implied set of users.

7.2 Quality Characteristics for Test Analysts

In general, test analysts are concerned with the functional suitability and the usability quality characteristics of the product under test.

The functionality is what the product can do. Without functionality we don't have a product at all. The functionality supports the users in their daily work or their leisure, as the case might be.

Functionality may be tested in all test subprocesses. In component testing, for example, we can test the functionality or partial functionality implemented in individual components, and in system testing we can test the full functionality implemented in the system across a number of integrated components. When we test how the functionality meets the expectations, we can use the testing techniques discussed in Chapter 6.

Usability is how the users experience the use of the product. This is at least if not more important than functionality. The functionality may be perfect in itself, but so time consuming to perform on the computer that it is more easily done manually.

The usability of a product should be tested as part of the requirements specification or at the latest during user interface design to determine what the most appropriate user interface for the product is. Late usability testing should only be done to ensure that the user interface has been implemented according to the approved design, as it may be too late to change serious flaws in the user interface late in the development life cycle.

7.2.1 Functional Suitability Testing

Functional suitability testing is performed to get information about the degree to which a product provides functions that meet stated and implied needs when used under specified conditions.

ISO 25010 breaks the functional suitability characteristics into the following subcharacteristics (the text in brackets describes the changes in relation to ISO 9126):

▶ Functional completeness (new);
▶ Functional correctness (was accuracy);
▶ Functional appropriateness (was suitability).

This list may be used as a checklist for producing requirements, as well as for structuring the functionality testing. Each of the subcharacteristics is discussed in more detail below.

7.2.1.1 Functional Completeness Testing

In functional completeness testing we test to provide information about the degree to which the set of functions covers all of the specified tasks and user objectives.

The basic way all software products work is to contain and/or to allow entry of appropriate data, to handle the data in correct ways, and to present the data and the handling results appropriately.

The very short story about what detailed functional completeness could be concerned with is:

▶ *Data availability:* how do we get data, both in terms of background or reference data and/or data from other systems and in terms of data input and data change facilities and the associated levels of data validations;

▶ *Data handling:* what is the data used for, for example as event-driven interrupts or signals, calculations, actions, etc., based on the data;

▶ *Result presentation:* output facilities in terms of, for example, forms and reports.

The story is by no means exhaustive. It should, however, give an idea of how functionality requirements may be structured.

Expectations regarding functional completeness may be expressed in formal requirements, but are also often seen expressed in use cases and/or user stories, because these provide a good way of describing what the users' tasks are and how the software product should support these.

The first thing to find out for a product is, therefore, how much of the expected functionality has actually been delivered. This quality characteristic is not about whether or not the delivered functionality is correct or appropriate, but simply about which functionality is present in the product.

Completeness testing may be done by assessing trace information from the specified tasks and user objective (requirements) to the product. If there is no such traceability, the specified tasks and user objective may serve as a checklist that can be used to test how much is covered by the product.

7.2.1.2 Functional Correctness Testing

In functional correctness testing we test to provide information about the degree to which a product provides the correct results with the needed degree of precision.

More detailed functional correctness specification could concern:

▶ Algorithmic correctness: calculation of a value from other values and the correctness of function representation;

▶ Calculation precision: precision of calculated values;

▶ Time correctness: correctness of time-related functionality;

▶ Time precision: precision of time-related functionality.

Correctness requirements are often implied. If in doubt about these quality characteristics during testing it is better to ask, rather than to assume, especially if you are not an absolute domain expert.

A few examples of functional correctness requirements could be:

> [230] The system shall ensure that during calculation all money values are rounded; except in the Japanese version, where money values shall be truncated.
>
> [231] The system shall ensure that all money calculations in Euros are performed to three decimals.
>
> [232] The system shall ensure that all money calculations in other currencies are performed to two decimals.
>
> [233] The system shall present all values for money with two decimals on the user interface and in reports.

Functional correctness can be tested in all test subprocesses; the earlier the better. Some functional correctness testing may even take place as static testing of design and code. Many of the techniques discussed in Chapter 6 can be used in correctness testing.

7.2.1.3 Functional Appropriateness Testing

In functional appropriateness testing we test to provide information about the degree to which the functions facilitate the accomplishment of specified tasks and objectives.

Remember that a software product is never the goal in itself. It is produced to support its users in doing their real jobs or in having more fun. Software is a tool to make work and fun faster and more reliable.

> An accountant's job is to keep accounts. This can be done entirely using pen and paper. However, the accountant may instead use a computer system to help. When the accountant has entered the data, the system may be able to store them, calculate sums from them, and produce reports presenting the data on the screen and on paper.
>
> If the computer system does not calculate the needed sums, the functional appropriateness would be lower than if it did.

Functional appropriateness testing can take place in all test subprocesses, but is usually done in a test subprocess including user acceptance testing. All the techniques discussed in Chapter 6 may be used in this kind of testing depending on the nature of the requirements.

7.2.2 Usability Testing

In usability testing we test to provide information about the degree to which a product or system can be used by specified users to achieve specified goals with effectiveness, efficiency, and satisfaction in a specified context of use. The *effectiveness* of a software product is based on its ability to enable users to achieve specified goals with accuracy and completeness. The *efficiency* of a product is its ability to enable users to expend appropriate amounts of re-sources in relation to the effectiveness achieved. The *satisfaction* of a product is its ability to please users.

7.2.2.1   Users Concerned with Usability

The usability quality attribute is related to the users of the product. It is important to get a complete overview of potential user groups or types, and to take any kind of user characteristics into account when working with usability.

A user group for a product is a group of people who will be affected in similar ways by the product. A user group is not just the people entering data into the product and looking at the screen, though this is certainly an important user group. This group may indeed be divided into frequent users, occasional users, and rare users, or other relevant subgroups. User groups may also consist of those in charge of installing the product, and those monitoring and maintaining it. User groups may also consist of those getting information from the product, for example, in the form of reports or letters, and those having to be near the product without actually interfering with it.

The list of appropriate user groups is of course very product sensitive, and care should always be taken not to forget a potential user group.

For each of the user groups, it is necessary to look at different character-istics. Examples include:

- Age (e.g., preschool, children, teens, young adults, mature adults, elderly);
- Attitude toward the product (e.g., hostile, neutral, enthusiastic);
- Education (e.g., no education yet, illiterate, basic education, middle education, workman, university education);
- Disabilities (e.g., people who are dyslexic, color-blind, blind, partial-ly sighted, deaf, mobility impaired, or cognitively disabled);
- Ability to learn and understand (slow, average, fast).

7.2.2.2   Usability Subattributes

The ISO 25010 standard classifies usability as a nonfunctional quality char-acteristic. It has got to do with how the functionality presents itself to the users. But there is more to it than meets the eye; usability covers much more than just the look and feel of the product.

ISO 25010 breaks the usability quality characteristic into the following subcharacteristics:

◗ Appropriateness recognizability;
◗ Learnability;
◗ Operability;
◗ User error protection;
◗ User interface aesthetics;
◗ Accessibility.

The *appropriateness recognizability* characteristic is the degree to which users can recognize whether a product is appropriate for their needs.

This has got to do with how difficult it is to recognize the logical concept of the product and figure out how to apply it in practice. This may cover:

◗ Extent to which the system maps the concepts employed in the business procedures;
◗ Extent to which existing nomenclature is used;
◗ Nature and presentation of structure of entities to work with;
◗ Presentation of connections between entities.

The *learnability* characteristic is the degree to which a product can be used by specified users to achieve specified goals of learning and to use the product with effectiveness, efficiency, freedom from risk, and satisfaction in a specified context of use.

This has got to do with the learning curve for the product, and it may cover:

◗ Extent to which a user of the system can learn how to use the system without external instruction;
◗ Presence and nature of online help facilities for specified parts of the system;
◗ Presence and nature of offline help facilities for specified parts of the system;
◗ Presence and nature of specific manuals.

The *operability* characteristic is the degree to which a product has attributes that make it easy to operate and control. This may cover:

◗ Presence and nature of facilities for interactions with the product;
◗ Consistency of the man–machine interface;
◗ Presence, nature, and ordering of elements on each form;
◗ Presence and nature of input and output formats;

◗ Presence and nature of means of corrections of input;

◗ Presence and nature of navigational means;

◗ Number of operations and/or forms needed to perform a specified task;

◗ Format, contents, and presentation of warnings and error messages;

◗ Presence and nature of informative messages;

◗ Pattern of human operational errors over stated periods of time under stated operational profiles according to defined reliability models.

The *user error protection* characteristic is the degree to which the system protects users against making errors.

This is the opposite of the old "joke" among programmers: "Garbage in, garbage out." This attitude is not tolerable today. The user error protection may consist of, for example:

◗ Defined and controlled syntax for input data;

◗ Appropriate default values for input;

◗ No default values where the active setting of a value is required (typically for safety critical products);

◗ Defined and controlled minimum and/or maximum values for input;

◗ Defined and controlled mandatory input;

◗ Defined and controlled dependencies between two or more inputs.

The *user interface aesthetics* characteristic is the degree to which the user interface enables pleasing and satisfying interaction for the user.

This has got to do with how the users like the system and what may make them choose to acquire it in the first place. It may cover:

◗ Use of colors;

◗ Use of fonts;

◗ Use of design elements, such as drawings and pictures;

◗ Use of music and sounds;

◗ Use of voices (for example, soprano or baritone), languages, and accents;

◗ Layout of user interfaces and reports;

◗ Presence and nature of nontechnical documentation material;

◗ Presence and nature of technical documentation material;

◗ Presence and nature of specified demonstration facilities;

◗ Presence and nature of marketing material.

The *accessibility* characteristic is the degree to which a product can be used by people with the widest range of characteristics and capabilities to achieve a specified goal in a specified context of use.

In recent years there has been more and more focus on equal opportunities, not least for people with disabilities. This also concerns software systems, which must be accessible and operable for everybody.

Rules are, for example, expressed in the Disability Discrimination Act covering the United Kingdom and Australia, and Section 508 for the United States.

In this context accessibility is the ease with which people with disabilities can operate the product.

Accessibility may cover:

◗ Use of colors, especially mixtures of red and green;

◗ Possibility of connecting special facilities, such as a speaker reading the text aloud, Braille keyboard, voice recognition, and touch screens;

◗ Possibility of using the product entirely by key strokes and/or voice commands;

◗ Facilities for multiple key pressure using only one finger or other pointing device;

◗ Possibility of enlarging forms and/or fonts;

◗ Navigation consistency.

A number of standards cover various aspects of accessibility, including Web Contents Accessibility Guidelines from the World Wide Web Consortium (W3C); an international consortium working on web standards.

7.2.2.3 Establishing Usability Requirements

Like all other requirements, usability requirements should be expressed as explicitly as possible. Usability requirements can be derived from usability assessments (sometimes unfortunately called by the misleading name "usability test" and also known as formative evaluation).

Usability assessment is a requirements elicitation technique—and it should be performed early, not on the finished product, when it usually is too late to make any changes.

A usability assessment is performed by representative users who are given tasks to complete on a prototype of the products. This can be hand-drawn sketches of forms or mockups of the forms made in, for example, Power-Point. Any thoughts and difficulties the users have in completing the tasks are recorded. This is best done if the users can be made to "think aloud" during the assessment.

After the usability assessment the comments are analyzed, the prototype may be changed and assessed again, and finally the usability requirements can be derived.

Usability assessments can be done very primitively by review of prototypes and storyboards, or in a very sophisticated manner by means of purpose-built usability labs with two-way mirrors and video equipment.

People with different skills may participate in the elicitation and documentation of usability requirements, for example, specialists in sociology, psychology, ergonomics, and so forth.

The usability requirements must be measurable. A requirement like this:

~~The user interface shall be nice to look at.~~

is seen all too often, but it is not helpful.

Below are a few examples of measurable usability requirements:

{UR.518} At least 95% of the primary users of the product shall answer either "Very good" or "Good" when asked about their opinion of the look and feel of the user interface in the survey to be carried out 2 months after deployment

{UR.523} At least 80% of estate agents with min. 5 years experience shall be able to complete the task described in use case {UC.78} in less than 30 minutes after 20 minutes of instruction.

{UR.542} All push buttons shall be placed right aligned at the bottom of the forms.

{UR.557} All forms shall have an online help facility describing the purpose and the syntax of all the fields on the form.

{UR.516} All tasks described in Section 4.1 shall be completable with a maximum of five clicks.

Note that these usability requirements are nonfunctional. They cannot be expressed independently of functionality, but must refer to the functionality to which they apply, whether it is the entire product or a smaller part of it.

7.2.2.4 Testing Usability

Usability may be tested in various ways during the development life cycle. Techniques to use include:

- ▶ Static testing;
- ▶ Verification and validation of the implementation;
- ▶ Surveys and questionnaires.

Static testing can be performed as technical reviews and/or inspections of usability requirements. This may include heuristic evaluation, in which the design of the user interface is verified against recognized usability principles. Static testing finds defects early and is hence very cost effective, not least for usability, where mistakes in the user interface may be very expensive to remedy late in the development life cycle. Static testing is further described in Chapter 4.

The *verification and validation* of the implementation of the usability requirements are performed on the working system. Here the focus is on the usability requirements associated with the functional requirements. Test procedures, use cases, or scenarios may be used to express what is to be done, whereas the actual usability testing is about whether the usability requirements are fulfilled.

The usability requirements may be in the form of requirements stated in natural languages, as the examples above show, or they may be expressed in terms of prototypes or drawings. These may be more difficult to test against, but it is important to verify that an implementation is in fact reflecting the prototype agreed on by the future users.

In this form of usability testing, it is particularly important for the test environment to reflect the operational environment, not least in terms of space, light, noise, and other disturbing factors.

Coverage may be measured using the usability requirements as the coverage element.

The ultimate validation is the user acceptance test where the finished product should be accepted by the users as being the system that fulfills their requirements, expectations, and needs. Obvious great care should be taken throughout the development process to ensure that acceptance may actually be the results of the acceptance testing. Serious defects and failures identified at this point in time may turn out to be very expensive.

Not all requirements can be tested with quantitative static and dynamic testing. *Surveys and questionnaires* may be used where subjective measures, such as the percentage of representative future users who like or dislike the user interface, are needed.

The questions must be worded to reflect what we want to know about the users feelings toward the product. We can make our own, or we may use standardized surveys such as SUMI or WAMMI.

SUMI, The *Software Usability Measurement Inventory,* is a tested and proven method of measuring software quality from the end user's point of view. It can assist with the detection of usability flaws before a product is shipped, and it is backed by an extensive reference database embedded in an effective analysis and report generation tool. SUMI provides concrete measurements of usability and these may be used as inspiration for usability requirements or completion criteria. See more at http://sumi.ucc.ie.

WAMMI is a web analytics service to help website owners accomplish their business goals by measuring and tracking user reactions to a website's ease of use. See more at http://www.wammi.com

7.3 Quality Characteristics for Technical Test Analysts

As important as the functionality of a product may be, it cannot stand alone. The functionality will always behave and present itself in certain ways. This is what we call the nonfunctional quality characteristics of a product.

Historically, these characteristics have been more or less neglected when requirements have been specified, and testers have "tested" some of the nonfunctional quality characteristics based on their experience. This testing was very often just a negative test: The basic idea was to get the product to fail to see how much it could cope with, without knowing what the needs and expectations were.

This ought not to happen. Nonfunctional requirements should be defined for all the functionality for the product in the requirements specification.

There are many suggestions for what nonfunctional requirements should cover. Some classic standards, which have been around for quite some time, are listed here with the quality attributes they include:

ISO 9126: functionality, reliability, usability, efficiency, maintainability, portability;

McCall and Matsumoto: integrity, correctness, reliability, usability, efficiency, maintainability, testability, flexibility, portability, interoperability, reusability;

IEEE 830: performance, reliability, availability, security, maintainability, portability;

ESA PSS-05: performance, documentation, quality, safety, reliability, maintainability.

The nonfunctional quality characteristics covered in this section are:

> ▶ Performance efficiency;
> ▶ Compatibility;
> ▶ Reliability;
> ▶ Security;
> ▶ Maintainability;

▶ Portability;

in accordance with ISO 25010.

The usability quality characteristic is covered in the previous section, since it is typically within the responsibility of the test analysts.

7.3.1 Technical Testing in General

To a large extent, nonfunctional testing is identical to functional testing; it should be based on expectation and use the test case design techniques discussed in Chapter 6 as much as possible.

Testers can, and should, help developers and analysts define these requirements from the beginning; and we should review the requirements to ensure that they are comprehensive and testable.

It is important for the nonfunctional requirements to be measurable and testable. This is not always easy, however, at least not in the beginning. All too many nonfunctional requirements are expressed using words such as "good," "fast," or "most of the time."

To overcome this, keep in mind that each nonfunctional requirement must be expressed using a scale, a specific goal, and possibly also acceptable limits. The circumstances under which the goal is to be achieved must also be specified. Further information (e.g., achieved records and future goals) could also be given to put the specified requirement value(s) in perspective.

Let's look at an example. First a typical way of expressing a performance expectation:

"Reports must not take too long to be created."

This should make you wonder which reports we are talking about, what "too long" means, and if this is a general expectation regardless of the circumstances.

The requirements could be reworded to:

"[P.65] The creation of a full report of all the clients as specified in Req. [F.89] shall not take more than 15 minutes if launched between 8:00 and 16:00 on normal weekdays."

This is much better. Now we know which report we are talking about, namely, the one specified in the functional requirement [F.89]; we know that 15 minutes is acceptable; and we know that this is the expectation for a report to be produced in a normal working day. The requirement could be even more specific, but the improvement in testability is already significant.

It can become a sport to dig behind imprecise nonfunctional expectations and find out what the real need is.

Apart from assisting during the requirements specification, technical testers must test the actual product in relation to the nonfunctional requirements. This can be done in different test subprocesses depending on the type of requirements.

The coverage for nonfunctional testing can be measured using nonfunctional requirements as the coverage element.

The testing of the nonfunctional quality characteristics must be executed in a realistic environment reflecting the specified circumstances. This can include hardware, network, other systems, timing, place, load patterns, and operational profiles.

An operational profile is a description of

▶ how many;
▶ of which user groups;
▶ will use what parts of the system;
▶ when; and
▶ how much and/or how often.

If care is not taken to ensure realistic circumstances, the testing may be a complete waste of time and, even worse, create a false sense of confidence in the product.

For some of the nonfunctional quality characteristics it not possible or not sufficient to provide requirements and test in a structured way against these. In this case the descriptions of the quality attributes can serve as inspiration for checklists to assist less structured testing.

7.3.2   Performance Efficiency Testing

In performance efficiency testing we test to provide information about performance relative to the amount of resources used under stated conditions.

In performance efficiency testing we test the expectations concerned with the product's ability to provide appropriate performance, relative to the amount of resources used, under stated conditions.

The ISO 25010 standard breaks the performance efficiency quality characteristic down into the following subcharacteristics:

▶ Time behavior;
▶ Resource utilization;
▶ Capacity.

These are described below.

7.3.2.1   Time Behavior Testing

 In time behavior testing we test to provide information about the degree to which the response and processing times and throughput rates of a product, when performing its functions under stated conditions, meet requirements.

In short, time behavior testing is concerned with how fast specified parts of the functionality work. This may cover requirements concerning:

- ▶ The response time for specified online tasks under specified conditions;
- ▶ The elapsed time for transfer of specified data under specified circumstances;
- ▶ The internal processing time (e.g., in CPU cycles) for specified tasks under specified conditions;
- ▶ The elapsed processing time for specified batch tasks under specified conditions.

Expectations toward performance must be expressed in performance requirements.

[P.65] The creation of a full report of all the clients as specified in Req. {F.89} shall not take more than 15 minutes if launched between 8:00 and 16:00 on normal weekdays.

[P.72] The creation of a full report of all the clients as specified in Req. {F.89} shall not use more than 35% of the CPU time.

Performance testing can be very expensive and time consuming to perform. It can be especially costly to establish the correct environment for testing.

It is important to be absolutely sure that the environment and conditions are correctly specified in performance requirements and correctly established for performance testing, not least in terms of hardware, operating system, middleware, and concurrent use patterns or operational profiles.

This is something that should be specified in connection with the requirements specification in order for the performance requirements and hence the performance test to be reliable.

Many tools support the testing of performance. The tools can report on response times and execution times, for example, for database look-ups or data transfer, and they can identify bottlenecks in the functions, either internally in the product and/or in the network for web-based products. Tools are discussed in Chapter 9.

In principle, performance testing verifies that performance requirements have been fulfilled. The coverage element is performance requirements and the coverage is hence measured as the percentage of all performance requirements tested in a test. As for all testing, failures must be reported, and retest and regression test must be performed after corrections.

7.3.2.2 Resource Utilization Testing

In resource utilization testing we test to provide information about the degree to which the product's use of appropriate amounts of resources when the software performs its functions under stated conditions meets requirements.

In short, resource utilization refers to what is used and what is needed. This may cover requirements concerning:

▶ The amount of CPU resources used for specified functions;
▶ The amount of internal memory resources used for specified functions;
▶ The amount of external memory resources used for specified functions;
▶ Levels of memory leakage;
▶ The presence, appropriateness, and availability of human resources, peripherals, external software, and various materials.

In modern systems memory is rarely a problem, but it may be in, for example, games and real-time embedded systems. In the latter, memory usage, also referred to as memory footprint, may be the object of precise specification and thorough testing.

7.3.2.3 Capacity Testing

In capacity testing we test to provide information about the degree to which the maximum limits of a product parameter meet requirements.

Capacity testing is a special subtype of performance testing concerned with the product's behavior under specified conditions.

Capacity has two aspects, namely:

▶ Multiuser with an ordinary realistic number of users;
▶ A large, though still realistic number (volume) of concurrent users.

The capacity that the product is expected to be able to handle and the applicable response times must be expressed in capacity requirements.

We need to think about capacity early on during requirements specification. It is important to strike a balance in the capacity requirements so that they are within reason, but still take the future into account.

Capacity testing can be quite expensive, and it is important not to go overboard. Sometimes we may have to question the requirements: Are they realistic or "wearing both belt and braces"? To keep the capacity testing expenses under control, we should use risk analysis to prioritize and plan the testing tasks.

Tools may be used to generate and/or simulate loads and other capacity elements.

Capacity testing and time behavior testing are sometimes related in the sense that capacity can be part of the condition specifications for time behavior requirements.

Another aspect of capacity is stress, an expression of the product's capability for handling extreme situations.

When planning requirements for stress handling, it is a good idea to remember old Murphy's law:

"If anything can go wrong, it will"

or

"The unthinkable sometimes happen anyway."

In stress handling requirements we are confronting the risk of the system not being able to handle extreme situations. We are dealing with risks concerning people, money, data, and the environment; risks that will materialize if the system can't cope in a stress situation.

[87] The system shall not crash, but issue an error message and stop execution after acknowledgment if too much data is loaded in the data load described in requirement [DL931].

Stress handling is closely related to other nonfunctional areas. The relationship between reliability and stress is that stress looks at reliability in extreme situations. With respect to usability, stress is about handling failures with grace, so that the user is not left in the dark about what is happening. Stress in connection with capacity is concerned with peak load over a short span of time.

When working with stress-related requirements, we will have to think about what can go wrong. For data, this could be in situations with too much data, too little data, or faulty data. For usage, it could be too many simultaneous users, extended use (same operation "umpteen" times, system to run without restart for many hours/days/months), or maybe dropping the product on the floor. External events such as power failure may also cause stress in the system.

Stress handling is particularly important for web applications, such as e-products and e-business, in telecommunication, safety and security critical systems, and real-time systems.

Stress on a system can to a large extent be handled by defensive programming. This means that stress test can start early with review of the design and code.

A stress test should have high "product" coverage. Even if some stress prevention works in one place, it may not work in another part of the system.

Stress testing should be imaginative, but on the other hand it should not go overboard. When planning a stress test, we need to make a risk analysis. Even the unthinkable may happen too rarely to warrant a test.

7.3.3   Compatibility Testing

In compatibility testing we test to provide information about the degree to which the product is compatible with other products in the landscape in which it has to work.

The ISO 25010 standard breaks the compatibility quality characteristic down into two subcharacteristics:

▶ Coexistence;
▶ Interoperability.

These are described below.

7.3.3.1   Coexistence Testing

In coexistence testing we test to provide information about the degree to which the software product can coexist with other independent software products in a common environment sharing common resources. Today with powerful servers, PC, and portables, and with more and more functionality in everything being controlled by software, the coexistence of systems is a growing issue.

As cars began to have more and more software installed to control the functions of the car, a common joke was that the windscreen wipers would only work if the passenger in the right backseat weighed less than 80 kilos.

This example may seem farfetched, but failed coexistence can have the strangest effects. Such failures may be caused by systems using the same area of memory and thus getting corrupted data, or by systems affecting each other's time behavior.

Coexistence can be very difficult to specify, because we don't always know into which environment our software product will be placed. Precautions can be taken in the form of resource utilization requirements, which may then be compared to resource utilization of any other systems our system is going to coexist with, and the available resources in the target environment.

Coexistence testing can also be very difficult to perform, since it is usually impossible to establish correct test environments for this. Often coexistence is tested after acceptance testing of the product and the installation in the target environment. This is obviously risky, and the decision to do so should be made based on a risk analysis.

7.3.3.2   Interoperability Testing

In interoperability testing we test to provide information about the degree to which our software system can interact with other specified systems.

No software system stands alone; it will always have to interact with other systems in the intended deployment environment, such as hardware, other software systems like operating systems, database systems, browsers, and bespoke systems, external data repositories, and network facilities.

The interoperability quality characteristic is concerned with the specifications of all the interfaces the software system has to the external world at the time of deployment. The external systems may be part of the complete product being delivered, or already existing products that we need to interface with.

Detailed interoperability could be concerned with:

▶ In-bound interoperability: ability to use output from standard, third-party, or in-house products as input;

▶ Out-bound interoperability: ability to produce output in the format used by standard, third-party, or in-house products;

▶ Spawnability: ability to activate other products;

▶ Activatability: ability to be activated by other products.

Testing interoperability can be a huge task because of the sheer number of possible combinations of interfaces for a system. It is often practically and/or economically impossible to achieve full coverage of all possible combinations. The combinatorial testing techniques discussed in Section 6.1.5 can be used to select combinations.

A few examples of high-level interoperability requirements could be:

[I.509] The system shall obtain a record of a patient's hospitalization history from the Central Health Register.

[I.87] When a patient is discharged, his or her hospitalization history shall be updated in the Central Health Register.

[I.4] A discharge letter shall be produced by the Letter-Writer module when a patient is discharged.

Interoperability testing usually takes place in a test subprocess including system integration testing.

7.3.4 Reliability Testing

In reliability testing we test to provide information about the degree to which a system performs specified functions under specified conditions for a specified period of time.

No defects
= 100% reliability

Many defects
= x% reliability

Concerning reliability we need to be realistic: It is impossible to produce 100% fault-free products!

Functional testing and reliability testing are connected. The goal of functional testing is to obtain the highest possible reliability of the product within the given limits. The goal of reliability testing is to evaluate the reliability we have obtained.

The test object is the complete product. The reliability testing should be based on operational profiles specified for the product, and reliability goals expressed in requirements. This is not always easy to set up. In fact, it is sometimes impossible to perform reliability testing before the product is in operation. Usually this is acceptable and the reliability test will be part of the final acceptance test.

A specific level of reliability may be used as a test completion for the system testing, allowing for earlier reliability testing.

During reliability testing it is essential to collect measurements for the evaluation. Failures are registered when they appear "spontaneously," and they must be categorized and countable. We must also collect other measurements as appropriate, such as time and number of transactions.

The test must go on until "reliable" data has been obtained. This can take quite a while, certainly days and maybe even weeks or months.

The ISO 25010 standard breaks the reliability quality characteristic down into a number of subcharacteristics. These are:

▶ Maturity;
▶ Availability;
▶ Fault tolerance;
▶ Recoverability.

These are described below.

7.3.4.1 Maturity Testing

In maturity testing we test to provide information about the degree to which a system meets the needs for reliability under normal operation.

A product's expected maturity is often expressed in terms of:

- Mean time between failures (MTBF);
- Failures per test hour;
- Failures per production time, typically months;
- Failures per number of transactions.

The metrics may be further detailed by categorizing the accepted types of failures, for example, by severity.

A few examples of reliability requirements are:

[34] The MTBF for the product shall be more than 1 month on average in the first year of production.

[72] The product shall have no more than two failures of severity 1 reported in the first 6 months of production.

[281] The product shall have fewer than three failures per 10.000 transactions.

For testing completion criterion we may have reliability goals like:
The testing can stop when less than 1 failure of severity 1 has been found during 20 hours of testing on average over at least 2 weeks of testing.

The results of the reliability testing can be graphical presentations of the measurements using a reliability growth model.

The figure below shows a reliability growth curve for a product where the reliability is getting better, but not achieving its goal (www.testingstandards.com.uk).

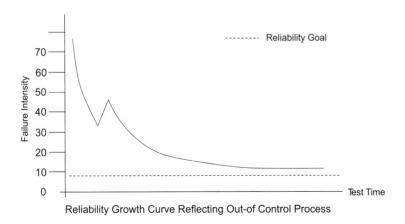

Reliability Growth Curve Reflecting Out-of Control Process

Another way to present reliability data is in an S-curve. Here the total number of failures found over time is plotted against time.

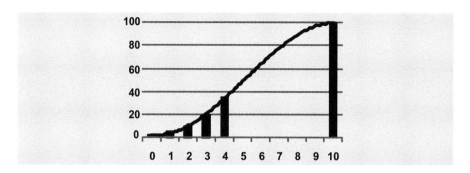

The figure shows an S-curve for the total number of failures for each test week. The expected number of failures after 10 weeks of testing is 100. So far it looks as if the pattern of failures found follows the expectations.

S-curves are often used to determine when to stop the testing. They are also useful for predicting when a reliability level will be reached. Furthermore S-curves may be used to demonstrate the impact on reliability of a decision to deliver the software NOW!

In cases where late or complete reliability testing is not acceptable, we must either reword the requirements, use statistical proof, or use analysis.

Reliability evaluation or reliability estimation is an activity where we analyze the fault-finding curves we have produced. We extrapolate from the curves and predict how many defects are left in the product.

Another way to predict remaining defects is to use estimation models based on the structure of the program, for example, knowledge of the size, the complexity, and the data transactions.

7.3.4.2   Availability Testing

In availability testing we test to provide information about the degree to which a system is operational and accessible when required for use.

A product's availability is the time it can be used in relation to the time it is supposed to be usable; that is, if the system cannot be used, or the use is reduced for any unexpected reason, the availability falls. The following factors can be used to calculate availability:

▶ Mean time between failures (MTBF);
▶ Mean time to repair (MTTR);

in that

Availability = MTBF/(MTBF + MTTR).

From this it can be seen that the smaller the MTTR is, the closer the availability is to 100%.

Therefore, what we have to test in availability testing is the time it takes to get the system running again when it fails. This includes the entire change control process, because it does not count much if a developer can change faulty code in a few minutes if it takes 2 hours for the change request to reach the developer.

Availability testing is often performed when the system is in production, but it can easily start long before that by simulating defects and testing the entire change control process.

7.3.4.3   Fault Tolerance Testing

In fault tolerance testing we test to provide information about the degree to which a system operates as intended despite the presence of hardware or software faults. This may cover the product's:

- ▶ Containment of failure to specified parts of the system;
- ▶ Reactions to failures of a given severity;
- ▶ Self-monitoring of the operations and self-identification of failures;
- ▶ Ability to allow specified work to continue after a failure of specified severity for specified parts of the product under specified conditions;
- ▶ Loss of specified operations (functionality requirement or set of functionality requirements) in case of failure of specified severities in specified periods of time for specified parts of the product;
- ▶ Loss of specified data in case of failure of specified severities in specified periods of time for specified parts of the product.

The failures to consider in fault tolerance testing are those forced on the product from external sources. Failures due to internal defects should be handled in the functional testing.

Failures from external sources could be caused, for example, by lack of external storage capacity, external data storage not found, external services not available, or lack of memory.

Fault tolerance testing can, like the other technical tests, start at the requirements level, with testers reviewing relevant requirements.

Even more important is review of design. Design can be made more or less defensive (i.e., more or less robust to external circumstances). A simple, though often overlooked way to make systems more fault tolerant is to check the return code of all system routine calls, and take action in the code when a system call is unsuccessful.

Lack of memory may be due to memory leaks. Possible memory leaks could be found using dynamic analysis, for example, in a test subprocess that includes component testing.

Testing fault tolerance in system testing and/or acceptance testing test subprocesses may require the use of simulators or other tools to expose the product to external problems that are otherwise difficult to produce.

7.3.4.4   Recoverability Testing

In recoverability testing we test to provide information about the degree to which, in the event of an interruption or a failure, a product can recover the data directly affected and reestablish the desired state of the system. This can cover aspects such as these:

▶ Downtime after a failure of specified severities in specified periods of time for specified parts of the system;

▶ Uptime during specified periods of time for specified parts of the system over a specified period of time;

▶ Downtime during specified periods of time for specified parts of the system over a specified period of time;

▶ Time to reestablish consistent data in case of failure causing inconsistent data;

▶ Built-in backup facilities;

▶ Need for duplication (stand-by server);

▶ Redundancy in the software system;

▶ Reporting of effects of a crash;

▶ "Advise" in connection with restart.

Downtime after a failure, including time to reestablish data, is measured as MTTR (mean time to repair).

7.3.5   Security Testing

In security testing we test to provide information about the degree to which a system protects its valuables so that people or other systems only have the degree of access appropriate to their types and levels of authorization.

The valuables we have in software systems are data kept in, for example, databases, and executable or interpretable code. This is what we need to protect, and security testing is about finding out if the system is able to withstand threats to these valuables.

Security testing can be split into functional security testing and technical security testing. In functional security testing we test the fulfillment of security-related requirements. In technical security testing we take on a much broader perspective.

It is impossible to express all security issues as testable requirements; there are simply too many ways in which things can go wrong and too many ways in which people with dishonest intentions can try to get to our valuables.

Another difficulty in security testing is that most of the testing techniques discussed in Chapter 6 usually have very little probability of finding security defects. The majority of the security defects are not defects in the sense that the product does not fulfill stated requirements or expectations in a narrow sense. Security issues may, for example, arise from the product having or allowing functionality that is not wanted by the future users and hence not specified, but implemented to ease the implementation or fulfill other requirements without regard to the possible security side effects this might have.

In a product protected by user identities and passwords, the passwords are normally stored in an encrypted way. But as long as a user is logged on, however, his or her password is stored in an unencrypted way in order to obtain better performance.

Already at the design stage of the system care should be taken to reduce the risks of these things happening. What designers need to do is to take on the most pessimistic and malicious minds they possibly can. This is not as easy as it sounds. Most people trust their neighbor to a large extent and find it difficult to think of ways in which they themselves may be cheated or threatened. This is why some professional hackers who have changed their ways may be employed as security consultants.

The next step is for testers to perform static testing on design and code implementation to look for vulnerabilities in the system at an early stage.

A more systematic approach is one supported by tools. A profile of the product in term of versions of operating software and middleware, identification of developers and users, and details about the internal network is created by the use of a tool. Based on this, tools can scan the product for known vulnerabilities, and this information can be used to develop targeted attack plans.

Note that there may be conflicts between security requirements and performance requirements, in the sense that higher security may cause lower performance.

The ISO 25010 standard breaks the security quality characteristic down into the following subcharacteristics:

- ▶ Confidentiality;
- ▶ Integrity;
- ▶ Nonrepudiation;

▶ Accountability;

▶ Authenticity.

These are described below.

7.3.5.1   Confidentiality Testing

In confidentiality testing we test to provide information about the degree to which a system ensures that data are accessible only to those authorized to have access.

This includes, for example, accessibility (i.e., access control mechanisms), in which groups or individual users are granted specific rights to handle specific data. These rights are usually expressed in terms of "CRUD rights"; that is, right or no right to Create, Read, Update, and/or Delete identified sets of data.

There are two aspects to this type of testing: static testing of how the rights are set up, and static and/or dynamic testing of how the setup is handled by the system. This testing can be both complicated and voluminous if many data sets can be handled in different ways by many different users or user groups.

Self-protectiveness (i.e., the ability to resist deliberate attempts to violate access control mechanisms) is also an issue related to confidentiality. The testing technique of attacks, discussed in Section 6.3.4 can be very useful for this security testing area. Checklists of effective attacks should be kept up to date.

7.3.5.2   Integrity Testing

In integrity testing we test to provide information about the degree to which a system prevents unauthorized access to, or modification of, computer programs or data.

Data can be jeopardized in a number of ways, typically:

▶ Read to obtain other valuables (e.g., credit card numbers to buy products or sensitive data to sell);

▶ Copied for use without paying (e.g., music or entire products);

▶ Added for harmful effects (e.g., viruses or access requests);

▶ Changed (e.g., sensitive information or code instructions);

▶ Deleted (e.g., data).

A special integrity issue is logical bombs or so-called Easter eggs, where harmful code has been written into the components during development. Static testing is the only technique that may find this.

Examples of logical bombs include:

> An IF clause that is only true on a specific date, where data might be erased.
>
> An IF clause that is only true for a specific bank account number, to which an extra amount of money is debited.

7.3.5.3 Nonrepudiation Testing

In nonrepudiation testing we test to provide information about the degree to which actions or events can be proven to have taken place, so that the events or actions cannot be repudiated later.

This can be obtained by log facilities for activities and actors. This is usually covered by relevant requirements for high-security risk systems, but may be overlooked in other systems.

Note that it may be possible for trespassers to erase or in others ways mess with logs of different types, since these are data in the system.

7.3.5.4 Accountability Testing

In accountability testing we test to provide information about the degree to which the actions of an entity can be traced uniquely to the entity. An entity in this respect is an actor and may, for example, be identifiable users or specific interfacing systems.

This area of security testing is also related to the system's logging features and the quality of the logged data.

7.3.5.5 Authenticity Testing

In authenticity testing we test to provide information about the degree to which the identity of a subject or resource can be proved to be the one claimed.

This can be very difficult, but can be handled by, for example, biological identification (e.g., using a fingerprint as identification). It may also be handled by multilayer identification (e.g., a text message with a code to enter being sent to a person trying to gain access to a system).

7.3.6 Maintainability Testing

In maintainability testing we test to provide information about the degree to which a system can be analyzed and modified. Modifications may include corrections of defects, improvements or adaptations of the software to changes in the environment, and enhancements or new functionality.

Maintainability testing can be performed as static testing, in which the structure, complexity, and other attributes of the code and the documentation are reviewed or inspected based on the pertinent maintenance requirements. Static analysis of the code may also be used to ensure its adherence to coding standards and to obtain measurements, such as complexity measures.

The maintainability test may also be performed dynamically in the sense that specified maintenance procedures are executed and compared to pertaining requirements. What is measured in this type of maintenance testing is typically effort involved in the maintenance activities and elapsed time to perform these.

The dynamic maintenance testing may be combined with other tests, typically functional testing, where the failures found and the underlying defects to be corrected may serve as those the maintainability procedures are tested with.

The ISO 25010 standard breaks the maintainability quality characteristic down into the subcharacteristics:

> ⟩ Modularity;
> ⟩ Reusability;
> ⟩ Analyzability;
> ⟩ Modifiability;
> ⟩ Testability.

These are described below.

7.3.6.1 Modularity Testing

In modularity testing we test to provide information about the degree to which a system design is modular.

The modularity of a system refers to the way it is divided into identified modules that interface with each other and together constitute the system. A sensible modularity splits coherent parts of the functionality over reasonably sized modules. This makes it easier to test changed code and, hence, less risky to change code during maintenance.

Measures for modularity include fan-in and fan-out. Fan-in is the number of modules that interface (call) a specific module, and fan-out is the number of other modules that a specific module interfaces with (are called by).

Modularity can only be tested with static test techniques including the use of static analysis tools.

7.3.6.2 Reusability Testing

In reusability testing we test to provide information about the degree to which the system reuses modules from other systems.

The more modules that are reused, the higher, in principle, the reliability of the system. Systems based on SOA principles have a high level of reusability.

Reusability can only be tested by static testing of the architectural design.

7.3.6.3 Analyzability Testing

In analyzability testing we test to provide information about the degree to which maintainers are able to identify deficiencies, diagnose the cause of failures, and identify areas requiring modification to implement required changes. The analyzability of a system contributes to its MTTR.

Analyzability can cover aspects such as these:

▶ Understandability: making the design documentation, including the source code, understood by maintainers;

▶ Design standard compliance: adherence to defined design standards;

▶ Coding standard compliance: adherence to defined coding standards;

▶ Diagnosability: presence and nature of diagnostic functions in the code;

▶ Traceability: presence of traces between elements, for example, between requirements and test cases, and requirements and design and code;

▶ Technical manual helpfulness: nature of any technical manual or specification.

7.3.6.4 Modifiability Testing

In modifiability testing we test to provide information about the degree to which a specified modification can be implemented in the product.

Modifiability can cover aspects such as these:

▶ Modularity: the structure of the software;

▶ Code change efficiency: capability for implementing required changes;

▶ Documentation change efficiency: capability for documenting implemented changes.

7.3.6.5 Testability Testing

In testability testing we test to provide information about the degree to which the modified system can be validated; that is, how easy it is to perform testing of changes, either new tests or retests, and how easy it is to perform regression testing.

This is influenced both by the structure of the system itself and by the structure of the test specification and other testware.

Testability is also influenced by how configuration management is performed. The better the control over the testware (not least the test data, the system, and the documentation of the relationships between system versions and testware versions), the better the testability.

7.3.7 Portability Testing

In portability testing we test to get information about the degree to which the system can be transferred into or out of its intended environment. The environment may include the organization in which the system is used and the hardware, software, and network environment.

The porting may be the first porting from a development or test environment into a deployment environment, or it may be the porting from one deployment environment to another at a later point in time.

Portability is primarily an issue for software systems or software subsystems, not so much for, for example, hardware subsystems. These are usually part of the environment into which the software subsystem or software system is being ported.

The ISO 25010 standard breaks the portability attributes down into the subattributes of:

- ▶ Adaptability;
- ▶ Installability;
- ▶ Replaceability.

These are described below.

7.3.7.1 Adaptability

In adaptability testing we test to provide information about the degree to which the system is able to be adapted to different specified environments without applying actions or means other than those provided for this purpose for the system.

Systems are rarely permanent and unchangeable for a long time these days, and it will often happen that a system our system interfaces with will have to be replaced by a newer version or a completely different system. In this case our system will have to be adapted to interface with the new system in the environment instead of with the old one.

Ease of changing interfacing systems may be achieved by using communication standards, or by constructing the software in such a way that it can itself detect and adjust to external communication needs.

Adaptability is primarily of interest to organizations developing commercial off-the-shelf (COTS) products or systems of systems.

Adaptability can cover aspects such as these:

▶ Hardware dependency: dependence on specific hardware for the system's adaptation to a different specified environment;

▶ Software dependency: dependence on specific external software for the system's adaptation to a different specified environment;

▶ Representation dependency: dependence on specific data representation for the system's adaptation to a different specified environment;

▶ Standard language conformance: conformance to the formal standard version of a programming language;

▶ Dependency encapsulation: the isolation of dependent code from independent code;

▶ Text convertability: the ability to convert text to fit a specified environment.

7.3.7.2 Installability Testing

In installability testing we test to provide information about the degree to which the system can be installed in a specified environment.

Installability can cover aspects such as these:

▶ Space demand: temporary space to be used during installation of the software in a specified environment;

▶ Checking prerequisites: facilities to ensure that the target environment is meeting the demands of the product in terms of, for example, operating system, hardware, and middleware;

▶ Installation procedures: existence and understandability of installation aids such as general or specific installation scripts, installation manuals, or wizards. This may also include requirements concerning the time and effort to be spent on the installation task.

▶ Completeness: facilities for checking that an installation is complete in terms of, for example, checklists from configuration management;

▶ Installation interruption: possibility of interrupting an installation and rolling any work done back to leave the environment unchanged;

▶ Customization: the capability for setting or changing parameters at installation time in a specified environment;

◗ Initialization: the capability for setting up initial information at installation time, both internal and external in a specified environment;

◗ Deinstallation: facilities for removing the product partly (downgrading) or completely from the environment.

7.3.7.3 Replaceability Testing

In replaceability testing we test to provide information about the degree to which the system can be used in place of another specified product for the same purpose in the same environment.

This is the opposite of adaptability, because in this case our system replaces an old one. The issues for adaptability therefore also apply for replaceability. There is also a certain overlap with installability.

Furthermore, replaceability can cover aspects such as these:

◗ Data loadability: facilities for loading existing data into permanent storage in our system;

◗ Data convertability: facilities for converting existing data to fit into our system.

Questions

1. Which quality characteristics are defined by ISO 25010?
2. How are quality characteristics divided in this book?
3. What are the subcharacteristics for functional suitability?
4. What are the three parts that illustrate functional completeness?
5. What do we need to be aware of concerning correctness testing?
6. What is functional appropriateness?
7. What is a user group?
8. What are the subcharacteristics for usability?
9. What is operability?
10. What may be included in user interface aesthetics?
11. Who may be especially concerned with accessibility?
12. What is SUMI?
13. How should usability requirements be expressed?
14. What is especially important when testing usability?
15. Why is nonfunctional testing traditionally a focus point for testing?

16. What are sources for nonfunctional attributes other than ISO 25010?
17. What are the nonfunctional quality characteristics in ISO 25020?
18. What is an operational profile?
19. What are the subcharacteristics for performance efficiency?
20. What must be specified as part of performance efficiency requirements?
21. What characterizes stress testing?
22. What are the subcharacteristics for compatibility?
23. Why is it necessary to perform interoperability testing?
24. What is reliability?
25. What are the subcharacteristics of reliability testing?
26. What is a reliability growth curve?
27. What is MTBF and MTTR?
28. What might be included in fault tolerance?
29. What might be included in recoverability?
30. Which other nonfunctional quality characteristic can security affect?
31. What are the subcharacteristics for security?
32. What is meant by nonrepudiation?
33. What are the subcharacteristics for maintainability?
34. What does analyzability contribute to?
35. What are the subcharacteristics of portability?
36. Who should be especially interested in adaptability?
37. What aspects are mentioned for replaceability?

Incident and Defect Management

A successful dynamic test provokes failures, and a successful static test detects defects. In addition to these dedicated testing activities, work products and products are used in the course of a product's life cycle and observations are made.

However, if the failures and defects detected during testing are not managed, the test effort is wasted. If observations are not managed, useful information may be missed.

The activity of managing failures and observations is usually called incident management, where an *incident* is an event occurring that requires investigation (ISTQB Glossary). Note that sometimes the synonym *anomaly* is used instead of *incident*, both in ISTQB and in other contexts.

Failures and observations may not originate from a defect; they could be misunderstandings, something too trivial for further attention, or an idea for an enhancement. One activity in incident management is to determine if a given incident is in fact due to a defect.

If it has been determined that a defect (or more defects) is (are) in fact the cause of an incident, this (or these) will have to be managed, that is, be subjected to defect management.

The ISTQB Foundation syllabus describes the incident management process, whereas the ISTQB Advanced Syllabi for test manager and test analysts describe the defect management only, but do mention that incidents (anomalies) may precede the identification of defects.

Incident and defect management is formally (in standards and maturity models) an activity in the configuration management process; that is, it is a support activity that may be used to support any process in an organization. We emphasize it here because it is so strongly connected to testing.

Incident management is about following all incidents from the *cradle to the grave*. Defect management is about following the defects from identification to solution. Both are also concerned with gathering information embedded in the incidents and/or defects, respectively defects.

Facilitating the gathering of this information is part of the goal of all testing. The information can be used to:

- ▶ Improve the product under development.
- ▶ Improve the decisions to be made about the product.
- ▶ Improve the processes used in both testing and development.

Models may be made for the defect and incident management. Two different models are provided for inspiration in Appendixes 8.B and 8.C.

8.1 Incident Detection

8.1.1 Incident Definition

This section is about incidents/anomalies. The section is based on the IEEE 1044 and IEEE 1044.1 standards in which the term anomaly is used, but we use the term incident here because it is, after all, the most widely used term.

8.1.2 Incident Causes

When a product is being developed, tested, deployed, and maintained, incidents are inevitable. It is human to make mistakes, so defects get introduced during development, requirements change over time, and the environment in which the product is deployed can evolve as well. In addition to this, people constantly develop their knowledge about their products and business processes and consequently get new ideas for evolving the product.

Testing is the obvious source of incidents, since the idea of testing is to ferret out things that make us think: "Oops—what was that?"

There are many synonyms for an "oops," for example:

- ▶ Anomaly;
- ▶ Bug;
- ▶ Deviation;
- ▶ Enhancement request;
- ▶ Event;
- ▶ Failure;
- ▶ Problem.

The term *incident* is considered more neutral than most of the others commonly used, and signifies that what we are dealing with is not necessarily a defect.

Incidents can be raised by all stakeholders within the organization or at the customer's organization. It is important for all incidents to be handled via a defined path and processed in a controlled way.

8.1.3   Incident Reporting and Tracking

All incidents should be registered or reported. Correct reporting of incidents is important for many reasons.

The more thorough and uniformly incidents are reported, the better the possibilities for making the right decisions in the life cycle of the incident.

Good reports enable exploitation of the information about a product and its processes. Incident reports can be analyzed to find trends in the failures and defects and subsequently for suggesting process improvement.

The incident report can be handled on paper or by the use of a tool. The latter is by far the most common these days, because modern tools provide facilities for communicating incident reports to those who need them and for producing statistics very easily.

The incident report must follow the incident through its entire life cycle.

8.2   Incident and Defect Life Cycles

When an incident is observed, something must happen. But that something is *NOT an immediate change.*

The incident must follow a controlled life cycle. The states in the life cycle defined in IEEE 1044 for an incident are:

▶ Recognition;
▶ Investigation;
▶ Action;
▶ Disposition.

This is illustrated in this simple state diagram.

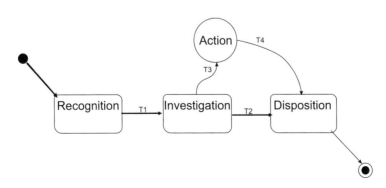

A complete state mode for incident and defect management is provided in Appendix 8.B.

Note that the state *Action* has a shape different from the other states. This is because the Action state is only relevant for actual defects, and because the defect life cycle takes place within the Action state. The Action state and hence the defect life cycle are described in Section 8.2.3.

It should be possible to trace incidents through their states and follow their progress. This is done by the use of an incident report that follows the incident and is updated as the incident changes its states.

For each of the states, the incident report must contain the following types of information according to IEEE 1044:

▶ Supporting data;

▶ Classification;

▶ Identified impact.

Again, these and the detailed incident and defect information mentioned here are merely suggestions.

The incident state model shown here does not indicate the roles or organizational units involved. The number of organizational units involved can range from one—in the case of incidents found and resolved during component testing performed in the development unit—to many different organizational units.

Special care must be taken during the life cycles of incidents in the case of outsourced development and/or testing where organizational units belonging to independent companies spread over large geographical (and cultural) distances may be involved.

8.2.1 Incident Recognition

Upon recognition of an incident, an incident report must be initialized. All incidents must be reported meticulously so that they can be investigated, re-created if needed, and their progress followed.

If the incident has been recognized during testing, this is the responsibility of the tester.

The initial state of an incident report may be for example "Open" or "Created" or something similar. Note that the states named here are only examples; each organization can choose its own, or use those proposed by the tool the organization uses.

The *supporting data* to provide in the incident report when an incident is first recognized includes the following:

▶ Identification of the incident, including unique number, heading, trigger event, proposed fix, if possible, and documentation (e.g., screen dumps);

▶ Identification of the environment, including hardware, software, vendor, item in which the incident was seen, and fix description, if any;

▶ Identification of the people involved, including originator and investigator;

▶ Related time information (e.g., system time and wall time as appropriate).

The information for *classification* should include:

▶ Project activity: What were you doing when the incident was recognized?

▶ Project phase: What phase was the project in when the incident was recognized?

▶ Symptom: What did you see when you recognized the incident?

It could also include information about suspected cause, repeatability, and product status.

Impact information should include:

▶ Severity;

▶ Estimated impact on project schedule;

▶ Estimated impact on project cost.

The information concerning impact could also include impact on priority, customer value, mission safety, project risk, project quality, and society.

The estimates may of course be rather uncertain at this point.

IEEE 1044 suggests standard values for the classification and impact categories. These are described below in Section 8.3.

An example of what an incident report template might look like is given below. Only recognition information is shown here—the other information will follow further below in the appropriate sections.

Note that this is a real-world example; the terms are not necessarily IEEE 1044 compliant.

Incident report
Recognition
  supporting data
  classification
  impact
Investigation
  supporting data
  classification
  impact
Action
  supporting data
  classification
  impact
Disposition
  supporting data
  classification
  impact

Incident Registration Form		
ID		
Short title		
Software product		
Version (n.m)		
Status = Open		
Registration created by		Date & time	
Incident observed by		Date & time	
Comprehensive description	Include references to attachments, if any.	
Observed during	Walk-through/Review/Inspection/Code & Build/Test/Use	
Observed in	Requirement/Design/Implementation/Test/Operation	
Symptom	Opr. system crash/Program hang-up/Program crash/ Input/Output/Total product failure/System error/ Other:	
User severity	Urgent/High/Medium/Low/None	

The incident report must now be handed over to the right people. Testers or others who initiate incident reports need to understand to whom the report should be given. This may depend on a number of factors, for example, the process during which the incident was recognized, what work product it was found in, and its estimated severity.

In the state model, this corresponds to the first transition:

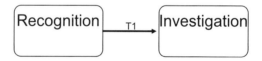

	Event	Action
T1	Incident report created and sent to CCB	State set to "Under investigation"

For the time being the incident is now out of the hands of the testers.

8.2.2   Incident Investigation

The *investigation* is performed based on the information provided in the incident report. Formally this is not testing but configuration management.

The investigation should be done by an authority appointed to do just that. This authority is normally called a CCB (change control board or configuration control board). A CCB must be formed by people with the right insight and the right power to be able to decide what is going to happen to an incident of a specific severity and/or impact. This includes technical, economic, and possibly political insight and power.

An organization should have an appropriate number of CCBs depending on the organizational structure and the nature of the product being developed or maintained. The wider the severity and/or impact, the more formal the CCB should be—and vice versa.

During component testing the CCB may be the developer or the developer and the project manager.

For high-impact incidents found in system testing, the CCB may include the project manager, the product manager, marketing, and the customer.

The investigation is about finding out what is wrong, if anything, and what should happen next. Many things could be wrong; for example, in the context of testing, it could be:

▶ Incorrect wording found during a review of a document;

▶ A coding defect found during a walk-through of a piece of source code;

▶ A failure found in the integration test;

▶ A wish to expand or enhance the finished product, arising when the product is in the acceptance testing phase;

▶ A change required in the code because of the upgrade to a new version of the middleware supporting the system (e.g., a new version of Microsoft Access, which in certain places is not backward compatible).

If something is indeed wrong, the investigation must try to determine the impact and what the cost of making the necessary correction(s) is. The cost of *not* making the correction(s) is also a consideration.

It is not always a simple matter to perform such an analysis, but it must be done thoroughly before an informed decision about what to do can be made.

Investigation

T5a
  T5b

Specific investigation

We can expand the state model with an extra state and two extra transitions, to show that the CCB may ask relevant people to investigate specific issues.

Information may have to be gathered from many sources, and in that case there may be a number of specific investigations going on in parallel and/or sequentially.

The CCB needs to make sure that all relevant information—including technical, economic, and political—is gathered before a decision is made.

Testers may also be asked to provide additional information and/or reproduce the incident.

The transitions for this part of the state model are:

	Event	Action
T5a	CCB requests information	State may be set to "Under further investigation"
T5b	Information (or no relevant information) provided to CCB	If state is changed, it should be reset to "Under investigation"

Incident report
Recognition
  supporting data
  classification
  impact
Investigation
  supporting data
  classification
  impact
Action
  supporting data
  classification
  impact
Disposition
  supporting data
  classification
  impact

The supporting data for the investigation primarily include:

▶ Identification of the people involved in the investigation, at least those responsible for any decisions made;
▶ Related time information.

The information for classification should include:

▶ Actual cause—where have we pinpointed the incident to come from at a high level?
▶ Source—in which work product(s) or product component(s) must changes be made?
▶ Type—what type of incident are we dealing with?

The impact information here is the same as for recognition: severity, project schedule, and project cost as mandatory. The estimations should now be less uncertain than in the recognition state.

IEEE 1044 suggests standard values for the classification and impact categories. These are discussed below in Section 8.3, but, of course, an organization is free to choose their own, unless they need to be IEEE 1044 compliant.

The investigation part of the example incident report is shown here.

Status = Under investigation			
Forwarded by		Date & time	
Investigated by		Date & time	
Actual cause	Software/Data/Test system/Platform/User/Unknown		
Source	Specification/Code/Database/Manual/Plan		
Overall problem type	Logical/Computation/Interface/Timing/Data handling/Data/Documentation/Document quality/ Enhancement/Failure caused by previous fix/ Performance/Other :		
Affected CIs State type from list above			
Estimated correction effort			
Estimated confirmation test and regression test effort			
Schedule impact	High/Medium/Low/None		
Cost impact	High/Medium/Low/None		
Evaluator severity	Urgent/High/Medium/Low/None		

The investigation is concluded with a decision about how to handle the incident. A CCB typically has the following options:

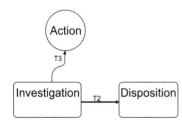

▶ Close the incident—no defect(s) after all or changes too costly;

▶ Defer incident—changes are postponed, either to a specific point in time or indefinitely;

▶ Action(s) must be taken to implement necessary changes.

The corresponding transitions in the state model are:

	Event	Action
T2	Decision made on disposition	State set to "Closed"
T3	Decision made on action	State set to "Action" and appropriate change request(s) created

If the incident is closed at this point the "Action" state is not activated. The "Disposition" state is described below in Section 8.2.4.

8.2.3   Defect Management = Incident Action

If investigation has shown that the incident is caused by one or more defects and it has been decided that the defect(s) must be corrected, then the defect(s) are subjected to defect management.

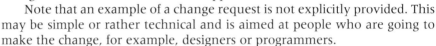
An incident encountered during system testing may be caused by a defect in the requirement specification, and the investigation has shown that changes will have to be made in the requirement specification as well as in the design, in the code, in the user manual, and maybe even in the project plan.

Specific change requests should be produced for each of the items (configuration items, if formal configuration management is in place) to be changed. The change requests must be connected to the originating incident report, so that it is possible to follow up on the progress of each change through its states: open, implemented, and approved, until all necessary changes for the incident have been approved.

Note that an example of a change request is not explicitly provided. This may be simple or rather technical and is aimed at people who are going to make the change, for example, designers or programmers.

The Action state is expanded to show the underlying change management state model. The figure below shows that more changes may be performed in parallel or sequentially. Each change will have to be approved by the appropriate CCB, and the corresponding defect report closed, before the final approval from the originating CBB can cause the incident to be closed.

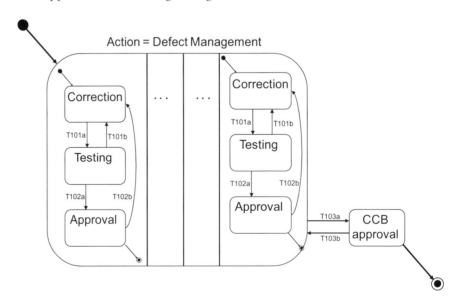

The testers participate in the incident handling in the approval stage by executing the necessary retests and regression tests to ensure that the changes have been made

correctly, and that they don't have any adverse effects on the areas that were working before the correction.

The necessary tests may be both dynamic and static.

The information for the incident classification should include:

▶ Resolution—when are we going to take action?

This part of the incident report from our example is shown here.

Status = Action				
Forwarded for decision by			Date & time	
CCB decided			Date & time	
Resolution	Immediate/Eventual change/Deferred/No fix			
Observer informed by			Date	
Change request(s) opened by		Ref.:	Date & time	
All change requests accepted closed by			Date & time	
Comprehensive solution description, if applicable	Include references to attachments, if any.			
Total actual change effort				
Total actual test effort				
Solution complete CCB signature			Date & time	

Note that action may result in one or more changes being returned for further investigation; this is not illustrated for the sake of simplicity.

8.2.4 Incident Disposition

If action has been taken, *disposition* can only happen once all the change requests have been approved. In this case the incident report is closed with information about how the corrections have been implemented and finally approved.

The information for classification pertaining to disposition should include:

▶ Disposition—Why was the incident closed?

The last bit of the example incident report is shown here.

Status = Closed		
Close condition	Closed/Deferred/Merged/Referred Reference:	
Conditions— if applicable	All new configuration items correctly identified	
	All new configuration items properly stored	
	All stakeholders informed of new configuration items	
Remarks		
Incident observer informed by		Date & time
CCB Signature		Date & time

Note that extra information can be provided for the closed state. For example, if the closure is due to the incident being a duplicate of another one, it can be marked as "Merged" and the identification of the identical incident report may be given as a reference.

8.3 Incident Fields

It can be difficult to get an overview of a large number of incidents, and to be able to see patterns in them, and use the embedded information to its full potential. To mitigate this, it is necessary to be systematic about the data being gathered.

A *classification scheme* provides a standard terminology and facilitates communication and information exploitation within or between projects and organizations.

IEEE 1044 defines a classification scheme for each of the life cycle states it defines for an incident, namely, Recognition, Investigation, Action, and Disposition as used in the sections above.

The defined classification has a hierarchical structure. This means that a varying number of layers of possible values exist for each category. In the standard each of the classification values has a code in the form of a unique identification determining its place in the life cycle and the hierarchy. This numbering scheme also means that organizations can use each others' classifications for incident reports even if the actual wording of the categories is different, for example, due to usage of the local language.

You can use the IEEE 1044 classification scheme as an inspiration to get more structure into the incident reporting.

If for some reason you need to be IEEE 1044 compliant (e.g., for safety critical software) you need to be aware of the numbering scheme and the fact that some of the categories are mandatory and some are optional.

An extract of the IEEE 1044 classification scheme is given in Appendix 8.A at the end of the chapter.

Do not learn the classification schemes by heart—but take them into your heart and use them as inspiration for an efficient and useful way of reporting incidents.

8.4 Metrics and Incident Management

There is no reason to collect information about incidents or defects if it is not going to be used for anything.

On the other hand, information that can be extracted from incident reports is essential for a number of people in the organization, including test management, project management, project participants, process improvement people, and organizational management.

If you are involved in the definition of incident reports, then ask these people what they need to know—and inspire them, if they do not yet have any wishes.

The primary areas for which incident report information can be used are:

▶ Estimation and progress;
▶ Incident distribution;
▶ Effectiveness of quality assurance activities;
▶ Ideas for process improvement.

Section 3.5 discusses metrics and measurements in details.

Direct measures may be interesting, but it gets even more interesting when we use them for calculation of more complex measurements.

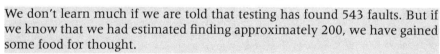
We don't learn much if we are told that testing has found 543 faults. But if we know that we had estimated finding approximately 200, we have gained some food for thought.

Some of the direct measures we can extract from incident reports at any given time are:

▶ Total number of incidents;
▶ The number of open incidents;
▶ The number of closed incidents;
▶ The time it took to close each incident report;
▶ Which changes have been made since the last release.

The incidents can be counted for specific classifications, and this is where life gets so much easier if a defined classification scheme has been used.

Just to mention a few of the possibilities, we may want to count the number of:

▶ Incidents found during review of the requirements;
▶ Incidents found during component testing;
▶ Incidents where the source was a specification;
▶ Incident where the type was a data problem.

We can also get associated time information from the incident reports and use this in connection with some of the above measures.

For *estimation and progress* purposes we can compare the actual time it took to close an incident to our estimate, and get wiser and better at estimating next time. We can also look at the development in open and closed incidents over time and use that to estimate when the testing can be stopped.

For *incident distribution* we can determine how incidents are distributed over the components and areas in the design. This helps us identify the more fault-prone and, hence, high-risk areas. We can also determine incident distribution in relation to work product characteristics, such as size, complexity, or technology; or we can determine distribution in relation to development activities, severity, or type.

For information about effectiveness of quality assurance activities we can calculate the defect detection percentage (DDP) of various quality assurance activities as time goes by.

The DDP is the percentage of defects in an object found in a specific quality assurance activity. The DDP falls over time as more and more defects are detected. The DDP is usually given for a specific activity with an associated time frame; for example DDP for system test after 3 months' use.

In the component test 75 defects are found. The DDP of the component test is 100% at the end of the component test activity (we have found all the defects we could). In the system test another 25 faults that could have been found in the component test are found. The DDP of the component test after system test can therefore be calculated to be only 75% (we only found 75% of what we now know we could have found).

The DDP may fall even further if more component test–related failures are reported from the customer.

The information extracted from incident reports may be used to analyze the entire course of the development and identify ideas for process improvement. Process improvement is, at least at the higher levels, concerned with defect prevention. We can analyze the information to detect trends and tendencies in the incidents, and identify ways to improve the processes to avoid making the same errors again and again; and to get a higher detection rate for those we do make.

There is more about monitoring and control of the testing process in Section 3.6.

8.5 Communicating Incidents

Careful incident reporting in written incident reports using an incident management system facilitates objective communication about incidents and defects. However, this cannot and should not eliminate verbal communication.

Communication about incidents is difficult. The first thing both testers and developers must be aware of is the danger of "Them and Us." We (the testers) may have a tendency to think that we are better than them: "We" are good, conscientious, and right while "they" are careless and stupid. They (analysts and developers) may have a tendency to think that they are better than we are: "They" are smart, fast, and pragmatic, while "we" are stupid, unknowing, and sticklers for the letter of the law.

It is tempting to fall into the trap of irritation and blame. The first and most important thing for testers and developers is to keep in mind that developers and others do not make defects on purpose to annoy us, or to tease us, or even to keep us busy. The next and equally important thing to remember is that testers and others do not report incidents to gloat and punish but as their contribution to a high-quality product.

Examples of what NOT to say:
Tester: "Now you have delivered some …. again—are you never going to get any better?!"
Developer: "It works on my machine—it must be your setup (or you) that is wrong!"

Have mutual respect! Managers and employees alike must work on the spirit of "We are in this together."

Another aspect of incident communication is concerned with what should be corrected and when. This is where it is important to establish CCBs before things get hot and to establish them in such a way that their decisions are trustworthy and respected.

If proper CCBs are not established, the decisions about what should happen to incidents and their relative prioritization can be arbitrary and counterproductive, or worse.

Questions

1. What can information from incidents help to improve?
2. Which process area does incident management formally belong to?
3. What is an incident?
4. What are some of the other names for an incident?

5. What are the four states in the incident life cycle according to IEEE 1044?

6. What types of information should be collected for an incident?

7. Name some of the information elements for the first incident life cycle state.

8. Which of the states in the incident life cycle are testers not directly involved in?

9. What is the responsibility of a CCB?

10. How many CCBs should an organization have?

11. What happens if it is discovered that an incident is due to a misunderstanding?

12. What is the prerequisite for closing an incident after the necessary changes have been made?

13. Why is it a good idea to use a classification scheme?

14. What is DDP and how is it calculated?

15. What are the two most important things to keep in mind when communicating about incidents?

Appendix 8.A: Standard Anomaly Classification
IEEE 1044-1993 Standard Classification for Software Anomalies (Extract)

Recognition
Supporting data
Classification
   Project activity
      Analysis
      Review
      Audit
      Inspection
   Code/compile/assemble
      Testing
      Validation
      Support/operational
      Walk-through
   Project phase
      Requirements
      Design
      Implementation
      Test
      Operation and maint.
      Retirement
   Suspected cause
   Repeatability
   Symptom
      Operating system crash
      Program hang-up
      Program crash
      Input problem
      Output problem
      Failed performance
      Perceived total failure
      System error message
      Other
   Product status
Impact

Investigation
Supporting data
Classification
   Actual cause
      Product
      Test system
      Platform
      Outside vendor
      User
      Unknown
   Source
      Specification
      Code
      Database
      Manual and guides
      Plans and procedures
      Reports
      Standards/policies
   Type
      Logical problem
      Computation problem
      Interface/timing problem
      Data handling problem
      Data problem
      Documentation problem
      Document quality prob.
      Enhancement
      Failure caused by fix
      Performance problem
      Interoperability
      Standards conformance
      Other problem
Impact

Action
Supporting data
Classification   Impact (applicable to all)
   Resolution   Severity
       Immediate   Urgent
       Eventual (next release)   High
       Deferred (future release)   Medium
       No fix   Low
   Corrective action   None
Impact   Priority
                                             Customer value
Disposition   Mission safety
Supporting data   Project schedule
Classification   High/Medium/Low/None
   Disposition   Project cost
   Closed   High/Medium/Low/None
   Deferred   Project risk
   Merged with another   Project quality
   Referred to another project   Societal
Impact

Note that only the values for the mandatory categories and only one layer of values are shown in the extract of IEEE 1044 above.

Also note that the impact classification is identical for each of the phases in the incident life cycle. It must be done by different people for each phase. In each phase the classification must reflect what the impact is estimated to be at that point in time based on the available information.

When you estimate the impact, it is important to remember that the nature of the fault does not necessarily reveal anything about the failure that may follow.

A spelling mistake may seem like an innocent fault, but on the home page of a company selling translation and writing services it can be perceived as a major failure.

A fault that looks really nasty, like a possible pointer list overflow, may never actually result in a failure, because there is no way the list can get filled up during the use of the system.

Appendix 8.B: Incident and Defect State Model

This appendix shows an example of a state diagram for an incident and the associated state diagram for changes necessary for the closure of the incident, if it is caused by one or more defects.

All of the states are depicted in the diagram as rounded boxes, except the Action state because the Action state is only relevant for actual defects, and because the defect life cycle takes place within the Action state (see below). The possible transitions between the states are shown as arrowhead lines with an identification of the transition ID, for example "T1."

The start state for a state diagram is shown by an arrow from a filled circle, and the end state is shown as an arrow pointing to a semifilled circle.

Note that the state diagram shown here illustrates that a closed incident may be reopened for investigation; this is not described in the text above.

Basic Incident State Model

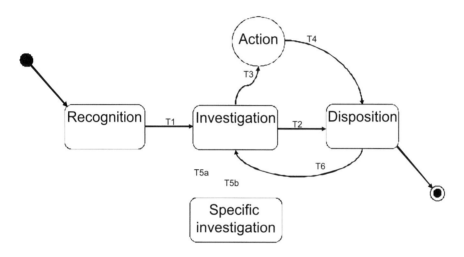

The possible transitions in the state model are:

	Event	Action
T1	Incident report created and sent to CCB	State set to "Under investigation"
T2	Decision made on disposition without any action	State set to "Closed"
T3	Decision made on action	State set to "Action" and appropriate change request(s) created
T4	Decision made on disposition after action	State set to "Closed"
T5a	CCB requests information	State may be set to "Under further investigation"
T5b	Information (or no relevant information) provided to CCB	If state is changed, it is reset to "Under investigation"
T6	Incident reopened	State set to "Under investigation"

Note that action may result in one or more changes being returned to Investigation; this is not illustrated for the sake of simplicity.

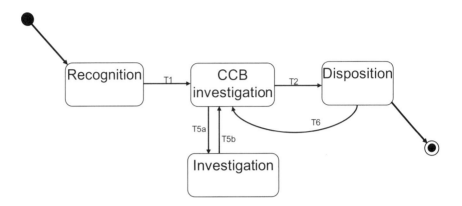

Action = Defect Management State Model
The possible transitions in the state model are:

	Event	Action
T101a	Change implemented and sent to test	State set to "Being tested"
T101b	Retest or regression test failed; change returned to correction	State set to "Correction"
T102a	Test succeeded; change sent to "local" CCB for approval	State set to "Approval"
T102b	Approval failed; change returned to correction	State set to "Correction"
T103a	All changes approved "locally" sent for CCB approval	State set to "Change approval"
T103b	Approval failed; change(s) returned to correction	State set to "Correction"

Appendix 8.C: Change Control Flow Diagram
This appendix shows an example of a process diagram for a change control process.

A number of processes are depicted in the diagram as a box with input and output sections (e.g., "Evaluation of event registration"). All of these

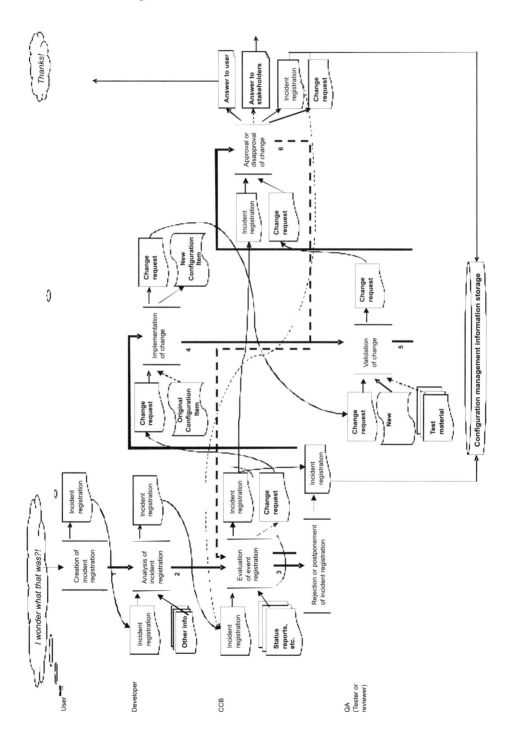

processes will have to be defined, preferably described, so that the involved people know what they need to do.

The thick lines illustrate the process flow, and the thin lines illustrate the information flow.

An arch across two lines is used to illustrate "either/or." A dashed line illustrates "maybe."

The column to the left holds the name of the role holding the responsibility for the processes shown in the right column—this is the "swim line principle."

Test Tools and Automation

The main purpose of using tools for testing is to automate as much as possible of the noncreative, repetitive, time-consuming, and boring parts of testing activities. Another purpose is to exploit the possibility of tools for storing and arranging large amounts of data.

Test tools and automation are an integral part of ISTQB. The ISTQB Foundation syllabus covers tool support for testing, and all of the ISTQB Advanced Syllabi cover test tools and automation, especially the advanced technical test analyst syllabus.

Test tools and automation are out of the scope of ISO 29119 as such, but Part 1, which is not mandatory, does include a small section about automation of test process activities.

A huge number of test tools are available on the market, and it is an area that is growing fast. Have a look in Appendix 9.A! Every test tool automates some test activities to a certain degree. No single tool automates everything completely. But there are test tools for all test activities, even though most testers first think about test execution tools when test automation is mentioned.

Test automation is not an easy task. An organization can be more or less ready for test automation. A certain level of test maturity is required to be able to use tools efficiently. Tools do not provide more maturity; they should only be implemented to support the existing maturity.

A certain amount of courage is also required to engage in test automation—both the courage to choose and the courage to refuse. It is important to select tools with great care so that they don't end up as "shelfware."

As difficult as it is to choose at tool, that is a cake walk compared to actually getting a tool introduced in an organization. And keeping it running efficiently is perhaps even more difficult.

9.1 Test Tool Categories

Many tools for the support of software development are available, and the selection is growing every day. This is also the case for tools aimed at supporting testing.

It is therefore impossible to list specific tools. The purpose of this section is to present different types of testing tools, and give an idea of their advantages and disadvantages.

Tools can be classified to get a better overview of what is available. There are different classification schemes for testing tools, for example, according to:

- ▶ The test activity they support;
- ▶ The test sub-process they primarily support;
- ▶ The types of failures or defects they can find;
- ▶ The test approach or test technique they support;
- ▶ The domain they apply to;
- ▶ Who the primary users of the tools are.

The last scheme is used here.

Tool support exists for the following primary users:

- ▶ All testers:
  - ▶ Test management tools, including configuration management tools;
- ▶ Test analysts and technical test analysts:
  - ▶ Test design tools;
  - ▶ Test data generation tools;
  - ▶ Test oracles;
  - ▶ Simulation and emulation tools;
  - ▶ Test execution tools;
  - ▶ Keyword-driven automation tools;
  - ▶ Comparison tools;
  - ▶ Fault seeding and fault injection tools;
  - ▶ Web testing tools;
- ▶ Technical test analysts only:
  - ▶ Static analysis tools;
  - ▶ Dynamic analysis tools;
  - ▶ Performance testing tools;

- ❯ Programmers (or technical test analysts writing and maintaining test scripts):
  - ❯ Debugging, tracing, and troubleshooting tools.

Not all of the tools in the areas listed here are test tools in a narrow sense, but they are all useful in testing and hence included in this overview. It must be stressed again here, that debugging is NOT a test activity, although it is tightly connected to testing, especially low-level tests.

9.1.1 Tools for All Testers
9.1.1.1 Test Management Tools

Test management, like all management, includes risk analysis, estimation, scheduling, monitoring and control, and communication. Test management is discussed in Chapter 3.

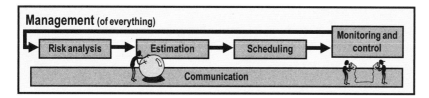

Test management tools cover these activities and support the project management aspects of testing. These tools can typically be used for registration of test activities, estimation, scheduling of tests, logging of results, and analysis and reporting of progress.

Most test management tools provide extensive reporting and analysis facilities.

Test management tools can support the handling of test documentation, such as plans, test specifications, and test procedures, and even traces between test cases and requirements.

The *advantage* of test management tools is that they can support the management of all test activities. They can provide an overview of the testing project and show the progress.

There are *no direct disadvantages* of test management tools. They are, however, often wedged between other tools, such as project management tools and configuration management tools. Most test management tools provide some of the facilities that these other tools also provide. Hence, there are often many interfaces and/or redundancies in connection with other tools used in the organization. The reason for this is—to some extent at least—that no single management tool provides all of the needed features for software development management.

Another reason for the confusion among tools is that the border lines between project management, configuration management, and test management are often blurred or not defined. This has a lot to do with the maturity of the organization. The more mature an organization is, the more the individual process areas are understood and clearly defined, and the easier it is to define what the tools should do and not do.

9.1.1.2 Tool Support for Configuration Management

Configuration management is identification, storage, change management, and reporting of configuration items. Configuration management for testers is discussed in Section 1.3.3.

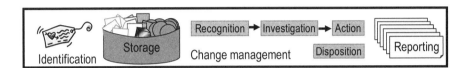

Configuration items are all work products, product components, and components that we want to control. This includes testware (e.g., test plans, test specifications, test environments including tools and test results) and requirements. Requirements are essential for testing and it is therefore of special interest to testers how requirements are managed.

Configuration management tools are used to support the configuration management activities. The main features of these tools are:

▶ Identification and storage of items;
▶ Traceability between items;
▶ Incident reporting and management of the life cycle of faults;
▶ Reporting and analysis.

Traceability and incident management are important features. Requirements and test cases should be traced to each other, and traceability tools allow the links between test cases and their corresponding test coverage items to be recorded. Changes to requirements must be communicated to testers and appropriate consequential changes implemented, for example, in related test cases. This is facilitated by trace information.

Changes to configuration items should always be initiated by an incident report, and the main supplier of incident reports is testing. A strong interface exists, therefore, between testing and configuration management. Only a few configuration management tools include full change management support, but a large number of more or less independent tools exist for this. Incident management tools (also known as defect tracking tools) may also have workflow-oriented facilities to track and control the allocation, correction, and retesting of incidents.

The main *advantage* of these tools is that they support the cumbersome and difficult information administration associated with the configuration management activities. Configuration management is difficult, if not impossible, to perform without some sort of tool support.

Most configuration management and incident management tools support analysis and reporting of configuration management information. This facilitates communication of the facts about how the development and testing processes are working.

The *pitfall* of these tools is redundancy in features and information and/or the need for transfer of data between tools, caused by unclear borders between tools, as described earlier.

9.1.2   Tools for Test Analysts and Technical Test Analysts
9.1.2.1   Test Design Tools

Test design tools support the creation of test specifications. They can analyze a specification of the product, often expressed as a model in a formal way, and generate high-level test cases and possibly test procedures or scripts based on this analysis.

This type of test tool can, for example:

- ▶ Derive high-level test cases from formally specified requirements, often managed by the same tool.
- ▶ Generate test cases based on specification of a model, for example, UML or state machines.
- ▶ Generate input for test cases based on input models, for example, input distribution specifications.
- ▶ Derive high-level test cases from actual source code.

The *advantage* of these tools is that test cases are systematically and comprehensively derived from the basis documentation. If the basis documentation is produced in accordance with specified rules, no test case will be missed, and they will all be correct.

The *pitfall* of these tools is that they only do half (or less) of the work. They cannot specify the expected results, so we have to elaborate the test input provided by the tool into test cases with the definition of the expected result and any preconditions.

Test design tools require very formally formatted basis documentation, and that can be regarded as both an advantage and a disadvantage.

9.1.2.2 Test Data Preparation Tools

Test input data preparation tools support:

▶ Selection (e.g., from an existing database);

▶ Creation;

▶ Generation;

▶ Manipulation; and

▶ Editing;

of test data for use in setting up preconditions for test procedures and individual test cases.

Some of these tools are data tool dependent, while the most sophisticated can deal with a range of file and database formats.

Test data can be selected and extracted from live data and scrambled to hide person-sensitive information. This enables tests to be performed on real data, which can be essential for systems in, for example, the public sector.

A test data preparation tool is able to extract live data from the tax authorities' database according to specific selection criteria for test runs of the implementation of a new tax law. The criteria may be 100 families with one income and at least three children, 100 people over 80 years of age with an income over a certain amount, and the 40 people with the highest income in a specific city. The tool scrambles identifying information (e.g., name and Social Security number) before the data can be used.

The *advantage* of these tools is that they make it possible to handle great volumes of data.

Use of this type of testing requires good configuration management of testware to identify which specific versions of the object, the test specification, and the test data belong to each other.

The *pitfall* here is that the tools may create too much useless data, if selection is not planned carefully.

9.1.2.3 Test Oracles

A test oracle is a special concept in testing; it is used to determine expected results from inputs. Some say that the best test oracle is the tester studying the test basis documentation and deriving the expected result from this. This is, however, sometimes not possible for time and/or cost reasons.

Automated test oracles are tools that can generate the expected result for specific input and hence facilitate the creation of test cases. Such "oracles" are hard to find. In principle, they must do exactly the same as the test object and may therefore seem redundant.

One of the situations in which an oracle can be found and can be very useful is when an old system is being replaced by a new one providing the same functionality. This is seen more and more often when old legacy systems are replaced with systems using new technology, for example, web access. In such a case test input is given to the old system and the result that this provides is regarded as the expected result for the new system.

Oracles can also be created in situations where nonfunctional requirements can be disregarded and a system simulating the functionality only can be developed at a much lower cost. This is especially the case where the real system has very strict performance requirements.

The *advantage* of oracles is that they make it possible to generate the expected results much faster than if we had to derive them manually. The use of oracles requires strict control over the oracle and the other testware.

The *disadvantage* of oracles is that they can give us a false sense of reliability. There is a risk that we will repeat faults from the old system, or between an oracle system and the real system. There is also a risk of not getting sufficient test coverage if we just test according to what the oracle provides without taking the structure of the new system into account.

9.1.2.4   Simulation Tools and Emulation Tools

Simulators are used to support tests where necessary code or other systems are either unavailable or impractical or even dangerous to use. I for one would rather not test the software supposed to handle a nuclear meltdown under real-world conditions.

Test harnesses and drivers fall into this category of tools. They are used where components or other test objects cannot be executed directly, for example, for testing of a component in isolation, embedded software without a user interface, or execution of many unrelated automated test scripts.

Some testing tools in the market provide harness and driver facilities, especially component testing tools. Very often, however, these tools are homemade and tailored precisely to the specific needs. The principle in stubs and drivers is illustrated below.

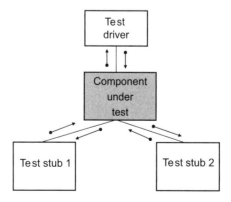

A special type of simulator is called an emulator because it is used to mimic hardware to which the software under test interfaces.

Simulation tools are almost always bespoke systems made for a specific test project.

The *advantage* of these tools is that they make otherwise impossible or difficult tests possible. These tools can save us a lot of money.

Emulators can make it possible to test in "slow motion," and they can act as debuggers as well.

These tools, like most other testing tools, require good configuration management of the testware, something that may be considered an advantage.

The *disadvantages* include that the use of these tools may give a false sense of reliability—after all, the simulators or emulators may be wrong. It may also be that the use of such tools "hides" defects, for example, performance and other time-related defects. Simulators and emulators can also be rather expensive to produce and set up, and the cost must be balanced carefully with the benefit.

Another disadvantage of these tools can be that they require the testers to be able to code or have access to people who can code. In practice, this is not a problem, since these tools are often used in testing being performed in close connection with the coding.

9.1.2.5 Test Execution Tools

This type of testing tool goes under many names—test execution tools, test running tools, or capture and replay tools—and is probably the most widely used category of testing tool.

These tools are primarily used for automation of regression testing. They can execute test scripts much faster and more reliably than human beings, and they can therefore reduce test execution time when tests are repeated and/or allow more tests to be executed.

All the tools in this category work according to the same basic principles, namely:

- ▶ Capture: a recording of all the tester's manual actions and the system's responses into a test script;
- ▶ Control points: a number of checkpoints added to the script by the tester during the capture;
- ▶ Playback: automatic (re)execution of the test script.

Test execution tools exist for graphical user interface (GUI) and for character-based interfaces. For GUI applications the tools can simulate mouse movement and button clicks and can recognize GUI objects such as windows, fields, buttons, and other controls.

When a script has been captured once, it may be executed at any given time again. If the software under test reacts differently from what was expected at the inserted checkpoints, the execution will report a failure. It is usually also possible to log information during execution.

Test scripts are captured in a specific scripting language. In newer versions of these tools, it is now possible to access the scripts that have been captured. These are often in a C or Visual Basic like code, and this offers the possibility for editing the scripts, so that, for example, forgotten operations, further control points, or changed values, can be added.

Experience shows that if the scripts are written from scratch, rather than captured, and good and systematic development principles are used, the scripts will be more maintainable. More and more of these tools are therefore used as test execution tools of coded scripts, rather than as capture/playback tools.

The *advantage* of these tools is that a lot of manual test execution can be done automatically. This is especially the case in iterative development and other development projects where a large number of regression tests are needed. These tools are indispensable in development where "frequent build and smoke test" principles are used. Builds can be made in the evening, and automated test suites can be set to run overnight. Testing results will then be ready in the morning.

The use of test scripts requires good configuration management to keep track of which versions of the test objects, test data, and test scripts belong together. Again a blessing (maybe) in disguise.

The *pitfall* for these tools is that it can be rather expensive to establish and maintain the test scripts. The requirements, specifications, and code undergo changes in the course of the development, especially in iterative development. This must be carefully considered in connection with the estimation of the continuous maintenance of the test scripts.

Another pitfall is that the work with the test scripts requires programming skills. If the necessary skills are not available, the use of test execution tools may be very cumbersome and inefficient.

At the same time, keep in mind that test scripts written by a programmer or tester are just like any other (software) product: made by humans and therefore not perfect. Defects are also introduced in test scripts, and test scripts should therefore be tested and corrected when defects are identified. The earlier this is done, the better since fewer defects in the test scripts reduce the possible uncertainty as to whether a failure is being caused by a defect in the test script or is indeed in the product under test.

9.1.2.6 Keyword-Driven Automation Tools

Keyword-driven testing is a way to execute test scripts at a higher level of abstraction. A keyword is defined to represent a script, and a tool can then act as a link between the keyword and the tool executing the corresponding test script.

One or more parameters may be associated with a keyword, so that the same script may be executed several times with different values given for the parameters. The idea is similar to that of a service or subroutine in programming where the same code may be executed with different values.

The tools make it possible to use parameter-driven test scripts without having to change the (often complicated) scripts in the execution tool.

Keywords are usually related to higher level functionality or business procedures. They may also reflect flows within use cases.

The tools for keyword-driven testing are also known as script wrappers, because they wrap the technical part of the test (the actual test scripts and the test execution tool) so that the testers only need to know about the high-level keywords.

Keywords and values for their parameters may be held in spreadsheets or tables, to enable automatic execution of several test scripts in sequence.

A test sequence defined by a list of keywords and values for their associated parameters may look like this:

Keyword	P1	P2	P3
Create customer	Mr.	Paul	Smith
Create customer	Ms.	Anna	Philipson
Find customer	Ms.	Anna	Philipson
Edit customer	, ,Philipsson		
Find customer	Mr.	Pail	Smith
Find customer	Mr.	Paul	Smith
Delete customer	Yes		

Each keyword has a number of parameters with specific meanings. See if you can figure out what the meanings are.

Keyword-driven testing is getting more and more sophisticated, introducing several levels of abstraction between the tester and the technical test scripts.

Test wrapping tools are available commercially and as open source, but they are also very often homemade and usually quite simple, yet very effective.

Keyword-driven testing requires a good overview of the test sub-process and a high level of abstraction as all parameterization does. This is demanding but can be rewarding for the test in the long run.

The *advantages* of these tools are primarily seen from the point of view of those controlling the test execution, especially if these are domain experts rather than test analysts. For test executioners it is easier to use keyword-driven testing rather than testing script directly for these reasons:

- Keywords that reflect the business can be chosen.
- Test execution can be done automatically by nontechnical people based on the keyword lists.
- The keyword lists are robust to minor changes in the software.
- The implementation of the keywords is independent of the implementation of the underlying scripts, so that the same keyword lists may be used with scripts in a number of different scripting languages being executed in different execution tools.

Using keyword-driven testing does not ease the work with the actual test scripts. They still need to be established (captured or written) and maintained, and they need to be able to be executed with different parameter values.

The *pitfall* here is that extra layers are placed between the test executer and the product under test. It requires more coordination and communications between the people involved to maintain the integrity of the layers in the testware.

Last but not least—and again a possible advantage rather than a pitfall—is the fact that keyword-driven testing requires extra care in configuration management. This kind of testing has several layers of testware instead of "just" test scripts to keep track of and to keep consistent.

9.1.2.7 Comparison Tools

Comparison tools are used to find differences between the expected and the actual results.

These tools range from very simple comparison facilities, as in Word, for example, to very advanced, dedicated tools. Test execution tools normally include some type of comparison facility.

The tools may be able to compare, for example, values in files or on screens, bitmaps, and positions.

The *advantage* is that these tools can compare large amounts of data very fast and reliably, and without getting tired.

The *pitfall* is that they may produce enormous amounts of reported data of which only a fraction is relevant. The tools can, and should, have filtering or masking possibilities (e.g., to allow them to ignore dates or to ignore positions of objects and concentrate on the contents).

A comparison tool I use quite often is the window in my office. When I need to compare two texts or two drawings on paper I place the papers on top of each other and hold them against the window. Differences are usually easy to spot.

9.1.2.8 Fault Seeding and Fault Injection Tools

These types of tool are used to support the defect-based test technique of fault injection (or fault seeding) discussed in Section 6.5.2.

The tools create or inject faults (or rather defects) into the software component under test. The tools can work either on the source code, changing the code in prespecified ways, or on the compiled code, changing the structure of the code.

In both cases new versions of the component under test are created with the defects.

The *advantage* of fault seeding and fault injection tools is that many defects may be injected in a systematic way to support these defect-based techniques.

The *disadvantage* of the tools is that the defects are not necessarily realistic. Also, care must be taken not to use the version with defects in production.

9.1.2.9 Web Tools

These days testing never stops. With more and more web-based products around, we need to constantly monitor that the products are doing well. Products being web based means that some issues are out of our hands (e.g., hyperlinks and server and network availability).

Hyperlink testing tools are used to check that no broken hyperlinks are present on a website.

These tools often have additional functionality such as HTML validation, spelling, and availability check. The facility is often built into other tools (e.g., HTML development tools).

Monitoring tools are used for web-based products, most typically e-commerce and e-business applications. The tools monitor the product's availability to customers and the service level (performance and resource usage). The tools will issue warnings if the monitoring shows that something is not as expected.

Many free web tools are available. Many are also proprietary, and they can be quite sophisticated.

The *advantage* of these tools is that they can check all hyperlinks very quickly. It is important for the trustworthiness of a website that there are no broken links. Links change very frequently; and it can be quite an eye opener to run such a check for the first time on your "perfect" website. The tools also give us a chance to determine if things are not working as they should before the users find out.

There is no *disadvantage* to using these tools. It should be an ongoing activity, at least once a day, to perform these checks.

9.1.3   Tools for Technical Test Analysts
9.1.3.1   Static Analysis Tools

Static analysis can be performed on code as well as on architecture. Static analysis is discussed in detail in Section 4.4. Most static testing is performed by people, but some types are supported by tools.

Static analysis tools examine the written code to detect, for example, variable anomalies, to check adherence to defined coding rules, and to collect measurements concerning the code (e.g., cyclomatic complexity and website balance).

The code is not executed in static analysis, and no test cases are executed either.

One *advantage* of automated static analysis is that the tools find all occurrences of the defects they are looking for. Tools do not get tired or "blind" to defects they have seen many times before.

Static analysis requires some coding standards to check against to find deviations, and that can also be considered an advantage. The more structured and uniformly the code is written, the easier it is to maintain.

The *disadvantage* of static analysis is that some tools—especially older tools—may find a number of "incidents" that are not defects after all. The reports for static analysis can be overwhelming with many things that can be disregarded, and that can make it difficult to find the "gold nuggets."

9.1.3.2   Dynamic Analysis Tools

Dynamic analysis tools are used to provide information about the behavior and state of software while it is being executed. These tools primarily give run-time information about memory handling and pointers.

Memory handling is concerned with the allocation, use, and deallocation of memory. The tools can detect memory leaks, where memory is gradually being filled up during extended use, long before it actually happens. Some coding languages prevent such defects from happening; others don't, for example, C and C++.

Pointers are used to handle dynamic allocation of memory, and the dynamic analysis tools can identify unassigned pointers; that is, pointers pointing at "who-knows-what." They can also detect defects in pointer arithmetic.

The *advantage* of these tools is that they can find defects, which it is almost impossible or very expensive to find in other ways. They don't need specific test cases, because they report on what is going on while other test cases or scenarios are executed.

There is no *disadvantage* of using this type of tools. One thing to be aware of, however, is that different dynamic test tools may report different types of problems because of the way they are implemented.

A special type of dynamic analysis tool is *coverage measurement tools* or analysis tools. These tools provide objective measurement for some structural or white-box test coverage metrics, for example:

- Statement coverage;
- Branch coverage.

The *advantage* of these tools is that objective measurements to be used in the checking against test completion criteria are delivered in a fast and reliable way.

Some tools can also deliver reports about uncovered areas. The more fancy ones produce colored reports where covered code is shown in one color and uncovered code in another. This is a great help when more test cases must be designed to obtain a higher coverage.

The *disadvantage* is that the code is instrumented, and that the tools log information during execution. This means that it is not strictly the "real" code we are testing. This can also have an adverse impact on performance, and that can pose problems if we are testing real-time software.

9.1.3.3   Performance Test Tools

Performance test tools are used to:

- Generate large volumes or loads on the product;
- Measure the performance of the product under controlled circumstances.

The tools can be used to create the volumes specified in the volume requirements and necessary for volume testing. This may be number of concurrent users, the amount of memory to be used, number of information items of a given type (e.g., customers or patients), or number of transactions per time unit.

The use of the tools for stress testing is similar to that described for volume testing.

For performance testing the tools can be used to measure what the performance is under given circumstances. Performance testing tools can provide very useful reports based on collected information, often in graphical form.

The *advantage* of these tools is that they can provide information about "bottleneck" areas relatively inexpensively before the product hits the real world. All too many products have no or insufficient performance requirements and turn out to be unable to cope with real-life volumes and loads. It is much better to test these aspects before the product breaks down when the first set of users starts using it.

The *disadvantages* are the additional knowledge and skills required to be able to use these tools effectively, the cost of commercial tools, and the possible lack of a technical match with the software under test or the test environment.

9.1.4 Tools for Programmers
9.1.4.1 Debugging Tools

Debugging tools are NOT testing tools!

They are, however, related to testing, since they are used by programmers to pinpoint defects. For this purpose they are a very efficient aid.

Debuggers allow programmers to:

▶ Execute the code line by line.

▶ Insert break points.

▶ Control and set values of variables at break points.

Note that when testers use debugging tools to locate defects in test tools, test scripts, or other types of testware, they do not do that in their capacity of testers, but as developers of testware. This may seem like quibbling, but for common understanding and communication purposes it is important to be able to distinguish between different roles, even when they are filled by the same person.

The *advantage* of these tools is that they can save the programmers a lot of time during detailed fault hunting. It can also be motivating for some testers with a development background to work with the programmers and use these tools to pinpoint not only the failure, but also the defect.

On the other hand, the *pitfall* is that programmers can waste a lot of time if the tools are used in an undisciplined way—or to play with.

9.2 Test Tool Acquisition

Many tools are bought in excitement. We find a tool—at an exhibition or in a magazine—and we are immediately convinced that this tool is the solution to all our problems. The tool is used for a short while, it appears that it was not quite what we expected, and sooner or later it ends up on a shelf and is completely forgotten about. Sound familiar?

In a professional organization it is important to treat the investment in (testing) tools as the serious decision it is. Tools are usually expensive, and even if they are not expensive to buy, they are expensive to implement and maintain in an organization.

Acquisition and introduction of a tool in a company requires a number of organizational considerations. It is not something you just rush in and do (like fools!); conscious decisions about what to do and how to do it in the company must be made before the work can commence.

The acquisition should include the following activities:

▶ Tool selection preparation;

▶ Tool evaluation;

> ◗ Selection of the winner.

9.2.1   Tool or No Tool?

The first thing we must do when the idea of automation occurs is find out what it is we are trying to achieve with the tool. What exactly is the problem?

Introduction of a test tool or test automation is not necessarily the answer to all problems.

A fool with a tool
is still a fool

If the problem is that we are not entirely sure how to perform a task or an activity, it may be tempting to get a tool to help us, but it is usually not a good idea. Only work that is well specified is appropriate for automation.

Work that requires creativity is not a candidate for automation either. We cannot get a computer to be creative and think outside of the box.

Automation may help solving problems caused by:

> ◗ Work that is to be repeated many times;
> ◗ Work that it is slower to do manually;
> ◗ Work that it is safer to do with a tool.

Once the problem is described and well understood, we can consider how to solve it. There may be a number of alternative solutions, including the acquisition of a tool.

Maybe it does seem like a tool is the best solution, and in that case we can go on with the selection preparation.

9.2.2   Tool Selection Team

The next step is to establish a team to perform the evaluation and selection of the tool. This team must be as broad as possible and include representatives for all potential stakeholders for the test tool.

The team must be composed of a team leader and representatives for all potential users of the test tool, including developers, professional testers, tool-responsible, process owner(s), and future product users.

The team members cannot be expected to be assigned full time to the selection and evaluation task. They must, however, be available when meetings are held and take an active part in the work.

9.2.3   Test Tool Strategy

The long-term test tool strategy for an organization must be reconsidered if it is already in place, or it must be produced if it is not.

The point to make clear is how a new tool will fit into the overall goals for the company (e.g., with regard to general process improvement or the achievement of a certain level of capability or a specific certification). This may have an impact on the type of tool to choose.

It must also be clear how large a part of the organization is going to use the new tool. Will everybody be involved such that we should choose a solution that covers the entire company; or will it be used on a project level so that we should choose a solution that only covers the needs of a single, independent project? This decision may have far-reaching consequences both with regard to direct cost and with regard to time to be spent.

At some point it is of course also important to establish who is going to pay for a new tool and for its continued usage and maintenance.

9.2.4 Preparation of a Business Case

In a business case we compare the cost of a solution with the benefits the solution is going to bring us.

The cost of selecting, implementing, and maintaining a tool is usually significant. It includes expenses for the following:

▶ Selection;
▶ Acquisition (list price minus possible discounts, open source, or own development);
▶ Licenses;
▶ Tailoring;
▶ Implementation;
▶ Training;
▶ Tool use;
▶ Maintenance of automated testware;
▶ Tool maintenance.

Some of these expenses are measured directly in money; others come from time being spent by employees; both must be considered in the calculation.

On the other side of the business case equation we have the benefits. Benefits from test automation are rarely, if ever, measurable in actual money. They come from savings we obtain because the tool helps us perform tasks faster and with fewer mistakes.

For test execution tools the cost/benefit depends very heavily on how often the automated tests will be executed, as illustrated below.

Tests that are only executed a few times during the entire lifetime of the product are usually not worth spending automation resources on.

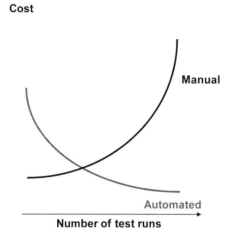

On the other hand, it may be well worth it to automate the tests that are being executed many times (e.g., tests used for extensive regression testing of high-risk areas).

It is of course possible to use a mixture of manual and automated tests.

9.2.5   Identification of Tool Requirements

A test tool is a software product, and just like all other software products it should satisfy a number of requirements. Part of the selection process is to identity the applicable requirements for the tool to be implemented.

First of all the tool needs to have some *functionality*. We must define what we require the tool to do. This must, of course, be consistent with the processes we are going to automate. Integration with other tools is another important part of the functionality we need to specify. If the tool is going to have web access, this must also be explicitly and thoroughly described.

Connected to the functional requirements, we have the *nonfunctional requirements*. These should at least include aspects of performance, usability, availability, and maintainability for the tool.

There are many aspects of performance, and these aspects may have a greater impact on everyday life than you may think. It may, for example, be the time it takes to execute a complete regression test suite, or the volume of something that the tool can handle.

Usability is a measure of how easy a test tool is to use. It may include aspects such as an intuitive interface, help facilities and user documentation, compatibility with existing procedures, and tailoring facilities.

Availability describes when we can use the tool. If the tool is running on a server somewhere, this can be fairly unpredictable.

We should also consider availability of support. Is it possible to get support in our own language during normal working hours, or do we have to call somewhere in the middle of night and try to explain our problems in a foreign language?

Maintainability is interesting, for example, in terms of upgrades. How often do we get new versions? Will they be backward-compatible? What about our own tailoring?

The *environmental requirements* or constraints are requirements forced on us by the environment around our organization. These can be in the form of existing products that the testing tool must be able to cooperate with or a specific platform that we need to use.

The last thing to consider is *project requirements* or constraints. The usual ones are resources, time, and money. They form the foundation of the requirements tower and they need to be "strong" enough to carry the tower. If not we must reduce the product quality requirements or increase the project requirements.

9.2.6 Buy, Open Source, or Do-It-Yourself

There are advantages and disadvantages to buying a standard tool, using an open source tool, or developing one's own tool. This is a consideration worth making, and it may be based on the aspects shown below.

Buy	Open Source	Do-It-Yourself
Some tailoring must always be foreseen, either to the tool or to the processes in the company, or both.	The tool may be changed and enhancements should be shared.	The tool can be made exactly as the company wants it (provided it knows what it wants).
The price is usually easy to calculate.	The tool is free but there may be license fees to pay.	It may be extremely difficult to estimate the final cost.
Usually the payment must be made within a relatively short period of time.	No immediate price needs to be paid.	The development and hence the "payment" can be done at the company's own pace.
Do what you do best—that is what the suppliers do.	The quality depends on the exposure, history, and use of the tool.	Maybe you are best suited to developing your own tool.

The table is by no means exhaustive, but it might be used as inspiration for the considerations.

If a company decides to develop its own tool, this must be undertaken like any other development project (i.e., at least as seriously as a project with an external customer).

We need to be aware that many tools come into existence because developers or testers have an urgent need for tool support for a specific task and are able to develop a tool themselves. This is often done as "hidden"

work, (i.e., the time spent is not registered anywhere). Such tools may be very efficient and they may be taken into consideration when selecting a more official tool solution. These tools must be evaluated to determine if they are sufficiently documented to build on and if they can handle the scaling involved in spreading the use to a larger user group.

9.2.7 Preparation of a Shortlist of Candidates

Many sources for information about test tools exist, for example, articles, suppliers' web pages, other companies, exhibitions, and research reports.

Based on the initial information, a number of possible candidates are identified by a fairly coarse evaluation method based on some really essential requirements like the platform on which a given tool will need to run.

It can be useful to supplement the evaluation with a look at the supplier. The supplier is the "family-in-law" that we will have to live with for a long time, so investigate for example:

- ▶ The supplier's employees—do they match ours?
- ▶ The supplier's own use of the tool;
- ▶ The supplier's financial status;
- ▶ The supplier's focus—is testing tools a niche?
- ▶ The supplier's acquaintances;
- ▶ The supplier's reputation;
- ▶ The supplier's support facilities.

9.2.8 Detailed Evaluation

After this first selection stricter and stricter evaluations are done until only two candidates are left in the field.

It is important for the evaluation group to agree on how the evaluation is to be made and precisely what is significant in the selection. An evaluation method includes:

- ▶ Description of the scale for the evaluation of fulfillment of the requirements, for example:
  - ▶ Fully, Almost, Partly, Not;
  - ▶ From 0 to 100%.
- ▶ Description of the selection criteria, based on the fulfillment evaluation, for example:
  - ▶ All priority 1 requirements fulfilled at least 80% and at least 50% of the priority 2 requirements fulfilled.

It is a good idea to define different criteria for different selection phases, which typically become more strict as the field narrows.

After the initial evaluation rounds, the list of candidates will have been reduced from a number of possible test tools to fewer and fewer candidates by the deployment of the defined evaluation method. In the end there should be only two left.

9.2.9   Performance of a Competitive Trial

The two finalists should undergo a detailed evaluation that should include at least one demonstration and preferably a trial period, so that the tools may be tried out under circumstances that are as realistic as possible.

Scenarios that reflect the functional requirements should be set up and run through.

At the same time the nonfunctional requirements can be tested. Performance aspects should be evaluated under realistic circumstances, that is, both locally and over great distances, if that is the need, and in an environment with the "normal" load, not just on an isolated test machine.

It may be important to investigate whether a tool can handle the volumes that the company or the project may have to handle. Volume may also be a question of a large number of users and/or a large number of platforms possibly distributed over large distances. Not just the company's current situation should be included in an evaluation; a test tool should be able to cope with the development in the company for at least the foreseeable future.

For testers it should not be difficult to test a tool they are going to use themselves. Even if we are really eager to start using test tools, it is worth remembering that advertising materials and salespeople may color things a bit.

The last thing to do for now is to

select the winner!

9.3   Testing Tool Implementation and Deployment

Now that the tool has been selected, the real challenge is to make the tool become part of everyday life, and to keep it alive long enough to profit on the investment.

The introduction or implementation of a tool in an organization is an organizational change project. The principles of process improvement in general are discussed in Section 1.4.1.

Management commitment is essential for the implementation to be a success. An implementation process must be described and followed closely to avoid the tool ending up as "shelfware," as so many tools unfortunately do.

An implementation process should include the following activities:

- ▶ Make necessary adjustments to the tool, if any.
- ▶ Perform a pilot project.
- ▶ Assess the pilot project.
- ▶ Produce a roll-out strategy.
- ▶ Make the roll-out happen.
- ▶ Follow up on the roll-out.

The necessary resources, both in terms of people, time, money, and training must be provided and sustained until the use of the new tool is an engraved part of everyday working life.

The roles that must be in place to make the tool implementation a success are:

- ▶ The sponsor;
- ▶ The target group;
- ▶ The champions;
- ▶ The change agents.

Furthermore, the introduction of a tool requires a *tool custodian*. This is a technical person who is responsible for the setup and maintenance of the tool. He or she provides internal help and support with technical issues and can be responsible for contact with the supplier of the tool for second-level support.

9.3.1   Necessary Adjustments

Generally the processes that a tool supports are generic, having been designed to be "all things to all people." It may therefore be necessary to make some adjustments or tailoring before a pilot can start.

This tailoring can range from merely making an adjustment to the tool to make it comply completely with the processes to using the tool as it is and tailoring the processes to the tool.

If the organization's processes are tried and tested within their context, it is much better to tailor the tool to the processes. Otherwise, it is easiest and most future-safe to tailor the processes to the tool.

9.3.2 Testing Tool Piloting

A pilot project should always be performed for the tool before we commit to implementing it across all projects.

There are a number of reasons for performing a small-scale pilot project. First of all we need to verify the business case and ensure that the benefits of the use of the test tool can really be achieved.

A goal for the pilot project is also to get some experience in the use of the test tool. The pilot should enable us to identify further adjustments needed to the processes and/or to the tool, as appropriate. The different tools of all the different tool types support different detailed processes. They also require interfaces with other tools and other processes, for example, configuration management of testware. Finally a pilot can help us refine the estimate for the actual costs and benefits for the implementation.

The length of the pilot depends on the type of tool. For a test execution tool it should take between 3 and 6 months; for a static analysis tool only 2 to 4 weeks may be needed. In any case the pilot should be followed closely.

9.3.3 Testing Tool Roll-Out

The roll-out of the testing tool should be based on a successful evaluation of the pilot project. Roll-out normally requires serious involvement of all the people who have roles in the test tool implementation, not least the users of the test tool, the target group.

A roll-out strategy that suits the nature of the organization must be defined. A "big bang" roll out, where everybody starts using the tool at a given point in time, works in some organizations. In other organizations a gradual implementation, where the tool is deployed as the need arises, will work better.

Regardless of how the roll-out is done, the most important activity at this point is to support the new users as the roll-out takes place. We must be prepared to

- ◗ support the users;
- ◗ support the users;
- ◗ support the users;
- ◗ support the users;

until the usage of the test tool is a completely integrated part of the work.

9.3.4 Testing Tool Deployment

A testing tool is a part of the test environment for our tests, and in many ways like any other (software) product. The tools we use should be kept under proper configuration management like the rest of the test environment and other testware.

It is important to be able to record with which version of a tool specific tests have been prepared and/or executed. The concepts of configuration management, especially for testers, is discussed further in Section 1.3.3.

Questions

1.   How can test tools be categorized?
2.   Which test tools category is used in this book?
3.   Which tool category does not contain testing tools?
4.   What do we need to be careful about in terms of using test management tools?
5.   What activities do configuration management tools support?
6.   What is the pitfall of these tools?
7.   What does a test design tool do?
8.   What are data preparation tools used for?
9.   What is an oracle in the context of testing?
10.   When should simulation tools be used?
11.   What are a test harness and drivers used for?
12.   What are test execution tools also called?
13.   What do test execution tools use for execution?
14.   What are advantages and disadvantages of test execution tools?
15.   What is keyword-driven testing?
16.   What are tools for keyword-driven testing also called, and why?
17.   What process needs to be considered carefully when keyword-driven testing is used?
18.   Where are comparison tools often found?
19.   What is a disadvantage of fault injection tools?
20.   What can web tools do?
21.   What are the advantages of static analysis tools?
22.   What are dynamic analysis tools providing information about?
23.   What can some advanced coverage measurement tools provide?
24.   What can performance test tools do?
25.   What is a debugging tool?
26.   What are the activities in the tool acquisition process?
27.   What is a fool with a tool; and what does that mean?
28.   Who should be in a tool selection team?
29.   What is a test tool strategy used for?
30.   What should be considered in a tool acquisition business case?
31.   What is the most important type of requirements for a tool?

32. What are the ways in which a tool can come into existence in an organization?
33. What should be investigated when choosing a test tool supplier?
34. What could an evaluation scale be like?
35. What is important in a trial?
36. What are the activities in tool implementation?
37. What are the roles in tool introduction?
38. What are the goals of a pilot project?
39. What is the most important part of an actual test tool roll-out?
40. What most be done with tools used in testing?

Appendix 9.A: List of Testing Tools

This list was found on the website http://www.aptest.com/resources.html on February 28, 2014.

Application Test Tools

AdaTEST
AQtime
BoundsChecker
Bullseye Coverage
CMT++
Code Coverage
CodeCheck
CodeWizard
CTA++, CTB
CTC++
devAdvantage
Diversity Analyzer
GlowCode
Hexawise
Insure++
LDRA Testbed
Leak Check
Logiscope
OSPC
Panorama

McCabe TQ
PolySpace Suite
Predictive Lite
Prevent
Purify
TCAT C/C++
Test Coverage
Testers Desk

Functional Test Tools

.TEST
AberroTest
AETG Web
Automated Test Designer
Avignon Acceptance Testing System
CAPBAK/X, CAPBAK/MSW
Certify
CitraTest
eggplant
GUITAR

Haven
Holodeck
JPdfUnit
MITS.GUI
PETA
PyUnit
QACenter
Repro
SAP Software Quality Assurance Testing Tools
ScriptTech
Silktest
Smalltalk Test Mentor
Squish
TALC2000
TestArchitect
TestComplete
TestWorks
Unified Test Pro
Vermont HighTest Plus
VNCRobot

WinRunner®

X-Unity

Performance Test Tools

AppLoader

AppsWatch

BugTimer

DB Stress

LoadeaTest

LoadRunner®

Monitor Master

IxLoad

QACenter Performance Edition Shunra\Storm

SilkPerformer

SSW Performance PRO! 97

WinFeedback

XtremeLoad

Java Test Tools

Abbot

AdaptiveCells/J

AgileTest

AppLoader

AppaWatch

Agitator

Bugkilla

Cactus

GJ-Coverage

GJTester

GUIdancer

JCover

Jemmy

JMeter

JStyle

JSystem

jtest

JUnit

JVerify

KCC

LiSA

Marathon Panorama

QEngine

QF-Test

QStudio Enterprise

TCAT/Java

Embedded Test Tools

Message Magic

Reactis Tester

TBrun

Tessy

TestQuest Pro

USBTester

VectorCAST

Database Test Tools

AETG

Data Generator

Datatect

DTM DB Stress

ER/Datagen

JennySQL DB Validator

SQL Profiler

SQS/Test Professional

TestIt!

TurboData

utPLSQL

Link and HTML Test Tools

AccVerify/AccRepair

ChangeAgent

CSE HTML Validator

Cyber Spyder Link Test

Dead Links

HTML PowerTools

HTML Tidy

InFocus

Link Checker Pro

LinkRunner

LinkScan

LinkSleuth

Link Validator

MOMspider

Ramp Ascend

Real Validator

Truwex website QA tool

WebLight

WebQA

On-line Link and HTML Test Services

Audit Blossom

CSSCheck

CSS Validation Service

Dr. Watson

HTML Validator

HTML Validation Service

Link Alarm

NetMechanic

Site Check

SiteTechnician

Validation Spider

W3C Link Checker

Weblint Gateway

Web Page Backward Compatibility Viewer

Web Page Purifier

XML Validation

Web Functional Test Tools

actiWATE

AppsWatch

Astra

Badboy

Canoo WebTest

eValid

IeUnit

Imprimatur

Internet Macros

HTTP::Recorder

iRise Application Simulator

ITP

LiSA

Netvantage Functional Tester

PesterCat

QA Wizard

Ranorex

RapidRep Test Suite

Rational Robot

Sahi

SAMIE

Selenium

SilkTest

SoapTest

soapui

Solex

Squish

swete

TestSmith

TestWeb

vTest

WatiN

Watir

WebAii

Webcorder

WebInject

WebKing

WET

WSUnit

Yawet

Web Security Test Tools

QA Inspect

Web Performance Test Tools

ANTS

Dotcom-Monitor

forecast

http_load

Jblitz

LoadTracer

Microsoft Application Center Test

NeoLoad

OpenLoad

OpenSTA

PowerProxy

Proxy Sniffer

PureLoad

Siege

SilkPerformer

StressIT

Site Tester 1.0

TestMaker

Wbox

Web Application Stress Tool

Webload

WebPartner TPC

Web Performance Trainer

Web Polygraph

WAPT

Webseam

Web Server Stress Tool

WebSizr

Web Performance Test Services

Load Gold

SiteStress

webStress

Web Based Bug Tracking

AceProject

AdminiTrack

ADT Web

Bug/Defect Tracking Expert

BugAware.com

bugcentral.com

BUGtrack

BugHost

BugStation

Bug Tracker

Bug Tracker Software

Bug Tracking

Bugvisor

Bugzero

Bugzilla

Census BugTrack

DefectTracker

Defectr

Dragonfly

ExDesk

FogBUGZ

Fast BugTrack

Footprints

IssueTrak

JIRA

Jitterbug

JTrac

Mantis

MyBugReport

OnTime Now!

Ozibug

Perfect Tracker

ProblemTracker

PR Tracker

QEngine

Soffront Defect and
Bug Tracking

SpeeDEV

Squish

Task Complete

teamatic

TestWave

TrackStudio

VisionProject

Woodpecker IT

yKAP

**Bug Tracking
Applications**

assyst

BridgeTrak

BugRat

BugSentry

Bug Trail

Defect Agent

Defect Manager

Fast BugTrack

GNATS

Intercept

IssueView

JIRA

OnTime

ProjecTrak

QAW

Support Tracker

SWBTracker

TestTrack Pro

ZeroDefect

**Test Management
Tools**

ApTest Manager

Extended Test Plan

QADirector

SilkPlan Pro

T-Plan Professional

TestDirectorTM

Test Manager
Adaptors

TestLog

Testuff

TestWave

API Test Tools

ADL project
repository

MITS.Comm

DejaGNU

TET

**Communications
Test Tools**

AdventNet Simulator

ANVL

Chariot

Cheetah

Drive Test

Emulation Engine XT

FanfareSVT

Fault Factory

InterWatch

iSoftTechTAS

LANTraffic

Maxwell

NetDisturb

NetworkTester

nGenius Performance
Monitor

NuStreams 2000

Silvercreek SNMP
Test Suite

SNAsim

Requirements Management Tools

Analyst Pro Blueprint Requirements Center Doors

Caliber

Gatherspace

RequisitePro

Other Products

Aprobe

Ascert

Bug Shot

KaNest

LogStomper

MPMM

ProjectManager.com

Project Manager Resources

Project Manager Templates

Project Planning Software

QACenter 3270 Edition

SOAPSonar

TestOOB

People Skills

Testers are people. Therefore, testing is not purely processes and techniques—it also has a human and psychological aspect. This is out of the scope of ISO 29119, but fortunately covered by ISTQB.

The ISTQB Foundation syllabus covers basic psychological aspects of testing and testers. Dealing with people in an organization is a management responsibility, and hence only the ISTQB Advanced Test Manager syllabus includes a people-related aspect in a chapter called People Skills. This chapter is structured in the same way as this syllabus.

People work for one single reason: We have to. There are, however, many explanations for *why* we have to—also some more specific to testers.

The individual's testing capability can be derived from experience and/or training in one or more of the following areas: users, development, and testing. Regardless of whom we are, interpersonal skills such as giving and receiving criticism, influencing, and negotiation are all important in the role of testing.

People are different, and it is an advantage to have a variety of personality types within the test team. The best combinations may be ensured at times of recruitment. Even if that is not possible, knowledge of certain patterns of behavior can help us enhance the team we are working with.

Testers work in many different organizations, and they all have different organizational structures for testing and for other activities. Communication within an organization is essential, not least in testing.

10.1   Individual Skills

Testing is a profession. It requires certain skills and capabilities of the individual testing practitioners. It also requires people with certain human characteristics or personality types.

People have individual personalities. A person's personality is very difficult to change; we are born with many of the traits and the rest have been chiseled in to us.

There are some common traits that will help professional testers in their position. A tester should preferably, and very generally speaking, be:

- ▶ Intelligent—testing is an intellectual type of work;
- ▶ Creative—testing needs to be inventive to be effective;
- ▶ Persevering/enduring—testing needs to go on and on despite resistance and pressure;
- ▶ Systematic—testing needs to have a trustworthy coverage;
- ▶ Pragmatic—testing is sampling in its nature;
- ▶ A good communicator—testing has many stakeholders;
- ▶ Courageous—testing can be perceived to bring bad news;
- ▶ Mature—testing is a demanding profession.

Personality types and how these can be deployed to the advantage of test teams are discussed in more detail in the next section.

Professional testers need to have training and experience in testing. Training includes:

- ▶ Education, either from an educational institution or in the form of courses, in testing theory. Testers should learn to remember and understand test related terms, concepts and statements.
- ▶ On-the-job training and mentoring. Testers should learn to apply their knowledge.
- ▶ Carrying out testing tasks. Testers should learn to see structures and principles, and divide a task into smaller tasks.
- ▶ Experience exchange and further education. The testers should learn to combine and think in abstract terms.

Even though testing is a specific profession, many testers have had other careers before they became testers. I have encountered a former dentist, a lawyer, several chemists, and many, many others. However, most of the testers who did not start out as testers either have a background in development or in the domain of the product with which they are working.

Some say that a tester must have a development background. That is not necessarily so, but it can help. Knowledge of how
software development is performed provides
invaluable insight into what could cause errors to be made and how defects can possibly
be introduced.

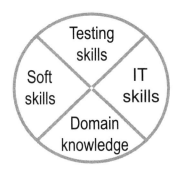

Having a background in the product
domain can also be a great help in a testing
career. It facilitates the understanding of the
requirements and the necessary test environment. Knowledge of the domain creates
valuable credibility from the point of view of the users of the product. In
fact, it can be a good investment to provide testers without relevant domain
knowledge with a feeling for where the products they are working on are
going when they are released.

Many testers in the economical sector have a background in banking.

10.1.1   Test Roles and Specific Skills

Testing is not just one single activity. If we take a close look at the test process and all of the tasks testers have to perform, we can see that a number of
different test roles are involved. Test roles can be defined as follows:

- ▶ Test leader (manager or responsible);
- ▶ Test analyst/designer;
- ▶ Test executor;
- ▶ Reviewer/inspector;
- ▶ Domain expert (user representative);
- ▶ Test environment responsible;
- ▶ (Test) tool responsible.

Each of these roles requires specific skills and capabilities of the people filling them, apart from the general traits and skills required for all testers. The
table below lists the most important ones:

	Should Have Training and/or Experience in
Test leader	Test policy and strategy for the organization Testing standards Test management: estimation, planning, monitoring, control, and reporting Managing people
Test analyst/designer	Analysis of requirements and other specifications Design of test cases Effective usage of test case design techniques Building and documenting test procedures
Test executor	Executing tests, recording, and checking test results
Reviewer/inspector	Static test techniques
Domain expert	Basic test principles
Test environment responsible	Platform(s) Test database administration
Test tool responsible	Platform(s) Specific tool(s)

10.1.2   Testing by Other Professionals

Even though testing is a profession in its own right, people in other professions can also participate and contribute to testing activities.

Users may be good testers. This applies to both future users of the new product and actual users of similar products or earlier versions of the product. The users obviously see the product from the users' perspectives. In other words, users have ideas about the future use of the product. This provides insight into where failures would have the greatest impact; that is, it provides input to the risk management.

Users are best involved in requirements analysis—this is where it all starts. But they can also be very useful during testing, even if in-depth knowledge of the domain does not reside with (naïve) users.

Developers may be good testers. They know how difficult requirements analysis is, how difficult design is, and how difficult coding is, and this means that they have insight into where errors may have been made, and hence where the defects may be.

Developers are best involved in static testing. They can also contribute during dynamic testing, not least in component testing and component integration testing.

10.1.3 Interpersonal Skills

Interpersonal skills are important in testing. Testers need to know how to:

▶ Give and receive criticism;
▶ Influence people;
▶ Negotiate.

Giving criticism is very difficult for most people. We don't want to hurt anybody—most people prefer to have peace rather then pointing out failures.

Again we need to consider what testing is. It may be seen as a destructive activity, since the tester has to find and register failures. But registration of failures is not criticizing the developer. Testing is a very constructive development activity—it contributes to the possibility of everybody reaching the common goal of delivering a product of good quality and to learning from the experience and becoming even better in the future.

Testers do, however, have to give criticism from time to time. Here are the basic rules for doing that:

▶ Stay calm.

T: "Is it convenient for you if we talk about my findings now?"

▶ Stick with the facts.

T: "During the last hour I have noted 27 incidents in the customer invoicing feature."

▶ Don't blame.

T: "We need to figure out how this situation can be stabilized—is there anything I can do?"

▶ Keep an open mind—you could be wrong!

T: "Oh, I didn't realize it was supposed to be like that."

Receiving criticism is just as difficult as giving it. We feel threatened, and some of our needs (respect, recognition, and security) seem to be jeopardized.

Testers do, however, have to take criticism from time to time if we want to get better at our job. Here are the basic rules for doing that:

> Listen carefully for the tiniest bit of truth.

D: "You keep disturbing me with all those * failures!"
T: "Yah, I'm sorry I come barging in here every 10 minutes. Would it be better if we talked once an hour?"

> Ask for clarification of view and goals.

T: "How do you suggest I go about reporting the failures?"

> Make concessions—when the criticism is legitimate, you have to admit to it frankly—otherwise you'll lose credibility!

Testing interacts with many development and supporting activities. We are dependent on other people's decisions and other people's schedules.

Often testers harbor a feeling of being victims. We find ourselves in impossible situations and we don't do much about it, because "This is just the way things are!" There is no reason for bending under this "law of necessity." In fact, testers usually have more influence than they think—especially if they start early.

Some of the areas where testers are dependent on others, but where we may also use our influence, are:

> Delivery order—by asking and explaining why;
> Delivery quality—by defining entry criteria;
> Delivery date—by negotiating with other managers;
> Planning of test activities—by talking to other managers;
> Allocation of resources—by negotiation with management;
> Classification of failures—by using an agreed-on scheme;
> Training—by asking and participating;
> Process improvement—by contributing and participating.

When we assert our influence on other people, it is useful to remember that demands create resentment, whereas requests for help usually create kindheartedness.

T: "It would be a great help for us if we could start testing the components xx and yy first. Would you be able to help us do that?"

As with all other communication, we need to listen first and then talk. When we listen, we must listen for reasons, goals, fears, and threats from the other party's point of view. And when we talk, we must explain. We have to explain our reasons, goals, fears, and threats.

Most of the time we can come to an agreement simply by talking and explaining our needs and constraints to each other.

But sometimes we get into a situation where we have to **negotiate**, that is, engage in bargaining to reach agreement.

A few basic rules about negotiations include the following:

◗ Look behind the positions to the real interests.

◗ Work with BATNAs—Best Alternative To A Negotiated Agreement.

◗ Walk away if the negotiations are going nowhere.

◗ Identify options as parts of the solution.

◗ Go for a win–win solution.

◗ Aim at an atmosphere of common problem solution.

10.2   Test Team Dynamics

Imagine if everybody were like you…

Would life be better or worse for that?

People have different personalities. This has been known since the ancient Greek philosophers defined four temperaments:

◗ Phlegmatic—relaxed and peaceful;

◗ Sanguine—pleasure seeking and sociable;

◗ Choleric—ambitious and leader-like;

◗ Melancholic—analytical and quiet.

The philosophers also said: "We all have our share of each—in different mixtures."

Others have studied personalities including Freud, Jung, and Myers-Briggs. Based on Jung's work, Myers-Briggs defines 16 personality types composed from four dimensions. The dimensions are:

◗ How do you get energy?

Extraversion (E)/Introversion (I);

◗ How do you collect information and knowledge?

Sensing (S)/Intuition (N);

◗ How do you decide?

Thinking (T)/Feeling (F);

◗ How do you act?

Judging (J)/Perceptive (P).

The Greek view is quite simple, the Myers-Briggs view rather complex, and they are both concerned with the individual person as just that: an individual.

10.2.1   Team Roles

Dr. Meredith Belbin and his team of researchers based at Henley Management College, England, studied the behavior of managers from all over the world for more than nine years. Their different core personality traits, intellectual styles, and behaviors were assessed during the research.

Results showed that there are a finite number of behaviors or team roles. A team role as defined by Belbin is "A tendency to behave, contribute and interrelate with others in a particular way."

Belbin has defined nine team roles based on his studies. They each describe a pattern of behavior that characterizes a person's behavior in relationship to others in a team.

The nine team roles are divided into three roles types to create an overview and a deeper understanding of how the roles work.

The Belbin roles are as follows:

Action Oriented (hands):

▶ Shaper;

▶ Implementer;

▶ Completer.

People Oriented (heart):

▶ Coordinator;

▶ Teamworker;

▶ Resource investigator.

Cerebral (head):

▶ Plant;

▶ Monitor;

▶ Specialist.

Each of the roles has some valuable contributions to the progress of the team in which it acts. They also have some weaknesses that may have an adverse effect on the team.

The contributions and weaknesses are summarized in the table below.

Team Role	Contributions	Weaknesses
Shaper	Challenging, dynamic, thrives on pressure. The drive and courage to overcome obstacles.	Prone to provocation. Offends people's feelings.
Implementer	Disciplined, reliable, conservative, and efficient. Turns ideas into practical actions.	Somewhat inflexible. Slow to respond to new possibilities.
Completer/ finisher	Painstaking, conscientious, anxious. Searches out errors and omissions. Delivers on time.	Inclined to worry unduly. Reluctant to delegate.
Coordinator	Mature, confident, a good chairperson. Clarifies goals, promotes decision making, delegates well.	Can often be seen as manipulative. Offloads personal work.
Teamworker	Cooperative, mild, perceptive, and diplomatic. Listens, builds, averts friction.	Indecisive in crunch situations.
Resource investigator	Extrovert, enthusiastic, communicative. Explores opportunities. Develops contacts.	Overly optimistic. Loses interest once initial enthusiasm has passed.
Plant	Creative, imaginative, unorthodox. Solves difficult problems.	Ignores incidentals. Too preoccupied to communicate effectively.
Monitor/ evaluator	Sober, strategic, and discerning. Sees all options. Judges accurately.	Lacks drive and ability to inspire others.
Specialist	Single-minded, self-starting, dedicated. Provides knowledge and skills in rare supply.	Contributes only on a narrow front. Dwells on technicalities.

Everybody is a mixture of more team roles, usually with one being dominant. An analysis of an individual's Belbin team role will give a team role profile showing the weight of each role in one's personality.

10.2.2 Forming Testing Teams

It is the test manager's responsibility to get the test team to work together as well as possible during a specific testing sub-process. And it is higher management's responsibility to choose a test manager with the right traits, skills, and capabilities to be a test manager.

There are two aspects to a team: the people and the roles assigned to the people. Each individual person in a team has his or her personal team role profile (for example, according to Belbin) and a number of skills and

capabilities. Each role has certain requirements toward the person or the people who are going to fill it. Apart from all that, the people in the team need to be able to work together and not have too many personality conflicts.

It can be quite a puzzle to form a synthesis of all this. But the idea is to choose people to match the requirements of the roles who will fit together as a team.

The ideal situation is, of course, when the manager can analyze the roles he or she has to find people for, and then hire exactly the right people. Advertisements, etc., can be tailored to the needs. The applicants can be tested, both for their personal traits and for their skills and capabilities. The team can then be formed by the most suitable people—and ahead we go.

Unfortunately, life is rarely that easy. In most cases the test manager either has an already defined group of people from which to form a team. Or he has a limited and specific group of people from which to choose. It might also be the case that the manager has to find one or more new people to fill vacancies on an existing team.

In all cases the knowledge of individuals' Belbin team role profiles is a great advantage. Even people in teams that have worked together for a long time can benefit from knowing their own and the other team members' team role profiles.

I once worked on a team with many frictions and mistrust. One of the team members had heard of the Belbin roles and we all had a test. That was a true revelation to us all. The two team members with the most friction between them were very different types. They had both been completely at a loss as to why the other acted as he did. Having understood that it was not ill will, but simply a question of being very different personalities, they worked much better together in the team.

The contributions as well as the weaknesses of each team role must be considered. A well-formed team is a strong team, and a team tailored for the task is the strongest team you can get.

Forming teams and getting them to work is not an easy task. There is no absolute solution, but some are better than others.

10.3   Fitting Testing into an Organization
10.3.1   Organizational Anchorage
Testing is always done within an organization, and it can be anchored in many different ways in that organization. It can, in fact, be anchored in several places during the course of a development project and the subsequent maintenance period when the product is in production.

Let's first take a look at some of the different organizational units involved in testing:

- Product management;
- Project management;
- Quality assurance department;
- Development department;
- Development team;
- Internal test department or test team;
- External test organization;
- Internal or internal consultants;
- Sales/marketing department;
- Support organization;
- Internal IT department;
- The customer;
- Present and future end users;
- Subcontractor(s);
- Process or method department.

Distributing the responsibility for the testing activities for the appropriate testing sub-processes and the defined testing roles over organizational units is a three-dimensional jigsaw puzzle.

A number of rules should be observed for this puzzle:

- Testing requires one or more test teams—we can, for example, have a test team for component and integration testing, and another team for system testing.
- Test teams are composed of a number of roles—all the roles must be covered for the entire test task for a project, but it could be that the component testing does not require a test environment responsible or a domain expert
- A role can be filled by one or more people—this depends on the size of the team. We may, for example, need one test responsible, a number of test designers, and an even greater number of test executors for a large test task.
- One person can fill one or more roles—again this depends on the size. The test designer can, for example, also be the test executor. Here it is important to remember that less than 25% assignment to a role = 0; that is, don't cut your slices too thinly.
- People may come from different organizations—the developers could be test designers and executors for the component testing, people from an independent test department could fill these roles

for system testing, and customer representatives could fill them for acceptance testing.

The distribution of the roles must be done with great care and documented explicitly and precisely in the test plan and/or other relevant plans.

10.3.2   Independence in Testing

Testing should be as objective as possible. The closer the tester is to the producer of the test object, the more difficult it is to be objective.

The producer herself usually finds it quite difficult to try and get her own product to fail. She has already done her best, so how can there be faults left in the product? Impossible! Furthermore, the producer carries any assumptions on which the production was based with her to the testing. We therefore don't get a new viewpoint on the item.

Identical considerations apply for the project team testing each others' products, even though to a smaller degree.

The concept of independence in testing has therefore been introduced. The degree or level of independence increases with the "distance" between the producer and the test analyst. Six levels are defined:

1. Producer tests his or her own product.
2. Tests are designed by a different person than the producer, but one with the same responsibilities, typically another developer.
3. Tests are designed by a tester who is a member of the same organization unit as the producer reporting to the same manager.
4. Tests are design by testers independent of the producing organizational unit, though still in-house.
5. Tests are designed by testers belonging to an external organization working in the production organization (consultants).
6. Tests are design by testers in an external organization (third party testing).

As can be seen from the list, the point is who designs the test cases. In structured testing the execution must follow the specifications, so the degree of independence should not be affected by who is executing the test. In less scripted tests, like exploratory testing, the independence is between the producer and the test executor.

The strategy must determine the necessary degree of independence for the test at hand. The higher the risk, the higher the degree of independence should be.

The independence usually varies for the different levels of testing. In component testing we often see the lowest level of independence (= no independence) even though the same concept in reviews does not seem acceptable. The higher the test level, the higher the independence usually is.

The three highest levels of independence include crossings of organizational borders. We have specific names for these types of test:

▶ Distributed testing, in which testing is carried out by people belonging to the same organization, but distributed geographically (or organizationally);

▶ In-sourced testing, in which testing is carried out in the development organization, but by people reporting to a different organization (consultants);

▶ Outsourced testing, in which testing is carried out in a different organization by this organization's own people.

These ways of placing responsibility have advantages and disadvantages, and they pose specific requirements on the organizations.

The obvious advantage is the inherent independence of testing. Other advantages may be lower wages and overcoming shortage of staff.

The disadvantages will have to be taken into account in the risk analysis for the testing project and mitigations must be planned. People not having taken close part in the development will be less prepared for the testing task and might take longer to produce test specifications.

The risks related to distributed, in-sourced, and outsourced testing fall within the areas of

▶ Process descriptions;
▶ Distribution of work;
▶ Quality of work;
▶ Culture;
▶ Trust.

The involved organizations must be aware of their own processes and the processes to which the other parties work. If processes cannot be shared, the interfaces between them must be made very clear.

The work breakdown structure for the task assignment must be performed to a rather large level of detail and all involved must agree. The most important is to agree on the distribution of the tasks, so that nothing is left out and nothing performed twice.

Test work to be done by people not having been closely involved in the development of a product requires precise and comprehensive basis documentation. A test team far away from the development team cannot easily go and ask what to expect when documentation is missing or difficult to interpret. This is perhaps a blessing in disguise: All other things equal, the better the basis documentation, the better the product will be.

For outsourced testing the quality assurance of the work being done is a specific risk. We test work by testing its results, but we cannot test the testing as such. We need to be prepared to do thorough review of work products produced by the outsource organization, and require comprehensive documentation of fulfilled completion criteria.

Without trust between the people working together and relying on each other, the work will not be done properly. This goes for all kinds of work, but especially when work is split up between different organizations. Mutual trust must be the starting point, but all parties should remember that trust is very easily lost and hard to earn back.

10.4 Motivation

Why do we work? And why do we test?

On the surface testing does not add any value—the object under test is in principle unchanged by the test.

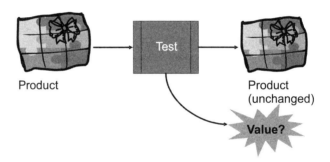

So is it really worth it—for the company and for us?

We have previously seen how testing brings value to the company by the way the information we collect during the testing is used. This is why our company pays us. But do we work just for money?

Traditionally, a company or organization has been regarded as a control system. The employees were a variable cost factor to be minimized through rationalization. The salary was the main purpose for the employees and a means to an end for the management. Today we see and know that at least in the Western world the salary is far from the only motivation.

A number of American scientists—Maslow, McGregor, Herzberg, and Hackman, as well as the Danish professor K. B. Madsen—have contributed to the understanding of why we work.

10.4.1   Maslow's Pyramid of Needs

Abraham Maslow, 1908–1970, had a Ph.D. in psychology from the University of Wisconsin. One of the many interesting things he noticed while working with monkeys early in his career was that some needs take precedence over others. For example, if you are hungry and thirsty, you will tend to try to take care of the thirst first. After all, you can do without food for weeks, but you can only do without water for a couple of days. Thirst is a "stronger" need than hunger. Likewise, if you are very very thirsty, but someone has put a choke hold on you and you can't breathe, which is more important? The need to breathe, of course.

This section is based on http://www.ship.edu/~cgboeree/

Based on these observations Maslow created his now famous *hierarchy of needs.*

Maslow laid out five layers: the physiological needs, the needs for safety and security, the needs for love and belonging, the needs for esteem, and the need to actualize the self, in that order.

1. *The physiological needs.* These include the needs we have for oxygen, water, minerals and vitamins, as well as to be active, to rest, to sleep, to get rid of wastes, and to avoid pain.
2. *The safety and security needs.* When the physiological needs are largely taken care of, this second layer of needs comes into play. You will become increasingly interested in finding safe circumstances, stability, and protection.
3. *The love and belonging needs.* When physiological needs and safety needs are, by and large, taken care of, a third layer starts to show up. You begin to feel the need for friends, a sweetheart, children, affectionate relationships in general, and even a sense of community.
4. *The esteem needs.* Next, we begin to look for self-esteem. Maslow noted two versions of esteem needs, a lower one and a higher

one. The lower one is the need for the respect of others, the need for status, fame, glory, recognition, even dominance. The higher form involves the need for self-respect, including such feelings as confidence, competence, achievement, mastery, independence, and freedom. Note that this is the "higher" form because, unlike the respect of others, *once you have self-respect, it's a lot harder to lose.*

All of these four levels Maslow calls *deficit needs,* or D-needs. If you don't have enough of something, that is, if you have a deficit, you feel the need. But if you get all you need, you feel nothing at all! In other words, they cease to be motivating.

In the Western world the basic needs are covered to a large degree for most people. Most people therefore start a couple of layers up in Maslow's pyramid and strive to go up from there. In the IT business where people usually have higher education and higher salaries, it is particularly the top two or tree layers in the pyramid that can be unsatisfied. We need to keep this in mind when we discuss motivation of testers.

10.4.2 Herzberg's Factors

In the late 1950s Frederick Herzberg's wrote *The Motivation to Work.* This has become one of the most replicated studies in the field of workplace psychology.

On the basis of interviews with engineers, politicians, scientists, accountants, officers, and others, Herzberg concludes that there are two factors in working situations: maintenance factors and motivation factors. The factors giving satisfaction and motivation are separate and different from the factors that create dissatisfaction. Satisfaction and dissatisfaction are not directly each other's contrast as illustrated here:

▶ The opposite of satisfaction with the work is not dissatisfaction, but rather no satisfaction.

▶ The opposite of dissatisfaction is not satisfaction, but rather no dissatisfaction.

Motivation factors are the factors that stimulate a need for personal development, and they are imbedded in the work, such as performance, recognition, responsibility, and promotion. Maintenance factors include company policies and administration, relations to colleagues, salary, status, and security. Hertzberg's main point is that only the work itself can give lasting motivation.

If we compare Maslow's pyramid with Herzberg's factors, we see that the motivation factors belong in the top two layers of the pyramid and the maintenance factors in the three lower.

10.4.3   K. B. Madsen's Motivation Theory

Both Maslow's and Herzberg's theories have been criticized: Maslow for not having described a universal motivational process, but one reflecting the American middle class. Herzberg for his interview form: If you ask people about good and bad aspects of their working life, they are inclined to attribute the bad ones to others, and the good ones to their own accomplishments.

The Danish professor K. B. Madsen has provided a synthesis of a number of motivation theories. He sees us as being driven by internal forces (needs = motives) and controlled by external forces (incentives).

Incentives can be split into primary and secondary. Primary incentives activate our innate reactions. Secondary incentives activate our acquired reactions. Some of the more important incentives are listed here:

	Innate	**Acquired**
Want to have	Food and drink Comfort Service Security	Money Recognition Honor and praise Respect
Want to avoid	Pain Punishment Aggression Humiliation	Sarcasm Danger signals Frustration Verbal threats

In connection with our working life, Madsen summarizes his and others' research in the following statements:

The most effective form of motivation is: Interest in the task.
Almost as effective is: Reward and praise.
Least effective forms of motivation are: Punishment and blame.

10.4.4 Testers' Motivation

Motivation theories are not particularly aimed at testers. But we can map the general motives to the testing world.

Testers are motivated by an interest in the task. This means that testers must think or feel that it is fun to find failures to be motivated to do their job. They must see it as an intellectual challenge to reveal as many faults as possible in the given time. This is in many ways in contradiction with "acceptable, nice behavior" and requires a very specific mind-set. Testers must sometimes work hard to convince both ourselves and others around us that we work together to produce a more reliable product—not to destroy it.

Testers are motivated by reward and praise. We can also say that testers must get recognition and respect—we certainly deserve it. This can be done by the management being very aware of the value testers add to the project and hence to the company. Remember what we create of value? Project information! The better we are at presenting the information and assisting the recipients in using it, the more recognition and respect we get.

The earlier the testers are involved in the project, the more we can prove our value. Testers involved in early static testing can be a great eye opener and motivator for everybody.

Testers are demotivated by punishment and blame. One (rather sophisticated) form of punishment can be lack of career path. It can be very demotivating if the organization ignores the testers and doesn't provide them with a way to climb up the organization's ladder. On a more day-to-day scale, lack of understanding of the value of testing ("Oh, you are just overhead") or direct blame ("Stop finding (read: producing) all those failures!") can make the working life of testers very uphill.

10.5 Team Communication

Testers need to communicate with people in all the organizational units involved in the testing. This means that testers have to communicate with many different people at many different organizational levels internally in their organization and externally, for example, with customers.

The first thing to remember is that *communication is difficult.* The perfect way of communicating where people understand each other absolutely perfectly and completely is not possible.

We are people and we are all "colored" by our personalities, our upbringing, and our experience—just to mention a fw factors.

But we have to communicate and we have to make an effort to make it work. One of the things we can do is to understand the type of people we are dealing with, both in terms of their personality types, their education and background, and their responsibilities and working conditions.

Another thing is to accept that it is the "sender" of the information who is responsible for making it understandable to the audience. We as testers must learn that other teams talk in different languages: management speaks "money"; users (and marketing and sales) speak "functionality and quality," developers speak "technique." All of our communication must be targeted to the audience.

The most important and perhaps the most difficult communication lines are those between the testers and

◗ Project management;
◗ Developers;
◗ Users.

Communication with project management is most often done by the test manager. Project management needs to inform about and discuss with testers aspects such as expectations, resources, constraints, quality criteria, and changes in plans. Testers for their part must inform project management about issues such as the progress of testing and the quality of the product under test. This communication is usually based on written documentation (i.e., test strategy, test plans, test progress reports, and test summary reports), but should also be accompanied by verbal communication.

The communication with development is usually done by test analysts and designers. Development needs to inform testing about issues like especially complex or difficult areas of the product, which areas are new development and which have "just" been updated, other areas that need special attention for various reasons, changes in requirements and/or design, changes in delivery schedule, specific difficulties during development, problems reproducing reported failures, and when and why new test objects are delivered for testing.

Testers need to inform development about failures found, problems arising during retesting of corrected defects, and problems concerning the number and/or types of failures.

These issues can be delicate to talk about. The information should be conveyed diplomatically as a means of improving the quality of the product—not as blame! Also here written documentation may constitute some of the communication, but verbal communication should not be eliminated completely.

The users may communicate with many different test roles depending on the organizational structure. Useful information can be provided by users to testers, for example, concerning their expectations regarding the new product, risk areas to the business in the product, assessment of the effect of identified risks, important areas in the product seen from the users' perspective, and background information about the business and the business processes. This information can be used to support the risk analysis and the prioritization of the testing. Users will often receive or see test results. Users with little knowledge of testing may need help interpreting these results.

Questions

1. What traits are useful for a tester to have?
2. What are the seven test roles that can be defined?
3. Which test role do you prefer and why?
4. What should you remember when giving criticism?
5. What should you remember when receiving criticism?
6. In what areas are testers dependent on other people?
7. What are the negotiation rules?
8. What are the four temperaments?
9. What are the four dimensions that Myers-Briggs defined?
10. What are the nine Belbin team roles?
11. How should test teams be formed?
12. Which organizational units might be involved in testing, and how?
13. What are the levels of test independence?
14. What are the differences between distributed testing, in-sourced testing, and outsourced testing?
15. What are the risk areas for these kinds of test organization?
16. Why do you work in testing (or in other areas as the case might be)?
17. What is the idea behind Maslow's hierarchy of needs?
18. What is special for self-respect compared to the other needs?

19.   What are Herzberg's two types of factors?
20.   What is the idea behind K. B. Madsen's motivation theory?
21.   What is the most effective form of motivation?
22.   Why is "perfect" communication impossible?
23.   Who do testers communicate with?
24.   What do we communicate about?

Selected Bibliography

Books

Beizer, B., *Black Box Testing*, Wiley, 1995.

Beizer, B., Software Testing Techniques, Wiley, 1990.

Black, R., *Managing the Testing Process*, Microsoft Press, 1999.

Buwalda, H., Janssen, D., and Pinkster, I., *Integrated Test Design and Automation*, Addison-Wesley, 2001.

Copeland, L., *A Practitioner's Guide to Software Test Design*, Artech House, 2003.

Crispin, L., and Gregory, J., Agile Testing: A Practical Guide for Testers and Agile Teams, Addison-Wesley, 2011.

Fewster, M., and Graham, D., *Software Test Automation*, Addison Wesley, 1999.

Gerrard, P., and Thompson, E., *Risk-Based E-Business Testing*, Artech House, 2002.

Gilb, T., *Software Inspection*, Addison-Wesley, 1993.

Hass, A. M. J., Configuration Management Principles and Practice, Addison-Wesley, 2003.

Hass, A. M. J., Requirements Development and Management, DF-17; Copenhagen, 2003.

International Software Testing Qualification Board, *Certified Tester, Foundation Level Syllabus, Version 2011.*

International Software Testing Qualification Board, *Certified Tester, Advanced Level Syllabus, Test Manager, Version 2012.*

International Software Testing Qualification Board, *Certified Tester, Advanced Level Syllabus, Test Analyst, Version 2012.*

International Software Testing Qualification Board, *Certified Tester, Foundation Advanced Level Syllabus, Technical Test Analyst, Version 2012.*

431

Kaner, C., Bach, J., and Pettichord, B., *Lessons Learned in Software Testing,* Wiley, 2002.

Kit, E., *Software Testing in the Real World,* Addison-Wesley, 1995.

Koomen, T., and Pol, M., *Test Process Improvement (TPI),* Addison-Wesley, 1999.

Myers, G., *The Art of Software Testing,* Wiley Interscience, 2004.

Perry, W. E., and Rice, R. W., *Surviving the Top Ten Challenges of Software Testing* Dorset House, 1997.

Pinkster, I., et al., *Successful Test Management,* Springer, 2004.

Pol, M., Teunissen, R., and Veenendaal, E. van, *Software Testing: A Guide to the TMap Approac,* Addison-Wesley, 2002.

Ryber,T., *Essential Software Test Design,* Unique Publishing Ltd., 2007.

Sogeti, *TPI Next—Business Driven Test Process Improvement,* Addison, 2009.

Tobar, Ltd., *Incredible Visual Illusions,* Arcturus Publishing Limited, 2005.

Veenendaal, E. van., *The Testing Practitioner,* UTN, 2002.

Vinter, O., *The prevention of Errors through error experience-driven test efforts,* DELTA rapport D-259.

Wiegers, K., *Peer Reviews in Software,* Addison-Wesley, 2002.

Standards

BS 7925-2 (1998) "Software Component Testing"

IEEE Std. 829-2008, "Standard for Software Testing Documentation"

IEEE Std. 1028—1997, "Standard for Software Reviews"

IEEE Std. 1044—1993, "Standards Classification for Software Incidents"

IEEE Std. 1044.1—1995, "Guide to Classification for Software Incidents"

ISO/IEC:2014, "SQuaRE Series"

ISO/IEC/IEEE 29119-1:2013, "Software and Systems Engineering—Software Testing—Part 1: Concepts and Definitions"

ISO/IEC/IEEE 29119-2:2013, "Software and Systems Engineering—Software Testing—Part 2: Test Processses"

ISO/IEC/IEEE 29119-3:2013, "Software and Systems Engineering—Software Testing—Part 3: Test Documentation"

ISO/IEC/IEEE DIS 29119-4.2, "Software and Systems Engineering—Software Testing—Part 4: Test Techniques"

ISO/IEC 9126—1:2001, "Software Engineering—Software Product Quality"

ISTQB "Glossary of Terms Used in Software Testing," Version 2.2, 2012

Web Sites

www.belbin.com

www.iso.org

www.istqb.org

http://neilsloane.com/oadir

www.softwaretestingstandard.org

http://whatisww.cmmiinstitute.com

About the Author

With a M.Sc.C.E. degree Anne Mette Hass has worked in IT since 1980. She started as a programmer; but gradually got more and more interested in testing. While working on two assignments in quality assurance for the European Space Agency in the early 1990s, she really discovered her passion for processes, testing, and compliance, and since then she has used and enhanced her experience working as a test, quality assurance, and process consultant.

The pervasiveness of IT has allowed Ms. Hass to work in many different businesses—from life science to games and also in the oil, banking, and insurance industries, the public sector, and universities. Ms. Hass has lived and worked in Denmark, where she comes from, and in Norway, England, France, and Italy for longer periods.

It is important to Ms. Hass to have a deep understanding of what she is doing, and therefore she mixes practical work and theory. She holds an ISEB Practitioner certification, corresponding to all ISTQB Advanced certifications, and she has taught ISTQB Foundation and ISTQB Advanced Test Manager and Test Analyst courses.

Ms. Hass also holds an IREB (International Requirement Engineering) certification and has taught this certification. She is very interested in requirements development and management as the basis for both development and testing.

Ms. was president of iNTCCM (iNTernational Certified Configuration Management) under ISQI from its start in 2006 until 2009. She was a member of the foundation syllabus working group, and has taught this certification as well.

With regard to processes and process improvement, Ms. Hass is certified CMMI assessor and certified ISO 15504 lead assessor, and she has performed more than 50 assessments in Denmark, Canada, and Poland for companies of all sizes and in many different branches.

Ms. Hass was secretary of the Danish Special Interest Group for Software Test and Test Management under TecPoint from 1998 to 2011. The group had more than 90 members at its highest and it celebrated its 50th meeting in spring 2010.

Since 2008 Ms. Hass has been a member of the working group for ISO 29119 Standard for Software Test, where she is editor for Part 3, Test Documentation. The first three parts of the standard were published in August 2013. The working group has members from over 20 countries.

Ms. Hass is a frequent speaker at national and international conferences. She was the Danish country coordinator for the EuroSTAR conference for 5 years and has been on the program committee. She has also served on the program committee for EuroQUEST 2007 and EuroQUEST 2008. Ms. Hass has been an external lecturer at the IT University in Copenhagen since 2007 and is currently teaching testing and database fundamentals.

Ms. Hass has written more than 30 papers, primarily about testing, but also about requirements and configuration management issues. She is author of the books Configuration Management Principles and Practice (Addison-Wesley, 2003) and Requirements Development and Management (DF-17 2002).

In addition to this Ms. Hass developed the team game "Process Contest," which provides a fun way to learn development concepts and terms. She is also creator of the posters "... at a Glance – or two" covering the themes of software testing, configuration management, and requirements handling. These posters are available from delta.dk. A new poster covering software testing has been developed to comply with this book.

Ms. Hass is married and has a daughter and a small dog. The family lives in the eastern part of Copenhagen.

Index

Recent Titles in the Artech House Computing Library

Achieving Software Quality through Teamwork, Isabel Evans

Action Focused Assessment for Software Process Improvement, Tim Kasse

Advanced Database Technology and Design, Mario Piattini and Oscar Díaz, editors

Advanced Standard SQL Dynamic Structured Data Modeling and Hierarchical Processing, Michael M. David

Agent-Based Software Development, Michael Luck, Ronald Ashri, and Mark d'Inverno

Agile Software Development, Evaluating the Methods for Your Organization, Alan S. Koch

Agile Systems with Reusable Patterns of Business Knowledge, A Component-Based Approach, Amit Mitra and Amar Gupta

Building Reliable Component-Based Software Systems, Ivica Crnkovic and Magnus Larsson, editors

Business Process Implementation for IT Professionals and Managers, Robert B. Walford

Data Modeling and Design for Today's Architectures, Angelo Bobak

Developing Secure Distributed Systems with CORBA, Ulrich Lang and Rudolf Schreiner

Discovering Real Business Requirements for Software Project Success, Robin F. Goldsmith

Engineering Wireless-Based Software Systems and Applications, Jerry Zeyu Gao, Simon Shim, Hsing Mei, Xiao Su

Future Codes: Essays in Advanced Computer Technology and the Law, Curtis E. A. Karnow

Global Distributed Applications with Windows® DNA, Enrique Madrona

Guide to Advanced Software Testing, Second Edition, Anne Mette Hass

Workflow Modeling: Tools for Process Improvement and Application Development, Alec Sharp and Patrick McDermott

For further information on these and other Artech House titles, including previously considered out-of-print books now available through our In-Print-Forever® (IPF®) program, contact:

Artech House
685 Canton Street
Norwood, MA 02062
Phone: 781-769-9750
Fax: 781-769-6334
e-mail: artech@artechhouse.com

Artech House
16 Sussex Street
London SW1V HRW UK
Phone: +44 (0)20 7596-8750
Fax: +44 (0)20 7630-0166
e-mail: artech-uk@artechhouse.com

Find us on the World Wide Web at: www.artechhouse.com